The Expositor's Bible
The First Book Of Kings

By

F. W. Farrar

The Expositor's Bible
The First Book Of Kings
by F. W. Farrar

Copyright © 2024

All Rights reserved.

ISBN: 978-93-61158-77-3

Published by

DOUBLE 9 BOOKS

2/13-B, Ansari Road
Daryaganj, New Delhi – 110002
info@double9books.com
www.double9books.com
Tel. 011-40042856

ABOUT THE AUTHOR

Farrar was born in Bombay, India, and attended King William's College on the Isle of Man, King's College, London, and Trinity College, Cambridge. In 1852, he was awarded the Chancellor's Gold Medal for Poetry at Cambridge. He was a master at Harrow School for a few years before becoming the headmaster of Marlborough College from 1871 to 1876. Farrar spent much of his career at Westminster Abbey. He was named canon there in 1876, then rector of St Margaret's (the church next door), and finally archdeacon of the Abbey in 1883. He then became Dean of Canterbury and a chaplain in ordinary, which meant he was associated to the Royal Household. Farrar was a classics professor and comparative philologist who applied Charles Darwin's branching descent theory to the relationships between languages, sparking a lengthy argument with anti-Darwinian linguist Max Müller. While Farrar was never convinced by the evidence for evolution in biology, he had no theological objections to the concept and argued that it should be studied only on scientific grounds. Farrar was elected to the Royal Society in 1866, following Darwin's recommendation for his philological work. When Darwin died in 1882, then-Canon Farrar assisted in obtaining church permission for him to be buried at Westminster Abbey and delivered the funeral sermon.

CONTENTS

BOOK I
INTRODUCTION

"Ich bin überzeugt, dass die Bibel immer schöner wird, je mehr man sie versteht, d.h. je mehr man einsieht und anschaut, dass jedes Wort, das wir allgemein auffassen und in Besondern auf uns anwenden, nach gewissen Umständen, nach Zeit- und Orts-verhältnissen einen, eigenen, besondern, unmittelbar individuellen Bezug gehabt hat." —Goethe.

"Es bleibt dabei, das beste Lesen der Bibel, dieses Göttlichen Buchs, ist *menschlich*. Ich nehme dies Wort im weitesten Umfang und in der andringendsten Bedeutung. Menschlich muss man die Bibel lesen: denn sie ist ein Buch durch Menschen für Menschen geschrieben; menschlich ist die Sprache, menschlich die äussern Hülfsmittel, mit denen sie geschrieben und aufbehalten ist.... Es darf also sicher geglaubt werden: je humaner (im besten Sinn des Worts) man das Wort Gottes liest, desto näher kommt man dem Zweck seines Urhebers, welcher Menschen zu seinem Bilde schuf ... und für uns menschlich handelt." —Herder.

CHAPTER I
THE HIGHER CRITICISM

"God shows all things in the slow history of their ripening." —
George Eliot.

God has given us many Bibles. The book which we call the Bible consists of a series of books, and its name represents the Greek plural τὰ Βίβλια. It is not so much a book, as the extant fragments of a literature, which grew up during many centuries. Supreme as is the importance of this "Book of God," it was never meant to be the sole teacher of mankind. We mistake its purpose, we misapply its revelation, when we use it to exclude the other sources of religious knowledge. It is supremely profitable for our instruction, but, so far from being designed to absorb our exclusive attention, its work is to stimulate the eagerness with which, by its aid, we are able to learn from all other sources the will of God towards men.

God speaks to us in many voices. In the Bible He revealed Himself to all mankind by His messages to the individual souls of some of His servants. But those messages, whether uttered or consigned to writing, were but one method of enabling us to hold communion with Him. They were not even an *indispensable* method. Thousands of the saints of God lived the spiritual life in close communion with their Father in heaven in ages which possessed no written book; in ages before any such book existed; in ages during which, though it existed, it was practically inaccessible; in ages during which it had been designedly kept out of their hands by priests. This fact should quicken our sense of gratitude for the inestimable boon of a Book wherein he who runs may now read, and respecting the main teaching of which wayfaring men, and even fools, need not err. But it should at the same time save us from the error of treating the Bible as though it were in itself an amulet or a fetish, as the Mohammedan treats his Koran. The Bible was written in human language, by men for men. It was written mainly in Judæa, by Jews, for Jews. "*Scripture,*" as the old theological rule said, "*is the sense of Scripture,*"[1] and the sense of Scripture can only be ascertained by the methods of study and the rules of criticism without which no ancient document or literature can be even approximately understood. In these respects the Bible cannot be arbitrarily or exceptionally treated. No *a priori* rules can be devised for its elucidation. It is what it is, not what we might have expected it to be. Language, at the best, is an imperfect and ever-varying instrument of thought. It is full of twilight, and of gracious shadows. Vast numbers of its words were originally metaphorical. When the light of metaphor has faded from them they come to mean different things at different times, under different conditions, in different contexts, on different lips. Language can at the best be but an *asymptote* to thought; in other words, it resembles the mathematical line which approaches nearer and nearer to the circumference of a circle, but which, even when infinitely extended, can never actually touch it. The fact that the Bible contains a Divine revelation does not alter the fact that it represents a nation's literature. It is the library of the Jewish people, or rather all that remains to us of that library, and all that was most precious in it. Holy men of old were moved by the Spirit of God, but as this Divine inspiration did not make them personally sinless in their actions, or infallible in their judgments, so neither does it exempt their messages from the limitation which attaches to all human conditions. Criticism would have rendered an inestimable service to every thoughtful reader of the Scriptures if it had done nothing more than impress upon them that the component books are not one, but complex and multiform, separated from each other by centuries of time, and of very varying value and preciousness. They too, like the greatest apostles of God, have their treasure in earthen vessels; and we not only may, but must, by the aid of that reason which is "the candle of the Lord," estimate both the value of the treasure, and the age and character of the earthen vessel in which it is contained.

There are hundreds of texts in Scripture which may convey to some souls a very true and blessed meaning, but which do not in the original possess any such meaning as that which is now attached to them. The words of Hebrew prophets often seem perfectly clear, but in some cases they had another set of connotations in the mouths of those by whom they were originally spoken. It requires a learned and a literary training to discover by philology, by history, or by comparison, what alone they could have meant when they were first spoken. In many cases their exact significance is no longer to be ascertained with certainty. It must be more or less conjectural. There are passages of Scripture which have received scores of differing interpretations. There are entire books of Scripture about the general scope of which there have been diametrically opposite opinions. The spiritual intuition of the saint may in some instances be keener to read aright than the laborious researches of the scholar, because spiritual things can only be spiritually discerned. But in general it is true that the *ex cathedra* assertions of ignorant readers, though they are often pronounced with an assumption of infallibility, are not worth the breath which utters them. All artificial dogmas as to what Scripture *must* be, and *must* mean, are worse than idle;

we have only to deal with what it *really is,* and what it *really says.* Even when opinions respecting it have been all but unanimously pronounced by the representatives of all the Churches, they have nevertheless been again and again shown to be absurdly erroneous. The slow light of scholarship, of criticism, of comparative religion, has proved that in many instances not only the interpretations of former ages, but the very *principles* of interpretation from which they were derived, had no basis whatever in fact. And the methods of interpretation—dogmatic, ecclesiastical, mystic, allegorical, literal—have changed from age to age.[2] The asserted heresy of yesterday has in scores of instances become the accepted commonplace of to-morrow. The duty of the Church in the present day is neither to make out that the Bible is what men have imagined that it was, nor to repeat the assertions of ancient writers as to what they declared it to be, but honestly and truthfully to discover the significance of the actual phenomena which it presents to the enlightened and cultivated intelligence.

If it were not so common a failing to ignore the lessons of the past, it might have been hoped that a certain modesty, of which the necessity is taught us by centuries of error, would have saved a multitude of writers from rushing into premature and denunciative rejection of results which they have not studied, and of which they are incapable to judge. St. Jerome complained that in his day there was no old woman so fatuous as not to assume the right to lay down the law about Scriptural interpretation. It is just the same in these days. Half-taught dogmatists—αὐτοσχέδιοι δογματισταὶ, as they have been called—may sweepingly condemn the lifelong researches of men far superior to themselves, not only in learning, but in love of truth; they may attribute their conclusions to faithless infatuation, and even to moral obliquity. This has been done over and over again in our own lifetime; and yet such self-constituted and unauthorised defenders of their own prejudices and traditions—which they always identify with the Catholic faith—are impotent to prevent, impotent even greatly to retard, the spread of real knowledge. Many of the now-accepted certainties of science were repudiated a generation ago as absurd and blasphemous. As long as it was possible to put them down by persecution, the thumbscrew and the stake were freely used by priests and inquisitors for their suppression. *E pur si muove.* Theologians who mingled the gold of Revelation with the clay of their own opinions have been driven to correct their past errors. Untaught by experience, religious prejudice is ever heaping up fresh obstacles to oppose the progress of new truths. The obstacles will be swept away in the future as surely as they have been in the past. The eagle, it has been said, which soars through the air does not worry itself how to cross the rivers.

It is probable that no age since that of the Apostles has added so much to our knowledge of the true meaning and history of the Bible as has been added by our own. The mode of regarding Scripture has been almost revolutionised, and in consequence many books of Scripture previously misunderstood have acquired a reality and intensity of interest and instructiveness which have rendered them trebly precious. A deeper and holier reverence for all eternal truth which the Bible contains has taken the place of a meaningless letter worship. The fatal and wooden Rabbinic dogma of verbal dictation — a dogma which either destroys intelligent faith altogether, or introduces into Christian conduct some of the worst delusions of false religion — is dead and buried in every capable and well-taught mind. Truths which had long been seen through the distorting mirage of false exegesis have now been set forth in their true aspect. We have been enabled, for the first time, to grasp the real character of events which, by being set in a wrong perspective, had been made so fantastic as to have no relation to ordinary lives. Figures which had become dim spectres moving through an unnatural atmosphere now stand out, full of grace, instructiveness and warning, in the clear light of day. The science of Biblical criticism has solved scores of enigmas which were once disastrously obscure, and has brought out the original beauty of some passages, which, even in our Authorised Version, conveyed no intelligible meaning to earnest readers. The Revised Version alone has corrected hundreds of inaccuracies which in some instances defaced the beauty of the sacred page, and in many others misrepresented and mistranslated it. Intolerance has been robbed of favourite shibboleths, used as the basis of cruel beliefs, which souls unhardened by system could only repudiate with a "God forbid!" Familiar error has ever been dearer to most men than unfamiliar truths; but truth, however slow may seem to be the beat of her pinions, always wins her way at last.

> "Thro' the heather an' howe gaed the creepin' thing,
> But abune was the waft of an angel's wing."

Can there be any doubt that mankind has everything to gain and nothing to lose from the ascertainment of genuine truth? Are we so wholly devoid of even an elementary faith as to think that man can profit by consciously cherished illusions? Does it not show a nobler confidence in facts to correct traditional prejudices, than to rest blindly content with conventional assertions? If we do not believe that God is a God of truth, that all falsity is hateful to Him,—and religious falsity most hateful of all, because it adds the sin of hypocrisy to the love of lies,—we believe in *nothing*. If our religion is to consist in a rejection of knowledge, lest it should disturb the convictions of times of ignorance, the dicta of "the Fathers," or dogmas which arrogate to themselves the sham claim of Catholicity—if we are to give only to the Dark Ages the title of the Ages of Faith, then indeed

> "The pillared firmament is rottenness,
> And earth's base built on stubble."

"There is and will be much discussion," says Goethe, "as to the advantage or disadvantage of the popular dissemination of the Bible. To me it is clear that it will be mischievous, as it always has been, if used dogmatically and capriciously; beneficial, as it always has been, if accepted didactically (for our instruction) and with feeling." There is abundance in the Bible for doctrine, for reproof, for correction, for instruction in righteousness;—we shall weaken its moral and spiritual force, and gain nothing in its place, if we turn it into an idol adorned with impossible claims which it never makes for itself, and if we support its golden image upon the brittle clay of an exegesis which is morally, critically, and historically false.

I do not see how there can be any loss in the positive results of what is called the Higher Criticism. Certainly its suggestions must never be hastily adopted. Nor is it likely that they will be. They have to fight their way through crowds of opposing prejudices. They are first held up to ridicule as absurd; then exposed to anathema as irreligious; at last they are accepted as obviously true. The very theologians who once denounced them silently ignore or readjust what they previously preached, and hasten, first to minimise the importance, then to extol the value of the new discoveries. It is quite right that they should be keenly scrutinised. All new sciences are liable to rush into extremes. Their first discoverers are misled into error by premature generalisations born of a genuine enthusiasm. They are tempted to build elaborate superstructures on inadequate foundations. But when they have established certain irrefragable principles, can the obvious deductions from those principles be other than a pure gain? Can we be the better for traditional delusions? Can mistakes and ignorance—can anything but the ascertained fact—be desirable for man, or acceptable to God?

No doubt it is with a sensation of pain that we are compelled to give up convictions which we once regarded as indubitable and sacred. That is a part of our human nature. We must say with all gentleness to the passionate devotees of each old erroneous *mumpsimus*—

"Disce; sed ira cadat naso rugosaque sanna
Cum veteres avias tibi de pulmone revello."

Our blessed Lord, with His consummate tenderness, and Divine insight into the frailties of our nature, made tolerant allowance for inveterate prejudices. "No man," He said, "having drunk old wine straightway desireth new: for he saith, The old is good." But the pain of disillusionment is blessed and healing when it is incurred in the cause of sincerity. There must always be more value in results earned by heroic labour than in conventions accepted without serious inquiry. Already there has been a silent revolution. Many of the old opinions about the Bible have been greatly modified. There is scarcely a single competent scholar who does not now admit that the Hexateuch is a composite structure; that much of the Levitical legislation, which was once called Mosaic, is in reality an aftergrowth which *in its present form* is not earlier than the days of the prophet Ezekiel; that the Book of Deuteronomy belongs, in its present form, whatever older elements it may contain, to the era of Hezekiah's or Josiah's reformation; that the Books of Zechariah and Isaiah are not homogeneous, but preserve the writings of more prophets than their titles imply; that only a small section of the Psalter was the work of David; that the Book of Ecclesiastes was not the work of King Solomon; that most of the Book of Daniel belongs to the era of Antiochus Epiphanes; and so forth. In what respect is the Bible less precious, less "inspired" in the only tenable sense of that very undefined word, in consequence of such discoveries? In what way do they touch the outermost fringe of our Christian faith? Is there anything in such results of modern criticism which militates against the most inferential expansion of a single clause in the Apostolic, the Nicene, or even the Athanasian Creed? Do they contravene one single syllable of the hundreds of propositions to which our assent is demanded in the Thirty-nine Articles? I would gladly help to mitigate the needless anxiety felt by many religious minds. When the Higher Criticism is in question I would ask them to distinguish between established premisses and the exorbitant system of inferences which a few writers have based upon them. They may rest assured that sweeping conclusions will not be hastily snatched up; that no conclusion will be regarded as proved until it has successfully run the gauntlet of many a jealous challenge. They need not fear for one moment that the Ark of their faith is in peril, and they will be guilty not only of unwisdom but of profanity if they rush forward to support it with rude and unauthorised hands. There never has been an age of deep thought and earnest inquiry which has not left its mark in the modification of some traditions or doctrines of theology. But the truths of essential Christianity are built upon a rock. They belong to things which cannot be shaken, and which remain. The intense labours of eminent scholars, English and German, thanklessly as they have been received, have not robbed us of so much as a fraction of a single precious element of revelation. On the contrary, they have cleared the Bible of many accretions by which its meaning was spoilt, and its doctrines wrested to perdition, and they have thus rendered it more profitable than before for every purpose for which it was designed, that the man of God may be perfect, throughly furnished unto all good works.

When we study the Bible it is surely one of our most primary duties to beware lest any idols of the caverns or of the forum tempt us "to offer to the God of truth the unclean sacrifice of a lie."[3]

CHAPTER II
THE BOOKS OF KINGS

The "Two Books of Kings," as we call them, are only one book (Sepher Melakîm), and were so regarded not only in the days of Origen (*ap.* Euseb., *H. E.*, vi. 25) and of Jerome (a.d. 420), but by the Jews even down to Bomberg's Hebrew Bible of 1518. They are treated as one book in the Talmud and the Peshito. The Western Bibles followed the Alexandrian division into two books (called the third and fourth of Kings), and Jerome adopted this division in the Vulgate (*Regum*, iii. et iv.). But if this separation into two books was due to the LXX. translators, they should have made a less awkward and artificial division than the one which breaks off the first book in the middle of the brief reign of Ahaziah. Jerome's version of the Books of Samuel and Kings appeared first of his translations, and in his famous *Prologus Galeatus* he mentions these facts.

The History was intended to be a continuation of the Books of Samuel. Some critics, and among them Ewald, assign them to the same author, but closer examination of the Book of Kings renders this more than doubtful. The incessant use of the prefix "King," the extreme frequency of the description "Man of God," the references to the law, and above all the constant condemnation of high places, counterbalance the minor resemblance of style, and prove a difference of authorship.

What has the Higher Criticism, as represented in historic sequence by such writers as Vatke, de Wette, Reuss, Graf, Ewald, Kuenen, Bleek, Wellhausen, Stade, Kittel, Renan, Klostermann, Cheyne, Driver, Robertson Smith, and others, to tell us about the structure and historic credibility of the Books of Kings? Has it in any way shaken their value, while it has undoubtedly added to their intelligibility and interest?

1. It emphasises the fact that they are a compilation. In this there is nothing either new or startling, for the fact is plainly and repeatedly acknowledged in the page of the sacred narrative. The sources utilised are:—

(1) The Book of the Acts of Solomon (1 Kings xi. 41).

(2) The Book of the Chronicles of the Kings of Judah (referred to fifteen times).

(3) The Book of the Chronicles of the Kings of Israel (referred to seventeen times).[4]

By comparing the authority referred to in 1 Kings xi. 41 with those quoted in 2 Chron. ix. 29, we see that "the Book of the Acts of Solomon" must have been to a large extent identical with the annals of that king's reign contained in "the Book (R.V., Histories) of Nathan the Prophet," the prophecy of Ahijah the Shilonite, and "the story (R.V., commentary) or visions of Iddo the Seer."[5] Similarly it appears that the Acts of Rehoboam, Abijam, Jehoshaphat, Uzziah, were compiled, at any rate in part, from the histories of Shemaiah, Jehu the son of Hanani,[6] Isaiah the son of Amoz, Hozai (2 Chron. xxxiii. 18, R.V.), and other seers. In the narrative of a history of 450 years (from b.c. 1016 to 562) the writer was of course compelled to rely for his facts upon more ancient authorities. Whether he consulted the original documents in the archives of Jerusalem, or whether he utilised some outline of them which had previously been drawn up, cannot easily be determined. The work would have been impossible but for the existence of the officials known as recorders and historiographers (*Mazkirim, Sopherim*), who first make their appearance in the court of David. But the *original* documents could hardly have survived the ravages of Shalmanezer in Samaria and of Nebuchadnezzar in Jerusalem, so that Movers is probably right in the conjecture that the author's extracts were made, not immediately, but from the epitome of an earlier compiler.[7]

2. Although no direct quotations are referred to other documents, it seems certain from the style, and from various minor touches, that the compiler also utilised detailed accounts of great prophets like Elijah, Elisha, and Micaiah son of Imlah, which had been drawn up by literary students in the Schools of the Prophets. The stories of prophets and men of God who are left unnamed were derived from oral traditions so old that the names had been forgotten before they had been committed to writing.[8]

3. The work of the compiler himself is easily traceable. It is seen in the constantly recurring formulæ, which come almost like the refrain of an epic poem, at the accession and close of every reign.

They run normally as follows. For the Kings of Judah:—

"And in the ... year of ... King of Israel reigned ... over Judah." "And ... years he reigned in Jerusalem. And his mother's name was ... the daughter of.... And ... did that which was {right/evil} in the sight of the Lord."

"And ... slept with his fathers, and was buried with his fathers in the City of David his father. And ... his son reigned in his stead." In the formulæ for the Kings of Israel *"slept with his fathers"* is omitted when the king was murdered; and *"was buried with his fathers"* is omitted because there was no unbroken dynasty and no royal burial-place. The prominent and frequent mention of the queen-mother is due to the fact that as *Gebira* she held a far higher rank than the favourite wife.

4. To the compiler is also due the moral aspect given to the annals and other documents which he utilised. Something of this religious colouring he doubtless found in the prophetic histories which he consulted; and the unity of aim visible throughout the book is due to the fact that his standpoint is identical with theirs. Thus, in spite of its compilation from different sources, the book bears the impress of one hand and of one mind. Sometimes a passing touch in an earlier narrative shows the work of an editor after the Exile, as when in the story of Solomon (1 Kings iv. 20-26) we read, "And he had dominion over all the region *on the other side of the river*," *i.e.*, west of the Euphrates, exactly as in Ezra iv. 10. Here the rendering of the A.V., "on this side the river," is certainly inaccurate, and is surprisingly retained in the R.V. also.[9]

5. To this high moral purpose everything else is subordinated. Like all his Jewish contemporaries, the writer attaches small importance to accurate chronological data. He pays little attention to discrepancies, and does not care in every instance to harmonise his own authorities.[10] Some contradictions may be due to additions made in a later recension,[11] and some may have arisen from the introduction of marginal glosses,[12] or from corruptions of the text which (apart from a miraculous supervision such as was not exercised) might easily, and indeed would inevitably, occur in the constant transcription of numerical letters closely resembling each other. "The numbers as they have come down to us in the Book of Kings," says Canon Rawlinson, "are untrustworthy, being in part self-contradictory, in part opposed to other Scriptural notices, in part improbable, if not impossible."[13]

6. The date of the book as it stands was *after* b.c. 542, for the last event mentioned in it is the mercy extended by Evil-merodach, King of Babylon, to his unfortunate prisoner Jehoiachin (2 Kings xxv. 27) in the thirty-seventh year of his captivity. The language—later than that of Isaiah, and earlier than that of Ezra—confirms this conclusion. That the book appeared before b.c. 536 is clear from the fact that the compiler makes no allusion to Zerubbabel, Jeshua, or the first exiles who returned to Jerusalem after the decree of Cyrus. But it is generally agreed that the book was *substantially* complete before the Exile (about b.c. 600), though some exilic additions may have been made by a later editor.[14] "The writer was already removed by

at least six hundred years from the days of Samuel, a space of time as long as that which separates us from the first Parliament of Edward I."

This date of the book—which cannot but have some bearing on its historic value—is admitted by all, since the peculiarities of the language from the beginning to the end are marked by the usages of later Hebrew.[15] The chronicler lived some two centuries later "in about the same chronological relation to David as Professor Freeman stands to William Rufus."[16]

7. Criticism cannot furnish us with the name of this great compiler. [17] Jewish tradition, as preserved in the Talmud,[18] assigned the Books of Kings to the prophet Jeremiah, and in the Jewish canon they are reckoned among "the earlier prophets." This would account for the strange silence about Jeremiah in the Second Book of Kings, whereas he is prominently mentioned in the Book of Chronicles, in the Apocrypha, and in Josephus. But unless we accept the late and worthless Jewish assertion that, after being carried to Egypt by Johanan, son of Kareah (Jer. xlii. 6, 7), Jeremiah escaped to Babylon,[19] he could not have been the author of the last section of the book (2 Kings xxv. 27-30).[20] Yet it is precisely in the closing chapters of the second book (in and after chap. xvii.) that the resemblances to the style of Jeremiah are most marked.[21] That the writer was a *contemporary* of that prophet, was closely akin to him in his religious attitude, and was filled with the same melancholy feelings, is plain; but this, as recent critics have pointed out, is due to the fact that both writers reflect the opinions and the phraseology which we find in the Book of Deuteronomy.

8. The critics who are so often charged with rash assumptions have been led to the conclusions which they adopt by intense and infinite labour, including the examination of various books of Scripture phrase by phrase, and even word by word. The sum total of their most important results as regards the Books of Kings is as follows:—

i. The books are composed of older materials, retouched, sometimes expanded, and set in a suitable framework, mostly by a single author who writes throughout in the same characteristic phraseology, and judges the actions and characters of the kings from the standpoint of later centuries. The annals which he consulted, and in part incorporated, were twofold—prophetic and political. The latter were probably drawn up for each reign by the official recorder (רִיכְזַמ), who held an important place in the courts of all the greatest kings (2 Sam. viii. 16, xx. 24; 1 Kings iv. 3; 2 Kings xviii. 18), and whose duty it was to write the "acts" or "words" of the "days" of his sovereign (םימיה ירבד).

ii. The compiler's work is partly of the nature of an epitome,[22] and partly consists of longer narratives, of which we can sometimes trace the Northern Israelitish origin by peculiarities of form and expression.

iii. The synchronisms which he gives between the reigns of the kings of Israel and Judah are computed by himself, or by some redactor, and only in round numbers.

iv. The speeches, prayers, and prophecies introduced are perhaps based on tradition, but, since they reflect all the peculiarities of the compiler, must owe their ultimate form to him. This accounts for the fact that the earlier prophecies recorded in these books resemble the tone and style of Jeremiah, but do not resemble such ancient prophecies as those of Amos and Hoshea.

v. The numbers which he adopts are sometimes so enormous as to be grossly improbable; and in these, as in some of the dates, allowance must be made for possible errors of tradition and transcription.

vi. "Deuteronomy," says Professor Driver, "is the standard by which the compiler judges both men and actions; and the history from the beginning of Solomon's reign is presented, not in a purely 'objective' form (as *e.g.* in 2 Sam. ix.-xx.), but from the point of view of the Deuteronomic code.[23]... The principles which, in his view, the history as a whole is to exemplify, are already expressed succinctly in the charge which he represents David as giving to his son Solomon (1 Kings ii. 3, 4); they are stated by him again in chap. iii. 14, and more distinctly in chap. ix. 1-9. Obedience to the Deuteronomic law is the qualification for an approving verdict; deviation from it is the source of ill success (1 Kings xi. 9-13, xiv. 7-11, xvi. 2; 2 Kings xvii. 7-18), and the sure prelude to condemnation. Every king of the Northern Kingdom is characterised as doing 'that which was evil in the eyes of Jehovah.' In the Southern Kingdom the exceptions are Asa, Jehoshaphat, Jehoash, Amaziah, Uzziah, Jotham, Hezekiah, Josiah—usually, however, with the limitation that 'the high places were not removed' as demanded by the Deuteronomic law.[24] The constantly recurring Deuteronomic phrases which most directly illustrate the point of view from which the history is regarded are, *'To keep the charge of Jehovah'*; *'to walk in the ways of Jehovah'*; *'to keep* (or execute) *His commandments, or statutes, and judgments'*; *'to do that which is right in the eyes of Jehovah'*; *'to provoke Jehovah to anger'*; *'to cleave to Jehovah.'* If the reader will be at the pains of underlining in his text the phrases here cited" (and many others of which Professor Driver gives a list), "he will not only realise how numerous they are, but also perceive how they seldom occur indiscriminately in the narrative as such, but are generally aggregated in particular passages (mostly comments on the history, or speeches) which are thereby distinguished from their context, and shown to be presumably the work of a different hand."[25]

vii. It must not be imagined that the late compilation of the book, or its subsequent recensions, or the dogmatic colouring which it may have insensibly derived from the religious systems and organisations of days subsequent to the Exile, have in the least affected the main historic veracity of the kingly annals. They may have influenced the omissions and the moral estimates, but the events themselves are in every case confirmed when we are able to compare them with any records and monuments of Phœnicia, Moab, Egypt, Assyria, or Babylon. The discovery and deciphering of the Moabite stone, and of the painted vaunts of Shishak at Karnak, and of the cuneiform inscriptions, confirm in every case the general truth, in some cases the minute details, of the sacred historian. In so passing an allusion as that in 2 Kings iii. 16, 17 the accuracy of the narrative is confirmed by the fact that (as Delitzsch has shown) the method of obtaining water is that which is to this day employed in the Wady el-Hasa at the southern end of the Dead Sea.[26]

viii. The Book of Kings consists, according to Stade,[27] of, (a) 1 Kings i., ii., the close of a history of David, in continuation of 1 and 2 Samuel. The continuity of the Scriptures is marked in an interesting way by the word "and," with which so many of the books begin. The Jews, devout believers in the work of a Divine Providence, saw no discontinuities in the course of national events.[28]

(b) 1 Kings iii.-xi., a conglomerate of notices about Solomon, grouped round chaps. vi., vii., which narrate the building of the Temple. They are arranged by the præ-exilic compiler, but not without later touches from the Deuteronomic standpoint of a later editor (e.g., iii. 2, 3). Chap. viii. 14-ix. 9 also belong to the later editor.

(c) 1 Kings xi.-2 Kings xxiii. 29, an epitome of the entire regal period of Judah and Israel, after the three first reigns over the undivided kingdom, compiled mainly before the Exile.

(d) 2 Kings xxiii. 30-xxv. 30, a conclusion, added, in its present form, after the Exile.

Two positions are maintained (A) as regards the text, and (B) as regards the chronology.

A. As regards the text no one will maintain the old false assertion that it has come down to us in a perfect condition. There are in the history of the text three epochs: 1, The Præ-Talmudic; 2, The Talmudic-Massoretic up to the time when vowel-points were introduced; 3, The Massoretic traditions of a later period. The marginal annotations known as Q'ri, "read" (plural, *Qarjan*), consist of glosses and euphemisms which were used in the service of the synagogue in place of the written text (K'zib); the oral tradition of these variations was known as the Massora (*i.e.*, tradition). The Greek version (Septuagint, LXX.), which is of immense importance for the history of the text, was begun in Alexandria under Ptolemy Philadelphus (b.c. 283-247). It presents many additions and variations in the Books of Kings.[30]

All Hebrew manuscripts, as is well known, are of comparatively recent date, owing to the strict rule of the Jewish Schools that any manuscript which had in the slightest degree suffered from time or use was to be instantly destroyed. The oldest Hebrew manuscript is supposed to be the Codex Babylonicus at St. Petersburg (a.d. 916), unless one recently discovered by Dr. Ginsburg in the British Museum be older. Most Hebrew manuscripts are later than the twelfth century.

The variations in the Samaritan Pentateuch, and in the Septuagint version—the latter of which are often specially valuable as indications of the original text—furnish abundant proof that no miracle has been wrought to preserve the text of Scripture from the changes and corruptions which always arise in the course of constant transcriptions.

A further and serious difficulty in the reproduction of events in their historic exactitude is introduced by the certainty that many books of the Bible, in their present form, represent the results arrived at after their recension by successive editors, some of whom lived many centuries after the events recorded. In the Books of Kings we probably see many *nuances* which were not introduced till after the epoch-making discovery of the Book of the Law (perhaps the essential parts of the Book of Deuteronomy) in the reign of Josiah, b.c. 621 (2 Kings xxii. 8-14). It is, for instance, impossible to declare with certainty what parts of the Temple service were really coæval with David and Solomon, and what parts had arisen in later days. There appear to be liturgical touches, or alterations as indicated by the variations of the text in 1 Kings viii. 4, 12, 13. In xviii. 29-36 the allusion to the *Minchah* is absent from the LXX. in verse 36, and in 2 Kings iii 20 another reading is suggested.

B. As regards the difficult question of *Chronology* we need add but little to what has been elsewhere said.[31] Even the most conservative critics admit that (1) the numbers of the Biblical text have often become corrupt or uncertain; and (2) that the ancient Hebrews were careless on the subject of exact chronology. The Chronology of the Kings, as it now stands, is historically true in its general outlines, but in its details presents us with data which are mutually irreconcilable. It is obviously artificial, and is dominated by slight modifications of the round number 40.[32] Thus from the Exodus to the Building of the Temple is stated at 480 years, and from that period to the fiftieth year of the Exile also at 480 years. In the Chronicles there are eleven high priests from Azariah ben-Ahimaaz to the Exile of Jozadak, which, with the Exile period, gives twelve generations of 40 years each. Again, from Rehoboam to the Fall of Samaria in the sixth year of Hezekiah, following the 40 years' reign of Saul, of David, and of Solomon, we have:—

Rehoboam, Abijah	20	years.
Asa	41	"
Jehoshaphat, Jehoram	40	"
Ahaziah, Athaliah		
Joash	40	"
Amaziah, Uzziah	81	"
Jotham, Ahaz, Hezekiah	38	"

After the Fall of Samaria we have:—

Hezekiah, Manasseh, Amon	80	"

and it can hardly be a mere accident that in these lists the number 40 is only modified by slight necessary details.

The history of the Northern Kingdom seems to be roughly trisected into 80 years before Benhadad's first invasion, 80 years of Syrian war, 40 years of prosperity under Jeroboam II., and 40 years of decline.[33] This is probably a result of chronological system, not uninfluenced by mystical considerations. For 480 = 40 × 12. *Forty* is repeatedly used as a sacred number in connexion with epochs of penitence and punishment. *Twelve* (4 × 3) is, according to Bähr (the chief student of numerical and other symbolism), "the signature of the people of Israel"—as a whole (4), in the midst of which God (3) resides. Similarly Stade thinks that 16 is the basal number for the reigns of kings from Jehu to Hoshea, and 12 from Jeroboam to Jehu.[34]

It is possible that the synchronistic data did not proceed from the compiler of the Book of Kings, but were added by the last redactor.

Are these critical conclusions so formidable? Are they fraught with disastrous consequences? Which is really dangerous—truth laboriously sought for, or error accepted with unreasoning blindness and maintained with invincible prejudice?

CHAPTER III
THE HISTORIAN OF THE KINGS

"The hearts of kings are in Thy rule and governance, and Thou dost dispose and turn them as it *seemeth best* to Thy godly wisdom."

Were we to judge the compiler or epitomator of the Book of Kings from the literary standpoint of modern historians, he would, no doubt, hold a very inferior place; but so to judge him would be to take a mistaken view of his object, and to test his merits and demerits by conditions which are entirely alien from the ideal of his contemporaries and the purpose which he had in view.

It is quite true that he does not ever aim at fulfilling the requirements demanded of an ordinary secular historian. He does not attempt to present any philosophical conception of the political events and complicated interrelations of the Northern and Southern Kingdoms. His method of writing the story of the Kings of Judah and Israel in so many separate paragraphs gives a certain confusedness to the general picture. It leads inevitably to the repetition of the same facts in the accounts of two reigns. Each king is judged from a single point of view, and that not the point of view by which his own age was influenced, but one arrived at in later centuries, and under changed conditions, religious and political. There is no attempt to show that

"God fulfils Himself in many ways,
Lest one good custom should corrupt the world."

The military splendour or political ability of a king goes for nothing. It has so little interest for the writer that a brilliant and powerful ruler like Jeroboam II. seems to excite in him as little interest as an effeminate weakling like Ahaziah. He passes over without notice events of such capital importance as the invasion of Zerah the Ethiopian (2 Chron. xiv. 9-15, xvi. 8); the wars of Jehoshaphat against Edom, Ammon, and Moab (2 Chron. xx. 1-25); of Uzziah against the Philistines (2 Chron. xxvi. 6-8); and of the Assyrians against Manasseh (2 Chron. xxxiii. 11-13). He neither tells us that Omri subdued Moab, nor that he was defeated by Syria. He scarcely more than mentions events of such deep interest as the conquest of Jerusalem by Shishak (1 Kings xiv. 25, 26); the war between Abijam and Jeroboam (1 Kings xv. 7); of Amaziah with Edom (2 Kings xiv. 7); or even the expedition of Josiah against Pharaoh-nechoh (2 Kings xxiii. 29).[35] For these events he is content to relegate us to the best authorities which he used, with the phrase "and the rest of his acts, his wars, and all that he did." The fact that Omri was the founder of so powerful a dynasty that the Kings of Israel were known to Assyria as "the House of Omri," does not induce him to give more than a passing notice to that king. It did not come within his province to record such memorable circumstances as that Ahab fought with the Aramæan host against Assyria at the battle of Karkar, or that the bloodstained Jehu had to send a large tribute to Shalmaneser II.

There is a certain monotony in the grounds given for the moral judgments passed on each successive monarch. One unchanging formula tells us of every one of the kings of Israel that *"he did that which was evil in the sight of the Lord,"* with exclusive reference in most cases to "the sins of Jeroboam the son of Nebat, wherewith he made Israel to sin." The unfavourable remark about king after king of Judah that *"nevertheless the high places were not taken away; the people offered and burnt incense yet in the high places"* (1 Kings xv. 14, xxii. 43; 2 Kings xii. 3, xiv. 4) makes no allowance for the fact that high places dedicated to Jehovah had been previously used unblamed by the greatest judges and seers, and that the feeling against them had only entered into the national life in later days.

It belongs to the same essential view of history that the writer's attention is so largely occupied by the activity of the prophets, whose personality often looms far more largely on his imagination than that of the kings. If we were to remove from his pages all that he tells us of Nathan, Ahijah of Shiloh, Shemaiah, Jehu the son of Hanani, Elijah, Elisha, Micaiah, Isaiah, Huldah, Jonah, and various nameless "men of God,"[36] the residuum would be meagre indeed. The silence as to Jeremiah is a remarkable circumstance which no theory has explained; but we must remember the small extent of the compiler's canvas, and that, even as it is, we should have but a dim insight into the condition of the two kingdoms if we did not study also the extant writings of contemporary prophets. His whole aim is to exhibit the course of events as so controlled by the Divine Hand that faithfulness to God ensured blessing, and unfaithfulness brought down His displeasure and led to national decline. So far from concealing this principle he states it, again and again, in the most formal manner.[37]

These might be objections against the author if he had written his book in the spirit of an ordinary historian. They cease to have any validity when we remember that he does not profess to offer us a secular history at all. His aim and method have been described as "prophetico-didactic." He writes avowedly as one who believed in the Theocracy. His epitomes from the documents which he had before him were made with a definite religious purpose. The importance or unimportance of kings in his eyes depended on their relation to the opinions which had come home to the conscience of the nation in the still recent reformation of Josiah. He strove to solve the moral problems of God's government as they presented themselves, with much distress and perplexity, to the mind of his nation in the days of its decadence and threatened obliteration. And in virtue of his method of dealing with such themes, he shares with the other historical writers of the Old Testament a right to be regarded as one of the *Prophetæ priores*.[38]

What were those problems?

They were the old problems respecting God's moral government of the world which always haunted the Jewish mind, complicated by the disappointment of national convictions about the promises of God to the race of Abraham and the family of David.

The Exile was already imminent—it had indeed partly begun in the deportation of Jehoiakin and many Jews to Babylon (b.c. 598)—when the book saw the light. The writer was compelled to look back with tears on "the days that were no more." The epoch of Israel's splendour and dominion seemed to have passed for ever. And yet, was not God the true Governor of His people? Had He not chosen Jacob for Himself, and Israel for His own possession? Had not Abraham received the promise that his seed should be as the sand of the sea, and that in his seed should all the nations of the earth be blessed? Or was it a mere illusion that "when Israel was a child I loved him, and out of Egypt I called My son"? The writer clung with unquenchable faith to his convictions about the destinies of his people, and yet every year seemed to render their fulfilment more distant and more impossible.

The promise to Abraham had been renewed to Isaac, and to Jacob, and to the patriarchs; but to David and his house it had been reiterated with special emphasis and fresh details. That promise, as it stood recorded in 2 Sam. vii. 12-16, was doubtless in the writer's hands. The election of Israel as "God's people" is "a world-historic fact, the fundamental miracle which no criticism can explain away."[39] And, in addition, God had sworn in His holiness that He would not forsake David. "When thy days be fulfilled," He had said, "and thou shalt sleep with thy fathers, I will set up thy seed after thee ... and will establish his kingdom. He shall build an house for My name, and *I will establish the throne of his kingdom for ever, I will be his father, and he shall be My son*. If he commit iniquity, I will chastise him with the rod of men, and with the stripes of the children of men. *But My mercy shall not depart from him, as I took it from Saul whom I put away before thee, and thy house and thy kingdom shall be established for ever before thee; thy throne shall be established for ever."* This promise haunted the imagination of the compiler of the Book of Kings. He repeatedly refers to it, and it is so constantly present to his mind that his whole narrative seems to be a comment, and often a perplexed and half-despairing comment, upon it.[40] Yet he resisted the assaults of despair. The Lord had made a faithful oath unto David, and He would *not* depart from it.

It is this that makes him linger so lovingly on the glories of the reign of Solomon. At first they seem to inaugurate an era of overwhelming and permanent prosperity. Because Solomon was the heir of David whom God had chosen, his dominion is established without an effort in spite of a formidable conspiracy. Under his wise, pacific rule the united kingdom springs to the zenith of its greatness. The writer dwells with fond regret upon the glories of the Temple, the Empire, and the Court of the wise king. He records God's renewed promises to him that there should not be any among the kings like unto him all his days. Alas! the splendid visions had faded away like an unsubstantial pageant. Glory had led to vice and corruption. Worldly policy carried apostasy in its train. The sun of Solomon set in darkness, as the sun of David had set in decrepitude and blood. "And the Lord was angry with Solomon, because his heart was turned from the Lord God of Israel, who had appeared unto him twice: ... but he kept not that which the Lord commanded. Wherefore the Lord said unto Solomon, Forasmuch as this is done of thee, and thou hast not kept My covenant, ... I will surely rend the kingdom from thee.... Notwithstanding in thy day I will not do it for David thy father's sake.... Howbeit I will not rend away all the kingdom; but will give one tribe to thy son, for David My servant's sake, and for Jerusalem's sake which I have chosen."[41]

Thus at one blow the heir of "Solomon in all his glory" dwindles into the kinglet of a paltry little province not nearly so large as the smallest of English counties. So insignificant, in fact, do the fortunes of the kingdom become, that, for long periods, it has no history worth speaking of. The historian is driven to occupy himself with the northern tribes because they are the scene of the activity of two glorious though widely different prophets. From first to last we seem to hear in the prose of the annalist the cry of the troubled Psalmist, "Lord, where are Thy old loving-kindnesses which Thou swarest unto David in Thy truth? Remember, Lord, the rebukes that Thy servants have, and how I do bear in my bosom the rebukes of many people wherewith thine enemies have blasphemed Thee, and slandered the footsteps of Thine anointed." And yet, in spite of all, with invincible confidence, he adds, "Praised be the Lord for evermore. Amen and Amen."

And this is one of the great lessons which we learn alike from Scripture and from the experience of every holy and humble life. It may be briefly summed up in the words, "Put thou thy trust in God and be doing good, and He shall bring it to pass." In multitudes of forms the Bible inculcates upon us the lesson, "Have faith in God," "Fear not; only believe." The paradox of the New Testament is the existence of joy in the midst of sorrow and sighing, of exultation (ἀγαλλίασις) even amid the burning fiery furnaces of anguish and persecution. The secret of both Testaments alike is the power to maintain an unquenchable faith, an unbroken peace, an indomitable trust amid every complication of disaster and apparent overthrow. The writer of the Book of Kings saw that God is patient, because He is eternal; that even the histories of nations, not individual lives only, are but as one ticking of a clock amid the eternal silence; that God's ways are not man's ways. And because this is so—because God sitteth above the water floods and remaineth a King for ever—therefore we can attain to that ultimate triumph of faith which consists in holding fast our profession, not only amid all the waves and storms of calamity, but even when we are brought face to face with that which wears the aspect of absolute and final failure. The historian says in the name of his nation what the saint has so often to say in his own, "Though He slay me, yet will I trust in Him." Amos, earliest of the prophets whose written utterances have been preserved, undazzled by the magnificent revival of the Northern Kingdom under Jeroboam II., was still convinced that the future lay with the poor fallen "booth" of David's royalty: "And I will raise up his ruins, and I will build it as in the days of old, ... saith the Lord that doeth this."[42] In many a dark age of Jewish affliction this fire of conviction has still burned amid the ashes of national hopes after it had seemed to have flickered out under white heaps of chilly dust.[43]

CHAPTER IV
GOD IN HISTORY

"The Lord remaineth a King for ever."

Had the compiler of the Book of Kings been so incompetent and valueless an historian as some critics have represented, it would indeed have been strange that his book should have kindled so immortal an interest, or have taken its place securely in the Jewish canon among the most sacred books of the world. He could not have secured this recognition without real and abiding merits. His greatness appears by the manner in which he grapples with, and is not crushed by, the problems presented to him by the course of events to him so dismal.

1. He wrote after Israel had long been scattered among the nations. The sons of Jacob had been deported into strange lands to be hopelessly lost and absorbed amid heathen peoples. The district which had been assigned to the Ten Tribes after the conquest of Joshua had been given over to an alien and mongrel population. The worst anticipations of northern prophets like Amos and Hoshea had been terribly fulfilled. The glory of Samaria had been wiped out, as when one wipeth a dish, wiping and turning it upside down. From the beginning of Israel's separate dominion the prophets saw the germ of its final ruin in what is called the "calf-worship" of Jeroboam, which prepared the way for the Baal-worship introduced by the House of Omri. In the two and a half centuries of Samaria's existence the compiler of this history finds nothing of eternal interest except the activity of God's great messengers. In the history of Judah the better reigns of a Jehoshaphat, of a Hezekiah, of a Josiah, had shed a sunset gleam over the waning fortunes of the remnant of God's people. Hezekiah and Josiah, with whatever deflections, had both ruled in the theocratic spirit. They had both inaugurated reforms. The reformation achieved by the latter was so sweeping and thorough as to kindle the hope that the deep wound inflicted on the nation by the manifold crimes of Manasseh had been healed. But it was not so. The records of these two best kings end, nevertheless, in prophecies of doom.[44] The results of their reforming efforts proved to be partial and unsatisfactory. A race of vassal weaklings succeeded. Jehoahaz was taken captive by the Egyptians, who set up Jehoiakim as their puppet. He submits to Nebuchadnezzar, attempts a weak revolt, and is punished. In the short

reign of Jehoiachin the captivity begins, and the futile rebellion of Zedekiah leads to the deportation of his people, the burning of the Holy City, and the desecration of the Temple. It seemed as though the ruin of the olden hopes could not have been more absolute. Yet the historian will not abandon them. Clinging to God's promises with desperate and pathetic tenacity he gilds his last page, as with one faint sunbeam struggling out of the stormy darkness of the exile, by narrating how Evil-merodach released Jehoiachin from his long captivity, and treated him with kindness, and advanced him to the first rank among the vassal kings in the court of Babylon. If the ruler of Judah must be a hopeless prisoner, let him at least occupy among his fellow-prisoners a sad pre-eminence!

2. The historian has been blamed for the perpetual gloom which enwraps his narrative. Surely the criticism is unjust. He did not invent his story. He is no whit more gloomy than Thucydides, who had to record how the brief gleam of Athenian glory sank in the Bay of Syracuse into a sea of blood. He is not half so gloomy as Tacitus, who is forced to apologise for the "hues of earthquake and eclipse" which darken his every page. The gloom lay in the events of which he desired to be the faithful recorder. He certainly did not love gloom. He lingers at disproportionate length over the grandeur of the reign of Solomon, dilating fondly upon every element of his magnificence, and unwilling to tear himself away from the one period which realised his ideal expectations. After that period his spirits sink. He cared less to deal with a divided kingdom of which only the smallest fragment was even approximately faithful. There could be nothing but gloom in the record of shortlived, sanguinary, and idolatrous dynasties, which succeeded each other like the scenes of a grim phantasmagoria in Samaria and Jezreel. There could be nothing but gloom in the story of that northern kingdom in which king after king was dogged to ruin by the politic unfaithfulness of the rebel by whom it had been founded. Nor could there be much real brightness in the story of humiliated Judah. There also many kings preferred a diplomatic worldliness to reliance on their true source of strength. Even in Judah there were kings who defiled God's own temple with heathen abominations; and a saint like Hezekiah had been followed by an apostate like Manasseh. Had Judah been content to dwell in the defence of the Most High and abide under the shadow of the Almighty, she would have been defended under His wings and been safe beneath His feathers; His righteousness and truth would have been her shield and buckler. He who protected her in the awful crisis of Sennacherib's invasion had proved that He never faileth them that trust Him. But her kings had preferred to lean on such a bruised reed as Egypt, which broke under the weight, and pierced the hand of all who relied on her assistance. "But ye said, Nay, but we will flee upon horses;

therefore shall ye flee: and, We will ride upon the swift; therefore shall they that pursue you be swift."[45]

3. And has not gloom been the normal characteristic of many a long period of human history? It is with the life of nations as with the life of men. With nations, too, there is "a perpetual fading of all beauty into darkness, and of all strength into dust." Humanity advances, but it advances over the ruins of peoples and the wrecks of institutions. Truth forces its way into acceptance, but its progress is "from scaffold to scaffold, and from stake to stake." All who have generalised on the course of history have been forced to recognise its agonies and disappointments. There, says Byron,

> "There is the moral of all human tales;
> 'Tis but the same rehearsal of the past;
> First Freedom, and then Glory — when that fails,
> Wealth, Vice, Corruption — Barbarism at last.
> And History, with all her volumes vast,
> Hath but one page: 'tis better written here
> Where gorgeous tyranny hath thus amassed
> All treasures, all delights that eye or ear,
> Heart, soul could seek, tongue ask."

Mr. J. R. Lowell, looking at the question from another side, sings: —

> "Careless seems the Great Avenger; History's pages but record
> One death-grapple in the darkness 'twixt all systems and the Word;
> Truth for ever on the scaffold, Wrong for ever on the throne —
> Yet that scaffold sways the Future, and behind the dim unknown
> Standeth God within the shadow, keeping watch above His own."

Mr. W. H. Lecky, again, considering the facts of national story from the point of view of heredity, and the permanent consequences of wrong-doing, sings: —

> "The voice of the afflicted is rising to the sun,
> The thousands who have perished for the selfishness of one;
> The judgment-seat polluted, the altar overthrown,
> The sighing of the exile, the tortured captive's groan,
> The many crushed and plundered to gratify the few,
> The hounds of hate pursuing the noble and the true."

Or, if we desire a prose authority, can we deny this painful estimate of Mr. Ruskin?—"Truly it seems to me as I gather in my mind the evidence of insane religion, degraded art, merciless war, sullen toil, detestable pleasure, and vain or vile hope in which the nations of the world have lived since first they could bear record of themselves, it seems to me, I say, as if the race itself were still half serpent, not extricated yet from its clay; a lacertine brood of bitterness, the glory of it emaciate with cruel hunger and blotted with venomous stain, and the track of it on the leaf a glittering slime, and in the sand a useless furrow."[46]

Dark as is the story which the author of the Book of Kings has to record, and hopeless as might seem to be the conclusion of the tragedy, he is responsible for neither. He can but tell the things that were, and tell them as they were; the picture is, after all, far less gloomy than that presented in many a great historic record. Consider the features of such an age as that recorded by Tacitus, with the "Iliad of woes" of which he was the annalist.[47] Does Jewish history offer us nothing but this horrible monotony of delations and suicides? Consider the long ages of darkness and retrogression in the fifth and following centuries; or the unutterable miseries inflicted on the seaboard of Europe by the invasions of the Norsemen—the mere thought of which drove Charlemagne to tears; or the long complicated agony produced by hundreds of petty feudal wars, and the cruel tyranny of marauding barons; or the condition of England in the middle of the fourteenth century when the Black Death swept away half of her population; or the extreme misery of the masses after the Thirty Years' War; or the desolating horror of the wars of Napoleon which filled Germany with homeless and starving orphans. The annals of the Hebrew monarchy are less grim than these; yet the House of Israel might also seem to have been chosen out for a pre-eminence of sorrow which ended in making Jerusalem "a rendezvous for the extermination of the race." When once the Jewish wars began—

> "Vengeance! thy fiery wing their race pursued,
> Thy thirsty poniard blushed with infant blood!
> Roused at thy call and panting still for game
> The bird of war, the Latin eagle came.
> Then Judah raged, by ruffian discord led,
> Drunk with the steamy carnage of the dead;
> He saw his sons by dubious slaughter fall,
> And war without, and death within the wall."

Probably no calamity since time began exceeded in horror and anguish the carnage and cannibalism and demoniac outbreak of every vile and furious passion which marked the siege of Jerusalem; and, in the dreary ages which followed, the world has heard rising from the Jewish people the groan of myriads of broken hearts.

"The fruits of the earth have lost their savour," wrote one poor Rabbi, the son of Gamaliel, "and no dew falls."

In the crowded Ghettos of mediæval cities, during the foul tyranny of the Inquisition in Spain, and many a time throughout Europe, amid the iron oppression of ignorant and armed brutality, the hapless Jews have been forced to cry aloud to the God of their fathers: "Thou feedest Thy people with the bread of tears, and givest them plenteousness of tears to drink!" "Thou sellest Thy people for nought, and givest no money for them."

When the eccentric Frederic William I. of Prussia ordered his Court chaplain to give him in one sentence a proof of Christianity, the chaplain answered without a moment's hesitation: "The Jews, your Majesty." Truly it might seem that the fortunes of that strange people had been designed for a special lesson, not to them only, but to the whole human race; and the general outlines of that lesson have never been more clearly and forcibly indicated than in the Book of Kings.

CHAPTER V
HISTORY WITH A PURPOSE

"History, as distinguished from chronicles or annals, must always contain a theory whether confessed by the writer or not. A sound theory is simply a general conception which co-ordinates a multitude of facts. Without this, facts cease to have interest except to the antiquarian." — Laurie.

The prejudice against history written with a purpose is a groundless prejudice. Herodotus, Thucydides, Livy, Sallust, had each his guiding principle, no less than Ammianus Marcellinus, St. Augustine, Orosius, Bossuet, Montesquieu, Voltaire, Kant, Turgot, Condorcet, Hegel, Fichte, and every modern historian worthy the name. They have all, as Mr. Morley says, felt the intellectual necessity for showing "those secret dispositions of events which prepared the way for great changes, as well as the momentous conjunctures which more immediately brought them to pass." Orosius, founding his epitome on the hint given by St. Augustine in his *De Civitate Dei*, begins with the famous words, "*Divina providentia agitur mundus et homo.*" Other serious writers may vary the formula, but in all their annals the lesson is essentially the same. "The foundation upon which, at all periods, Israel's sense of its national unity rested was religious in its character." "The history of Israel," says Stade, "is essentially a history of religious ideas."[48]

Of course the history is rendered valueless if, in pursuing his purpose, the writer either falsifies events or intentionally manipulates them in such a way that they lead to false issues. But the man who is not inspired by his subject, the man to whom the history which he is narrating has no particular significance, must be a man of dull imagination or cold affections. No such man can write a true history at all. For history is the record of what has happened to men in nations, and its events are swayed by human passions, and palpitate with human emotions. There is no great historian who may not be charged with having been in some respects a partisan. The ebb and flow of his narrative, the "to-and-fro-conflicting waves" of the struggles which he records, must be to him as idle as a dance of puppets if he feels no special interest in the chief actors, and has not formed a distinct judgment of the sweep of the great unseen tidal forces by which they are determined and controlled.

The greatness of the sacred historian of the Kings consists in his firm grasp of the principle that God is the controlling power and sin the disturbing force in the entire history of men and nations.

Surely he does not stand alone in either conviction. Both propositions are confirmed by all experience. In all life, individual and national, sin is weakness; and human life without God, whether isolated or corporate, is no better than

> "A trouble of ants 'mid a million million of suns."

"Why do the heathen so furiously rage together," sang the Psalmist, "and why do the people imagine a vain thing?... He that dwelleth in the heavens shall laugh them to scorn; the Lord shall have them in derision." Even the oldest of the Greek poets, in the first lines of the *Iliad*, declares that amid those scenes of carnage, and the tragic fate of heroes, Διὸς δ' ἐτέλειετο βουλή: —

> "Achilles' wrath, to Greece the direful spring
> Of woes unnumbered, Heavenly Goddess sing;
> That wrath which hurled to Pluto's gloomy reign
> The souls of countless chiefs untimely slain;
> Whose limbs, unburied on the naked shore,
> Devouring dogs and hungry vultures tore:
> Since great Achilles and Atreides strove,
> Such was the sovereign doom, and such the will of Jove!"

In the *Odyssey* the same conviction is repeated, where Odysseus says that "it is the fate-fraught decree of Zeus which stands by as arbiter, when it is meant that miserable men should suffer many woes."[49] The heathen, too, saw clearly that,

> "Though the mills of God grind slowly,
> Yet they grind exceeding small;"

and that, alike for Trojans and Danaans, the chariot-wheels of Heaven roll onward to their destined goal.

Such words express a belief in the hearts of pagans identical with that in the hearts of the early disciples when they exclaimed: "Of a truth in this city against Thy holy Servant Jesus, whom Thou didst anoint, both Herod and Pontius Pilate, with the Gentiles and the peoples of Israel, were gathered together, *to do whatsoever Thy hand and Thy counsel foreordained to come to pass.*"[50]

The ever-present intensity of these convictions leads the historian of the Kings to many shorter or longer "homiletic excursuses," in which he develops his main theme. And if he inculcates his high faith in the form of speeches and other insertions which perhaps express his own views more distinctly than they could have been expressed by the earlier prophets and kings of Judah, he adopts a method which was common in past ages and has always been conceded to the greatest and most trustworthy of ancient historians.

CHAPTER VI
LESSONS OF THE HISTORY

"Great men are the inspired texts of that Divine Book of Revelation of which a chapter is completed from epoch to epoch, and by some named History." —Carlyle.

Thus history becomes one of the most precious books of God. To speak vaguely of "a stream of tendency not ourselves which makes for righteousness," is to endow "a stream of tendency" with a moral sense. Philosophers may talk of "dass unbekannte höhere Wesen das wir ahnen"; but the great majority, alike of the wisest and the humblest of mankind, will give to that moral "Not-ourselves" the name of God. The truth was more simply and more religiously expressed by the American orator when he said that "One with God is always in a majority," and "God is the only final public opinion." Only thus can we account for the fact that events apparently the most trivial have repeatedly been overruled to produce the most stupendous issues, and opposition apparently the most overwhelming has been made to further the very ends which it most fiercely resisted. "The fierceness of man shall turn to Thy praise, and the fierceness of them shalt Thou restrain."

St. Paul expresses his sense of this fact when he says, "Not many wise after the flesh, not many mighty, not many noble, are called: but God chose the foolish things of the world, and the weak things of the world, and the base things of the world, and the things that are despised did God choose, and the things that are not, that He might bring to nought the things that are":[51] and that "because the foolishness of God is wiser than men, and the weakness of God is stronger than men."[52]

The most conspicuous instance of these laws in history is furnished by the victories of Christianity. It was against all probability that a faith not only despised but execrated—a faith whose crucified Messiah kindled unmitigated contempt, and its doctrine of the Resurrection unmingled derision—a faith confined originally to a handful of ignorant peasants drawn from the dregs of a tenth-rate and subjugated people—should prevail over all the philosophy, and genius, and ridicule, and authority of the world, supported by the diadems of all-powerful Cæsars and the swords of thirty legions. It was against all probability that a faith which, in the world's judgment, was so abject, should in so short a space of time achieve so complete a triumph, not by aggressive force, but by meek non-resistance, and that it should win its way through armed antagonism by the sole powers of innocence and of martyrdom—"not by might, nor by power, but by My Spirit, saith the Lord of Hosts."

But though the thoughtful Israelite had no such glorious spectacle as this before him, he saw something analogous to it. The prophets had been careful to point out that no merit or superiority of its own had caused the people to be chosen by God from among the nations for the mighty functions for which it was destined, and which it had already in part fulfilled. "And thou shalt answer before the Lord thy God, and say, A Syrian ready to perish was my father; he went down to Egypt, and sojourned there, few in number."[53] The chosen people could boast of no loftier ancestry than that they sprang from a fugitive from the land of Ur, whose descendants had sunk into a horde of miserable slaves in the hot valley of Egypt. Yet from that degraded and sensuous serfdom God had led them into the wilderness "through parted seas and thundering battles," and had spoken to them at Sinai in a voice so mighty that its echoes have rolled among the nations for evermore. If through their sins and shortcomings they had once more been reduced to the rank of captive strangers in a strange land, the historian knew that even then their lot was not so abject as it once had been. They had at least heroic memories and an imperishable past. He believed that though God's face was darkened to them, the light of it was neither utterly nor finally withdrawn. Nothing could henceforth shake his trust that, even when Israel walked in the valley of the shadow of death, God would still be with His people; that "He would *love* their souls out of the pit of destruction."[54] The vain-glorious efforts of the heathen were foredoomed to final impotence, for God ruled the raging of the sea, the noise of his waves, and the madness of the people.

If this high faith seemed so often to lead only to frustrate hopes, the historian saw the reason. His philosophy of history reduced itself to the one rule that "Righteousness exalteth a nation, but sin is the reproach of any people." It is a sublime philosophy, and no other is possible. It might be written as the comment on every history in the world. The prophets write it large, and again and again, as in letters of blood and fire. Upon their pages, even from the days of Balaam,

> "In outline dim and vast
> Their mighty shadows cast
> The giant forms of Empires on their way
> To ruin: one by one
> They tower, and they are gone!"

Balaam had uttered his denunciation on Moab and Amalek and the Kenite. Amos hurled defiance on Moab, Ammon, and the Philistines. Isaiah taunted Egypt with her splendid impotence, and had said of Babylon: "How art thou fallen from heaven, O Lucifer, son of the morning!" As the sphere of national life enlarged, Nahum had poured forth his exultant dirge over the falling greatness of Assyria; and Ezekiel had painted the desolation which should come on glorious Tyre. These great prophets had read upon the palace-walls of the mightiest kingdoms the burning messages of doom, because they knew that (to quote the words of a living historian) "for every false word and unrighteous deed, for cruelty and oppression, for lust and vanity, the price has to be paid at last.... Justice and truth alone endure and live. Injustice and falsehood may be long-lived, but doomsday comes to them at last."

Has the course of ages at all altered the incidence of these eternal laws? Do modern kingdoms offer any exceptions to the universal experience of the past? Look at Spain. Corrupted by her own vast wealth, by the confusion of religion with the indolent acceptance of lies which paraded themselves as catholic orthodoxy, and by the fatal disseverance of religion from the moral law, she has sunk into decrepitude. Read in the utter collapse and ruin of her great Armada the inevitable Nemesis on greed, indolence, and superstition. Look at modern France. When the inflated bubble of her arrogance collapsed at Sedan as with a touch, two of her own writers, certainly not prejudiced in favour of Christian conclusions—Ernest Renan and Alexandre Dumas, *fils*—pointed independently to the causes of her ruin, and found them in her irreligion and her debauchery. The warnings which they addressed to their countrymen in that hour of humiliation, on the sanctity of family life and the eternal obligations of national righteousness, were identical with those addressed to the Israelites of old by Amos or Isaiah. The only difference was that the form in which they were uttered was modern and came with incomparably less of impassioned force.

The historian who, six hundred years before Christ, saw so clearly, and illustrated with such striking conciseness, the laws of God's moral governance of the world stands far above the casual censure of those who judge him by a mistaken standard. We owe him a debt of the deepest gratitude, not only because he has preserved for us the national records which might otherwise have perished, but far more because he has seen and pointed out their true significance. Imagine an English writer trying to give a sketch of English history since the death of Henry VI. in a thin volume of sixty or seventy octavo pages! Is it conceivable that even the most gifted and brilliant of our historians could in so short a space have rendered such a service as this sacred historian has rendered to all mankind? Do we owe nothing to the vivid insight which enabled him to set so many characters clearly before us with a few strokes of the pen? It is true that it is the *history* which is inspired rather than the *record* of the history; but the record itself is of quite exceptional value. It is true that the prophetic historian and the scientific historian must be judged by wholly different canons of criticism; but may not the prophetic historian be much the greater of the two? By the light of his histories we can read all histories, and see the common lesson taught us by the life of nations, as by the life of individuals — which is, that obedience to God's law is the only path of safety, the only condition of permanence. To fear God and keep His commandments is the end of the matter, and is the whole duty of man. To one who follows the guiding clue of these convictions history becomes "Providence made visible."

Bossuet, like St. Augustine, found the key to all events in a Divine Will controlling and overruling the course of human destinies by a constant exercise of superhuman power. Even Comte "ascribed a hardly less resistible power to a Providence of his own construction, directing present events along a groove cut ever more and more deeply for them by the past." And Mr. John Morley admits that "whether you accept Bossuet's theory or Comte's — whether men be their own Providence, or no more than instruments or secondary agents in other hands — this classification of either Providence equally deserves study and meditation."

Thus, though the Jews were a small and insignificant people — though their kings were mere local sheykhs in comparison with the Pharaohs, or the kings of Assyria and Babylon; though they had none of that sense of beauty which gave immortality to the arts of Greece; though their temple was an altogether trivial structure when compared with the Parthenon or the Serapeum; though they had no drama which can be distantly compared with the Oresteia of Æschylus, and no epic which can be put beside the Iliad or the Nibelungen; though they had nothing which can be dignified with the name of a system of Philosophy — yet their influence on the human race — rendered permanent by their literature, or by that fragment of it which we call "The Books" as though there were none other in the world worth speaking of — has been more powerful than that of all nations upon the development of humanity. Millions have known the names of David or Isaiah, who never so much as heard of Sesostris or of Plato. The influence of the Hebrew race upon mankind has been a moral and a religious influence. Leaving Christianity out of sight — though Christianity itself was nursed in the cradle of Judaism, and was the fulfilment of the Messianic idea which was the most characteristic element in the ancient religion of the Hebrews — the history of Israel is more widely known a million-fold than any history of any people. Professor Huxley is an unsuspected witness to this truth. He has declared that he knows of no other work in the world by the study of which children could be so much humanised, and made to feel that each figure in that vast historical procession fills, like themselves, but a momentary space in the interval between the two eternities. What other nation has contributed to the treasure of human thought elements so immeasurably important as the idea of monotheism, and the Ten Commandments, and the high spiritual teaching by which the prophets brought home to the consciousness of our race the nearness, the holiness, and the love of God? We do not underrate the value of Eternal Inspiration in the "richly-variegated wisdom" which "multifariously and fragmentarily" the Creator has vouchsafed to man; but the Jews will ever be the most interesting of nations, chiefly because to them were entrusted the oracles of God.[55]

BOOK II
DAVID AND SOLOMON

CHAPTER VII
DAVID'S DECREPITUDE

1 Kings i. 1-4

"Praise a fair day at night."

The old age of good men is often a beautiful spectacle. They show us the example of a mellower wisdom, a larger tolerance, a sweeter temper, a more unselfish sympathy, a clearer faith. The setting sun of their bright day tinges even the clouds which gather round it with softer and more lovely hues.

We cannot say this of David's age. After the oppressive splendour of his heroic youth and manhood there was no dewy twilight of honoured peace. We see him in a somewhat pitiable decrepitude. He was not really old; the expression of our Authorised Version, "stricken in years," is literally "entered into days," but the Book of Chronicles calls him "old and full of days."[56] Josephus says that when he died he was only seventy years old. He had reigned seven years and a half in Hebron and thirty-three years in Jerusalem.[57] At the age of seventy many men are still in full vigour of strength and intellect, but the conditions of that day were not favourable to longevity. Solomon does not seem to have survived his sixtieth year; and it is doubtful whether any one of the kings of Israel or Judah—excepting, strange to say, the wicked Manasseh—attained even that moderate age. Threescore years and ten have always been the allotted space of human life, and few who long survive that age find that their strength then is anything but labour and sorrow.

But the decrepitude of David was exceptional. He was drained of all his vital force. He took to his bed, but though they heaped clothes upon him he could get no warmth. "He remained cold amid the torrid heat of Jerusalem." Then his physicians recommended the only remedy they knew, to give heat to his chilled and withered frame. It was the primitive and not ineffectual remedy—which was suggested twenty-two centuries later to the great Frederic Barbarossa—of contact with the warmth of a youthful frame. [58] So they sought out the fairest virgin in all the coasts of Israel to act as the king's nurse, and their choice fell on Abishag, a maiden of Shunem in Issachar.[59] There was no question of his taking another wife. He had already many wives and concubines, and what the bed-ridden invalid required was a strong and youthful nurse to cherish him. We are surprised at such total failure of life's forces. But David had lived through a youth of toil and exposure, of fight and hardship, in the days when his only home had been the dark and dripping limestone caves, and he had been hunted like a partridge on the mountains by the furious jealousy of Saul. The sun had smitten him by day and the moon by night, and the chill dews had fallen on him in the midnight bivouacs among the crags of Engedi. Then had followed the burdens and cares of royalty with guilty anxieties and deeds which shook his pulses with wrath and fear. Coincident with these were the demoralising luxuries and domestic sensualism of a polygamous palace. Worst of all, he had sinned against God, and against light, and against his own conscience. For a time his moral sense had slumbered, and retribution had been delayed. But when he awoke from his sensual dream, the belated punishment burst over him in thunder and his conscience with outstretched finger and tones of menace must often have repeated to the murderous adulterer the doom of Nathan and the stern sentence, "Thou art the man!" Many a vulgar Eastern tyrant would hardly have regarded David's sin as a sin at all; but when such a man as David sins, the fact that he has been admitted into a holier sanctuary adds deadliness to the guilt of his sacrilege. True he was forgiven, but he must have found it terribly hard to forgive himself. God gave back to him the clean heart, and renewed a right spirit within him; but the sense of forgiveness differs from the sweetness of innocence, and the remission of his sins did not bring with it the remission of their consequences. From that disastrous day David was a changed man. It might be said of him as of the Fallen Spirit:—

> "His face
> Deep scars of thunder had entrenched, and care
> Sat on his faded cheek."

The Nemesis of sin's normal consequences pursued him to the end. Dark spirits walked in his house. Joab knew his guilty secrets, and Joab became the tyrannous master of his destiny. Those guilty secrets leaked out, and he lost his charm, his influence, his popularity among his subjects. He was haunted by an ever-present sense of shame and humiliation. Joab was a murderer, and went unpunished; but was not he too an unpunished murderer? If his enemies cursed him, he sometimes felt with a sense of despair, "Let them curse. God hath said unto them, Curse David." His past carried with it the inevitable deterioration of his present. In the overwhelming shame and horror which rent his heart during the rebellion of Absalom, he must often have felt tempted to the fatalism of desperation, like that guilty king of Greek tragedy who, burdened with the curse of his race, was forced to exclaim,—

"Ἔπει τὸ πρᾶγμα καρτ' ἐπισπέρχει θεός
Ἴτω κατ' οὖρον, κῦμα Κωκυτοῦ λαχόν,
Θεῷ στυγηθὲν πᾶν το Λαΐου γένος."[60]

Curses in his family, a curse upon his daughter, a curse upon his sons, a curse upon himself, a curse upon his people,—there was scarcely one ingredient in the cup of human woe which, in consequence of his own crimes, this unhappy king had not been forced to taste. Scourges of war, famine, and pestilence—of a three years' famine, of a three years' flight before his enemies, of a three days' pestilence—he had known them all. He had suffered with the sufferings of his subjects, whose trials had been aggravated by his own transgressions. He had seen his sons following his own fatal example, and he had felt the worst of all sufferings in the serpent's tooth of filial ingratitude agonising a troubled heart and a weakened will. It is no wonder that David became decrepit before his time.

Yet what a picture does he present of the vanity of human wishes, of the emptiness of all that men desire, of the truth which Solon impressed on the Lydian king that we can call no man happy before his death! David's youth had been a pastoral idyll; his manhood an epic of war and chivalry; his premature age becomes the chronicle of a nursery. What different pictures are presented to us by David in his sweet youth and glowing bloom, and David in his unloved and disgraced decline! We have seen him a beautiful ruddy boy, summoned from his sheepfolds, with the wind of the desert on his cheek and its sunlight in his hair, to kneel before the aged prophet and feel the hands of consecration laid upon his head. Swift and strong, his feet like hart's feet, his arms able to bend a bow of steel, he fights like a good shepherd for his flock, and single-handed smites the lion and the bear. His harp and song drive the evil spirit from the tortured soul of the demoniac king. With a sling and a stone the boy slays the giant champion, and the maidens of Israel praise their deliverer with songs and dances. He becomes the armour-bearer of the king, the beloved comrade of the king's son, the husband of the king's daughter. Then indeed he is driven into imperilled outlawry by the king's envy, and becomes the captain of a band of freebooters; but his influence over them, as in our English legends of Robin Hood, gives something of beneficence to his lawlessness, and even these wandering years of brigandage are brightened by tales of his splendid magnanimity. The young chieftain who had mingled a loyal tenderness and genial humour with all his wild adventures—who had so generously and almost playfully spared the life of Saul his enemy—who had protected the flocks and fields of the churlish Nabal—who, with the chivalry of a Sydney, had poured on the ground the bright drops of water from the Well of Bethlehem for which he had thirsted, because they had been won by imperilled lives—sprang naturally into the idolised hero and poet of his people. Then God had taken him from the sheepfolds, from following the ewes great with young ones, that he might lead Jacob His people and Israel His inheritance. Generous to the sad memories of Saul and Jonathan, generous to the princely Abner, generous to the weak Ishbosheth, generous to poor lame Mephibosheth, he had knit all hearts like the heart of one man to himself, and in successful war had carried all before him, north and south, and east and west. He enlarged the borders of his kingdom, captured the City of Waters, and placed the Moloch-crown of Rabbah on his head. Then in the mid-flush of his prosperity, in his pride, fulness of bread, and abundance of idleness, "the tempting opportunity met the susceptible disposition," and David forgat God who had done so great things for him.

The people must have felt how deep was the debt of gratitude which they owed to him. He had given them a consciousness of power yet undeveloped; a sense of the unity of their national life perpetuated by the possession of a capital which has been famous to all succeeding ages. To David the nation owed the conquest of the stronghold of Jebus, and they would feel that "as the hills stand about Jerusalem so standeth the Lord round about them that fear Him."[61] The king who associates his name with a national capital—as Nebuchadnezzar built great Babylon, or Constantine chose Byzantium—secures the strongest claim to immortality. But the choice made by David for his capital showed an intuition as keen as that which has immortalised the fame of the Macedonian conqueror in the name of Alexandria. Jerusalem is a city which belongs to all time, and even under the curse of Turkish rule it has not lost its undying interest. But David had rendered a still higher service in giving stability to the national religion. The prestige of the Ark had been destroyed in the overwhelming defeat of Israel by the Philistines at Aphek, when it fell into the hands of the uncircumcised. After that it had been neglected and half forgotten until David brought it with songs and dances to God's holy hill of Zion. Since then every pious Israelite might rejoice that, as in the Tabernacle of old, God was once more in the midst of His people. The merely superstitious might only regard the Ark as a fetish—the fated Palladium of the national existence. But to all thoughtful men the presence of the Ark had a deeper meaning, for it enshrined the Tables of the Moral Law; and those broken Tables, and the bending Cherubim which gazed down upon them, and the blood-sprinkled gold of the Mercy-Seat were a vivid emblem that God's Will is the Rule of Righteousness, and that if it be broken the soul must be reconciled to Him by repentance and forgiveness. That meaning is beautifully brought out in the Psalm which says, "Who shall ascend into the hill of the Lord, or who shall rise up into the holy place? Even he that hath clean hands and a pure heart: who hath not lifted up his mind unto vanity, nor sworn to deceive his neighbour."

To David more than to any man that conviction of the supremacy of righteousness must have been keenly present, and for this reason his sin was the less pardonable. It "tore down the altar of confidence" in many hearts. It caused the enemies of the Lord to blaspheme, and was therefore worthy of a sorer punishment. And God in His mercy smote, and did not spare.

He sinned: then came earthquake and eclipse. His earthly life was shipwrecked in that place where two seas meet—where the sea of calamity meets the sea of crime.[62] Then followed the death of his infant child; the outrage of Amnon; the blood of the brutal ravisher shed by his brother's hands; the flight of Absalom; his insolence, his rebellion, his deadly insult to his father's household; the long day of flight and shame and weeping and curses, as David ascended the slope of Olivet and went down into the Valley of Jordan; the sanguinary battle; the cruel murder of the beloved rebel; the insolence of Joab; the heartrending cry, "O Absalom, my son, my son Absalom; would God I had died for thee, O Absalom, my son, my son!"

Not even then had David's trials ended. He had to endure the fierce quarrel between Israel and Judah; the rebellion of Sheba; the murder of Amasa, which he dared not punish. He had to sink into the further sin of pride in numbering the people, and to see the Angel of the Plague standing with drawn sword over the threshing-floor of Araurah, while his people— those sheep who had not offended—died around him by thousands. After such a life he was made to feel that it was not for blood-stained hands like his to rear the Temple, though he had said, "I will not suffer mine eyes to sleep nor mine eyelids to slumber, neither the temples of my head to take any rest till I find a place for the tabernacle of the Lord, a habitation for the mighty God of Jacob." And now we see him surrounded by intrigues; alienated from the friends and advisers of his youth, shivering in his sick-room; attended by his nurse; feeble, apathetic, the ghost and wreck of all that he held been, with little left him of his life but its "glimmerings and decays."

It is an oft-repeated story. Even so we see great Darius

"Deserted at his utmost need
By those his former bounty fed;
On the bare ground exposed he lies
Without a friend to close his eyes."

So we see glorious Alexander the Great, dying as a fool dieth, remorseful, drunken, disappointed, at Babylon. So we see our great Plantagenet:—

"Mighty victor, mighty lord,
Low on his funeral couch he lies!
No pitying heart, no eye afford
A tear to grace his obsequies."

So we see Louis XIV., *le grand monarque*, peevish, *ennuyé*, fortunate no longer, an old man of seventy-seven left in his vast lonely palace with his great-grandson, a frivolous child of five, and saying to him, *"J'ai trop aime la guerre; ne m'imitez point."* So we see the last great conqueror of modern times, embittering his dishonoured island-exile by miserable disputes with Sir Hudson Lowe about etiquette and champagne. But among all the "sad stories of the deaths of kings" none ends a purer glory with a more pitiful decline than the poet-king of Israel, whose songs have been to so many thousands their delight in the house of their pilgrimage. Truly David's experience no less than his own may have added bitterness to the traditional epitaph of his son on all human glory: "Vanity of vanities, saith the Preacher, vanity of vanities; all is vanity."

CHAPTER VIII
AN EASTERN COURT AND HOME

1 Kings i

"Pride, fulness of bread, and abundance of idleness."—Ezek. xvi. 49.

A man does not choose his own destiny; it is ordained for higher ends than his own personal happiness. If David could have made his choice, he might, indeed, have been dazzled by the glittering lure of royalty; yet he would have been in all probability happier and nobler had he never risen above the simple life of his forefathers. Our saintly king in Shakespeare's tragedy says:—

"My crown is in my heart, not on my head;
Not decked with diamonds and Indian stones,
Nor to be seen. My crown is called Content;
And crown it is which seldom kings enjoy."

David assuredly did not enjoy that crown. After his establishment at Jerusalem it is doubtful whether he could count more happy days than Abderrahman the Magnificent, who recorded that amid a life honoured in peace and victorious in war he could not number more than fourteen.

We admire the generous freebooter more than we admire the powerful king. As time went on he showed a certain deterioration of character, the inevitable result of the unnatural conditions to which he had succumbed. Saul was a king of a very simple type. No pompous ceremonials separated him from the simple intercourse of natural kindliness. He did not tower over the friends of his youth like a Colossus, and look down on his superiors from the artificial elevation of his inch-high dignity. "In himself was all his state," and there was something kinglier in his simple majesty when he stood under his pomegranate at Migron, with his huge javelin in his hand, than in

"The tedious pomp which waits
On princes, when their rich retinue long
Of horses led, and grooms besmeared with gold
Dazzles the crowd, and sets them all agape."

We should not have assumed beforehand that there was anything in David's character which rendered external pomp and ceremony attractive to him. But the inherent flunkeyism of Eastern servility made his courtiers feed him with adulation, and approach him with genuflexions. Apparently he could not rise superior to the slowly corrupting influences of autocracy which gradually assimilated the court of the once simple warrior to that of his vulgar compeers on the neighbouring thrones. There is something startling to see what a chasm royalty has cleft between him and the comrades of his adversity, and even the partner of his guilt who had become his favourite queen. We see it throughout the story of the last scenes in which he plays a part. He can only be addressed with periphrases and in the third person. "Let there be sought for *my lord the king* a young virgin; and let her stand before *the king*, and let her lie in thy bosom, that *my lord the king* may get heat." Bathsheba can only speak to him in such terms as, "Didst not thou, my lord, O king, swear unto thy handmaid?" and even she, when she enters the sick-chamber of his decrepitude, prostrates herself and does obeisance. Every other word of her speech is interlarded with "my lord the king," and "my lord, O king"; and when she leaves "the presence" she again bows herself with her face to the earth, and does reverence to the king[63] with the words, "May my lord, King David, live for ever." The anointed dignity of the prophet who had once so boldly rebuked David's worst crime does not exempt him from the same ceremonial, and he too goes into the inner chamber bowing his face before the king to the earth.

Insensibly David must have come to require it all, and to like it. Yet the unsophisticated instincts of his more natural youth would surely have revolted from it. He would have deprecated it as sternly as the Greek conqueror in the mighty tragedy who hates to walk to his throne on purple tapestries, and says to his queen:—

> "Ope not the mouth to me, nor cry amain
> As at the footstool of a man of the East,
> Prone on the ground: so stoop not thou to me;"

or, as another has more literally rendered it:—

> "Nor like some barbarous man
> Gape thou upon me an earth-grovelling howl."[64]

But the royal position of David brought with it a surer curse than that which follows the extreme exaltation of a man above his fellows. It brought with it the permitted luxury of imaginary necessity for polygamy, and the man-enervating, woman-degrading paraphernalia of an Eastern harem. Jesse and Boaz, in their paternal fields at Bethlehem, had been content with one wife, and had known the true joys of love and home. But monogamy was thought unsuitable to the new grandeur of a despot, and under the curse of polygamy the joy of love, the peace of home, are inevitably blighted. In that condition man gives up the sweetest sources of earthly blessing for the meanest gratifications of animal sensuousness. Love, when it is pure and true, gilds the life of man with a joy of heaven, and fills it with a breath of Paradise. It renders life more perfect and more noble by the union of two souls, and fulfils the original purpose of creation. A home, blessed by life's most natural sanctities, becomes a saving ark in days of storm.

> "Here Love his golden shafts employs, here lights
> His constant lamp, and waves his purple wings,
> Reigns here and revels."

But in a polygamous household a home is exchanged for a troubled establishment, and love is carnalised into a jaded appetite. The Eastern king becomes the slave of every wandering fancy, and can hardly fail to be a despiser of womanhood, which he sees only on its ignoblest side. His home is liable to be torn by mutual jealousies and subterranean intrigues, and many a foul and midnight murder has marked, and still marks, the secret history of Eastern seraglios. The women—idle, ignorant, uneducated, degraded, intriguing—with nothing to think of but gossip, scandal, spite, and animal passion; hating each other worst of all, and each engaged in the fierce attempt to reign supreme in the affection which she cannot monopolise—spend wasted lives of *ennui* and slavish degradation. Eunuchs, the vilest products of the most corrupted civilisation, soon make their loathly appearance in such courts, and add the element of morbid and rancorous effeminacy to the general ferment of corruption. Polygamy, as it is a contravention of God's original design, enfeebles the man, degrades the woman, corrupts the slave, and destroys the home. David introduced it into the Southern Kingdom, and Ahab into the Northern;—both with the most calamitous effects.

Polygamy produces results worse than all the others upon the children born in such families. Murderous rivalry often reigns between them, and fraternal affection is almost unknown. The children inherit the blood of deteriorated mothers, and the sons of different wives burn with the mutual animosities of the harem, under whose shadowing influence they have been brought up. When Napoleon was asked the greatest need of France, he answered in the one laconic word, *"Mothers"*; and when he was asked the best training ground for recruits, he said, *"The nurseries, of course."* Much of the manhood of the East shows the taint and blight which it has inherited from such mothers and such nurseries as seraglios alone can form.

The darkest elements of a polygamous household showed themselves in the unhappy family of David. The children of the various wives and concubines saw but little of their father during their childish years. David could only give them a scanty and much-divided attention when they were brought to him to display their beauty. They grew up as children, the spoiled and petted playthings of women and debased attendants, with nothing to curb their rebellious passions or check their imperious wills. The little influence over them which David exercised was unhappily not for good. He was a man of tender affections. He repeated the errors of which he might have been warned by the effects of foolish indulgence on Hophni and Phinehas, the sons of Eli, and even on the sons of the guide of his youth, the prophet Samuel. The wild careers of David's elder sons show that they had inherited his strong passions and eager ambition, and that in their case, as well as Adonijah's, he had not displeased them at any time in saying, "Why hast thou done so?"

The consequences which followed had been frightful beyond precedent. David must have learnt by experience the truth of the exhortation, "Desire not a multitude of unprofitable children, neither delight in ungodly sons. Though they multiply, rejoice not in them, except the fear of the Lord be with them: for one that is just is better than a thousand; and better it is to die without children, than to have those that are ungodly."[65]

David's eldest son was Amnon, the son of Ahinoam of Jezreel; his second Daniel or Chileab, son of Abigail, the wife of Nabal of Carmel; the third Absalom, son of Maacah, daughter of Talmai, King of Geshur; the fourth Adonijah, the son of Haggith. Shephatiah and Ithream were the sons of two other wives, and these six sons were born to David in Hebron. When he became king in Jerusalem he had four sons by Bathsheba, born after the one that died in his infancy, and at least nine other sons by various wives, besides his daughter Tamar, sister of Absalom. He had other sons by his concubines. Most of these sons are unknown to fame. Some of them probably died in childhood. He provided for others by making them priests.[66] His line, down to the days of Jeconiah, was continued in the descendants of Solomon, and afterwards in those of the otherwise unknown Nathan. The elder sons, born to him in the days of his more fervent youth, became the authors of the tragedies which laid waste his house. They were youths of splendid beauty, and, as they bore the proud title of "the king's sons," they were from their earliest years encircled by luxury and adulation.[67]

Amnon regarded himself as the heir to the throne, and his fierce passions brought the first infamy into the family of David. By the aid of his cousin Jonadab, the wily son of Shimmeah, the king's brother, he brutally dishonoured his half-sister Tamar, and then as brutally drove the unhappy princess from his presence. It was David's duty to inflict punishment on his shameless heir, but he weakly condoned the crime. Absalom dissembled his vengeance for two whole years, and spoke to his brother neither good nor evil. At the end of that time he invited David and all the princes to a joyous sheep-shearing festival at Baal Hazor. David, as he anticipated, declined the invitation, on the plea that his presence would burden his son with needless expense. Then Absalom asked that, as the king could not honour his festival, at least his brother Amnon, as the heir to the throne, might be present. David's heart misgave him, but he could refuse nothing to the youth whose magnificent and faultless beauty filled him with an almost doting pride, and Amnon and all the princes went to the feast. No sooner was Amnon's heart inflamed with wine, than, at a preconcerted signal, Absalom's servants fell on him and murdered him. The feast broke up in tumultuous horror, and in the wild cry and rumour which arose, the heart of David was torn with the intelligence that Absalom had murdered all his brothers. He rent his clothes, and lay weeping in the dust surrounded by his weeping servants. But Jonadab assured him that only Amnon had been murdered in revenge for his unpunished outrage, and a rush of people along the road, among whom the princes were visible riding on their mules, confirmed his words. But the deed was still black enough. Bathed in tears, and raising the wild cries of Eastern grief, the band of youthful princes stood round the father whose incestuous firstborn had thus fallen by a brother's hand, and the king also and all his servants "wept greatly with a great weeping."

Absalom fled to his grandfather the King of Geshur; but his purpose had been doubly accomplished. He had avenged the shame of his sister, and he was now himself the eldest son and heir to the throne.[68] His claim was strengthened by the superb physique and beautiful hair of which he was so proud, and which won the hearts both of king and people. Capable, ambitious, secure of ultimate pardon, the son and the grandson of a king, he lived for three years at the court of his grandfather. Then Joab, perceiving that David was consoled for the death of Amnon, and that his heart was yearning for his favourite son,[69] obtained the intercession of the wise woman of Tekoah, and got permission for Absalom to return. But his offence had been terrible, and to his extreme mortification the king refused to admit him. Joab, though he had manœuvred for his return, did not come near him, and twice refused to visit him when summoned to do so. With characteristic insolence the young man obtained an interview by ordering his servants to set fire to Joab's field of barley. By Joab's request the king once more saw Absalom, and, as the youth felt sure would be the case, raised him from the ground, kissed, forgave, and restored him to favour.

For the favour of his weakly-fond father he cared little; what he wanted was the throne. His proud beauty, his royal descent on both sides, fired his ambition. Eastern peoples are always ready to concede pre-eminence to splendid men. This had helped to win the kingdom for stately Saul and ruddy David; for the Jews, like the Greeks, thought that "loveliness of person involves the blossoming promises of future excellence, and is, as it were, a prelude of riper beauty."[70] It seemed intolerable to this prince in the zenith of glorious life that he should be kept out of his royal inheritance by one whom he described as a useless dotard. By his personal fascination, and by base intrigues against David, founded on the king's imperfect fulfilment of his duties as judge, "he stole the hearts of the children of Israel." After four years[71] everything was ripe for revolt. He found that for some unexplained reason the tribe of Judah and the old capital of Hebron were disaffected to David's rule. He got leave to visit Hebron in pretended fulfilment of a vow, and so successfully raised the standard of revolt that David, his family, and his followers had to fly hurriedly from Jerusalem with bare feet and cheeks bathed in tears along the road of the Perfumers. Of that long day of misery—to the description of which more space is given in Scripture than to that of any other day except that of the Crucifixion—we need not speak, nor of the defeat of the rebellion. David was saved by the adhesion of his warrior-corps (the *Gibborim*) and his mercenaries (the Krêthi and Plêthi). Absalom's host was routed. He was in some strange way entangled in the branches of a tree as he fled on his mule through the forest of Rephaim.[72] As he hung helpless there, Joab, with needless cruelty, drove three wooden staves through his body in revenge for his past insolence, leaving his armour-bearer to despatch the miserable fugitive. To this day every Jewish child flings a contumelious stone at the pillar in the King's Dale, which bears the traditional name of David's Son, the beautiful and bad.[73]

The days which followed were thickly strewn with calamities for the rapidly ageing and heart-broken king. His helpless decline was yet to be shaken by the attempted usurpation of another bad son.

CHAPTER IX
ADONIJAH'S REBELLION

1 Kings i. 5-53

"The king's word hath power; and who may say unto him,
What doest thou?"—Eccles. viii. 4.

The fate of Amnon and of Absalom might have warned the son who
was now the eldest, and who had succeeded to their claims.

Adonijah was the son of Haggith, "the dancer." His father had piously
given him the name, which means "Jehovah is my Lord." He, too, was "a
very goodly man," treated by David with foolish indulgence, and humoured
in all his wishes. Although the rights of primogeniture were ill-defined, a
king's eldest son, endowed as Adonijah was, would naturally be looked on
as the heir; and Adonijah was impatient for the great prize. Following the
example of Absalom "he exalted himself, saying, I will be king," and, as an
unmistakable sign of his intentions, prepared for himself fifty runners with
chariots and horsemen.[74] David, unwarned by the past, or perhaps too ill
and secluded to be aware of what was going on, put no obstacle in his way.
The people in general were tired of David, though the spell of his name
was still great. Adonijah's cause seemed safe when he had won over Joab,
the commander of the forces, and Abiathar, the chief priest. But the young
man's precipitancy spoiled everything. David lingered on. It was perhaps a
palace-secret that a strong court-party was in favour of Solomon, and that
David was inclined to leave his kingdom to this younger son by his favourite
wife. So Adonijah, once more imitating the tactics of Absalom, prepared
a great feast at the Dragon-stone by the Fullers' Well, in the valley below
Jerusalem.[75] He sacrificed sheep and fat oxen and cattle, and invited all
the king's fifteen sons, omitting Solomon, from whom alone he had any
rivalry to fear. To this feast he also invited Joab and Abiathar, and all the
men of Judah, the king's servants, by which are probably intended "all the
captains of the host" who formed the nucleus of the militia forces.[76] At
this feast Adonijah threw off the mask. In open rebellion against David, his
followers shouted, "God save king Adonijah!"

The watchful eye of one man—the old prophet-statesman, Nathan—
saw the danger. Adonijah was thirty-five; Solomon was comparatively a

child. "Solomon, my son," says David, "is young and tender."[77] What his age was at the date of Adonijah's rebellion we do not know. Josephus says that he was only twelve, and this would well accord with the fact that he seems to have taken no step on his own behalf, while Nathan and Bathsheba act for him. It accords less well with the calm magnanimity and regal decisiveness which he displayed from the first day that he was seated on the throne. The Greek proverb says, Ἀρχὴ ἄνδρα δείκνυσιν, "Power shows the man." Perhaps Solomon, hitherto concealed in the seclusion of the harem, was, up to this time, ignorant of himself as well as unknown to the people. Being unaware of the boy's capacity, many were taken in by the more showy gifts of the handsome Adonijah, whose age might seem to promise greater stability to the kingdom.

But Solomon from his birth upwards had been Nathan's special charge. [78] No sooner had he been born than David had entrusted the infant to the care of the man who had awakened his slumbering conscience to the heinousness of his offence, and had prophesied his punishment in the death of the child of adultery. An oracle had forbidden him to build the Temple because his hands were stained with blood, but had promised him a son who should be a man of rest, and in whose days Israel should have peace and quietness.[79] Long before, in Hebron, David, yearning for peace, had called his eldest son Absalom ("the father of peace"). To the second son of Bathsheba, whom he regarded as the heir of oracular promise, he gave the sounding name of Shelōmoh ("the Peaceful").[80] But Nathan, perhaps with reference to David's own name of "the Beloved," had called the child Jedidiah ("the beloved of Jehovah").

The secret of his destiny was probably known to few, though it was evidently suspected by Adonijah. To have proclaimed it in a crowded harem would have been to expose the child to the perils of poison, and to have doomed him to certain death if one of his unruly brothers succeeded in seizing the royal authority. The oath to Bathsheba that her son should succeed must have been a secret known at the time to Nathan only. It is evident that David had never taken any step to secure its fulfilment.

The crisis was one of extreme peril. Nathan was now old. He had perhaps sunk into the courtly complaisance which, content with one bold rebuke, ceased to deal faithfully with David. He had at any rate left it to Gad the Seer to reprove him for numbering the people. Now, however, he rose to the occasion, and by a prompt *coup d'état* caused the instant collapse of Adonijah's conspiracy.

Adonijah had counted on the jealousy of the tribe of Judah, on the king's seclusion and waning popularity, on the support of "all the captains of the host," on the acquiescence of all the other princes, and above all on the favour of the ecclesiastical and military power of the kingdom as represented by Abiathar and Joab. To Solomon himself, as yet a shadowy figure and so much younger, he attached no importance. He treated his aged father as a cipher, and Nathan as of no particular account.[31] He overlooked the influence of Bathsheba, the prestige which attached to the nomination of a reigning king, and above all the resistance of the body-guard of mercenaries and their captain Benaiah.

Nathan had no sooner received tidings of what was going on at Adonijah's feast than he shook off his lethargy and hurried to Bathsheba. She seems to have retained the same sort of influence over David that Madame de Maintenon exercised over the aged Louis XIV. "Had she heard," asked Nathan, "that Adonijah's coronation was going on at that moment? Let her hurry to King David, and inquire whether he had given any sanction to proceedings which contravened the oath which he had given her that her son Solomon should be his heir." As soon as she had broken the intelligence to the king, he would come and confirm her words.[32]

Bathsheba did not lose a moment. She knew that if Adonijah's conspiracy succeeded her own life and that of her son might not be worth a day's purchase. The helplessness of David's condition is shown by the fact that she had to make her way into "the inner chamber" to visit him. In violation of the immemorial etiquette of an Eastern household, she spoke to him without being summoned, and in the presence of another woman, Abishag, his fair young nurse. With profound obeisances she entered, and told the poor old hero that Adonijah had practically usurped the throne, but that the eyes of all Israel were awaiting his decision as to who should be his successor. She asked whether he was really indifferent to the peril of herself and of Solomon, for Adonijah's success would mean their doom.[33]

While she yet spoke Nathan was announced, as had been concerted between them, and he repeated the story of what was going on at Adonijah's feast. It is remarkable that he says nothing to David either about consulting the Urim, or in any way ascertaining the will of God. He and Bathsheba rely exclusively on four motives—David's rights of nomination, his promise, the danger to Solomon, and the contempt shown in Adonijah's proceedings. "The whole incident," says Reuss, "is swayed by the ordinary movements of passion and interest."[84] The news woke in David a flash of his old energy. With instant decision he summoned Bathsheba, who, as custom required, had left the chamber when Nathan entered. Using his strong and favourite adjuration, "As the Lord liveth, that hath redeemed my soul out of all distress,"[85] he pledged himself to carry out that very day the oath that Solomon should be his heir. She bowed her face to the earth in adoration with the words, "Let my lord, King David, live for ever." He then summoned Zadok, the second priest, Nathan, and Benaiah, and told them what to do. They were to take the body-guard[86] which was under Benaiah's command, to place Solomon on the king's own she-mule[87] (which was regarded as the highest honour of all honours), to conduct him down the Valley of Jehoshaphat to Gihon,[88] where the pool would furnish the water for the customary ablutions, to anoint him king, and then to blow the consecrated ram's horn (*shophar*)[89] with the shout, "God save King Solomon!" After this the boy was to be seated on the throne, and proclaimed ruler over Israel and Judah.

Benaiah was one of David's twelve chosen captains, who was placed at the head of one of the monthly courses of 24,000 soldiers in the third month. The chronicler calls him a priest.[90] His available forces made him master of the situation, and he joyfully accepted the commission with, "Amen! So may Jehovah say!" and with the prayer that the throne of Solomon might be even greater than the throne of David. Joab was commander-in-chief of the army, but his forces had not been summoned or mobilised. Accustomed to a bygone state of things he had failed to observe that Benaiah's palace-regiment of six hundred picked men could strike a blow long before he was ready for action. These guards were the Krêthi and Plêthi,[91] "executioners and runners," perhaps an alien body of faithful mercenaries originally composed of Cretans and Philistines. They formed a compact body of defenders, always prepared for action. They resemble the Germans of the Roman Emperors, the Turkish Janissaries, the Egyptian Mamelukes, the Byzantian Varangians, or the Swiss Guard of the Bourbons. Their one duty was to be ready at a moment's notice to carry out the king's behests. Such a picked regiment has often held in its hands the prerogative of Empire. They were, originally at any rate, identical with the *Gibborim*,[92] and had been at first commanded by men who had earned rank by personal prowess. But for their intervention on this occasion Adonijah would have become king.

While Adonijah's followers were wasting time over their turbulent banquet, the younger court-party were carrying out the unexpectedly vigorous suggestions of the aged king. While the eastern hills echoed with "Long live King Adonijah!" the western hills resounded with shouts of "Long live King Solomon!" The young Solomon had been ceremoniously mounted on the king's mule, and the procession had gone down to Gihon. There, with the solemnity which is only mentioned in cases of disputed succession,[93] Nathan the prophet and Zadok as priest anointed the son of Bathsheba with the horn of perfumed oil which the latter had taken from the sacred tent at Zion.[94] These measures had been neglected by Adonijah's party in the precipitation of their plot, and they were regarded as of the utmost importance, as they are in Persia to this day.[95] Then the trumpets blew, and the vast crowd which had assembled shouted, "God save King Solomon!" The people broke into acclamations, and danced, and played on pipes, and the earth rang again with the mighty sound.[96] Adonijah had fancied, and he subsequently asserted, that "all Israel set their faces on me that I should reign." But his vanity had misled him. Many of the people may have seen through his shallow character, and may have dreaded the rule of such a king. Others were still attached to David, and were prepared to accept his choice. Others were struck with the grave bearing and the youthful beauty of the son of Bathsheba. The multitude were probably opportunists ready to shout with the winner whoever he might be.

The old warrior Joab, perhaps less dazed with wine and enthusiasm than the other guests of Adonijah, was the first to catch the sound of the trumpet blasts and of the general rejoicing, and to portend its significance. As he started up in surprise the guests caught sight of Jonathan, son of Abiathar, a swift-footed priest who had acted as a spy for David in Jerusalem at Absalom's rebellion,[97] but who now, like his father Abiathar and so many of his betters, had gone over to Adonijah. The prince welcomed him as a "man of worth," one who was sure to bring tidings of good omen;[98] but Jonathan burst out with, "Nay, but our Lord king David hath made Solomon king." He does not seem to have been in a hurry to bring this fatal intelligence; for he had not only waited until the entire ceremony at Gihon was over, but to the close of the enthronisation of Solomon in Jerusalem.[99] He had seen the young king seated on the throne of state in the midst of the jubilant people. David had been carried out upon his couch, and, bowing his head in worship before the multitude, had said, "Blessed be the Lord God of Israel, which hath given one to sit on my throne this day, mine eyes even seeing it."

This intelligence fell like a thunderbolt among Adonijah's unprepared adherents. A general flight took place, each man being only eager to save himself. The straw fire of their enthusiasm had already flared itself away. Deserted by every one, and fearing to pay the forfeit of his life, Adonijah fled to the nearest sanctuary, where the Ark stood on Mount Zion under the care of his supporter the high priest Abiathar.[100] There he caught hold of the horns of the altar—wooden projections at each of its corners, overlaid with brass. When a sacrifice was offered the animal was tied to these horns of the altar,[101] and they were smeared with the victim's blood just as in after days the propitiatory was sprinkled with the blood of the bull and the goat on the Great Day of Atonement. The mercy-seat thus became a symbol of atonement, and an appeal to God that He would forgive the sinful priest and the sinful nation who came before Him with the blood of expiation. The mercy-seat would have furnished an inviolable sanctuary had it not been enclosed in the Holiest Place, unapproachable by any feet but that of the high priest once a year. The horns of the altar were, however, available for refuge to any offender, and their protection involved an appeal to the mercy of man as to the mercy of God.[102]

There in wretched plight clung the fallen prince, hurled down in one day from the summit of his ambition. He refused to leave the spot unless King Solomon would first of all swear that he would not slay his servant with the sword.[103] Adonijah saw that all was over with his cause. "God," says the Portuguese proverb, "can write straight on crooked lines;" and as is so often the case, the crisis which brought about His will was the immediate result of an endeavour to defeat it.

Solomon was not one of those Eastern princes who

"Bear like the Turk no brother near the throne."

Many an Eastern king has begun his reign as Baasha, Jehu, and Athaliah did, by the exile, imprisonment, or execution of every possible rival. Adonijah, caught red-handed in an attempt at rebellion, might have been left with some show of justice to starve at the horns of the altar, or to leave his refuge and face the penalty due to crime. But Solomon, unregarded and unknown as he had hitherto been, rose at once to the requirements of his new position, and magnanimously promised his brother a complete amnesty[104] so long as he remained faithful to his allegiance. Adonijah descended the steps of the altar, and having made sacred obeisance to his new sovereign[105] was dismissed with the laconic order, "Go to thine house." If, as some have conjectured, Adonijah had once urged on his father the condign punishment of Absalom, he might well congratulate himself on receiving pardon.[106]

CHAPTER X
DAVID'S DEATH-BED

1 Kings ii. 1-11

"Omnibus idem exitus est, sed et idem domicilium."—
Petron., *Satyr.*

In the Book of Samuel we have the last words cf David in the form of a brief and vivid psalm, of which the leading principle is, "He that ruleth over men must be just, ruling in the fear of God." A king's justice must be shown alike in his gracious influence upon the good and his stern justice to the wicked. The worthless sons of Belial are, he says, "to be beaten down like thorns with spear-shafts and iron."[107]

The same principle dominates in the charge which he gave to Solomon, perhaps after the magnificent public inauguration of his reign described in 1 Chron. xxviii., xxix. He bade his young son to show himself a man, and be rigidly faithful to the law of Moses, earning thereby the prosperity which would never fail to attend true righteousness.[108] Thus would the promise to David—"There shall not fail thee a man on the throne of Israel"—be continued in the time of Solomon.

With our Western and Christian views of morality we should have rejoiced if David's charge to his son had ended there. It is painful to us to read that his last injunctions bore upon the punishment of Joab who had so long fought for him, and of Shimei whom he had publicly pardoned. Between these two stern injunctions came the request that he would show kindness to the sons of Barzillai,[109] the old Gileadite sheykh who had extended such conspicuous hospitality to himself and his weary followers when they crossed the Jordan in their flight from Absalom. But the last words of David, as here recorded, are: "his (Shimei's) hoar head bring thou down to the grave with blood."[110]

In these avenging behests there was nothing which was regarded as unnatural, nothing that would have shocked the conscience of the age. The fact that they are recorded without blame by an admiring historiographer shows that we are reading the annals of times of ignorance which God "winked at." They belong to the era of imperfect moral development, when it was said to them of old time, "Thou shalt love thy neighbour and hate thine enemy," and men had not fully learnt the lesson, "Vengeance is Mine; I will repay, saith the Lord." We must discriminate between the *vitia temporis* and the *vitia hominis*. David was trained in the old traditions of the "avenger of blood"; and we cannot be astonished, though we may greatly regret, that his standard was indefinitely below that of the Sermon on the Mount. He may have been concerned for the safety of his son, but to us it must remain a proof of his imperfect moral attainments that he bade Solomon look out for pretexts to "smite the hoary head of inveterate wickedness," and use his wisdom not to let the two offenders go down to the grave in peace.

The character of Joab furnishes us with a singular study. He, Abishai, and Asahel were the brave, impetuous sons of Zeruiah, the sister or half-sister of David. They were about his own age, and it is not impossible that they were the grandsons of Nahash, King of Ammon.[111] In the days of Saul they had embraced the cause of David, heart and soul. They had endured all the hardships and fought through all the struggles of his freebooting days. Asahel, the youngest, had been in the front rank of his *Gibborim*, and his foot was fleet as that of a gazelle upon the mountain. Abishai had been one of the three who, with jeopardy of their lives, had burst their way to Bethlehem when David longed to drink of the water of its well beside the gate. He had also, on one occasion, saved David's life from the giant Ishbi of Gath, and had slain three hundred Philistines with his spear. His zeal was always ready to flash into action in his uncle's cause. Joab had been David's commander-in-chief for forty years. It was Joab who had conquered the Ammonites and Moabites and stormed the City of Waters. It was Joab who, at David's bare request, had brought about the murder of Uriah. It was Joab who, after wise but fruitless remonstrance, had been forced to number the people. But David had never liked these rough imperious soldiers, whose ways were not his ways. From the first he was unable to cope with them, or keep them in order. In the early days they had treated him with rude familiarity, though in late years they, too, were obliged to approach him with all the forms of Eastern servility. But ever since the murder of Uriah, Joab knew that David's reputation and David's throne were in his hand. Joab himself had been guilty of two wild acts of vengeance for which he would have offered some defence, and of one atrocious crime. His murder of the princely Abner, the son of Ner, might have been excused as the duty of an avenger of blood, for Abner, with one back-thrust of his mighty spear, had killed the young Asahel, after the vain warning to desist from pursuing him. Abner had only killed Asahel in self-defence; but, jealous of Abner's power as the cousin of King Saul, the husband of Rizpah, and the commander of the northern army, Joab, after bluntly rebuking David for receiving him, had without hesitation deluded Abner back to Hebron by a false message and treacherously murdered him. Even at that early period of his reign David was either unable or unwilling to punish the outrage, though he ostentatiously deplored it.

Doubtless in slaying Absalom, in spite of the king's entreaty, Joab had inflicted an agonising wound on the pride and tenderness of his master. But Absalom was in open rebellion, and Joab may have held that David's probable pardon of the beautiful rebel would be both weak and fatal. This death was inflicted in a manner needlessly cruel, but might have been excused as a death inflicted on the battle-field, though probably Joab had many an old grudge to pay off besides the burning of his barley field. After Absalom's rebellion David foolishly and unjustly offered the commandership of the army to his nephew Amasa. Amasa was the son of his sister Abigail by an Ishmaelite father, named Jether.[112] Joab simply would not tolerate being superseded in the command which he had earned by lifelong and perilous services. With deadly treachery, in which men have seen the antitype of the world's worst crime, Joab invited his kinsman to embrace him, and drove his sword into his bowels. David had heard, or perhaps had seen, the revolting spectacle which Joab presented, with the blood of war shed in peace, dyeing his girdle and streaming down to his shoes with its horrible crimson. Yet, even by that act, Joab had once more saved David's tottering throne. The Benjamite Sheba, son of Bichri, was making head in a terrible revolt, in which he had largely enlisted the sympathy of the northern tribes, offended by the overbearing fierceness of the men of Judah. Amasa had been either incompetent or half-hearted in suppressing this dangerous rising. It had only collapsed when the army welcomed back the strong hand of Joab. But whatever had been the crimes of Joab they had been condoned. David, on more than one occasion, had helplessly cried, "What have I to do with you, ye sons of Zeruiah?" "I am this day weak though anointed king, and these men, the sons of Zeruiah, are too hard for me." But he had done nothing, and, whether with or against his will, they continued to hold their offices near his person. David did not remind Solomon of the murder of Absalom, nor of the words of menace — words as bold as any subject ever uttered to his sovereign — with which Joab had imperiously hushed his wail over his worthless son. Those words had openly warned the king that, if he did not alter his line of conduct, he should be king no more. They were an insult which no king could pardon, even if he were powerless to avenge. But Joab, like David himself, was now an old man. The events of the last few days had shown that his power and influence were gone. He may have had something to fear from Bathsheba as the wife of Uriah and the granddaughter of Ahithophel; but his adhesion to the cause of Adonijah had doubtless been chiefly due to jealousy of the ever-growing influence of the priestly soldier Benaiah, son of Jehoiada, who had so evidently superseded him in his master's favour. However that may be, the historian faithfully records that David, on his death-bed, neither forgot nor forgave; and all that we can say is, that it would be unfair to judge him by modern or by Christian principles of conduct.

The other victim whose doom was bequeathed to the new king was Shimei, the son of Gera. He had cursed David at Bahurim on the day of his flight, and in the hour of his extremest humiliation. He had walked on the opposite side of the valley, flinging stones and dust at David,[113] cursing him with a grievous curse as a man of Belial and a man of blood, and telling him that the loss of his kingdom was the retribution which had fallen upon him for the blood of the House of Saul which he had shed. So grievous was the trial of these insults that the place where the king and his people rested that night received the pathetic name of *Ayephim*, "the place of the weary."[114] For this conduct Shimei might have pleaded the pent-up animosities of the House of Saul, which had been stripped by David of all its honours, and of which poor lame Mephibosheth was the only scion left, after David had impaled Saul's seven sons and grandsons in human sacrifice at the demand of the Gibeonites. Abishai, indignant at Shimei's conduct, had said, "Why should this dead dog curse my lord the king?" and had offered, then and there, to cross the valley and take his head. But David rebuked his generous wrath, and when Shimei came out to meet him on his return with expressions of penitence, David not only promised but swore that he should not die. No further danger surely could be anticipated from the ruined and humiliated House of Saul; yet David bade Solomon to find some excuse for putting Shimei to death.

How are we to deal with sins which are recorded of God's olden saints on the sacred page, and recorded without a word of blame?

Clearly we must avoid two errors—the one of injustice, the other of dishonesty.

1. On the one hand, as we have said, we must not judge Abraham, or Jacob, or Gideon, or Jael, or David, as though they were nineteenth-century Christians. Christ Himself taught us that some things inherently undesirable were yet permitted in old days because of the hardness of men's hearts; and that the moral standards of the days of ignorance were tolerated in all their imperfection until men were able to judge of their own deeds in a purer light. "The times of ignorance God overlooked," says St. Paul, "but now He commandeth men that they should all everywhere repent."[115] "Ye have heard that it was said, Thou shalt love thy neighbour, and hate thine enemy.

But *I say unto you, Love your enemies*," said our Lord.[116] When Bayle and Tindal and many others declaim against "the immorality of the Bible" they are unfair in a high degree. They pass judgment on men who had been trained from infancy in opinions and customs wholly unlike our own, and whose conscience would not be wounded by many things which we have been rightly taught to regard as evil. They apply the enlightenment of two millenniums of Christianity to criticise the more rudimentary conditions of life a millennium before Christ. The wild justice inflicted by an avenger of blood, the rude atrocity of the *lex talionis*, are rightly abhorrent to us in days of civilisation and settled law: they were the only available means of restraining crime in unsettled times and half-civilised communities. In his final injunctions about his enemies, whom he might have dreaded as enemies too formidable for his son to keep in subjection, David may have followed the view of his day that his former condonations had only been co-extensive with his own life, and that the claims of justice *ought* to be satisfied.[117]

2. But while we admit every palliation, and endeavour to judge justly, we must not fall into the conventionality of representing David's unforgiving severity as otherwise than reprehensible *in itself*. Attempts to gloss over moral wrong-doing, to represent it as blameless, to invent supposed Divine sanctions and intuitions in defence of it, can but weaken the eternal claims of the law of righteousness. The rule of right is inflexible: it is not a leaden rule which can be twisted into any shape we like. A crime is none the less a crime though a saint commits it; and imperfect conceptions of the high claims of the moral law, as Christ expounded its Divine significance, do not cease to be imperfect though they may be sometimes recorded without comment on the page of Scripture. No religious opinion can be more fatal to true religion than that wrong can, under any circumstances, become right, or that we may do evil that good may come. Because an act is relatively pardonable, it does not follow that it is not absolutely wrong. If it be dangerous to judge the essential morality of any earlier passage of Scripture by the ultimate laws which Scripture itself has taught us, it is infinitely more dangerous, and essentially Jesuitical, to explain away misdeeds as though, under any circumstances, they could be pleasing to God or worthy of a saint. The total omission of David's injunctions and of the sanguinary episodes of their fulfilment by the author of the Books of Chronicles, indicates that, in later days, they were thought derogatory to the pure fame both of the warrior-king and of his peaceful son.

David slept with his fathers, and passed before that bar where all is judged of truly. His life is an April day, half sunshine and half gloom. His sins were great, but his penitence was deep, lifelong, and sincere. He gave occasion for the enemies of God to blaspheme, but he also taught all who love God to praise and pray. If his record contains some dark passages, and his character shows many inconsistencies, we can never forget his courage, his flashes of nobleness, his intense spirituality whenever he was true to his better self. His name is a beacon-light of warning against the glamour and strength of evil passions. But he showed us also what repentance can do, and we are sure that his sins were forgiven him because he turned away from his wickedness. "The sacrifices of God are a troubled spirit: a broken and a contrite heart, O God, Thou wilt not despise." "I go the way of all the earth," said David. "In life," says Calmet, "each one has his particular route: one applies to one thing, another to another. But in the way to death they are all re-united. They go to the tomb by one path."[118]

David was buried in his own city—the stronghold of Zion; and his sepulchre—on the south part of Ophel, near the pool of Siloam—was still pointed out a thousand years later in the days of Christ.[119] As a poet who had given to the people splendid specimens of lyric songs; as a warrior who had inspired their youth with dauntless courage; as a king who had made Israel a united nation with an impregnable capital, and had uplifted it from insignificance into importance; as the man in whose family the distinctive Messianic hopes of the Hebrews were centred, he must remain to the end of time the most remarkable and interesting figure in the long annals of the Old Dispensation.

CHAPTER XI
AVENGING JUSTICE

1 Kings ii. 13-46

"The wrath of a king is as messengers of death." — Prov. xvi. 14.

The reign of Solomon began with a threefold deed of blood. An Eastern king, surrounded by the many princes of a polygamous family, and liable to endless jealousies and plots, is always in a condition of unstable equilibrium; the *death* of a rival is regarded as his only safe imprisonment. [120] On the other hand, it must be remembered that Solomon allowed his other brethren and kinsmen to live; and, in point of fact, his younger brother Nathan became the ancestor of the Divine Messiah of his race.[121]

It was the restless ambition of Adonijah which again brought down an avalanche of ruin. He and his adherents were necessarily under the cold shadow of royal disfavour, and they must have known that they had sinned too deeply to be forgiven. They felt the position intolerable. "In the light of the king's countenance is life, and his favour is as a cloud of the latter rain"; but Adonijah, in the prime of strength and the heyday of passion, beautiful and strong, and once the favourite of his father, could not forget the banquet at which all the princes and nobles and soldiers had shouted, "Long live King Adonijah!" That the royalty of one delirious day should be succeeded by the dull and suspected obscurity of dreary years was more than he could endure, if, by any possible subtlety or force, he could avert a doom so unlike his former golden dreams. Was not Solomon at least ten or fifteen years younger than himself? Was not his seat on the throne of his kingdom still insecure? Were not his own followers powerful and numerous?

Perhaps one of those followers — the experienced Joab, or Jonathan, son of Abiathar — whispered to him that he need not yet acquiesce in the ruin of his hopes, and suggested a subtle method of strengthening his cause, and keeping his claim before the eyes of the people.

Every one knew that Abishag, the fair damsel of Shunem, the ideal of Hebrew maidenhood, was the loveliest virgin who could be found throughout all the land of Israel. Had she been in the strict sense David's wife or concubine, it would have been regarded as a deadly contravention of the Mosaic law that she should be wedded to one of her stepsons. But as she had only been David's nurse, what could be more suitable than that so bright a maiden should be united to the handsome prince?

It was understood in all Eastern monarchies that the harem of a predecessor belonged to the succeeding sovereign. The first thing that a rival or a usurper aimed at was to win the prestige of possessing the wives of the royal house. Nathan reminds David that the Lord had given his master's wives into his bosom.[122] Ishbosheth, weak as he was, had been stung into indignation against his general and great-uncle the mighty Abner, because Abner had taken Rizpah, the daughter of Aiah, Saul's concubine, to wife, which looked like a dangerously ambitious encroachment upon the royal prerogative. Absalom, by the vile counsel of Ahithophel, had openly taken possession of the ten concubines whom his father, in his flight from Jerusalem, had left in charge of the palace. The pseudo-Smerdis, when he revolted against the absent Cambyses, at once seized his seraglio.[123] It is noted even in our English history that the relations between the Earl of Mortimer and Queen Isabella involved danger to the kingdom; and when Admiral Seymour married Queen Catharine Parr, widow of Henry VIII., he at once entered into treasonable conspiracies. Adonijah knew well that he would powerfully further his ulterior purpose if he could secure the hand of the lovely Shunamite.

Yet he feared to make the request to Solomon, who had already inspired him with wholesome awe. With pretended simplicity he sought the intercession of the *Gebira* Bathsheba, who, being the queen-mother, exercised great influence as the first lady of the land.[124] She it was who had placed the jewelled bridal crown with her own hand on the head of her young son.[125]

Alarmed at his visit she asked, "Comest thou peaceably?" He came, he humbly assured her, to ask a favour. Might she not think of his case with a little pity? He was the elder son; the kingdom by right of primogeniture was his; all Israel, so he flattered himself, had wished for his accession. But it had all been in vain, Jehovah had given the kingdom to his brother. Might he not be allowed some small consolation, some little accession to his dignity? at least some little source of happiness in his home?

Flattered by his humility and his appeal, Bathsheba encouraged him to proceed, and he begged that, as Solomon would refuse no request to his mother, would she ask that Abishag might be his wife?

With extraordinary lack of insight, Bathsheba, ambitious as she was, failed to see the subtle significance of the request, and promised to present his petition.

She went to Solomon, who immediately rose to meet her, and seated her with all honour on a throne at his right hand.[126] She had only come, she said, to ask "a small petition."

"Ask on, my mother," said the king tenderly, "for I will not say thee nay."

But no sooner had she mentioned the "small petition" than Solomon burst into a flame of fury. "Why did she not ask for the kingdom for Adonijah at once? He was the elder. He had the chief priest and the chief captain with him. They must be privy to this new plot. But by the God who had given him his father's kingdom, and established him a house, Adonijah had made the request to his own cost, and should die that day."

The command was instantly given to Benaiah, who, as captain of the body-guard, was also chief executioner. He slew Adonijah that same hour, and so the third of David's splendid sons died in his youth a death of violence.

We pause to ask whether the sudden and vehement outburst of King Solomon's indignation was only due to political causes? If, as seems almost certain, Abishag is indeed the fair Shulamite of the Song of Songs, there can be little doubt that Solomon himself loved her,[127] and that she was "the jewel of his seraglio."[128] The true meaning of Canticles is not difficult to read, however much it may lend itself to mystical and allegorical applications. It represents a rustic maiden, faithful to her shepherd lover, resisting all the allurements of a king's court, and all the blandishments of a king's affection. It is the one book of Scripture which is exclusively devoted to sing the glory of a pure love. The king is magnanimous; he does not force the beautiful maiden to accept his addresses. Exercising her freedom, and true to the dictates of her heart, she rejoicingly leaves the perfumed atmosphere of the harem of Jerusalem for the sweet and vernal air of her country home under the shadow of its northern hills. Solomon's impetuous wrath would not be so unaccountable if an unrequited affection added the sting of jealousy to the wrath of offended power. The scene is the more interesting because it is one of the very few personal touches in the story of Solomon, which is chiefly composed of external details, both in Scripture and in such fragments as have been preserved of the pagan historian Dios,

Eupolemos, Nicolas Polyhistor, and those referred to by Josephus, Eusebius, and Clemens of Alexandria.

The fall of Adonijah involved his chief votaries in ruin. Abiathar had been a friend and follower of David from his youthful days. When Doeg, the treacherous Edomite, had informed Saul that the priests of Nob had shown kindness to David in his hunger and distress, the demoniac king had not shrunk from employing the Edomite herdsman to massacre all on whom he could lay his hands. From this slaughter of eighty-five priests who wore linen ephods, Abiathar had fled to David, who alone could protect him from the king's pursuit.[129] In the days when the outlaw lived in dens and caves, the priest had been constantly with him, and had been afflicted in all wherein he was afflicted, and had inquired of God for him. David had recognised how vast was his debt of gratitude to one whose father and all his family had been sacrificed for an act of kindness done to himself. Abiathar had been chief priest for all the forty years of David's reign. In Absalom's rebellion he had still been faithful to the king. His son Jonathan had been David's scout in the city. Abiathar had helped Zadok to carry the Ark to the last house by the ascent to the Mount of Olives, and there he had stood under the olive tree by the wilderness[130] till all the people had passed by. If his loyalty had been less ardent than that of his brother-priest Zadok, who had evidently taken the lead in the matter, he had given no ground for suspicion. But, perhaps secretly jealous of the growing influence of his younger rival, the old man, after some fifty years of unswerving allegiance, had joined his lifelong friend Joab in supporting the conspiracy of Adonijah, and had not even now heartily accepted the rule of Solomon. Assuming his complicity in Adonijah's request, Solomon sent for him, and sternly told him that he was "a man of death," *i.e.*, that death was his desert. But it would have been outrageous to slay an aged priest, the sole survivor of a family slaughtered for David's sake, and one who had so long stood at the head of the whole religious organisation, wearing the Urim and carrying the Ark. He was therefore summarily deposed from his functions, and dismissed to his paternal fields at Anathoth, a priestly town about six miles from Jerusalem.[131] We hear no more of him; but Solomon's warning, "I will not *at this time* put thee to death," was sufficient to show him that, if he mixed himself with court intrigues again, he would ultimately pay the forfeit with his life. Solomon, like Saul, paid very little regard to "benefit of the clergy."[132]

The doom fell next on the arch-offender Joab, the white-haired hero of a hundred fights, "the Douglas of the House of David." He had, if the reading of the ancient versions be correct, "turned after Adonijah, and *had not turned after Solomon.*" Solomon could hardly have felt at ease when a general so powerful and so popular was disaffected to his rule, and Joab read his own sentence in the execution of Adonijah. On hearing the news the old hero fled up Mount Zion, and clung to the horns of the altar. But Abiathar, who might have asserted the sacredness of the asylum, was in disgrace, and Joab was not to escape. "What has happened to thee that thou hast fled to the altar?" was the message sent to him by the king. "Because," he answered, "I was afraid of thee, and fled unto the Lord."[133] It was Solomon's habit to give his autocratic orders with laconic brevity. "Go, fall upon him," he said to Benaiah.

The scene which ensued was very tragic.

The two rivals were face to face. On the one side the aged general, who had placed on David's head the crown of Rabbah, who had saved him from the rebellions of Absalom and of Sheba, and had been the pillar of his military glory and dominion for so many years; on the other the brave soldier-priest, who had won a chief place among the *Gibborim* by slaying a lion in a pit on a snowy day, and "two lion-like men of Moab,"[134] and a gigantic Egyptian whom he had attacked with only a staff, and out of whose hand he had plucked a spear like a weaver's beam and killed him with his own spear. As David lost confidence in Joab he had reposed more and more confidence in this hero. He had placed him over the body-guards, whom he trusted more than the native militia.

The Levite-soldier had no hesitation about acting as executioner, but he did not like to slay any man, and above all such a man, in a place so sacred,[135]—in a place where his blood would be mingled with that of the sacrifices with which the horns of the altar were besmeared.

"The king bids thee come forth," he said.

"Nay," said Joab, "but I will die here."

Perhaps he thought that he might be protected by the asylum, as Adonijah had been; perhaps he hoped that in any case his blood might cry to God for vengeance, if he was slain in the sanctuary of Mount Zion, and on the very altar of burnt offering.

Benaiah naturally scrupled under such circumstances to carry out Solomon's order, and went back to him for instruction. Solomon had no such scruples, and perhaps held that this act was meritorious.[136] "Slay him," he said, "where he stands! He is a twofold murderer; let his blood be on his head." Then Benaiah went back and killed him, and was promoted to his vacant office. Such was the dismal end of so much valour and so much glory! He had taken the sword, and he perished by the sword. And the Jews believed that the curse of David clung to his house for ever, and that among his descendants there never lacked one that was a leper, or a lame man, or a suicide, or a pauper.[137]

Shimei's turn came next. A watchful eye was fixed implacably on this last indignant representative of the ruined House of Saul. Solomon had sent and ordered him to leave his estate at Bahurim, and build a house at Jerusalem, forbidding him to go "any whither,"[138] and telling him that if on any pretence he passed the wady of Kidron he should be put to death. As he could not visit Bahurim, or any of his Benjamite connexions, without passing the Kidron, all danger of further intrigues seemed to be obviated.[139] To these terms the dangerous man had sworn, and for three years he kept them faithfully. At the end of that time two of his slaves fled from him to Achish, son of Maachah, King of Gath.[140] When informed of their whereabouts, Shimei, apparently with no thought of evil, saddled his mule and went to demand their restoration. As he had not crossed the Kidron, and had merely gone to Gath on private business, he thought that Solomon would never hear of it, or would at any rate treat the matter as harmless. Solomon, however, regarded his conduct as a proof of retributive dementation. He sent for him, bitterly upbraided him, and ordered Benaiah to slay him. So perished the last of Solomon's enemies; but Shimei had two illustrious descendants in the persons of Mordecai and Queen Esther.[141]

Solomon perhaps conceived himself to be only acting up to the true kingly ideal. "A king that sitteth on the throne of judgment scattereth away all evil with his eyes." "A wise king scattereth the wicked, and bringeth the wheel over them." "An evil man seeketh only rebellion; therefore a cruel messenger shall be sent against him." "The fear of a king is as the roaring of a lion, whoso provoketh him to anger endangereth his own soul."[142] On the other hand, he continued hereditary kindness to Chimham, son of the old chief Barzillai the Gileadite, who became the founder of the Khan at Bethlehem in which a thousand years later Christ was born.[143]

The elevation of Zadok to the high priesthood vacated by the disgrace of Abiathar restored the priestly succession to the elder line of the House of Aaron. Aaron had been the father of four sons: Nadab, Abihu, Eleazar, and Ithamar. The two eldest had perished childless in the wilderness, apparently for the profanation of serving the tabernacle while in a state of intoxication and offering "strange fire" upon the altar.[144] The son of Eleazar was the fierce priestly avenger Phinehas. The order of succession was as follows:—

```
                    AARON.
                      |
       +---------+------+
       |                |
  Eleazar.         Ithamar.
  Phinehas.        (gap.)
  Abishua.         Eli.
  Bukki.           Phinehas.
  Uzzi.            Ahitub.
  Zerahiah.        Ahiah (1 Sam. xiv. 3).
  Meraioth.        Ahimelech.
  Amariah.         Abiathar (1 Sam. xxii. 20).
  Ahitub.
  Zadok.[145]
```

The question naturally arises how the line of succession came to be disturbed, since to Eleazar, and his seed after him, had been promised "the covenant of an everlasting priesthood."[146] As the elder line continued unbroken, how was it that, for five generations at least, from Eli to Abiathar, we find the *younger* line of Ithamar in secure and lineal possession of the high priesthood? The answer belongs to the many strange reserves of Jewish history. It is clear from the silence of the Book of Chronicles that the intrusion, however caused, was an unpleasant recollection. Jewish tradition has perhaps revealed the secret, and a very curious one it is. We are told that Phinehas was high priest when Jephthah made his rash vow, and that his was the hand which carried out the human sacrifice of Jephthah's daughter. But the inborn feelings of humanity in the hearts of the people were stronger than the terrors of superstition, and arising in indignation against the high priest who could thus imbrue his hands in an innocent maiden's blood, they drove him from his office and appointed a son of Ithamar in his place. The story then offers a curious analogy to that told of the Homeric hero Idomeneus, King of Crete. Caught in a terrible storm on his return from Troy, he too vowed that if his life were saved he would offer up in sacrifice the first living thing that met him. His eldest son came forth with gladness to meet him. Idomeneus fulfilled his vow, but the Cretans rose in revolt against the ruthless father, and a civil war ensued, in which a hundred cities were destroyed and the king was driven into exile. The Jewish tradition is one which could hardly have been invented. It is certain that Jephthah's daughter *was* offered up in sacrifice, in accordance with his rash vow. This could hardly have been done by any but a priest, and the ferocious zeal of Phinehas would not perhaps have shrunk from the horrible consummation. Revolting, even abhorrent, as is such a notion from our views of God, and decisively as human sacrifice is condemned by all the highest teaching of Scripture, the traces of this horrible tendency of human guilt and human fear are evident in the history of Israel as of all other early nations. Some thought akin to it must have lain under the temptation of Abraham to offer up his son Isaac. Twelve centuries later Manasseh "made his son pass through the fire," and kindled the furnaces of Moloch at Tophet in Gehenna, the valley of the sons of Hinnom.[147] His grandfather Ahaz had done the same before him, offering sacrifice and burning his children in the fire.[148] Surrounded by kindred tribes, to which this worship was familiar, the Israelites, in their ignorance and backsliding, were not exempt from its fatal fascination. Solomon himself "went after," and built a high place for Milcom, the abomination of the Ammonites, on the right hand of "the hill that is before Jerusalem," which from this desecration got the name of "The Mount of Corruption." These high places continued, and it must be supposed, had their votaries on "that opprobrious hill," until good Josiah dismantled and defiled them about the year 639, some three centuries after they had been built.

But whether this legend about Phinehas be tenable or not, it is certain that the House of Ithamar fell into deadly disrepute and abject misery. In this the people saw the fulfilment of an old traditional curse, pronounced by some unknown "man of God" on the House of Eli, that there should be no old man in his house for ever; that his descendants should die in the flower of their age; and that they should come cringing to the descendants of the priest whom God would raise up in his stead, to get some humble place about the priesthood for a piece of silver and a morsel of bread.[149]

The prolongation of the curse in the House of Joab and of Eli furnishes an illustration of the menacing appendix to the second commandment— "For I the Lord thy God am a jealous God, visiting the sins of the fathers upon the children to the third and fourth generation of them that hate Me, and showing mercy unto thousands (of generations) of them that love Me and keep My commandments."

There is in families, as in communities, a solidarity alike of blessing and curse. No man perishes alone in his iniquity, whether he be an offender like Achan or an offender like Joab. Families have their inheritance of character, their prerogative examples of misdoing, their influence of the guilty past flowing like a tide of calamity over the present and the future! The physical consequences of transgression remain long after the sins which caused them have ended. Three things, however, are observable in this, as in every faithfully recorded history. One is that mercy boasteth over justice, and the area of beneficent consequence is more permanent and more continuous than that of the entailed curse, as right is always more permanent than wrong. A second is that, though man at all times is liable to troubles and disabilities, no innocent person who suffers temporal afflictions from the sins of his forefathers shall suffer one element of unjust depression in the eternal interests of life. A third is that the ultimate prosperity of the children, alike of the righteous and of sinners, is in their own control; each soul shall perish, and shall only perish, for its own sin. In this sense, though the fathers have eaten sour grapes, the teeth of the children shall *not* be set on edge. In the long generations the line of David no less than the line of Joab, the line of Zadok no less than that of Abiathar, was destined to feel the Nemesis of evil-doing, and to experience that, of whatever parentage men are born, the law remains true—"Say ye of the righteous, that it shall be well with him: for they shall eat the fruit of their doings. Woe unto the wicked! it shall be ill with him: for the reward of his hands shall be given him."[150]

CHAPTER XII
THE BOY-KING'S WISDOM

1 Kings iii. 1-28

"An oracle is upon the lips of a king."—Prov. xvi. 10 (Heb.).

"A king that sitteth on the throne of judgment scattereth away all evil with his eye."—Prov. xx. 8.

> "Ch' ei fu Rè, che chiese senno
> Acciochè Rè sufficiente fosse."
>
> Dante, *Parad.*, xiii. 95.

"Deos ipsos precor ut mihi ad finem usque vitæ quietam et intelligentem humani divinique juris mentem duint."—Tac., *Ann.*, iv. 38.

It would have thrown an interesting light on the character and development of Solomon, if we had been able to conjecture with any certainty what was his age when the death of David made him the unquestioned king. The pagan historian Eupolemos, quoted by Eusebius, says that he was twelve; Josephus asserts that he was fifteen. If Rehoboam was indeed as old as forty-one when he came to the throne (1 Kings xiv. 21), Solomon can hardly have been less than twenty at his accession, for in that case he must have been married before David's death (1 Kings xi. 42). But the reading "forty-one" in 1 Kings xiv. 21 is altered by some into "twenty-one," and we are left in complete uncertainty. Solomon is called "a child" (1 Kings iii. 7), "young and tender" (1 Chron. xxix. 1); but his acts show the full vigour and decision of a man.[151]

The composite character of the Books of Kings leads to some disturbance of the order of events, and 1 Kings iii. 1-4 is perhaps inserted to explain Solomon's sacrifice at the high place of Gibeon,[152] where stood the brazen altar of the old Tabernacle.[153] But no apology is needed for that act.[154] The use of high places, even when they were consecrated to the worship of Jehovah, was regarded in later days as involving principles of danger, and became a grave offence in the eyes of all who took the Deuteronomic standpoint. But high places to Jehovah, as distinct from those dedicated to idols, were not condemned by the earlier prophets, and the resort to them was never regarded as blameworthy before the establishment of the central sanctuary.

After the frightful massacre of the descendants of Aaron at Nob, the old "Tabernacle of the congregation" and the great brazen altar of burnt offerings had been removed to Gibeon from a city defiled by the blood of priests.[155] Gibeon stood on a commanding elevation within easy distance of Jerusalem, and was henceforth regarded as "the great high place," until the Temple on Mount Zion was finished. Thither Solomon went in that imposing civil, religious, and military procession of which the tradition may be preserved in the name of Wady Suleiman still given to the adjoining valley. There, with Oriental magnificence, like Xerxes at Troy, he offered what the Greeks called a *chiliombe*, that is, a tenfold hecatomb of burnt offerings.[156] This "thousandfold holocaust," as the Septuagint terms it, must have been a stately and long-continued function, and in approval of his sacrifice Jehovah granted a vision to the youthful king. Will the Lord be pleased with thousands of rams and ten thousands of rivers of oil, when all the beasts of the forest are His, and the cattle upon a thousand hills? "Thinkest thou," He asked, in the words of the Psalmist, "that I will eat bull's flesh or drink the blood of goats?" No; but God always accepts a willing sacrifice in accordance with the purpose and sincerity of the giver. In reward for the pure intention of the king He appeared to Solomon in a dream, and said, "Ask what I shall give thee."

The Jews recognised three modes of Divine communication—by dreams; by Urim, and by prophets. The highest and most immediate illumination was the prophetic. The revelation by means of the primitive Urim and Thummin, the oracle and jewelled breastplate of the high priest, was the poorest, the most elementary, the most liable to abuse. It was analogous to the method used by the Egyptian chief priests, who wore round their necks a sapphire ornament called Thmei, or "truth," for purposes of divination. [157] After the death of David the Urim and Thummin fell into such absolute desuetude, as a survival of primitive times, that we do not read of its being consulted again in a single instance. It is not so much as mentioned during the five centuries of the history of the kings, and we do not hear of it afterwards. Solomon never once inquired of the priests as David did repeatedly. In the reign of Solomon the voice of prophecy, too, was silent, until disasters began to cloud its close. Times of material prosperity and autocratic splendour are unfavourable to the prophet's function, and sometimes, as in the days of Ahab, the prophets themselves "philippised" in Jehovah's name. But revelation by dreams occurs in all ages. In his prophecy of the great future, Joel says, "Your old men shall see visions, your young men shall dream dreams." It is true that dreams must always have a subjective element, yet, as Aristotle says, "The visions of the noble are better than those of common men."[158] The dreams of night are reflections of the thoughts of day. "Solomon worships God by day; God appears to Solomon by night. Well may we look to enjoy God, when we have served Him."[159] Full of the thoughts inspired by an intense devotion, and a yearning desire to rule aright, the sleeping soul of Solomon became bright with eyes,[160] and in his dream he made a worthy answer to the appeal of God.

"Ask what I shall give thee!" That blessed and most loving offer is made to every human soul. To the meanest of us all God flings open the treasuries of heaven. The reason why we fatally lose them is because we are blinded by the glamour of temptation, and snatch instead at glittering bubbles or Dead Sea fruits. We fail to attain the best gifts, because so few of us earnestly desire them, and so many disbelieve the offer that is made of them. Yet there is no living soul to which God has not given the choice of good and evil. "He hath set fire and water before thee: stretch forth thy hand unto whether thou wilt. Before man is life and death; and whether him liketh shall be given him."[161] Even when our choice is not evil it is often desperately frivolous, and it is only too late that we rue the folly of having rejected the better and chosen the worse.

> "Damsels of Time the hypocritic days,
> Muffled and dumb like barefoot dervishes,
> And marching single in an endless file,
> Bring diadems and fagots in their hands.
> To each they offer gifts after his will, —
> Bread, kingdoms, stars, and sky that holds them all.
> I, in my pleachèd garden, watched the pomp,
> Forgot my morning wishes; hastily
> Took a few herbs and apples, and the Day
> Turned and departed silent. I, too late,
> Under her solemn fillet saw the scorn."[162]

But Solomon made the wise choice. In his dream he thanked God for His mercifully fulfilled promise to David his father, and with the touching humble confession, "I am but a little child: I know not how to go out or come in,"[163] he begged for an understanding heart to judge between right and wrong in guiding his great and countless people.[164]

God was pleased with the noble, unselfish request. The youthful king might have besought the boon of "many days," which was so highly valued before Christ had brought life and immortality to light; or for riches, or for victory over his enemies. Instead of this he had asked for "understanding, to discern judgment," and the lesser gifts were freely accorded him. "Seek ye first the kingdom of God, and His righteousness, and all these things shall be added unto you."[165] God promised him that he should be a king of unprecedented greatness. He freely gave him riches and honour, and, conditionally on his continued faithfulness, a long life. The condition was broken, and Solomon was not more than sixty years old when he was called before the God whom he forsook.[166]

"And Solomon awoke, and behold it was a dream." But he knew well that it was also more than a dream, and that "God giveth to His beloved even sleeping."[167]

In reverential gratitude he offered a second sacrifice of burnt offerings before the ark on Mount Zion, and added to them peace offerings, with which he made a great feast to all his servants. Twice again did God appear to Solomon; but the second time it was to warn, and the third time to condemn.

In the parallel account given by the chronicler, Solomon says, "Give me now wisdom and knowledge," and God replies, "Wisdom and knowledge is granted unto thee." There is a wide difference between the two things. Knowledge may come while wisdom still lingers, and wisdom may exist in Divine abundance where knowledge is but scant and superficial. The wise may be as ignorant as St. Antony, or St. Francis of Assisi; the masters of those who know may show as little 'wisdom for a man's self' as Abélard, or as Francis Bacon. "Among the Jews one set of terms does service to express both intellectual and moral wisdom. The 'wise' man means the righteous man; the 'fool' is one who is godless. Intellectual terms that describe knowledge are also moral terms describing life." No doubt in the ultimate senses of the words there can be no true knowledge, as there can be no perfect wisdom, without goodness. This was a truth with which Solomon himself became deeply impressed. "The fear of the Lord," he said, "is the beginning of wisdom, but fools despise knowledge and understanding." The lineaments of "a fool" are drawn in the Book of Proverbs, and they bear the impress of moral baseness and moral aberrations.

To Solomon both boons were given, "wisdom and understanding exceeding much, and largeness of heart, even as the sand that is on the sea shore." Of his many forms of intellectual eminence I will speak later on. What he longed for most was evidently moral insight and practical sagacity. He felt that "through justice shall the throne be established."

Practical wisdom was eminently needed for the office of a judge. [168] Judgeship was a main function of Eastern royalty, and rulers were called *Shophetim* or judges.[169] The reality of the gift which Solomon had received from God was speedily to be tested.[170] Two harlots came before him.[171] One had overlaid her child in the night, and stealing the living child of the other she put her dead child in its place. There was no evidence to be had. It was simply the bare word of one disreputable woman against the bare word of the other. With instant decision, and a flash of insight into the springs of human actions, Solomon gave the apparently childish order to cut the children in two, and divide them between the claimants. The people laughed,[172] and the delinquent accepted the horrible decision; but the mother of the living child yearned for her babe, and she cried out, "O my lord, give her the living babe,[173] and in no wise slay it." "*Give her the living babe, and in no wise slay it,*" murmured the king to himself, repeating the mother's words; and then he burst out with the triumphant verdict, "Give *her* the living child! *she* is the mother thereof!"[174]

The story has several parallels. It is said by Diodorus Siculus that when three youths came before Ariopharnes, King of Thrace, each claiming to be the only son of the King of the Cimmerians, he ordered them each to hurl a javelin at their father's corpse. Two obeyed, one refused, and Ariopharnes at once proclaimed him to be the true son.[175] Similarly an Indian story tells that a woman, before she bathed, left her child on the bank of the pool, and a female demon carried it off. The goddess, before whom each claimed the child, ordered them to pull it in two between them, and consigned it to the mother who shuddered at the test.[176] A judgment similarly founded on filial instinct is attributed to the Emperor Claudius. A mother refused to acknowledge her son; and as there were no proofs Claudius ordered her to marry the youth, whereupon she was obliged to acknowledge that he was her son.[177]

Modern critics, wise after the event, express themselves very slightingly of the amount of intelligence required for the decision; but the people saw the value of the presence of mind and rapid intuition which settled the question by bringing an individual dilemma under the immediate arbitrament of a general law. They rejoiced to recognise the practical wisdom which God had given to their young king. The word *Chokhmah*, which is represented by one large section of Jewish literature, implied the practical intelligence derived from insight or experience, the power to govern oneself and others. Its conclusions were expressed chiefly in a gnomic form, and they pass through various stages in the Sapiential Books of the Old Testament. The chief books of the *Chokhmah* are the Books of Proverbs, Job, and Ecclesiastes, followed by such books as Wisdom and Ecclesiasticus. On the Divine side Wisdom is the Spirit of God, regarded by man under the form of Providence (Wisdom i. 4, 7, vii. 7, 22, ix. 17); and on the human side it is trustworthy knowledge of the things that are (*id.* vii. 17). It is, in fact, "a knowledge of Divine and human things, and of their causes" (4 Macc. ii. 16). This branch of wisdom could be repeatedly shown by Solomon at the city gate and in the hall of judgment.

2. His varied *intellectual* wisdom created deeper astonishment. He spake, we are told, "of trees from the cedar which is in Lebanon even unto the hyssop that springeth out of the wall: he spake also of beasts and fowl and of creeping things and of fishes." This knowledge has been misunderstood and exaggerated by later tradition. It is expanded in the Book of Wisdom (viii. 17) into a perfect knowledge of kosmogony, astronomy, the alterations of solstices, the cycles of years, the natures of wild beasts, the forces of spirits, the reasonings of men, the diversities of plants. Solomon became to Eastern legend

> "The warrior-sage, whose restless mind
> Through nature's mazes wandered unconfined,
> Who every bird, and beast, and insect knew,
> And spake of every plant that quaffs the dew."

His knowledge, however, does not seem to have been even empirically scientific. It consisted in the moral and religious illustration of truth by emblems derived from nature.[178] He surpassed, we are told, the ethnic gnomic wisdom of all the children of the East—the Arabians and Chaldæans, and all the vaunted scientific and mystic wisdom of Egypt.[179] Ethan and Heman were Levitic poets and musicians;[180] Chalcol and Darda[181] were "sons of the choir," *i.e.*, poets (Luther), or sacred singers;[182] and all four were famed for wisdom; but Solomon excelled them all. Of his one thousand and five songs, the majority were probably secular. Only two psalms are even traditionally assigned to him.[183] Of his three thousand proverbs not more than two hundred survive, even if all in the Book of Proverbs be his. Tradition adds that he was a master of "riddles" or "dark sayings," by which he won largely in fines from Hiram, whom he challenged for their solution, until the Tyrian king defeated him by the aid of a sharp youth named Abdemon.[184] Specimens of these riddles with their answers may be found in the Book of Proverbs,[185] for the Hebrew word "proverb" (*Mashal*) probably means originally, an illustration. This book also contains various ambiguous hard sayings of which the skilful construction awoke admiration and stimulated thought.[186] The Queen of Sheba is said to have tested Solomon by riddles.[187] The tradition gradually spread in the East that Solomon was also skilled in magic arts, that he knew the language of the birds,[188] and possessed a seal which gave him mastery over the genii. In the Book of Wisdom he is made to say, "All such things as are either secret or manifest, them I know." Josephus attributes to him the formulæ and spells of exorcism, and in Eccles. ii. 8 the words rendered "musical instruments" (shiddah and shiddoth; R.V., "concubines very many") were understood by the Rabbis to mean that he was the lord over male and female demons.[189]

3. Far more precious than practical or intellectual ability is the gift of *moral* wisdom, which Solomon so greatly appreciated but so imperfectly attained. Yet he felt that "wisdom is the principal thing, therefore get wisdom." The world gives that name to many higher and lower manifestations of capacity and attainment, but wisdom is in Scripture the one law of all true life. In that magnificent outburst of Semitic poetry, the twenty-eighth chapter of the Book of Job, after pointing out that there is such a thing as natural knowledge—that there is a vein for the silver, and ore of gold, and a place of sapphires, and reservoirs of subterranean fire—the writer asks: "But where shall wisdom be found? and where is the place of understanding?" After showing with marvellous power that it is beyond man's unaided search—that the depths and the seas say, "It is not in us," and destruction and death have but heard the fame thereof with their ears—he adds with one great crash of concluding music, "God understandeth the way thereof, and He knoweth the place thereof.... And unto man He said, *Behold, the fear of the Lord, that is wisdom; and to depart from evil is understanding.*"[190] And again we read, "*The fear of the Lord is the beginning of knowledge.*"[191] The sated cynic of the Book of the Ecclesiastes, or one who had studied, not without dissatisfaction, his sad experience, adds, "*Fear God, and keep His commandments: for this is the whole duty of man.*" And in answer to the question "*Who is a wise man and endued with knowledge among you?*" St. James, the Lord's brother, who had evidently been a deep student of the Sapiential literature, does not answer, "He who understands all mysteries," or, "He who speaks with the tongue of men or of angels," but, "Let him show out of a good conversation his works with meekness of wisdom." Men whom the world has deemed wise have often fallen into utter infatuation, as it is written, "He taketh the wise in their own craftiness"; but heavenly wisdom may belong to the most ignorant and simplehearted. It is "first pure, then peaceable, gentle, and easy to be entreated, without partiality and without hypocrisy."

We should observe, however, that the *Chokhmah*, or wisdom-literature of the Jews, while it incessantly exalts morality, and sometimes almost attains to a perception of the spiritual life, was neither prophetic nor priestly in its character. It bears the same relation to the teaching of the prophets on the one hand, and the priests on the other, as morality does to religion and to externalism. Its teaching is loftier and truer than the petty insistence of Pharisaism on meats and drinks and divers washings, in that it deals with the weightier matters of the law; but it does not attain to the passionate spirituality of the greater Hebrew seers. It cares next to nothing for ritual, and therefore rises above the developed Judaism of the post-exilic epoch. It is lofty and true inasmuch as it breathes the spirit of the Ten Commandments, but it has not learnt the freedom of love and the beatitudes of perfect union with God. In one word, it finds its culmination in Proverbs and Ecclesiasticus, rather than in the spirit of the Sermon on the Mount and the Gospel of St. John.

We cannot better conclude this chapter than with the eulogy of the son of Sirach: "Solomon reigned in a peaceable time and was honoured; for God made all quiet round about him, that he might build a house in His name and prepare His sanctuary for ever. How wise wast thou in thy youth, and, as a flood, filled with understanding! Thy soul covered the whole earth, and thou filledst it with dark parables. Thy name went far unto the islands, and for thy peace thou wast beloved. The countries marvelled at thee for thy songs, and proverbs, and parables, and interpretations. By the name of the Lord God, who is called the Lord God of Israel, thou didst gather gold as tin, and didst multiply silver as lead."[192]

CHAPTER XIII
SOLOMON'S COURT AND KINGDOM

1 Kings iv. 1-34

"But what more oft in nations grown corrupt
And by their vices brought to servitude,
Than to love bondage more than liberty,
Bondage with ease than strenuous liberty?
"*Samson Agonistes.*

When David was dead, and Solomon was established on his throne, his first thoughts were turned to the consolidation of his kingdom. He was probably quite a youth.[193] He was not, nor did he ever desire to be, a warlike prince; but he was compelled to make himself secure from two enemies—Hadad and Rezon—who began almost at once to threaten his frontiers. Of these, however, we shall speak later on, since it is only towards the close of Solomon's reign that they seem to have given serious trouble. If the second psalm is by Solomon it may point to some early disturbances among heathen neighbours which he had successfully put down.

The only actual expedition which Solomon ever made was one against a certain Hamath-Zobah, to which, however, very little importance can be attached. It is simply mentioned in one line in the Book of Chronicles, and it is hard to believe—considering that Rezon had possession of Damascus—that Solomon was master of the *great* Hamath.[194] He made a material alteration in the military organisation of his kingdom by establishing a standing army of fourteen hundred war-chariots, and twelve thousand horsemen, whom he dispersed in various cities and barracks, keeping some of them at Jerusalem.[195]

In order to save his kingdom from attack Solomon expended vast sums on the fortification of frontier towns. In the north he fortified Hazor; in the north-west Megiddo. The passes to Jerusalem on the west were rendered safe by the fortresses at Upper and Nether Bethhoron. The southern districts were overawed by the building of Baalath and Tamar, "the palm-city," which is described as "in the wilderness in the land,"—perhaps in the desolate tract on the road from Hebron to Elath.[196] Movers thinks that

Hazezon-Tamar or Engedi is meant, as this town is called Tamar in Ezek. xlvii. 19.

As the king grew more and more in power he gave full reins to his innate love of magnificence. We can best estimate the sudden leap of the kingdom into luxurious civilisation if we contrast the royalty of Saul with that of Solomon. Saul was little more than a peasant-prince, a local emîr, and such state as he had was of the humblest description. But Solomon vied with the gorgeous secular dynasts of historic empires.

His position had become much more splendid owing to his alliance with the King of Egypt—an alliance of which his humbler predecessors would scarcely have dreamed. We are not told the name of his Egyptian bride, but she must have been the daughter of one of the last kings of the twenty-first Tanite dynasty—either Psinaces, or Psusennes II.[197] The dynasty had been founded at Tanis (Zoan) about b.c. 1100 by an ambitious priest named Hir-hor. It only lasted for five generations. Whatever other dower Solomon received with this Egyptian princess, his father-in-law rendered him one signal service. He advanced from Egypt with an army against the Canaanite town of Gezer, which he conquered and destroyed.[198] Solomon rebuilt it as an outpost of defence for Jerusalem. Further than this the Egyptian alliance did not prove to be of much use. The last king of this weak twenty-first dynasty was succeeded b.c. 990 by the founder of a new Bubastite dynasty, the great Shishak I. (Shesonk, Σεσόνχωσις), the protector of Jeroboam and the plunderer of Jerusalem and its Temple. Ker'amat, niece of the last king of the dynasty, married Shishak, the founder of the new dynasty, and was the mother of U-Sark-on I. (Zerah the Ethiopian).

It has been a matter of dispute among the Rabbis whether Solomon was commendable or blameworthy for contracting this foreign alliance. If we judge him simply from the secular standpoint, nothing could be more obviously politic than the course he took. Nor did he break any law in marrying Pharaoh's daughter. Moses had not forbidden the union with an Egyptian woman. Still, from the religious point of view, it was inevitable that such a connexion would involve consequences little in accordance with the theocratic ideal. The kings of Judah must not be judged as though they were ordinary sovereigns. They were meant to be something more than mere worldly potentates. The Egyptian alliance, instead of flattering the pride, only wounded the susceptibilities of the later Jews. The Rabbis had a fantastic notion that Shimei had been Solomon's teacher, and that the king did not fall into the error of wedding an alien[199] until Shimei had been driven from Jerusalem.[200] That there was some sense of doubt in Solomon's mind appears from the statement in 2 Chron. viii. 11, that he deemed it unfit for his bride to have her residence on Mount Moriah, a spot hallowed by the presence of the Ark of God.[201] That she became a proselytess has been suggested, but it is most unlikely. Had this been the case it would have been mentioned in contrast with the heathenism of the fair idolatresses who in later years beguiled the king's heart. On the other hand, the princess, who was his chief if not his earliest bride, does not seem to have asked for any shrine or chapel for the practice of her Egyptian rites. This is the more remarkable since Solomon, ashamed of the humble cedar house of David—which would look despicable to a lady who had lived in "the gigantic edifices, and labyrinthine palace of Egyptian kings"[202]— expended vast sums in building her a palace which should seem worthy of her royal race.

From this time forward the story of Solomon becomes more the record of a passing pageant preserved for us in loosely arranged fragments. It can never be one tithe so interesting as the history of a human heart with its sufferings and passions. "Solomon in all his glory," that figure so unique, so lonely in its wearisome pomp, can never stir our sympathy or win our affection as does the natural, impetuous David, or even the fallen, unhappy Saul. "The low sun makes the colour." The bright gleams and dark shadows of David's life are more instructive than the dull monotony of Solomon's magnificence.

The large space of Scripture devoted to him in the Books of Kings and Chronicles is occupied almost exclusively with the details of architecture and display. It is only in the first and last sections of his story that we catch the least glimpse of the man himself. In the central section we see nothing of him, but are absorbed in measurements and descriptions which have a purely archæological, or, at the best, a dimly symbolic significance. The man is lost in the monarch, the monarch in the appurtenances of his royal display. His annals degenerate into the record of a sumptuous parade.

The fourth chapter of the Book of Kings gives us the constitution of his court as it was in the middle of his reign, when two of his daughters were already married. It need not detain us long.

The highest officers of the kingdom were called *Sarim*, "princes," a title which in David's reign had been borne almost alone by Joab, who was *Sar-ha-zaba*, or captain of the host. The son of Zadok[203] is named first as "the priest." The two chief secretaries (*Sopherim*) were Elihoreph and Ahiah. They inherited the office of their father Shavsha (1 Chron. xviii. 16),[204] who had been the secretary of David. It was their duty to record decrees and draw up the documents of state. Jehoshaphat, the son of Ahilud, continued to hold the office of annalist or historiographer (*Mazkîr*), the officer known as the Waka Nuwish in Persian courts.[205] Azariah was over the twelve prefects (*Nitzabim*), or farmers-general, who administered the revenues. [206] His brother Zabud became "priest" and "king's friend."[207] Ahishar was "over the household" (*al-hab-Baith*); that is, he was the chamberlain, vizier, or mayor of the palace, wearing on his shoulder the key which was the symbol of his authority.[208] Adoniram or Adoram, who had been tax-collector for David, still held that onerous and invidious office,[209] which subsequently, in his advanced old age, cost him his life. Benaiah succeeded to the chief-captaincy of Joab. We hear nothing more of him, but the subsequent history shows that when David gathered around him this half alien and wholly mercenary force in a country which had no standing army, he turned the sovereignty into what the Greeks would have called a tyranny. As the only armed force in the kingdom the body-guard overawed opposition, and was wholly at the disposal of the king. These troops were to Solomon at Jerusalem what the Prætorians were to Tiberius at Rome.

The chief points of interest presented by the list are these:—

1. First we mark the absence of any prophet. Neither Nathan nor Gad is even mentioned. The pure ray of Divine illumination is overpowered by the glitter of material prosperity.

2. Secondly, the priests are quite subordinate. They are only mentioned fifth in order, and Abiathar is named with Zadok, though after his deposition he was living in enforced retirement.[210] The sacerdotal authority was at this time quite overshadowed by the royal. In all the elaborate details of the pomp which attended the consecration of the Temple, Solomon is everything, the priests comparatively nothing. Zadok is not even mentioned as taking any part in the sacrifices in spite of his exalted rank. Solomon acts throughout as supreme head of the Church. Nor was this unnatural, since the two capital events in the history of the worship of Jehovah—the removal of the Ark to Mount Zion, and the suggestion, inception, and completion of the building of the Temple—were due to Solomon and David, not to Zadok or Abiathar. The priests, throughout the monarchy, suggest nothing, inaugurate nothing. They are lost in functions and formal ceremonies. They are but obedient administrative servants, and, so far from protecting religion, they acquiesce with tame indifference in every innovation and every apostasy. History has few titles which form so poor a claim to distinction as that of Levitic priest.

3. Further, we have two curious and significant phenomena. The title "the priest" is given to Azariah, who is first mentioned among the court functionaries. Solomon had not the least intention to allow either the priestly or the much loftier prophetic functions to interfere with his autocracy. He did not choose that there should be any danger of a priest usurping an

exorbitant influence, as Hir-hor had done in Egypt, or Ethbaal afterwards did in the court of Tyre, or Thomas à-Becket in the court of England, or Torquemada in that of Spain. He was too much a king to submit to priestly domination. He therefore appointed one who should be "the priest" for courtly and official purposes, and should stand in immediate subordination to himself.

4. The Nathan whose two sons, Azariah and Zabud, held such high positions, was in all probability not Nathan the Prophet, who is rarely introduced without his distinctive title, but Nathan, the younger brother of Solomon, in whose line the race of David was continued after the extinction of the elder branch in Jeconiah. Here again we note the union of *civil* with priestly functions. Zabud is called "a priest" though he is a layman, a prince of the tribe of Judah. Nor was this the first instance in which princes of the royal house had found maintenance, occupation, and high official rank by being in some sort engaged in the functions of the priesthood. Already in David's reign we find the title "priests" (*Kohanim*) given to the sons of David in the list of court officials[211]—"*and David's sons were priests.*" In this we trace the possible results of Phœnician influences.

5. Incidentally it is pleasing to find that, though Solomon put Adonijah to death, he stood in close and kindly relations with his other brothers, and gave high promotions to the sons of the brothers who stood nearest to him in age, in one of whom we see the destined ancestor of the future Messiah. [212]

6. The growth of imposing officialism, and its accompanying gulf between the king and his people, is marked by the first appearance of "the chamberlain" as a new functionary. On him fell the arrangement of court pageants and court etiquette. The chamberlain in despotic Eastern courts becomes a personage of immense importance, because he controls the right of admission into the royal presence. Such officers, even when chosen from the lowest rank of slaves—like Eutropius the eunuch-minister of Arcadius,[213] or Olivier le Daim, the barber-minister of Louis XI.—often absorb no mean part of the influence of the sovereign with whom they are brought into daily connexion. In the court of Solomon the chamberlain stands only ninth in order; but three centuries later, in the days of Hezekiah, he has become the greatest of the officials, and "Eliakim who was over the household" is placed before Shebna, the influential scribe, and Joah, the son of Asaph the recorder.[214]

7. Last on the list stands the minister who has the ominous title of *al-ham-Mas*, or "over the tribute." The Mas means the "levy," corvée, or forced labour. In other words, Adoram was overseer of the soccagers. Saul had

required an overseer of the flocks, and David a guardian of the treasury, but Adoram is not mentioned till late in his reign.[215] The *gravamen* of David's numbering of the people seems to have lain in the intention to subject them to a poll tax, or to personal service, such as had become necessary to maintain the expenses of the court. It is obvious that as royalty developed from the conception of the theocratic king to that of the Oriental despot, the stern warning of Samuel to the people of Israel was more and more fulfilled. They had said, "Nay, but we will have a king to reign over us, when Jehovah was their king"; and Samuel had told them how much less blessed was bondage with ease than their strenuous liberty. He had warned them that their king would take their sons for his runners and charioteers and reapers and soldiers and armourers, and their daughters for his perfumers and confectioners; and that he would seize their fields and vineyards for his courtiers, and claim the tithes of their possession, and use their asses, and put their oxen to his work. The word *"Mas"* representing soccage, serfdom, forced labour (corvée; Germ., *Frohndienst*), first became odiously familiar in the days of Solomon.

Solomon was an expensive king, and the Jewish kings had no private revenue from which the necessary resources could be supplied. In order to secure contributions for the maintenance of the royal establishment, Solomon appointed his twelve Prefects. The list of them is incorporated from a document so ancient that in several instances the names have dropped out, and only "son of" remains.[216] The districts entirely and designedly ignored the old tribal limits, which Solomon probably wished to obliterate. Ben-Hur administered the hill country of Ephraim; Ben-Dekar had his headquarters in Dan; Ben-Hesed had the maritime plain; Ben-Abinadab the fertile region of Carmel, and he was wedded to Solomon's daughter Taphath;[217] Baana, son of Ahilud, managed the plain of Esdraelon; Ben-Geber the mountainous country east of Jordan, including Gilead and Argob with its basaltic towns; Ahinadab, son of Iddo, was officer in Mahanaim; Ahimaaz in Naphtali (he was married to Solomon's daughter Basmath, and was perhaps the son of Zadok); Baanah, son of David's faithful Hushai, was in Asher; Shimei, son of Elah, in Benjamin; Jehoshaphat in Issachar. Geber administered alone the ancient dominions of Sihon and Og. We see with surprise that Judah seems to have been exempted from the burdens imposed on the other districts, and if so the impolitic exemption was a main cause of the subsequent jealousies.[218]

The chief function of these officers was to furnish provisions for the immense numbers who were connected with the court. The curious list is given of the provision required for one day—thirty measures of fine flour, sixty of bread,[219] ten fat oxen, twenty pasture oxen, and one hundred sheep, besides the delicacies of harts, gazelles, fallow-deer, and fatted guinea-hens or swans.[220] Bunsen reckons that this would provide for about fifteen thousand persons. In this there is nothing extraordinary, though the number is disproportionate to the smallness of the kingdom. About the same number were daily supported by the kings of the great empire of Persia.[221] We see how rapidly the state of royalty had developed when we compare Solomon's superb surroundings with the humble palace of Ishbosheth less than fifty years earlier—a palace of which the only guard was a single sleepy woman, who had been sifting wheat in the noontide, and had fallen asleep over her task in the porch.[222]

Yet in the earlier years of the reign, while the people, dazzled by the novel sense of national importance, felt the stimulus given to trade and industry, the burden was not painfully felt. They multiplied in numbers, and lived under their vines and fig trees in peace and festivity.[223] But much of their prosperity was hollow and shortlived. Wealth led to vice and corruption, and in place of the old mountain breezes of freedom which purified the air, the nation, like Issachar, became like an ass crouching between two burdens, and bowing its shoulders to the yoke in the hot valley of sensuous servitude.

"Ill fares the land, to hastening ills a prey,
Where wealth accumulates and men decay!"

It is impossible to overlook the general drift of Jewish royalty towards pure materialism in the days of Solomon. We search in vain for the lofty spirituality which survived even in the rough epoch of the Judges and the rude simplicity of David's earlier reign. The noble aspirations which throb in one Davidic psalm are worth all the gorgeous formalism of the Temple service. Amid the luxuries of plenty and the feasts of wine on the lees there seems to have been an ever-deeping famine of the Word of God.

There was one innovation, which struck the imagination of Solomon's contemporaries, but was looked on with entire disfavour by those who had been trained in the old pious days. Solomon had immense stables for his chariot horses (*susim*), and the swift riding horses of his couriers (*parashim*).[224] It seems to have been Solomon's ambition to equal or outshine "the chariots of Pharaoh,"[225] with which his Egyptian queen had been familiar at Tanis. This feature of his reign is dwelt upon in the Arabian legends, as well as in all the historical records of his greatness.[226] But the maintenance of a cavalry force had always been discouraged by the religious teachers of Israel. The use of horses in war is forbidden in Deuteronomy.[227] Joshua had houghed the horses of the Canaanites, and burned their chariots at Misrephoth-maim. David had followed his example. Barak had defeated the iron chariots of Sisera, and David the splendid cavalry of Hadadezer with the simple infantry of Israel.[228] The spirit of the olden faithfulness spoke in such words as, "Some put their trust in chariots, and some in horses; but we will trust in the name of the Lord our God." Solomon's[229] successors discovered that they had not gained in strength by adopting this branch of military service in their hilly and rocky land. They found that "a horse is but a vain thing to save a man, neither shall he deliver any man by his great strength."[230]

For a time, however, Solomon's strenuous centralisation was successful. His dominion extended, at least nominally, from Tiphzah (Thapsacus), beside the ford on the west bank of the Euphrates, to the Mediterranean; over the whole domain of the Philistines; and from Damascus to "the river of Egypt," that is, the Rhinokolura or Wady el-Areesh. The names Jeroboam and Rehoboam imply that they were born in an epoch of prosperity.[231] But the sequel proves that it was that sort of empire which,

> "Like expanded gold,
> Exchanges solid strength for feeble splendour."[232]

CHAPTER XIV
THE TEMPLE

1 Kings v., vi., vii

"And his next son, for wealth and wisdom famed,
The clouded Ark of God, till then in tents
Wandering, shall in a glorious temple enshrine."
Paradise Lost, xii. 340.

After the destructive battle of Aphek, in which the Philistines had defeated Israel, slain the two sons of Eli, and taken captive the Ark of God, they had inflicted a terrible vengeance on the old sanctuary at Shiloh. They had burnt the young men in the fire, and slain the priests with the sword, and no widows were left to make lamentation.[233] It is true that, terrified by portents and diseases, the Philistines after a time restored the Ark, and the Tabernacle of the wilderness with its brazen altar still gave sacredness to the great high place at Gibeon, to which apparently it had been removed. [234] Nevertheless, the old worship seems to have languished till it received a new and powerful impulse from the religious earnestness of David. He had the mind of a patriot-statesman as well as of a soldier, and he felt that a nation is nothing without its sacred memories. Those memories clustered round the now-discredited Ark. Its capture, and its parade as a trophy of victory in the shrine of Dagon, had robbed it of all its superstitious prestige as a fetish; but, degraded as it had been, it still continued to be the one inestimably precious historic relic which enshrined the memories of the deliverance of Israel from Egypt, and the dawn of its heroic age.

As soon as David had given to his people the boon of a unique capital, nothing could be more natural than the wish to add sacredness to the glory of the capital by making it the centre of the national worship. According to the Chronicles, David—feeling it a reproach that he himself should dwell in palaces ceiled with cedar and painted with vermilion while the Ark of God dwelt between curtains—had made unheard-of preparations to build a house for God. But it had been decreed unfit that the sanctuary should be built by a man whose hands were red with the blood of many wars, and he had received the promise that the great work should be accomplished by his son.[235]

Into that work Solomon threw himself with hearty zeal in the month Zif[236] of the fourth year of his reign, when his kingdom was consolidated. [237] It commanded all his sympathies as an artist, a lover of magnificence, and a ruler bent on the work of centralisation. It was a task to which he was bound by the solemn exhortation of his father, and he felt, doubtless, its political as well as its religious importance. With his sincere desire to build to God's glory was mingled a prophetic conviction that his task would be fraught with immense issues for the future of his people and of all the world. The presence of the Temple left its impress on the very name of Jerusalem. Although it has nothing to do with the Temple or with Solomon, it became known to the heathen world as Hierosolyma, which, as we see from Eupolemos (Euseb., *Præp. Evang.*, ix. 34), the Gentile world supposed to mean "the Temple (*Hieron*) of Solomon."

The materials already provided were of priceless value. David had consecrated to God the spoils which he had won from conquered kings. We must reject, as the exaggerations of national vanity, the monstrous numbers which now stand in the text of the chronicler; but a king whose court was simple and inexpensive was quite able to amass treasures of gold and silver, brass and iron, precious marbles and onyx stones. Solomon had only to add to these sacred stores.[238]

He inherited the friendship which David had enjoyed, with Hiram, King of Tyre, who, according to the strange phrase of the Vatican Septuagint, sent his servants "to anoint" Solomon. The friendliest overtures passed between the two kings in letters, to which Josephus appeals as still extant. A commercial treaty was made by which Solomon engaged to furnish the Tyrian king with annual revenues of wheat, barley, and oil,[239] and Hiram put at Solomon's disposal the skilled labour of an army of Sidonian wood-cutters and artisans.[240] The huge trunks of cedar and cypress were sent rushing down the heights-of Lebanon by schlittage, and laboriously dragged by road or river to the shore. There they were constructed into immense rafts, which were floated a hundred miles along the coast to Joppa, where they were again dragged with enormous toil for thirty-five miles up the steep and rocky roads to Jerusalem. For more than twenty years, while Solomon was building the Temple and his various royal constructions, Jerusalem became a hive of ceaseless and varied industry. Its ordinary inhabitants must have been swelled by an army of Canaanite serfs and Phœnician artisans to whom residences were assigned in Ophel. There lived the hewers and bevellers of stone; the cedar-cutters of Gebal or Biblos;[241] the cunning workmen in gold or brass; the bronze-casters who made their moulds in the clay ground of the Jordan valley; the carvers and engravers; the dyers who stained wool with the purple of the murex, and the scarlet dye of the trumpet fish; the weavers and embroiderers of fine linen. Every class of labourer was put into requisition, from the descendants of the Gibeonite *Nethinim*, who were rough hewers of wood and drawers of water, to the trained artificers whose beautiful productions were the wonder of the world. The "father," or master-workman, of the whole community was a half-caste, who also bore the name of Hiram, and was the son of a woman of Naphtali by a Tyrian father.[242]

Some writers have tried to minimise Solomon's work as a builder, and have spoken of the Temple as an exceedingly insignificant structure which would not stand a moment's comparison with the smallest and humblest of our own cathedrals. Insignificant in size it certainly was, but we must not forget its costly splendour, the remote age in which the work was achieved, and the truly stupendous constructions which the design required. Mount Moriah was selected as a site hallowed by the tradition of Abraham's sacrifice, and more recently by David's vision of the Angel of the Pestilence with his drawn sword on the threshing-floor of the Jebusite Prince Araunah.[243] But to utilise this doubly consecrated area involved almost superhuman difficulties, which would have been avoided if the loftier but less suitable height of the Mount of Olives could have been chosen. The rugged summit had to be enlarged to a space of five hundred yards square, and this level was supported by Cyclopean walls, which have long been the wonder of the world.[244] The magnificent wall on the east side, known as "the Jews' wailing-place," is doubtless the work of Solomon, and after outlasting "the drums and tramplings of a hundred triumphs," it remains to this day in uninjured massiveness. One of the finely bevelled stones is 38½ feet long and 7 feet high, and weighs more than 100 tons. These vast stones were hewn from a quarry above the level of the wall, and lowered by rollers down an inclined plane. Part of the old wall rises 30 feet above the present level of the soil, but a far larger part of the height lies hidden 80 feet under the accumulated *débris* of the often captured city. At the south-west angle, by Robinson's arch, three pavements were discovered, one beneath the other, showing the gradual filling up of the valley; and on the lowest of these were found the broken *voussoirs* of the arch. In Solomon's day the whole of this mighty wall was visible. On one of the lowest stones have been discovered the Phœnician paint-marks which indicated where each of the huge masses, so carefully dressed, edge-drafted, and bevelled, was to be placed in the structure. The caverns, quarries, water storages, and subterranean conduits hewn out of the solid rock, over which Jerusalem is built, could only have been constructed at the cost of immeasurable toil. They would be wonderful even with our infinitely more rapid methods and more powerful agencies; but when we remember that they were made three thousand years ago we do not wonder that their massiveness has haunted the imagination of so many myriads of visitors from every nation.

It was perhaps from his Egyptian father-in-law that Solomon, to his own cost, learnt the secret of forced labour which alone rendered such undertakings possible. In their Egyptian bondage the forefathers of Israel had been fatally familiar with the ugly word *Mas*, the labour wrung from them by hard task-masters.[245] In the reign of Solomon it once more became only too common on the lips of the burdened people.[246]

Four classes were subject to it.

1. The lightest labour was required from the native freeborn Israelites (*ezrach*). They were not regarded as bondsmen (מַס־עֹבֵד), yet 30,000 of these were required in relays of 10,000 to work, one month in every three, in the forest of Lebanon.[247]

2. There were the strangers, or resident aliens (*Gerim*), such as the Phœnicians and Giblites, who were Hiram's subjects and worked for pay.

3. There were three classes of slaves—those taken in war, or sold for debt, or home-born.

4. Lowest and most wretched of all, there were the vassal Canaanites (*Toshabim*), from whom were drawn those 70,000 burden-bearers, and 80,000 quarry-men, the Helots of Palestine, who were placed under the charge of 3600 Israelite officers. The blotches of smoke are still visible on the walls and roofs of the subterranean quarries where these poor serfs, in the dim torchlight and suffocating air, "laboured without reward, perished without pity, and suffered without redress." The sad narrative reveals to us, and modern research confirms, that the purple of Solomon had a very seamy side, and that an abyss of misery heaved and moaned under the glittering surface of his splendour.[248] Jerusalem during the twenty years occupied by his building must have presented the disastrous spectacle of task-masters, armed with rods and scourges, enforcing the toil of gangs of slaves, as we see them represented on the tombs of Egypt and the palaces of Assyria. The sequel shows the jealousies and discontents even of the native Israelites, who felt themselves to be "scourged with whips and laden with heavy burdens." They were bondmen in all but name, for purposes which bore very little on their own welfare. But the curses of the wretched aborigines must have been deeper, if not so loud. They were torn from such homes as the despotism of conquest still left to them, and were forced to hopeless and unrewarded toil for the alien worship and hateful palaces of their masters. Five centuries later we find a pitiable trace of their existence in the 392 *Hierodouloi*, menials lower even than the enslaved *Nethinim*, who

are called *"sons of the slaves of Solomon"* — the dwindling and miserable remnant of that vast levy of Palestinian serfs.

Apart from the lavish costliness of its materials the actual Temple was architecturally a poor and commonplace structure. It was quite small — only 90 feet long, 35 feet broad, and 45 feet high. It was meant for the symbolic habitation of God, not for the worship of great congregations. It only represented the nascent art and limited resources of a tenth-rate kingdom, and was totally devoid alike of the pure and stately beauty of the Parthenon and the awe-inspiring grandeur of the great Egyptian temples with their avenues of obelisks and sphinxes and their colossal statues of deities and kings

"Staring right on with calm, eternal eyes."

When Justinian boastfully exclaimed, as he looked at his church, *"I have vanquished thee, O Solomon,"*[249] and when the Khalif Omar, pointing to the Dome of the Rock, murmured, *"Behold, a greater than Solomon is here,"* they forgot the vast differences between them and the Jewish king in the epoch at which they lived and the resources which they could command. The Temple was built in "majestic silence."

"No workman's axe, no ponderous hammer rung,
Like some tall palm the noiseless fabric sprung."

This was due to religious reverence. It could be easily accomplished, because each stone and beam was carefully prepared to be fitted in its exact place before it was carried up the Temple hill.

The elaborate particulars furnished us of the measurements of Solomon's Temple are too late in age, too divergent in particulars, too loosely strung together, too much mingled with later reminiscences, and altogether too architecturally insufficient, to enable us to re-construct the exact building, or even to form more than a vague conception of its external appearance. Both in Kings and Chronicles the notices, as Keil says, are "incomplete extracts made independently of one another," and vague in essential details. Critics and architects have attempted to reproduce the Temple on Greek,[250] Egyptian,[251] and Phœnician[252] models, so entirely unlike each other as to show that we can arrive at no certainty.[253] It is, however, most probable that, alike in ornamentation and conception, the building was predominantly Phœnician.[254] Severe in outline, gorgeous in detail, it was more like the Temple of Venus-Astarte at Paphos than any other. Fortunately the details, apart from such dim symbolism as we may detect in them, have no religious importance, but only an historic and antiquarian interest.[255]

The Temple—called *Baith* (תַּיִב) or *Hêkâl* (לְכַיָה)—was surrounded by the thickly clustered houses of the Levites, and by porticoes[256] through which the precincts were entered by numerous gates of wood overlaid with brass. A grove of olives, palms, cedars, and cypresses, the home of many birds, probably adorned the outer court.[257] This court was shut from the "higher court,"[258] afterwards known as "the Court of the Priests," by a partition of three rows of hewn stones surmounted by a cornice of cedar beams. In the higher court, which was reached by a flight of steps, was the vast new altar of brass, 15 feet high and 30 feet long, of which the hollow was filled with earth and stones, and of which the blazing sacrifices were visible in the court below.[259] Here also stood the huge molten sea, borne on the backs of twelve brazen oxen, of which three faced to each quarter of the heavens. [260] It was in the form of a lotus blossom, and its rim was hung with three hundred wild gourds in bronze, cast in two rows. Its reservoir of eight hundred and eighty gallons of water was for the priestly ablutions necessary in the butcheries of sacrifice, and its usefulness was supplemented by ten brazen caldrons on wheels, five on each side, adorned like "the sea," with pensile garlands and cherubic emblems.[261] Whether "the brazen serpent of the wilderness," to which the children of Israel burnt incense down to the days of Hezekiah, was in that court or in the Temple we do not know.

On the western side of this court, facing the rising sun, stood the Temple itself, on a platform elevated some sixteen feet from the ground. Its side chambers were "lean-to" annexes (Heb., ribs; LXX., μέλαθρα; Vulg., *tabulata*), in three stories, all accessible by one central entrance on the outside. Their beams rested on rebatements in the thickness of the wall, and the highest was the broadest. Above these were windows "skewed and closed," as the margin of the A.V. says; or "broad within and narrow without"; or, as it should rather be rendered, "with closed crossbeams," that is, with immovable lattices, which could not be opened and shut, but which allowed the escape of the smoke of lamps and the fumes of incense. These chambers must also have had windows. They were used to store the garments of the priests and other necessary paraphernalia of the Temple service, but as to all details we are left completely in the dark.

Of the external aspect of the building in Solomon's day we know nothing. We cannot even tell whether it had one level roof, or whether the Holy of Holies was like a lower chancel at the end of it; nor whether the roof was flat or, as the Rabbis say, ridged; nor whether the outer surface of the three-storeyed chambers which surrounded it was of stone, or planked with cedar, or overlaid with plinths of gold and silver;[262] nor whether, in any case, it was ornamented with carvings or left blank; nor whether the cornices only were decorated with open flowers like the Assyrian rosettes. Nor do we know with certainty whether it was supported within by pillars[263] or not. In the state of the records as they have come down to us, all accurate or intelligible descriptions are slurred over by compilers who had no technical knowledge and whose main desire was to impress their countrymen with the truth that the holy building was—as indeed for its day it was—"exceeding magnifical of fame and of glory throughout all countries."

In front of or just within the porch were two superb pillars, regarded as miracles of Tyrian art, made of fluted bronze, 27 feet high and 18 feet thick. Their capitals of 7½ feet in height resembled an open lotos blossom, surrounded by double wreaths of two hundred pensile bronze pomegranates, supporting an abacus, carved with conventional lily work. Both pomegranates and lilies had a symbolic meaning.[264] The pillars were, for unknown reasons, called Jachin and Boaz.[265] Much about them is obscure. It is not even known whether they stood detached like obelisks, or formed Propylæa; or supported the architraves of the porch itself, or were a sort of gateway, surmounted by a *melathron* with two *epithemas*, like a Japanese or Indian *toran*.

The porch (*Olam*), which was of the same height as the house (*i.e.*, 45 feet high),[266] was hung with the gilded shields of Hadadezer's soldiers which David had taken in battle,[267] and perhaps also with consecrated armour, like the sword of Goliath,[268] to show that "unto the Lord belongeth our shield" (Psalm lxxxix. 18), and that "the shields of the earth belong unto God" (Psalm xlvii. 9).

A door of cypress wood, of two leaves, made in four squares, 7½ feet broad and high, turning on golden hinges overlaid with gold, and carved with palm branches and festoons of lilies and pomegranates, opened from the porch into the main apartment. This was the *Mikdash* (מִקְדָּשׁ), Holy Place, or Sanctuary, and sometimes specially called in Chaldee "the Palace" (*Hêkâl*, or *Bîrah*) (Ezra v, 14, 15, etc.). Before it, as in the Tabernacle, hung an embroidered curtain (*Māsak*). It was probably supported by four pillars on each side. In the interspaces were five tables on each side, overlaid with gold, and each encircled by a wreath of gold (*zêr*). On these were placed the cakes of shewbread.[269] At the end of the chamber, on each side the door of the Holiest, were five golden candlesticks with chains of wreathed gold hanging between them. In the centre of the room stood the golden altar of incense, and somewhere (we must suppose) the golden candlestick of the Tabernacle, with its seven branches ornamented with lilies, pomegranates, and calices of almond flowers. Nothing which was in the darkness of the Holiest was visible except the projecting golden staves with which the Ark had been carried to its place. The Holy Place itself was lighted by narrow slits.

The entrance to the Holiest, the *Debir*, or oracle,[270] which corresponded to the Greek *adytum*, was through a two-leaved door of olive wood, 6 feet high and broad, overlaid with gold, and carved with palms, cherubim, and open flowers. The partition was of cedar wood. The floor of the whole house was of cedar overlaid with gold. The interior of this "Oracle," as it was called — for the title "Holy of Holies" is of later origin — was, at any rate in the later Temples, concealed by an embroidered veil of blue, purple, and crimson, looped up with golden chains.

The Oracle, like the New Jerusalem of the Apocalypse, was a perfect cube, 30 feet broad and long and high, covered with gold, but shrouded in perpetual and unbroken darkness.[271] No light was ever visible in it save such as was shed by the crimson gleam of the thurible of incense which the high priest carried into it once a year on the Great Day of Atonement.[272] In the centre of the floor must apparently have risen the mass of rock which is still visible in the Mosque of Omar, from which it is called *Al Sakhra*, "the Dome of the Rock." Tradition pointed to it as the spot on which Abraham had laid for sacrifice the body of his son Isaac, when the angel restrained the descending knife. It was also the site of Araunah's threshing-floor, and had been therefore hallowed by two angelic apparitions.[273] On it was deposited with solemn ceremony the awful palladium of the Ark, which had been preserved through the wanderings and wars of the Exodus and the troublous days of the Judges.[274] It contained the most sacred possession of the nation, the most priceless treasure which Israel guarded for the world. This treasure was the Two Tables of the Ten Commandments, graven (in the anthropomorphic language of the ancient record) by the actual finger of God; the tables which Moses had shattered on the rocks of Mount Sinai as he descended to the backsliding people.[275] The Ark was covered with its old "Propitiatory," or "Mercy-seat," overshadowed by the wings of two small cherubim; but Solomon had prepared for its reception a new and far more magnificent covering, in the form of two colossal cherubim, 15 feet high, of which each expanded wing was 7½ feet long. These wings touched the outer walls of the Oracle, and also touched each other over the centre of the Ark.

Such was the Temple.

It was the "forum, fortress, university, and sanctuary" of the Jews, and the transitory emblem of the Church of Christ's kingdom. It was destined to occupy a large share in the memory, and even in the religious development, of the world, because it became the central point round which crystallised the entire history of the Chosen People. The kings of Judah are henceforth estimated with almost exclusive reference to the relation in which they stood to the centralised worship of Jehovah. The Spanish kings who built and decorated the Escurial caught the spirit of Jewish annals when, in the Court of the Kings, they reared the six colossal statues of David the originator, of Solomon the founder, of Jehoshaphat, Hezekiah, Josiah, and Manasseh the restorers or purifiers of the Temple worship.[276]

It required the toil of 300,000 men for twenty years to build one of the pyramids. It took two hundred years to build and four hundred to embellish the great Temple of Artemis of the Ephesians. It took more than five centuries to give to Westminster Abbey its present form. Solomon's Temple only took seven and a half years to build; but, as we shall see, its objects were wholly different from those of the great shrines which we have mentioned. The wealth lavished upon it was such that its dishes, bowls, cups, even its snuffers and snuffer trays, and its meanest utensils, were of pure gold. The massiveness of its substructions, the splendour of its materials, the artistic skill displayed by the Tyrian workmen in all its details and adornments, added to the awful sense of its indwelling Deity, gave it an imperishable fame. Needing but little repair, it stood for more than four centuries. Succeeded as it was by the Temples of Zerubbabel and of Herod, it carried down till seventy years after the Christian era the memory of the Tabernacle in the wilderness, of which it preserved the general outline, though it exactly doubled all the proportions and admitted many innovations.[277]

The dedication ceremony was carried out with the utmost pomp. It required nearly a year to complete the necessary preparations, and the ceremony with its feasts occupied fourteen days, which were partly coincident with the autumn Feast of Tabernacles.[278]

The dedication falls into three great acts. The first was the removal of the Ark to its new home (1 Kings viii. 1-11); then followed the speech and the prayer of Solomon (vv. 12-61); and, finally, the great holocaust was offered (vv. 62-66).

The old Tabernacle, or what remained of it, with its precious heirlooms, was carried by priests and Levites from the high place at Gibeon, which was henceforth abandoned.[279] This procession was met by another, far more numerous and splendid, consisting of all the princes, nobles, and captains, which brought the Ark from the tent erected for it on Mount Zion by David forty years before.

The Israelites had flocked to Jerusalem in countless multitudes, under their sheykhs and emîrs[280] from the border of Hamath on the Orontes,[281] north of Mount Lebanon, to the Wady el-Areesh.[282] The king, in his most regal state, accompanied the procession, and the Ark passed through myriads of worshippers crowded in the outer court, from the tent on Mount Zion into the darkness of the Oracle on Mount Moriah, where it continued, unseen perhaps by any human eye but that of the high priest once a year, until it was carried away by Nebuchadnezzar to Babylon.[283] To indicate that this was to be its rest for ever, the staves, contrary to the old law, were drawn out of the golden rings through which they ran, in order that no human hand might touch the sacred emblem itself when it was borne on the shoulders of the Levitic priests. "And there they are unto this day," writes the compiler from his ancient record, long after Temple and Ark had ceased to exist.[284]

The king is the one predominant figure, and the high priest is not once mentioned. Nathan is only mentioned by the heathen historian Eupolemos. Visible to the whole vast multitude, Solomon stood in the inner court on a high scaffolding of brass. Then came a burst of music and psalmody from the priests and musicians, robed in white robes, who densely thronged the steps of the great altar.[285] They held in their hands their glittering harps and cymbals, and psalteries in their precious frames of red sandal wood, and twelve of their number rent the air with the blast of their silver trumpets as Solomon, in this supreme hour of his prosperity, shone forth before his people in all his manly beauty.

At the sight of that stately figure in its gorgeous robes the song of praise was swelled by innumerable voices, and, to crown all, a blaze of sudden glory wrapped the Temple and the whole scene in heaven's own splendour (2 Chron. v. 13, 14). First, the king, standing with his back to the people, broke out into a few words of prophetic song. Then, turning to the multitude, he blessed them—he, and not the high priest—and briefly told them the history and significance of this house of God, warning them faithfully that the Temple after all was but the *emblem* of God's presence in the midst of them, and that the Most High dwelleth not in temples made with hands, neither is worshipped with men's hands as though He needed anything. After this he advanced to the altar, and kneeling on his knees (2 Chron. vi. 13)—a most unusual attitude among the Jews, who, down to the latest ages, usually stood up to pray—he prayed with the palms of his hands upturned to heaven, as though to receive in deep humility its outpoured benefits. The prayer, as here given, consists of an introduction, seven petitions, and a conclusion. It was a passionate entreaty that God would hear, both individually and nationally, both in prosperity and in adversity, the supplications of His people, and even of strangers, who should either pray in the courts of that His house, or should make it the *Kibleh* of their devotions.[286]

After the dedicatory prayer both the outer and the inner court of the Temple reeked and swam with the blood of countless victims—victims so numerous that the great brazen altar became wholly insufficient for them. [287] At the close of the entire festival they departed to their homes with joy and gladness.[288]

But whatever the Temple might or might not be to the people, the king used it as his own chapel. Three times a year, we are told, he offered—and for all that appears, offered with his own hand without the intervention of any priest—burnt offerings and peace offerings upon the altar. Not only this, but he actually "burnt incense therewith upon the altar which was before the Lord,"—the very thing which was regarded as so deadly a crime in the case of King Uzziah.[289] Throughout the history of the monarchy, the priests, with scarcely any exception, seem to have been passive tools in the hands of the kings. Even under Rehoboam—much more under Ahaz and Manasseh—the sacred precincts were defiled with nameless abominations, to which, so far as we know, the priests offered no resistance.

CHAPTER XV
THE IDEAL SIGNIFICANCE OF THE TEMPLE

1 Kings vii. 13-51, viii. 12-61

"The hour cometh when ye shall neither in this mountain, nor yet at Jerusalem, worship the Father.... But the hour cometh, and now is, when the true worshippers shall worship the Father in spirit and in truth."—John iv. 21, 23.

Five long chapters of the First Book of Kings are devoted to the description of Solomon's Temple, which occupies a still larger space in the Books of Chronicles. The Temple was regarded as the permanent form of the ancient Tabernacle,[290] which is described with lengthy and minute detail in Exodus. It might seem, therefore, that there must be some clear explanation of the idea which this sacred building was intended to embody. Yet it is by no means easy to ascertain what this idea was, and those who have deeply studied the question have in age after age been led to widely different views.

1. Philo and Josephus,[291] with certain variations of detail, regard it as a symbol of the universe—the world of idea and the world of sense. Thus the seven-branched candlestick represents the seven planets; the twelve cakes of shewbread are the twelve signs of the Zodiac, the court is the earth; the sanctuary the sea; and the oracle the heavens. The theory derives no importance from its authorship. Neither Philo nor Josephus, nor the Rabbis, nor the Fathers who adopted their views,[292] have the least authority in such matters; and Philo, who led the way in mystical interpretation, abounds in fantasies which are ludicrously impossible, and are now universally rejected.

2. The Talmudists held that the Tabernacle was the exact copy of one in heaven,[293] and that its services reflected those of the heavenly hierarchy. This view went into the extreme of literalism, as the other did into the extreme of spiritualisation. It was based on the text, "Look that thou make them after their pattern, which was showed thee in the mount."[294] The Book of Chronicles goes so far in this direction as to say that David received from Jehovah the exact pattern of the Temple down to its minutest details, together with the entire priestly and Levitic organisation of its services. "All

this," says David to Solomon, "the Lord made me to understand *in writing*, by His hand upon me, even all the works in the pattern."

3. Christian writers have seen in the Temple an emblem of the visible, the invisible, and the triumphant Church. Such symbolic interpretation depends on the most arbitrary combinations, and does not rise higher than an exercise of fancy. It has not the smallest exegetic importance.

4. Luther thought that the Tabernacle and Temple were emblems of human nature:—the court, the sanctuary, and the oracle corresponding to the body, the soul, and the spirit. Later writers have pushed this opinion, already sufficiently baseless, into the absurdest detail.

5. The much simpler view of Maimonides[295] who is followed by our learned Spencer, is that the Temple was simply the palace of Jehovah, with its vestibule, its audience hall, its Presence-chamber, its attendant courtiers, its throne, and its offerings of food and wine and sacrifice. The simplicity of this conception seems to be in accordance with what we know of ancient forms of worship, and it is certain that in many heathen temples the offerings of food and wine were supposed to be consumed by the god. The name "palace" is, however, only given to the Temple in one chapter (1 Chron. xxix. 1, 19); and the Hebrew, or rather the Persian,[296] word so rendered (*bîrah*) may also be rendered "fortress."

6. In truth we cannot be sure that the idea of the Temple remained single and definite through so many ages. It was probably a composite and varying emblem, of which the original significance had become mingled with many later elements. It is, however, certain that many numbers and details were symbolical, and there was a deep insight and magnificent completeness in the manner in which certain truths were shadowed forth by its construction and its central service.

The book in which its symbolism is most thoroughly worked out is Bähr's *Symbolik.* He elaborates, in a simpler form, the opinion of Philo, that the Temple represented "the structure which God has erected, the house in which God lives." So far the fact cannot be disputed for, in Exod. xxix. 45 we are told that the Tabernacle is called the "House of God" because "I will dwell in the midst of the children of Israel, and will be their God." But Bähr takes a great leap when he proceeds to explain the house of God as "the creation of heaven and earth." If his views were true *as a whole*, it would indeed be strange that they are not indicated in a single passage either of the Old or New Testaments.

The Tabernacle was called "the Tabernacle of the Testimony" because its two tables of stone were a witness of the covenant between God and man.

It was also called "the Tabernacle of Meeting," by which is not meant the place where Israel assembled, but the place where God met Moses and the children of Israel.[297] "For there will I meet with thee, and I will commune with thee from above the mercy-seat," says Jehovah to Moses;[298] and "at the entrance of the tent of meeting I will meet with you to speak there unto thee, and there I will meet with the children of Israel."[299] Thus, in its broadest idea, the Temple brought before the soul of every thoughtful Israelite the three great beliefs, (1) that God deigned to dwell in the midst of His people; (2) that, in His infinite mercy and condescension, He admitted a reciprocity between Himself and His human children; and (3) that the most absolute expression of His will was the moral law, obedience to which was the condition of heavenly favour and earthly happiness.

"In the Porch," says Bishop Hall, "we may see the regenerate soul entering into the blessed society of the Church; in the Holy Place we may see a figure of the Communion of the true visible Church on earth; in the Holy of Holies the glories of Heaven opened to us by our true High Priest Christ Jesus, who entered once for all to make an Atonement betwixt God and man."

CHAPTER XVI
THE ARK AND THE CHERUBIM

1 Kings vi. 23-30, viii. 6-11

"Jehovah, thundering out of Sion, throned
Between the cherubim."
Milton.

The inculcation of truths so deep as the unity, the presence, and the mercy of God would alone have sufficed to give preciousness to the national sanctuary, and to justify the lavish expenditure with which it was carried to completion. But as in the Tabernacle, so in the Temple, which was only a more rich and permanent structure, the numbers, the colours, and many details had a real significance. The unity of the Temple shadowed forth the unity of the Godhead; while the concrete and perfect unity, resulting from the reconciliation of unity with difference and opposition (1 2), is "the signature of the Deity." Hence, as in our English cathedrals, three was the predominant number. There were three divisions,—Porch, Holy Place, Oracle. Each main division contained three expiatory objects. Three times its width (which was 3 × 10) was the measure of its length. The number ten is also prominent in the measurements. It includes all the cardinal numbers, and, as the completion of multiplicity, is used to indicate a perfect whole. The seven pillars which supported the house, and the seven branches of the candlestick, recalled the sacredness of the seventh day hallowed by the Sabbath, by circumcision, and by the Passover. The number of the cakes of shewbread was twelve, "the signature of the people of Israel, a whole in the midst of which God resides, a body which moves after Divine laws." Of the colours predominant in the Temple, *blue*, the colour of heaven, symbolises revelation; *white* is the colour of light and innocence; *purple*, of majesty and royal power; *crimson*, of life, being the colour of fire and blood. Every gem on the high priest's pectoral had its mystic significance, and the bells and pomegranates which fringed the edge of his ephod were emblems of devotion and good works.

Two instances will suffice to indicate how deep and rich was the significance of the truths which Moses had endeavoured to engraft in the minds of his people, and to which Solomon, whether with full consciousness or not, gave permanence in the Temple.

1. Consider, first, *the Ark.*

Every step towards the Holiest was a step of deepening reverence. The Holy Land was sacred, but Jerusalem was more sacred than all the rest. The Temple was the most sacred part of the city; the Oracle was the most sacred part of the Temple; the Ark was the most sacred thing in the Oracle; yet the Ark was only sacred because of that which it contained.

And what did it contain? What was it which enshrined in itself this quintessence of all sanctitude? When we pierce to the inmost recesses of a pyramid, we find there only the ashes of a dead man, or even of an animal. Within the adytum of an Egyptian temple we might have found "an ox wallowing on purple tapestry." The Egyptians, too, had their arks, as the Greeks had the cyst of Cybele, and the *vannus* of Iacchus. What did *they* contain? At the best phallic emblems, the emblems of prolific nature. But the Ark of Jehovah contained nothing but the stone tablets on which were carved the Ten Words of the Covenant, the briefest possible form of the moral law of God. In the inmost heart of the Temple was its most inestimable treasure,—a protest against all idolatry; a protest against all polytheism, or ditheism, or atheism; a protest, too, against the formalism which the Temple itself and its services might tend to produce in its least spiritually minded worshippers. Thus the entire Temple was a glorification of the truth that "the fear of the Lord is the beginning of wisdom," and that the one end to be produced by the fear of the Lord is obedience to His commandments. The Ark and its unseen treasure taught that no religion can be of the least value which does not result in conformity with the plain moral laws:—Be obedient; be kind; be pure; be honest; be truthful; be contented; and that this obedience can only spring from faith in the one God whom all real worshippers must worship in spirit and truth.

Obvious as this lesson might seem to be, it was entirely missed by the Jews in general. The Ark, too, was degraded into a fetish, and Jeremiah says (iii. 16) of the exiles, "They shall say no more, The ark of the covenant of the Lord: neither shall it come to mind: neither shall they miss it: neither shall it be made any more" (Heb.). When a symbol has been perverted into a source of materialism and superstition, it becomes not only useless but positively dangerous. No religions have fallen so absolutely dead as those which have sunk into petty formalism. The Ark, for all its quintessential sacredness, had been suffered to fall into the hands of uncircumcised Philistines, and to be placed in their Dagon temple, to show that it was no mere idolatrous amulet. Ultimately it was carried away to Babylon, to adorn the palace of a heathen tyrant, and probably to perish by fire in his captured city. In the second Temple there was no ark. Nothing remained but the rock of Araunah's threshing-floor, on which it once had stood.

2. Consider, next, the meaning of *the Cherubim.*

(1) The infinite sanctity given to the conception of the moral law was enhanced by the introduction of these overshadowing figures. We are never told in the entire books of Scripture what was the form of these cherubim; nor is their function anywhere specially defined; nor, again, can we be at all certain of the derivation of the name. That the cherubim over the Ark were not identical with the fourfold-visaged four of Ezekiel's cherub-chariot we know, because they certainly had but one face. But we now know that among the Assyrians, Persians, Egyptians, and other nations nothing was more common than these cherubic emblems, which were introduced into their palaces and temples under the forms of winged lions, oxen, men, and eagle-headed human figures. We see also that in the Tabernacle,[300] and to a still greater extent in the Temple, a tacit exception to the stringency of the Second Commandment seems to have been made in favour of the component parts of these cherubic figures. If Solomon was aware (as he surely must have been) of the existence of the law, "*Thou shalt not make to thyself any graven image,*" he must either have laid stress on the words "*to thyself,*" and have excused the brazen oxen which supported his great laver on the ground that they could not be turned into objects of worship, or he must have held, as Ezekiel apparently did, that the ox was the predominant form in the cherubic emblem.[301] From the Vision of Ezekiel we see that the cherubim — like the "Immortalities" ($\zeta\tilde{\omega}\alpha$) of the Apocalypse, which had faces of the ox, the eagle, the lion, and the man — were conceived of as "living creatures" upholding the sapphire Throne of God. They had wings, and the similitude of hands under their wings. They flashed to and fro like lightning in the midst of a great cloud, and an enfolding fire, and a rolling mass of amber-coloured flame. Of the form of this "changeable hieroglyphic" we need say no more. Perhaps originally suggested by the wreathing fires and rolling stormclouds, which were regarded as immediate signs of the Divine proximity, the cherubim came to be regarded as the genius of the created universe in its richest perfection and energy, at once revealing and shrouding the Presence of God.[302] Their eyes represent His omniscience, for "the eyes of the Lord are in every place"; their wings and straight feet represent the speed and fiery gliding of His omnipresence;[303] each element of their fourfold shape indicates His love, His patience, His power, His sublimity. Their wheels imply that "the dread magnificence of the unintelligent creation" is under His entire control; and, as a whole, they symbolise the dazzling beauty of the universe, alike conscious and material. They were

the ideal *anima animantium*—the perfection of existence emanating from and subject to the Divine Creator whose tender mercy is over all His works. Their function, when they are first introduced in the Book of Genesis, is at once vengeful and protective; vengeful of the violated law, protective of the treasure of life.[304] They are here the Erinnyes of the Dawn, revealing and avenging the works of darkness. Their "dreadful faces and fiery arms" at the gate of Eden typify guilty awakenment, realised retribution, conscious alienation from God, the universe siding with His awakened anger.

(2) But when next they are mentioned. God says to Moses, "Thou shalt make a mercy-seat of pure gold, and thou shalt make two cherubim of gold at the two ends of the mercy-seat." But for their presence on the mercy-seat how terrible would have been the symbolism of the Holy of Holies—God's darkness, man's crime, a broken law! It would have represented Him who hath clouds and darkness round about Him, and dwelleth in darkness which no man can approach unto; and the Ark would only have treasured up, as a witness against man's apostasy, the shattered slabs of the words of Sinai.[305] But over that Ark, and its saddening because dishallowed treasure, bent once more these mystic figures, these "cherubim of glory." They bent down as though at once to protect with outspread wings, and to regard with awful contemplation, that mystic gift of a law promulgated to all nations as their moral heritage and as the revealed will of God. These are no longer cherubim of vengeance or awakened wrath, for they stand on the *Capporeth*, the "covering," or "propitiatory" of the Ark.[306] They gleamed out in the red light of the high priest's golden brazier on the one day when human foot entered the darkness in which they were shrouded; and even by him they were but dimly discerned through the ascending wreaths of fragrant incense. But he stood before them, where, on their spreading wings, the light of the Divine presence was deemed to dwell; and with the blood of expiation he sprinkled seven times the mercy-seat over which these adoring figures leaned. The wrathful cherubim of the lost Eden had driven man from a treasure which he had forfeited; but these, though they guard the ten words of a law which man had broken, were cherubim of mercy and reconciliation. Those of Eden were armed with swords of flame; those of the Temple were reddened with the blood of forgiveness. Those typified a covenant destroyed and ended; these a covenant broken yet renewed. Those spoke of awakened wrath; these of covenanted mercy. Those kept men back from the Tree of Life; these guarded that which is a Tree of Life to them that love it.

Could the whole covenant of the law and the gospel have been symbolised more simply, yet with Diviner force? The Temple itself, with all its sacrifices, with all its service and ceremonial and all the gorgeous vestments of Aaron's vestry, served but to teach the infinite worth of simple righteousness. The heart of the Mosaic legislation was nothing so poor, so paltry, so material as the promotion of liturgical Levitism, and the pomp of ritual, and the organisation of priestly functions—as though these in themselves had any value in the sight of God. It lay in the lesson that "Obedience is better than sacrifice, and to hearken than the fat of rams." The law of Moses—the ten words which constituted the inmost preciousness of his legislation—was, alas! a violated law. For the disobedient it had no message but the wrathful menace of death. But to show that God has not abandoned His disobedient children, but would still enable them to keep that law, and to repent for its transgression, the cherubim are there. Their presence on the propitiatory was meant to reveal the glory of the gospel. The high priest, who alone saw them on the Great Day of Israel, was a type of Him who, not with the blood of bulls and goats, but in His own blood (*i.e.*, in the glory of the life outpoured for man), entered into God's presence within the veil.

(3) In the dazzling living creatures before the throne in the Revelation of St. John, we see once more these cherubim of Eden, who, having indicated at the Fall an awful warning, and represented in the Tabernacle a blessed hope, symbolise, in the last book of the Bible, a Divine fulfilment. They are there no longer with fiery swords, in wrathful aspect, in repellent silence; but, gracious and beautiful, they join in the new song of the redeemed multitude under the shadow of the Tree of Life, to which all have free access in that recovered Eden. In the Temple—glimmering through the rising fumes of incense, which were the type of accepted prayer, their golden plumage sprinkled with the blood of the atoning sacrifice—they became a type both of all creation, up to its most celestial beings, gazing in adoration on the will of God, and of all creation, in its groaning and travailing, restored through the precious blood that speaketh better things than the blood of Abel. Not all, of course, of these deep meanings were present to the souls of Israel's worshippers; but the best of them might with joy see something of the things which we see when we say that in these glorious figures are summed up the three chief images of all Scripture: first, the Primæval Dispensation, "*In the day that thou eatest thereof, thou shalt surely die*"; next, in the wilderness, "*This do, and thou shalt live*"; last of all, in the Gospel Dispensation, "*Thou wast slain, and hast redeemed us to God by Thy blood out of every kindred and tongue and people and nation, and hast made us unto our God kings and priests.*"

CHAPTER XVII
THE GRADUAL GROWTH OF
THE LEVITIC RITUAL

1 Kings viii. 1-66

"Behold, to obey is better than sacrifice." —1 Sam. xv. 22.

Before we enter on the subject of the Temple worship, it is necessary to emphasise a fact which will meet us again and again in many forms as we consider the history of the Chosen People: it is the amazing ignorance which seems to have prevailed among them for centuries as to the most central and decisive elements of nearly the whole of the Mosaic law as we now read it in the Pentateuch.

1. Take, for instance, the law of a central sanctuary. It is strongly laid down, and incessantly insisted on, throughout the Book of Deuteronomy. [307] Yet that law does not seem to have been so much as noticed by any of the earlier prophets or judges, or by Saul, or by David. The judges and early kings offer sacrifices at any place which they regard as sacred—Bochim, Ophrah, Mizpeh, Gilgal, Bethel, Bethlehem, etc.[308] The rule of one place for sacrifice was not regarded for a moment by the kings of the Northern Kingdom. The transgression of it was not made a subject of complaint by Elijah, Elisha, or any of the earlier prophets. Not one of the kings, even of the most pious kings—Asa, Jehoshaphat, Joash, Amaziah, Uzziah, Jotham—rigidly enforced it until the reign of Josiah. The law seems to have remained an absolutely dead letter for hundreds of years. Now this would be amply accounted for if the Deuteronomic and Levitic Codes only belonged in reality to the days of Josiah and of the Exile; for in "the Book of the Covenant" (Exod. xxiv. 7), which is the most ancient part of these codes, and comprises Exod. xx.-xxviii. 33, and is briefly repeated in Exod. xxxiv. 10-28, there is not only no insistence on a central shrine, but many of the regulations would have been rendered impossible had such a shrine existed (e.g., Exod. xxi. 6, xxii. 7, 8, where "the judges" should be "God," as in the R.V.). Indeed, so far from insistence on one Temple, we expressly read (Exod. xx. 24), "An altar of earth shalt thou make Me, and shalt sacrifice thereon thy burnt offerings

and thy peace offerings, thy sheep and thine oxen, *in all places where I record My name,* and I will come unto thee and bless thee."

2. Again, the Book of Leviticus lays down a singularly developed code of ritual, "extending to the minutest details of worship and of life." Yet there is scarcely the shadow of a trace of the observance of even its most reiterated and important provisions during centuries of Israelitish history. It is emphatically a priestly book; yet from the days of David down to those of Josiah, the priests, with few exceptions, are almost ignored in the national records. They took the colour of their opinions from the reigning kings, even in matters which were contrary to the whole extent and spirit of the Mosaic Code. Samuel, who was not a priest, nor even a Levite, performed every function of a priest, and of a high priest, all his life long.

3. Again, as we have seen, in spite of the positive distinctness of the Second Commandment, not only is the "calf-worship" established, with scarcely a protest, throughout the Northern Kingdom; but Solomon even ventures, without question or reproof, to place twelve oxen under his brazen sea, and to adorn the steps of his throne with golden lions.

4. Again, no ceremony was more awful, or more strikingly symbolical, in the later religion of Israel, than that of the Great Day of Atonement. It was the *only* appointed fast in the Jewish year,[309] a day so sacred that it acquired the name of *Yoma,* "the Day." Yet the Day of Atonement, with its arresting ceremonies and intense significance, is not so much as once mentioned outside the Levitical Code by a single prophet, or priest, or king. It is not even mentioned—which is exceedingly strange—in the post-exilic Books of Chronicles. Between the Book of Leviticus (with its supposed date of 1491 b.c.), down to the days of Philo, Josephus, and the New Testament, there is not so much as a hint of the observance of this central ceremony of the whole Levitic law! What is more perplexing is, that, in the ideal legislation of Ezekiel, where alone anything distantly resembling the Day of Atonement is alluded to (Ezek. xlv. 18-20), the time, manner, and circumstances are as absolutely different as if Ezekiel had never read the Levitic law at all. How would any prophet have dared to ignore or alter, without a word of reference or apology, a rite of Divine origin and immemorial sanctity, if he had been aware of its existence?

5. Nor is this only the case with the Day of Atonement. It seems certain that at Jerusalem there was not for centuries anything distantly resembling the due Levitic observance of the three great yearly feasts. Nehemiah, for instance, tells us in so many words that since the days of Joshua the son of Nun down to b.c. 445—perhaps for a thousand years—the Feast of

Tabernacles had never been observed in the most characteristic of all its appointed rites — the dwelling in booths.[310]

6. Again, although there are slight allusions in some of the Prophets to "laws" and "statutes" and "commandments," their silence about, if not their absolute ignorance of, anything which resembles the Levitic legislation as a whole is a startling problem. Thus, even a late prophet like Jeremiah alludes, without a word of reprobation, to men cutting and making themselves bald for the dead (Jer. xvi. 6; comp. xli. 5) in a way which the Levitic law (Lev. xix. 28; Deut. xiv. 1) strenuously forbids.

7. Again, as is well known, there is a fundamental difference between the three codes as to the relative position of the priests and Levites. (i) In Exod. xix. 6 all Israel is regarded as "a kingdom of priests and an holy nation," and in Exod. xxiv. 5 the young men of the children of Israel "offer burnt offerings and sacrifice peace offerings." (ii) In Numb. iii. 44-51 the Levites are set aside for the service of the Tabernacle in place of the firstborn. But neither in "the Book of the Covenant" nor in Deuteronomy is there any *distinction* between the services of the priests and the Levites. (iii) In Deut. x. 8 every Levite may become a priest. All priestly functions are open to the Levites, and the arrangements for the Levites are wholly different from those of Numbers. (iv) But in the Priestly Code only the sons of Aaron are to be priests (Numb. vi. 22-27, xviii. 1-7; Lev. i. 5, 8). The Levites are to minister to them in more or less menial functions, and are permitted a share in the tithes, but not (as in Deut. xviii. 1) in the firstfruits. We have first identity of priests and Levites, then partial, then absolute separation.[311] The earliest trace of this degradation of the Levites is propounded as something quite new in Ezek. xliv. 10-16, which distinctly implies (see verse 13) that up to that time the Levites had enjoyed full priestly rites.

It must be admitted that these facts are not capable of easy explanation, nor is it strange that they have led the way to unexpected conclusions. We have to face the certainty that, for ages together, the Levitic law was not only a dead letter among the people for whom it was intended, but that its very existence does not seem to have been known. "For long periods," says Professor Robertson, "the people of Israel seem to have been as ignorant of their own religion as the people of Europe were of theirs in the Dark Ages."[312] But the problem, were we to pursue it into its details, is far more perplexing than can be accounted for by the very partial and misleading parallel which Professor Robertson adduces. The parallel would be nearer if, throughout the Dark Ages for a thousand years together, scarcely a single trace were to be found, even under the best popes and the most pious kings, and even in theologic and sacred literature, of so much as the existence of a New Testament, or of any observance of the most distinctive festivals and sacraments of Christianity. And this, as Professor Robertson knows, is infinitely far from being the case. It is true that an argument *ex silentio* may easily be pushed too far; but we cannot ignore it when it is so striking as this, and when it is also strengthened by so many positive and corroborative facts.

A solution of this phenomenon—which becomes most salient in the Book of Kings—is proposed by the criticism which has received the title of "The Higher Criticism," because it is historic and constructive, and rises above purely verbal elements. That solution is that the Pentateuch is not only a composite structure (which all would concede), but that it was written in very different ages, and that much of it is of very late origin. Critics of the latest school believe that it consists of three well-marked and entirely different codes of laws—namely, "the Book of the Covenant" (Exod. xx. 23-xxiii.); the "Deuteronomic Code," first brought into prominence in the reign of Josiah, and written shortly before that reign; and the "Levitical" or "Priestly Code," which comprises most of Exodus, and nearly all Leviticus, and was not introduced till after the Exile. This would be indeed a radical conclusion, and cannot yet be regarded as having been conclusively established. But so remarkable has been the rapidity with which the opinion of religious critics has advanced on the subject, that now even the strongest opponents of this extreme view admit that *the existence of the three separate codes* has been demonstrated, although they still think that all three may belong to the Mosaic age.[313] It is obvious, however, that this view leaves many of the difficulties entirely untouched. Criticism has not yet spoken her last word upon the subject, but we ought to take her views into account in considering the judgments pronounced by the historian of the Kings. They were judgments which, in their details, though not as regards broad moral principles, were based on the standpoint of a later age. The views of that later age must be discounted if we have to admit that some of the ritual innovations and legal transgressions of the kings were transgressions of laws of the very existence of which they were profoundly ignorant. That they *were* thus ignorant of them is not only implied throughout, but appears from the direct statements of the sacred historians.[314]

CHAPTER XVIII
THE TEMPLE WORSHIP

1 Kings viii. 1-11

"Trust ye not in lying words, saying, The temple of the Lord, the temple of the Lord, the temple of the Lord, are these.... Behold, ye trust in lying words, that cannot profit." —Jer. vii. 4, 8.

The actual Temple building, apart from its spacious courts, was neither for worshippers nor for priests, neither for sacrifice nor for prayer. It existed only for symbolism and, at least in later days, for expiation. No prayer was offered in the sanctuary. The propitiatory was the symbol of expiation, but even after the introduction of the Day of Atonement the atoning blood was only carried into it once a year.

All the worship was in the outer court, and consisted mainly, (1) of praise, and (2) of offerings. Both were prominent in the Dedication Festival.

"It is written," said our Lord, "My house shall be called a House of Prayer, but ye have made it a den of robbers." The quotation is from the later Isaiah, and represents a happy advance in spiritual religion. Among the details of the Levitic Tabernacle no mention is made of prayer, though it was symbolised both in the incense and in the sacrifices which have been called "unspoken prayers."[315] *Let my prayer be set forth as incense,* says the Psalmist, *"and the lifting up of my hands as the evening sacrifice."* In the New Testament we read that "the whole multitude of the people were praying without at the time of incense." But during the whole history of the first Temple we only hear—and that very incidentally—of *private* prayer in the Temple. Solomon's prayer was public, and combined prayer with praises and benedictions. But no fragments of Jewish liturgies have come down to us which we can with any probability refer to the days of the kings. The Psalms which most clearly belong to the Temple service are mainly services of praise.

In the mind of the people the *sacrifices* were undoubtedly the main part of the Temple ritual. This fact was specially emphasised by the scene which marked the Festival of the Dedication.

It is difficult to imagine a scene which to our unaccustomed senses would have been more revolting than the holocausts of a great Jewish Festival like that of Solomon's Dedication. As a rule the daily sacrifices, exclusively of such as might be brought by private worshippers, were the lambs slain at morning and evening. Yet Maimonides gives us the very material and unpoetic suggestion that the incense used was to obviate the effluvium of animal sacrifice. The suggestion is unworthy of the great Rabbi's ability, and is wholly incorrect; but it reminds us of the almost terrible fact that, often and often, the Temple must have been converted into one huge and abhorrent *abattoir*, swimming with the blood of slaughtered victims, and rendered intolerably repulsive by heaps of bloody skins and masses of offal. The smell of burning flesh, the swift putrescence caused by the tropic heat, the unlovely accompaniments of swarms of flies, and ministers with blood-drenched robes would have been inconceivably disagreeable to our Western training—for no one will believe the continuous miracle invented by the Rabbis, who declare that no fly was ever seen in the Temple, and no flesh ever grew corrupt.[316] No doubt the brazen sea and the movable caldrons were in incessant requisition, and there were provisions for vast storages of water. These could have produced a very small mitigation of the accompanying pollutions during a festival which transformed the great court of the Temple into the reeking shambles and charnel-house of sheep and oxen "which could not be told nor numbered for multitude."

Had such spectacles been frequent, we should surely have had to say of the people of Jerusalem as Sir Monier Williams says of the ancient Hindus, "The land was saturated with blood, and people became wearied and disgusted with slaughtered sacrifices and sacrificing priests."[317] What infinite, and what revolting labour, must have been involved in the right burning of "the two kidneys and the fat," and the due disposition of the "inwards" of all these holocausts! The groaning brazen altar, vast as it was, failed to meet the requirements of the service, and apparently a multitude of other altars were extemporised for the occasion.

When the festival was over God appeared to Solomon in vision, as He had done at Gibeon. So far Solomon had not gravely or consciously deflected from the ideal of a theocratic king. Anything which had been worldly or mistaken in his policy—the oppression into which he had been led, the heathen alliances which he had formed, his crowded harem, his evident fondness for material splendour which carried with it the peril of selfish pride—were only signs of partial knowledge and human frailty. His heart was still, on the whole, right with God. He was once more assured in nightly vision that his prayer and supplication were accepted. The promise was renewed that if he would walk in integrity and uprightness his throne should be established for ever; but that if he or his children swerved into apostasy Israel should be driven into exile, and, as a warning to all lands, "this house, which I have hallowed for My name, will I cast out of My sight, and Israel shall be a proverb and a byword among all people."

Here, then, we are brought face to face with problems which arise from the whole system of worship in the Old Dispensation. Whatever it was, to whatever extent it was really carried out and was not merely theoretical, at whatever date its separate elements originated, and however clear it is that it has utterly passed away, there must have been certain ideas underlying it which are worthy of our study.

1. Of the element of praise, supported by music, we need say but little. It is a natural mode of expressing the joy and gratitude which fill the heart of man in contemplating the manifold mercies of God. For this reason the pages of Scripture ring with religious music from the earliest to the latest age. We are told in the Chronicles that triumphant praise was largely introduced into the great festival services, and that the Temple possessed a great organisation for vocal and orchestral music. David was not only a poet, but an inventor of musical instruments.[318] Fifteen musical instruments are mentioned in the Bible, and five of them in the Pentateuch. Most important among them are cymbals, flutes, silver trumpets, rams' horns, the harp (*Kinnor*) and the ten-stringed lute (*Nevel*).[319] The remark of Josephus that Solomon provided 40,000 harps and lutes and 200,000 silver trumpets is marked by that disease of exaggeration which seems to infect the mind of all later Jewish writers when they look back with yearning to the vanished glories of their past. There can, however, be no doubt that the orchestra was amply supplied, and that there was a very numerous and well-trained choir.[320] We read in the Psalms and elsewhere of tunes which they were trained to sing. Such tunes were "The Well," and "The Bow," and "The Gazelle of the morning," and "All my fresh springs shall be in Thee," and "Die for the son" (*Muth-labben*).[321] In the second Temple female singers were admitted;[322] in Herod's Temple Levite choir-boys took their place. [323] The singing was often antiphonal. Some of the music still used in the synagogue must date from these times, and there is no reason to doubt that in the so-called Gregorian *tones* we have preserved to us a close approximation to the ancient hymnody of the Temple. This element of ancient worship calls for no remark. It is a religious instinct to use music in the service of God; and perhaps the imagination of St. John in the Revelation, when he describes the rapture of the heavenly host pouring forth the chant "Alleluia, for the Lord God omnipotent reigneth," was coloured by reminiscences of gorgeous functions in which he had taken part on the "Mountain of the House."

2. When we proceed to speak of *the Priesthood* we are met by difficulties, to which we have already alluded, as to the date of the varying regulations respecting it. "It would be difficult," says Dr. Edersheim, "to conceive arrangements more thoroughly or consistently opposed to what are commonly called 'priestly pretensions' than those of the Old Testament."[324] According to the true ideal, Israel was to be "a kingdom of priests and an holy nation";[325] but the institution of *ministering* priests was of course a necessity, and the Jewish priesthood, which is now utterly abrogated, was, or gradually became, representative. Representatively they had to mediate between God and Israel, and typically to symbolise the "holiness," *i.e.*, the consecration of the Chosen People. Hence they were required to be free from every bodily blemish. It was regarded as a deadly offence for any one of them to officiate without scrupulous safeguard against every ceremonial defilement, and they were specially adorned and anointed for their office. They were an extremely numerous body, and from the days of David are said to have been divided into twenty-four courses. They were assisted by an army of attendant Levites, also divided into twenty-four courses, who acted as the cleansers and keepers of the Temple. But the distinction of priests and Levites does not seem to be older than "the Priestly Code," and criticism has all but demonstrated that the sections of the Pentateuch known by that name belong, in their present form, not to the age of Moses, but to the age of the successors of Ezekiel. The elaborate priestly and Levitic arrangements ascribed to the days of Aaron by the chronicler, who wrote six hundred years after David's day, are unknown to the writers of the Book of Kings.

In daily life they wore no distinctive dress. In the Temple service, all the year round, their vestments were of the simplest. They were of white *byssus* to typify innocence,[326] and four in number to indicate completeness. They consisted of a turban, breeches, and seamless coat of white linen, together with a girdle, symbolic of zeal and activity, which was assumed during actual ministrations.[327] The only magnificent vestments were those worn for a few hours by the high priest once a year on the Great Day of Atonement. These "golden vestments" were eight in number. To the ordinary robes were added the robe of the ephod (*Meil*) of dark blue, with seventy-two golden bells, and pomegranates of blue, purple, and scarlet; a jewelled pectoral containing the Urim and Thummim; the mitre; and the golden frontlet (*Ziz*), with its inscription of "Holiness to the Lord." The ideal type was fulfilled, and the poor shadows abolished for ever, by Him of whom it is said, "Such an high priest became us, who is holy, harmless, undefiled, separate from sinners."

The priests were poor; they were very often entirely unlettered; they seem to have had for many centuries but little influence on the moral and spiritual life of the people. Hardly any good is recorded of them as a body throughout the four hundred and ten years during which the first Temple stood, as very little good had been recorded of them in the earlier ages, and not much in the ages which were to follow. We read of scarcely a single moral protest or spiritual awakenment which had its origin in the priestly body. Their temptation was to be absorbed in their elaborate ceremonials. As these differed but little from the ritual functions of surrounding heathendom they seem to have relapsed into apostasy with shameful readiness, and to have submitted without opposition to the idolatrous aberrations of king after king, even to the extent of admitting the most monstrous idols and the most abhorrent pollutions into the sacred precincts of the Temple, which it was their work to guard. When a prophet arose out of their own supine and torpid ranks he invariably counted his brethren amongst his deadliest antagonists. They ridiculed him as they ridiculed Isaiah; they smote him on the cheek as they smote Jeremiah. The only thing which roused them was the spirit of revolt against their vapid ceremonialism, and their abject obedience to kings. The Presbyterate could have no worse ideal, and could follow no more pernicious example, than that of the Jewish priesthood. The days of their most rigid ritualism were the days also of their most desperate moral blindness. The crimes of their order culminated when they combined, as one man, under their high priest Caiaphas and their sagan Annas[328] to reject Christ for Barabbas, and to hand over to the Gentiles for crucifixion the Messiah of their nation, the Lord of Life.

CHAPTER XIX
THE TEMPLE SACRIFICES

1 Kings viii. 62-66, ix. 25.

"I have chosen this house to Myself for an house of sacrifice." —2 Chron. vii. 12.

"Gifts and sacrifices, that cannot, as touching the conscience, make the worshipper perfect, being only ... carnal ordinances, imposed until a time of reformation." —Heb. ix. 9, 10.

The whole sacrificial system with which our thoughts of Judaism are perhaps erroneously, and much too exclusively identified, furnishes us with many problems.

Whether it was originally of Divine origin, or whether it was only an instinctive expression, now of the gratitude, and now of the guilt and fear, of the human heart, we are not told. Nor is the basal idea on which it was founded ever explained to us. Were the ideas of "atonement" or propitiation (*Kippurim*) really connected with those of substitution and vicarious punishment? Or was the main conception that of *self*-sacrifice, which was certainly most prominent in the burnt offerings? Doubtless the views alike of priests and worshippers were to a great extent indefinite. We are not told what led Cain and Abel to present their sacrifices to God; nor did Moses—if he were its founder—furnish any theories to explain the elaborate system laid down in the Book of Leviticus. The large majority of the Jews probably sacrificed simply because to do so had become a part of their religious observances, and because in doing so they believed themselves to be obeying a Divine command. Others, doubtless, had as many divergent theories as Christians have when they attempt to explain the Atonement. The *"substitution"* theory of the "sin offering" finds little or no support from the Old Testament; not only is it never stated, but there is not a single clear allusion to it. It is emphatically asserted by later Jewish authorities, such as Rashi, Aben Ezra, Moses ben-Nachman, and Maimonides, and is enshrined in the Jewish liturgy. Yet Dr. Edersheim writes: "The common idea that the burning, either of part or the whole of the sacrifice, pointed to its destruction, and symbolised the wrath of God and the punishment due to sin, does not seem to accord with the statements of Scripture."[329]

Sacrifices were of two kinds, bloody (*Zebach*; LXX., θυσία), or unbloody (*minchah, korban*; LXX., δῶρον, προσφορά). The latter were oblations. Such were the cakes of shewbread, the meal and drink offerings, the first sheaf at Passover, the two loaves at Pentecost. In almost every instance the *minchah* accompanied the offering of a sacrificial victim.

The two general rules about all victims for sacrifice were, (1) that they should be without blemish and without spot, as types of perfectness; and (2) that every sacrifice should be salted with salt, as an antiseptic, and therefore a type of incorruption.[330]

Sacrificial victims could only be chosen from oxen, sheep, goats, turtle doves, and young pigeons—the latter being the offering of the poor who could not afford the costlier victims.

Sacrifices were also divided generally (1) into free, or obligatory; (2) public, or private; and (3) most holy or less holy, of which the latter were slain at the north and the former at the east side of the altar.[331] The offerer, according to the Rabbis, had to do five things—to lay on hands, slay, skin, dissect, and wash the inwards. The priest had also to do five things at the altar itself—to catch the blood, sprinkle it, light the fire, bring up the pieces, and complete the sacrifices.

Sacrifices are chiefly dwelt upon in the Priestly Code; but nowhere in the Old Testament is their significance formally explained, nor for many centuries was the Levitic ritual much regarded.[332]

The sacrifices commanded in the Pentateuch fall under four heads. (1) The burnt offering (*Olah, Kalil*),[333] which typified complete self-dedication, and which even the heathen might offer; (2) the sin offering (*Chattath*),[334] which made atonement for the offender; (3) the trespass offering (*Ashâm*),[335] which atones for some special offence, whether doubtful or certain, committed through ignorance; and (4) the thank offering, eucharistic peace offering (*Shelem*),[336] or "offering of completion," which followed the other sacrifices, and of which the flesh was eaten by the priest and the worshippers.[337]

The oldest practice seems only to have known of burnt offerings and thank offerings, and the former seem only to have been offered at great sacrificial feasts. Even in Deuteronomy a common phrase for sacrifices is "eating before the Lord," which is almost ignored in the Priestly Code. Of the sin offering, which in that code has acquired such enormous importance, there is scarcely a trace—unless Hosea iv. 8 be one, which is doubtful—before Ezekiel, in whom the *Ashâm* and *Chattath* occur in place of the old pecuniary fines (2 Kings xii. 16). Originally sacrifice was a glad meal, and even in the oldest part of the code (Lev. xvii.-xxvi.) sacrifices are comprised under the *Olam* and *Zebach*. The turning-point of the history of the sacrificial system is Josiah's reformation, of which the Priestly Code is the matured result.[338]

It is easy to see that sacrifices in general were eucharistic, dedicatory, and expiatory.

The eucharistic sacrifices (the meal and peace offerings) and the burnt offerings, which indicated the entire sacrifice of self, were the offerings of those who were in communion with God. They were recognitions of His absolute supremacy. The sin and trespass offerings were intended to recover a lost communion with God. And thus the sacrifices were, or ultimately came to be, the expression of the great ideas of thanksgiving, of self-dedication, and of propitiation. But the Israelites, "while they seem always to have retained the idea of propitiation and of eucharistic offering, constantly ignored the self-dedication, which is the link between the two, and which the regular burnt offering should have impressed upon them as their daily thought and duty." Had they kept this in view they would have been saved from the superstitions and degeneracies which made their use of the sacrificial system a curse and not a blessing. The expiatory conception, which was probably the latest of the three, expelled the others, and was perverted into the notion that God was a God of wrath, whose fury could be averted by gifts and His favour won by bribes. There was this truth in the notion of propitiation—that God hates, and is alienated by, and will punish, sin; and yet that in His mercy He has provided an Atonement for us. But in trying to imagine *how the sacrifice affected God*, the Israelites lost sight of the truth that *this* is an inexplicable mystery, and that all which we can know is the effect which *it can produce on the souls of man*. If they had interpreted the sacrifices as a whole to mean this only—that man is guilty and that God is merciful; and that though man's guilt separates him from God, reunion with Him can be gained by confession, penitence, and self-sacrifice, by virtue of an Atonement which He had revealed and would accept—then the effect of them would have been spiritually wholesome and ennobling. But when they came to think that sacrifices were presents to God, which might be put in the place of amendment and moral obedience, and that the punishment due to their offences might be thus mechanically diverted upon the heads of innocent victims, then the sacrificial system was rendered not only nugatory but pernicious. Nor have Christians been exempt from a similar corruption of the doctrine of the Atonement. In treating it as vicarious and expiatory they have forgotten that it is unavailing unless it be also representative. In looking upon it as the atonement *for* sin they have overlooked that there can be no such atonement unless it be accompanied by redemption *from* sin. They have tacitly and practically acted on the notion, which in the days of St. Paul some even avowed, that "we may continue in sin that grace may abound." But in the great work of redemption the will of man cannot be otiose. He must himself die with Christ. As Christ was sacrificed for him he, too, must offer his body a living sacrifice, holy, acceptable unto God. "Without the sin offering of the Cross," says Bishop Barry, "our burnt offering (of self-dedication) would be impossible; so also without the burnt offering the sin offering will, to us, be unavailing."[339]

Many of the crudities, and even horrors, which, alike in Jewish and Christian times, have been mixed up with the idea of bloody sacrifices, would have been removed if more attention had been paid to the prominence and real significance of *blood* in the entire ritual. As taught by some revivalists the doctrine of the blood adds the most revolting touches to theories which assimulate God to Moloch; but the true significance of the phrase and of the symbol elevates the entire doctrine of sacrifice into a purer and more spiritual atmosphere.

The central significance of the whole doctrine lies in the ancient opinion that "the blood" of the sacrifice was "its life." This was why an expiatory power was ascribed to the blood. There was certainly no transfer of guilt to the animal, *for its blood remained clean and cleansing.* Nor was the animal supposed to undergo the transgressor's punishment; first, because this is nowhere stated, and next, because had that been the case, fine flour would certainly not have been permitted (as it was) as a sin offering.[340] Moreover, no wilful offence, no offence "with uplifted hand," *i.e.,* with evil premeditation, *could* be atoned for either by sin or trespass offerings;—though certainly so wide a latitude was given to the notion of sin as an *involuntary* error as to tend to break down the notion of moral responsibility. The sin offering was further offered for some purely accidental and ceremonial offences, which could not involve any real consciousness of guilt.[341] "The blood of the covenant" (Exod. xxiv. 4-8) was not of the *sin* offering, but of peace and burnt offerings; and though, as Canon Cook says, we read of blood in paganism as a propitiation to a hostile demon, "we seem to seek in vain for an instance in which the blood, as a natural symbol for the soul, was offered as an atoning sacrifice."[342] "The atoning virtue of the blood lies not in its material substance, but in the life of which it is the vehicle," says Bishop Westcott. "The blood always includes the thought of the life preserved and active beyond death. It is not simply the price by which the redeemed were purchased, but the power by which they were quickened so as to be capable of belonging to God." "To drink the blood of Christ," says Clement of Alexandria, "is to partake of the Lord's incorruption."[343]

Besides the points to which we have alluded, there is a further difficulty created by the singular silence *respecting sin offerings of any kind,* except in that part of the Old Testament which has recently acquired the name of the Priestly Code.[344]

The word *Chattath,* in the sense of sin offering, occurs in Exod. xxix., xxx., and many times in Leviticus and Numbers, and six times in Ezekiel. Otherwise in the Old Testament it is barely mentioned, except in the post-exilic Books of Chronicles (2 Chron. xxix. 24) and Ezra (viii. 25).[345] It is not mentioned in any other historic book; nor in any prophet except Ezekiel. Again, as we have seen, the Day of Atonement leaves not a trace in any of the earlier historic records of Scripture, and is found only in the authorities above mentioned. Through all the rest of Scripture the scape-goat is unmentioned, and Azazel is ignored. Dr. Kalisch goes so far as to say that "there is conclusive evidence to prove that the Day of Atonement was instituted considerably more than a thousand years after the death of Moses and Aaron.[346] For even in Ezekiel, who wrote b.c. 574, there is no Day of Atonement on the tenth day of the seventh month, but on the first and seventh of the first month (Abib, Nisan)." He thinks it utterly impossible that, had it existed in his time, Ezekiel could have blotted out the holiest day of the year, and substituted two of his own arbitrary choice.[347] The rites, moreover, which he describes differ wholly from those laid down in Leviticus. Even in Nehemiah there is no notice of the Day of Atonement, though a day was observed on the twenty-fourth of the month. Hence this learned writer infers that even in B.C. 440 the Great Day of Atonement was not yet recognised, and that the pagan element of sending the scape-goat to Azazel, the demon of the wilderness, proves the late date of the ceremony.

It is interesting to observe how utterly the sacrificial priestly system, in the abuses which not only became involved in it, but seemed to be almost inseparable from it, is condemned by the loftier spiritual intuition which belongs to phases of revelation higher than the external and the typical.

Thus in the Old Testament no series of inspired utterances is more interesting, more eloquent, more impassioned and ennobling, than those which insist upon the utter nullity of all sacrifices in themselves, and their absolute insignificance in comparison with the lightest element of the moral law. On this subject the Prophets and the Psalmists use language so sweeping and exceptionless as almost to repudiate the desirability of sacrifices altogether. They speak of them with a depreciation akin to scorn. It may be doubted whether they had the Mosaic system with all its details, as we know it, before them. They do not enter into those final elaborations which it assumed, and not one of them so much as alludes to any service which resembles the powerfully symbolic ceremonial of the Great Day of

Atonement. But they speak of the ceremonial law in such fragments and aspects of it as were known to them. They deal with it as priests practised it, and as priests taught—if they ever taught anything—respecting it. They speak of it as it presented itself to the minds of the people around them, with whom it had become rather a substitute for moral efforts and an obstacle in the path of righteousness, than an aid to true religion. And this is what they say:—

"Hath the Lord as great delight in sacrifice," asks the indignant Samuel, "as in obeying the voice of the Lord? Behold, to obey is better than sacrifice, and to hearken than the fat of rams."[348]

"I hate, I despise your feasts," says Jehovah by Amos, "and I will take no delight in your solemn assemblies. Yea, though ye offer Me your burnt offerings and meal offerings, I will not accept them: neither will I regard the peace offerings of your fat beasts. Turn thou away from Me the noise of thy songs; for I will not hear the melody of thy viols. But let judgment roll down as waters, and righteousness as a mighty stream."[349]

"Wherewith shall I come before the Lord," asks Micah, "and bow myself before the most high God? Shall I come before Him with burnt offerings, with calves of a year old? Will the Lord be pleased with thousands of rams, or with ten thousands of rivers of oil? Shall I give my firstborn for my transgression, the fruit of my body for the sin of my soul? He hath showed thee, O man, what is good: and what doth the Lord require of thee, but to do justly, and to love mercy, and to walk humbly with thy God?"[350]

Hosea again in a message of Jehovah, twice quoted on different occasions by our Lord, says: "I desire mercy and not sacrifice, and the knowledge of God more than burnt offerings."[351]

Isaiah also, in the word of the Lord, gives burning expression to the same conviction: "To what purpose is the multitude of your sacrifices unto Me? saith the Lord: I am full of the burnt offerings of lambs, and the fat of fed beasts; and I delight not in the blood of bullocks, or of lambs, or of he-goats. When ye come to appear before Me, who hath required this at your hands, to trample My courts? Bring no more vain oblations; incense is an abomination unto Me; new moon and sabbath, the calling of assemblies,—I cannot away with iniquity and the solemn meeting. Your new moons and your appointed feasts My soul hateth: they are a cumbrance unto Me; I am weary to bear them.... Wash you, make you clean!"[352]

The language of Jeremiah's message is even more startling: "*I spake not unto your fathers*, nor commanded them in the day that I brought them out of the land of Egypt, concerning burnt offerings or sacrifices: but this thing

I commanded them, saying, Obey My voice." And again—in the version of the LXX., given in the margin of the Revised Version for the unintelligible rendering of the Authorised Version—he asks: "Why hath the beloved wrought abomination in My house? Shall vows and holy flesh take away from thee thy wickedness, or shalt thou escape by these?"[353]

Jeremiah is, in fact, the most anti-ritualistic of the prophets. So far from having hid and saved the Ark, he regarded it as entirely obsolete (iii. 16). He cares only for the spiritual covenant written on the heart, and very little, if at all, for Temple services and Levitic scrupulosities (vii. 4-15, xxxi. 31-34). [354]

The Psalmists are no less clear and emphatic in putting sacrifices nowhere in comparison with righteousness:—

> "I will not reprove thee for thy sacrifices;
> Nor for thy burnt offerings which are continually before
> Me.
> I will take no bullock out of thine house,
> Nor he-goats out of thy folds.
>
> Will I eat the flesh of bulls,
> Or drink the blood of goats?
> Offer unto God thanksgiving;
> And pay thy vows unto the Most High."[355]

And again:—

> "For Thou desirest not sacrifice, else would I give it Thee:
> Thou delightest not in burnt offering.
> The sacrifices of God are a broken spirit:
> A broken and contrite heart, O God, Thou wilt not
> despise."[356]

And again:—

> "Sacrifice and offering Thou hast no delight in;
> Mine ears hast thou opened:
> Burnt offering and sin offering hast Thou not
> required."[357]

And again:—

> "To do justice and judgment
> Is more acceptable to the Lord than sacrifice."[358]

And again:—

> "I will praise the name of God with a song,
> And magnify it with thanksgiving.

> This also shall please the Lord
> Rather than a bullock that hath horns and hoofs."[359]

Surely the most careless and conventional reader cannot fail to see that there is a wide difference between the standpoint of the prophets, which is so purely spiritual, and that of the writers and redactors of the Priestly Code, whose whole interest centred in the sacrificial and ceremonial observances.

Nor is the intrinsic nullity of the sacrificial system less distinctly pointed out in the New Testament. The better-instructed Jews, enlightened by Christ's teaching, could give emphatic testimony to the immeasurable superiority of the moral to the ceremonial. The candid scribe, hearing from Christ's lips the two great commandments, answers, "Of a truth, Master, Thou hast well said that He is one; and there is none other but He: and to love Him with all the heart, ... and to love his neighbour as himself, is much more than all whole burnt offerings and sacrifices."[360]

And our Lord quoted Hosea with the emphatic commendation, "Go ye and learn what that meaneth, I desire mercy, and not sacrifice."[361] And on another occasion: "But if ye had known what this meaneth, I desire mercy, and not sacrifice, ye would not have condemned the guiltless."[362]

The presenting of our bodies, says St. Paul, as a living sacrifice is our reasonable service; and St. Peter calls all Christians a holy priesthood to offer up spiritual sacrifice.[363]

"It is impossible," says the writer of the Epistle to the Hebrews, "that the blood of bulls and goats should take away sins;" and he speaks of the priests "daily offering the same sacrifice, the which can never take away sins."[364]

And again:—

"To do good and to distribute forget not: for with *such* sacrifices God is well pleased."[365]

The wisest fathers of Jewish thought in the post-exilic epoch held the same views. Thus the son of Sirach says: "He that keepeth the law bringeth offerings enough."[366] And Philo, echoing an opinion common among the best heathen moralists from Socrates to Marcus Aurelius,[367] writes, "The mind, when without blemish, is itself the most holy sacrifice, being entirely and in all respects pleasing to God."[368]

And what is very remarkable, modern Judaism now emphasises its belief that "neither sacrifices nor a Levitical system belong to the essence of the Old Testament."[369] Such was the view of the ancient Essenes, no less than of Maimonides or Abarbanel. Modern Rabbis even go so far as to argue that the whole system of Levitical sacrifice was an alien element, introduced into Judaism from without, tolerated indeed by Moses, but only as a concession to the immaturity of his people and their hardness of heart. [370]

Such, too, was the opinion of the ancient Fathers,—of the author of the Epistle of Barnabas, of Justin Martyr, Origen, Tertullian, Jerome, Chrysostom, Epiphanius, Cyril, and Theodoret, who are followed by such Roman Catholic theologians as Petavius and Bellarmine.[371]

This at any rate is certain:—that the Judaic system is not only abrogated, but rendered impossible. Whatever were its functions, God has stamped with absolute disapproval any attempt to continue them. They are utterly annulled and obliterated for ever.

"I am come to repeal the sacrifices." Such is the ἄγραφον δόγμα ascribed to Christ; "and unless ye desist from sacrificing, the wrath of God will not desist from you."[372] The argument of St. Paul in the Epistles to the Romans and Galatians, and of the writer of the Epistle to the Hebrews, show us why this was inevitable; and they were but following the initiative of Christ and the teaching of His Spirit. It is a mistake to imagine that our Lord merely repudiated the inane pettinesses of Pharisaic formalism. He went much further. There is not the slightest trace that He personally observed the requirements of the ceremonial law. It is certain that He broke them when He touched the leper and the dead youth's bier. The law insisted on the centralisation of worship, but Jesus said, "The day cometh, and now is, when neither in Jerusalem, nor yet in this mountain, shall men worship the Father. God is a Spirit, and they that worship Him must worship Him in spirit and in truth." The law insisted, with extreme emphasis, on the burdensome distinctions between clean and unclean meats. Jesus said that it is not that which cometh from without, but that which cometh from within which defileth a man, and this He said *making all meats clean.*"[373] St. Paul, when the types of Mosaism had been for ever fulfilled in Christ, and the antitype had thus become obsolete and pernicious, went further still. Taking circumcision, the most ancient and most distinctive rite of the Old Dispensation, he called it "concision" or mere mutilation, and said thrice over, "Circumcision is nothing, and uncircumcision is nothing, but 'a new creature'"; "but faith working by love," "but the keeping of the commandment of God." The whole system of Judaism was local, was external, was minute, was inferior, was transient, was a concession to infirmity, was a yoke of bondage: the whole system of Christianity is universal, is spiritual, is simple, is unsacrificial, is unsacerdotal, is perfect freedom. Judaism was a religion of a temple, of sacrifices, of a sacrificial priesthood: Christianity is a religion in which the Spirit of God

"Doth prefer
Before all temples the upright heart and pure."

It is a religion in which there is no more sacrifice for sin, because the one perfect and sufficient sacrifice, oblation and satisfaction, has been consummated for ever. It is a religion in which there is no altar but the Cross; in which there is no priest but Christ, except so far as *every* Christian is by metaphor a priest to offer up spiritual sacrifices which alone are acceptable to God.

The Temple of Solomon lasted only four centuries, and they were for the most part years of dishonour, disgrace, and decadence.[374] Solomon was scarcely in his grave before it was plundered by Shishak. During its four centuries of existence it was again stripped of its precious possessions at least six times, sometimes by foreign oppressors, sometimes by distressed kings. It was despoiled of its treasure by Asa, by Jehoash of Judah, by Jehoash of Israel, by Ahaz, by Hezekiah, and lastly by Nebuchadnezzar. After such plunderings it must have completely lost its pristine splendour. But the plunder of its treasures was nothing to the pollutions of its sanctity. They began as early as the reigns of Rehoboam and Abijah. Ahaz gave it a Syrian altar, Manasseh stained it with impurities, and Ezekiel in its secret chambers surveyed "the dark idolatries of alienated Judah."

And in the days when Judaism most prized itself on ritual faithfulness, the Lord of the Temple was insulted in the Temple of the Lord, and its courts were turned by greedy priests and Sadducees into a cowshed, and a dovecot, and a fair, and a usurer's mart, and a robber's den.

From the first the centralisation of worship in the Temple must have been accompanied by the danger of dissociating religious life from its daily social environments. The multitudes who lived in remote country places would no longer be able to join in forms of worship which had been carried on at local shrines. Judaism, as the prophets so often complain, tended to become too much a matter of officialism and function, of rubric and technique, which always tend to substitute external service for true devotion, and to leave the shell of religion without its soul.[375]

Even when it had been purified by Josiah's reformation, the Temple proved to be a source of danger and false security. It was regarded as a sort of Palladium. The formalists began to talk and act as though it furnished a mechanical protection, and gave them licence to transgress the moral law. Jeremiah had sternly to warn his countrymen against this trust in an idle formalism. "Amend your ways and your doings," he said. "Behold, ye trust in lying words which cannot profit. Will ye steal, murder, and commit adultery, and swear falsely, and burn incense unto Baal, and walk after other gods whom ye have not known, and come and stand before Me in this house, which is called by My name, and say, We are delivered; that ye may do all these abominations?"

The Temple of Solomon was defaced and destroyed and polluted by the Babylonians, but not until it had been polluted by the Jews themselves with the blood of prophets, by idolatries, by chambers of unclean imagery. It was rebuilt by a poor band of disheartened exiles to be again polluted by Antiochus Epiphanes, and ultimately to become the headquarters of a narrow, arrogant, and intriguing Pharisaism. It was rebuilt once more by Herod, the brutal Idumean usurper, and its splendour inspired such passionate enthusiasm that when it was wrapped in flames by Titus, it witnessed the carnage of thousands of maddened and despairing combatants.

> "As 'mid the cedar courts and gates of gold
> The trampled ranks in miry carnage rolled
> To save their Temple every hand essayed,
> And with cold fingers grasp'd the feeble blade;
> Through their torn veins reviving fury ran
> And life's last anger warm'd the dying man."

Yet that last Temple had been defiled by a worse crime than the other two. It had witnessed the priestly idols and the priestly machinations which ended in the murder of the Son of God. From the Temple sprang little or nothing of spiritual importance. Intended to teach the supremacy of righteousness, it became the stronghold of mere ritual. For the development of true holiness, as apart from ceremonial scrupulosity, its official protectors rendered it valueless.

We are not surprised that Christianity knows no temple but the hearts of all who love the Lord Jesus Christ in sincerity and truth; and that the characteristic of the New Jerusalem, which descends out of heaven like a bride adorned for her husband, is:—

"And I saw no temple therein."[376]

Abundantly was the menace fulfilled in which Jehovah warned Solomon after the Feast of Dedication that if Israel swerved into immorality and idolatry, that house should be an awful warning—that its blessing should be exchanged into a curse, and that every one who passed by it should be astonished and should hiss.[377]

CHAPTER XX
SOLOMON IN ALL HIS GLORY

1 Kings x. 1-29

"O Luxury! thou curs'd by Heaven's decree!
How do thy potions with insidious joy
Diffuse their pleasures only to destroy!
Kingdoms by thee to sickly greatness grown
Boast of a florid vigour not their own."
Goldsmith, *Deserted Village.*

"The Queen of the South shall rise up in judgment against this generation, and shall condemn it. For she came from the uttermost parts of the earth to hear the wisdom of Solomon."—Matt. xii. 42.

The history of the Temple is the event which gives supreme religious importance to the reign of one who became in other respects a worldly and irreligious king. It is for this reason that I have dwelt upon its significance, and on the many interesting questions which its worship naturally suggests. Solomon gave an impulse to outward service, not to spiritual life. His religion was mainly that form of externalism which rose but little above the

"Gay religions full of pomp and gold"

of the surrounding heathens. The other fragments of his story which have been preserved for us are mainly of a political character. They point us to Solomon in his wealth and ostentation, and contain nothing specially edifying. Our Lord thought less of all this splendour than of the flower of the field. "Consider the lilies of the field, how they grow; they toil not, neither do they spin: yet I say unto you, that Solomon in all his glory was not arrayed like one of these."

Princes who have once begun to build find a certain fascination in the task. After the seven years devoted to the Temple, Solomon occupied thirteen more in building "halls of Lebanoniac cedar" for himself, for his audience-chamber, and for Pharaoh's daughter.

Chief of these were:—

1. The house of the forest of Lebanon, a sort of arsenal so called from its triple rows of cedar pillars, on which hung the golden shields for the king's guards when they attended his great visits to the Temple.

2. The justice hall, the "Sublime Porte" of Jerusalem, built of gold and cedar. It contained the famous Lion Throne of gold and ivory, with two lions on each of its six steps.[378] It is not known whether these buildings formed part of the palace and harem of Solomon, nor is it worth while to waste time on the impossible attempt to reconstruct them.

Solomon also built the fortification of Jerusalem known as the "Millo," and the wall of Jerusalem, and repaired the breaches of the city of David,[379] as well as the fortresses and treasure cities to which we have already alluded, and the summer palaces in the region of Lebanon known as "the delights of Solomon."[380] Amid these records of palatial architecture we hear next to nothing of the religious life.

He further dazzled his people by an extensive system of foreign commerce. His land-traffic with Arabia familiarised them with spicery (*necoth*), gum tragacanth, frankincense, myrrh, aloes, and cassia and with precious stones of all kinds. From Egypt he obtained horses and chariots. They were brought from Tekoa, by his merchants, and kept by Solomon, or sold at a profit.[381]

He found a ready market for them among the Hittite and Aramæan kings. Emulating the Phœnicians, and apparently invading the monopoly of Tyre, he had—if we may take the chronicler literally—a fleet of "ships of Tarshish" which sailed along the coasts of Spain.[382] Above all, he made the daring attempt to establish a fleet of Tarshish-ships at Ezion-Geber, the port of Elath, at the north of the Gulf of Akaba. This fleet sailed down the Red Sea to Ophir—perhaps Abhîra, at the mouth of the Indus—and amazed the simple Hebrews with the sight of gorgeous iridescent peacocks, wrinkled chattering apes, the red and richly scented sandal wood of India, and the large tusks of elephants from which cunning artificers carved the smooth ivory to inlay furniture, thrones, and ultimately even houses, with lustrous ornamentation. Cinnamon came to him from Ceylon, and "sapphires" (*lapis lazuli*) from Babylon.[383] Other services which he rendered to his capital and kingdom were more real and permanent.

1. Jerusalem may have been in part indebted to Solomon for its supply of water. The magnificent springs of pure gushing water at Etam are still called "Solomon's fountains," and it is believed that he used their rocky basins as reservoirs from which to irrigate his garden in the Wady Urtas (Lat., *Hortus*). Etam is two hours distant from Jerusalem, and if Solomon built the aqueduct which once conveyed its water supply to the city he

proved himself a genuine benefactor.[384] There was immense need of the "fons perennis aquæ" of which Tacitus speaks for the purifications of the Temple, soiled by the reek and offal of so many holocausts.

2. Maritime allusions now began to appear in Hebrew literature;[385] and maritime enterprise produced the marvellous effect it always produces on the character and progress of the nation. Along the black basalt roads—the king's highways—of which the construction was necessitated by the outburst of commercial activity flocked hundreds of foreign visitors, not only merchantmen and itinerant traffickers, but governors of provinces, and vassal or allied princes. The isolated and stationary tribes of Palestine suddenly found themselves face to face with a new and splendid civilisation. Admiring visitors flocked to see the great king's magnificence and to admire his foreign curiosities, bringing with them presents of gold and silver, armour[386] and spicery, horses and mules, the broidered garments of Babylon, and robes rich with the crimson, purple, and scarlet dyes of Tyre. [387] Instead of riding like his predecessors on a humble mule, the king made his royal progress to his watered garden at Etam drawn by steeds magnificently caparisoned. He reclined in "Pharaoh's chariot" richly chased and brilliantly coloured. He was followed by a train of archers riding on war-horses and clothed in purple, and was escorted by a body-guard of youths tall and beautiful, whose dark and flowing locks glittered with gold dust. In the heat of summer, if we may accept the poetic picture of the Song of Songs, he would be luxuriously carried to some delicious retreat amid the hills of myrrh and leopard-haunted woods of Lebanon, in a palanquin of cedar wood with silver pillars, purple cushions, and richly embroidered curtains, wearing the jewelled crown which his mother placed on his head on the day of his espousals.[388] Or he would sit to do justice on his throne of ivory and gold,[389] with its steps guarded by golded lions leaning upon the golden bull of Ephraim which formed its back,[390] in all his princely beauty, "anointed with the oil of gladness," his lips full of grace, his garments breathing of perfume. On great occasions of state his Queen, and the virgins that bore her company, would stand among the crowd of inferior princesses, in garments of the wrought gold of Ophir, in which she had been carried from the inner palace upon tapestries of needlework. In the pomp of such ceremonials, amid bursts of rejoicing melody, the people began to believe that not even the Pharaohs of Egypt, or the Tyrian kings with "every precious stone as their covering," could show a more glorious pageant of royal state.[391]

This career of magnificence culminated in the visit of Balkis, the Queen of Sheba,[392] who came to him across the desert with "a very great train of her camels, bearing spices and very much gold and precious stones." She saw his abounding prosperity, his peaceful people, his houses, his vineyards at Beth-Haccerem, his parks and gardens, his pools and fruit trees, his herds of cattle, his horses, chariots, and palanquins, and all the delight of the sons of men. She saw his men singers and women singers with their harps of red sandal wood and gold. She saw him at the banquet at his golden table covered in boundless profusion with delicacies brought from every land. She saw his hosts of beautiful and richly dressed slaves with lavers, dishes, and goblets all made of the gold of Uphaz. She saw him dispensing justice in his pillared hall of cedar, seated on his lion-throne. She saw the golden shields and targets[393] carried before him as he went in state to the Temple over the Mount, across the valley, and mounted from the palace to the sacred courts by the gilded staircase with its balustrades of aromatic sandal wood. [394] Perhaps she was present as a spectator at some great Temple festival. And when she had tested his wisdom by communing with him of all that was in her heart, "there was no more spirit in her." She confessed that the half of his wisdom and glory had not been reported to her. Happy were his servants, happy the courtiers who stood by him and heard his words! Blessed was the Lord his God who delighted in him, and who, out of love for Israel, had given them such a king to do justice and judgment among them. The visit ended with an interchange of royal presents.[395] Solomon, we are vaguely told, "gave unto her all her desire, whatsoever she asked," and sent her away glad-hearted to her native land, leaving behind her a trail of legends. Before her departure she opened her treasures, and gave him vast stores of spicery and gold.[396]

And to sum up the accounts, which read like a page of the story of Haroun al Raschid, the king made silver to be as stones in Jerusalem, so that it was nothing accounted of in the day of Solomon,[397] and the cedars made he to be as the sycomores which are in the "Shefelah" for multitude.

It is around this epoch of Solomon's career that the legends of the East mainly cluster. They have received a larger development from the allusions to Mohammed in the Qur'an.[398] They take the place of the personal incidents of which so few are recorded, although Solomon occupies so large a space in sacred history. "That stately and melancholy figure—in some respects the grandest and the saddest in the Sacred Volume—is in detail little more than a mighty 'shadow.' Yet in later Jewish records he is scarcely mentioned. Of all the characters in the sacred history he is the most purely secular; and merely secular magnificence was an excrescence, not a native growth of the chosen people."[399]

CHAPTER XXI
HOLLOW PROSPERITY

1 Kings xi

"Vanity of vanities, saith the Preacher, vanity of vanities; all is vanity." — Eccles. i. 2.

"At every draught more large and large they grow
A bloated mass of rank unwieldy woe,
Till, sapp'd their strength, and every part unsound,
Down, down they sink, and spread a ruin round.
"Goldsmith.

There was a *ver rongeur* at the root of all Solomon's prosperity. His home was afflicted with the curse of his polygamy, his kingdom with the curse of his despotism. Failure is stamped upon the issues of his life.

1. His Temple was a wonder of the world; yet his own reign was scarcely over before it was plundered by the Egyptian king who had overthrown the feeble dynasty on alliance with which he had trusted. Under later kings its secret chambers were sometimes desecrated, sometimes deserted. It failed to exercise the unique influence in support of the worship of Jehovah for which it had been designed. Some of Solomon's successors confronted it with a rival temple, and a rival high priest, of Baal, and suffered atrocious emblems of heathen nature-worship to profane its courts. He himself became an apostate from the high theocratic ideal which had inspired its origin.

2. His long alliance and friendship with Hiram ended, to all appearance, in coolness and disgust, even if it be true that a daughter of Hiram was one of the princesses of his harem.[400] For his immense buildings had so greatly embarrassed his resources that, when the day for payment came, the only way in which he could discharge his obligations was by alienating a part of his dominions. He gave Hiram "twenty cities in the land of Galilee." The kings of Judah, down to the days of Hezekiah, and even of Josiah, show few traces of any consciousness that there was such a book as the Pentateuch and such a code as the Levitic law. Solomon may have been unaware that Phœnicia itself was part of the land which God had promised to His people. If that gift had lapsed through their inertness,[401] the law still remained,

which said, "The land shall not be sold for ever; for the land is Mine, for ye are strangers and sojourners with Me." It was a strong measure to resign any part of the soil of Judæa, even to discharge building debts, much more to pay for mercenaries and courtly ostentation. The transaction, dubious in every particular, was the evident cause of deep-seated dissatisfaction. Hiram thought himself ill-paid and unworthily treated. He found, by a personal visit, that these inland Galilæan towns, which were probably inhabited in great measure by a wretched and dwindling remnant of Canaanites,[402] were useless to him, whereas he had probably hoped to receive part, at least, of the Bay of Acco (Ptolemais).[403] They added so little to his resources, that he complained to Solomon. He called the cities by the obscure, but evidently contemptuous name "Cabul," and gave them back to Solomon in disgust as not worth having.[404] What significance lies in the strange and laconic addition, "And Hiram sent to the king six-score talents of gold," it is impossible for us to understand. If the Tyrian king gave as a present to Solomon a sum which was so vast as at least to equal £720,000—"apparently," as Canon Rawlinson thinks, "to show that, although disappointed, he was not offended!"—he must have been an angel in human form.

3. Solomon's palatial buildings, while they flattered his pride and ministered to his luxury, tended directly, as we shall see, to undermine his power. They represented the ill-requited toil of hopeless bondmen, and oppressed freedmen, whose sighs rose, not in vain, into the ears of the Lord God of Sabaoth.

4. His commerce, showy as it was, turned out to be transitory and useless. If for a time it enriched the king, it did not enrich his people. At Solomon's death, if not earlier, it not only languished but expired. Horses and chariots might give a pompous aspect to stately pageants, but they were practically useless in the endless hills of which Palestine is mainly composed. Apes, peacocks, and sandal wood were curious and interesting, but they certainly did not repay the expense incurred in their importation. No subsequent sovereign took the trouble to acquire these wonders, nor are they once mentioned in the later Scriptures. Precious stones might gleam on the necks of the concubine, or adorn the housings of the steed, but nothing was gained from their barren splendour. At one time the king's annual revenue is stated to have been six hundred and sixty-six talents of gold; but the story of Hiram, and the impoverishment to which Rehoboam succeeded, show that even this exchequer had been exhausted by the sumptuous prodigalities of a too luxurious court. And, indeed, the commerce of Solomon gave a new and untheocratic bias to Hebrew development. The ideal of the old Semitic life was the pastoral and agricultural ideal. No other

is contemplated in Exod. xxi.-xxix. Commerce was left to the Phœnicians and other races, so that the word for "merchant" was "Canaanite." But after the days of Solomon in Judah, and Ahab in Israel, the Hebrews followed eagerly in the steps of Canaan, and trade and commerce acting on minds materialised into worldliness brought their natural consequences. "He is a merchant," says Hosea (xii. 7); "the balances of deceit are in his hand: he loveth to defraud." Here the words "he is a merchant" may equally well be rendered "as for Canaan"; and by Canaan is here meant Canaanised or commercial Ephraim. And the prophet continues, "And Ephraim said, Surely I am become rich, I have found me wealth: in all my labour they shall find in me none iniquity that were sin." In other words, these influences of foreign trade had destroyed the moral sense of Israel altogether: "Howl, ye inhabitants of Maktesh"—*i.e.,* "The Mortar," a bazaar of that name in Jerusalem—"for all the people of Canaan" (*i.e.,* the merchants) "are brought to silence." But the hypnotising influence of wealth became more and more a potent factor in the development of the people. By an absolute reversal of their ancient characteristics they learnt, in the days of the Rabbis, utterly to despise agriculture and extravagantly to laud the gains of commerce. Of too many of them it became true, that they

> "With dumb despair their country's wrongs behold,
> And dead to glory, only burn for gold."

It was the mighty hand of Solomon which first gave them an impulse in this direction, though he seems to have managed all his commerce with exclusive reference to his own revenues.

In the wake of commerce, and the inevitable intercourse with foreign nations which it involves, came as a matter of course the fondness for luxuries; the taste for magnificence; the fraternisation with neighbouring kings; the use of cavalry; the development of a military caste; the attempts at distant navigation; the total disappearance of the antique simplicity. In the train of these innovations followed the disastrous alterations of the old conditions of society of which the prophets so grievously complain—extortions of the corn market; the formation of large estates; the frequency of mortgages; the misery of peasant proprietorship, unable to hold its own against the accumulations of wealth; the increase of the wage-receiving class; and the fluctuations of the labour market. These changes caused, by way of consequence, so much distress and starvation that even freeborn Hebrews were sometimes compelled to sell themselves into slavery as the only way to keep themselves alive.

So that the age of Solomon can in no respect be regarded as an age of gold. Rather, it resembled that grim Colossus of Dante's vision, which not only rested on a right foot of brittle clay, but was cracked and fissured through and through, while the wretchedness and torment which lay behind the outward splendour ever dripped and trickled downward till its bitter streams swelled the rivers of hell:—

"Abhorrèd Styx, the flood of deadly hate,
Sad Acheron of sorrow black and deep,
Corytus named of lamentation loud
Heard on its rueful stream, fierce Phlegethon,
Whose waves of torrent fire inflame with rage."

But there was something worse even than this. The Book of Proverbs shows us that, as in Rome, so in Jerusalem, foreign immoralities became fatal to the growing youth. The *picta lupa barbara mitrâ*, with her fatal fascinations, and her banquets of which the guests were in the depths of Hades, became so common in Jerusalem that no admonitions of the wise were more needful than those which warned the "simple ones" that to yield to her seductive snares was to go as an ox to the slaughter, as a fool to the correction of the stocks.

5. Even were there no disastrous sequel to Solomon's story—if we saw him only in the flush of his early promise, and the noon of his highest prosperity—we could still readily believe that he passed through some of the experiences of the bitter and sated voluptuary who borrows his name in the Book of Ecclesiastes. The human pathos, the fresh and varied interest, which meet us at every page of the annals of David, are entirely lacking in the magnificent monotony of the annals of Solomon. The splendours of materialism, which are mainly dwelt upon, could never satisfy the poorest of human souls. There are but two broad gleams of religious interest in his entire story—the narrative of his prayer for wisdom, and the prayer, in its present form of later origin, attributed to him at the Dedication Festival. All the rest is a story of gorgeous despotism, which gradually paled into

"The dim grey life and apathetic end."

"There was no king like Solomon: he exceeded all the kings of the earth," we are told, "for riches and for wisdom." But all that we know of such kings furnishes fresh proof of the universal experience that "the kingdoms of the world and the glory of them" are absolutely valueless for all the contributions they can lend to human happiness. The autocrats who have been most conspicuous for unchecked power and limitless resources have also been the most conspicuous in misery. We have but to recall Tiberius *"tristissimus ut constat hominum,"* who, from the enchanted isle which he had degraded into the stye of his infamies, wrote to his servile senate that "all the gods and goddesses were daily destroying him"; or Septimius Severus, who, rising step by step from a Dalmatian peasant and common soldier to be emperor of the world, remarked with pathetic conviction, "*Omnia fui et nihil expedit*"; or Abderrahman the Magnificent, who, in all his life of success and prosperity, could only count fourteen happy days; or Charles V., over-eating himself in his monastic retreat at San Yuste in Estremadura; or Alexander,[405] dying "as a fool dieth"; or Louis XIV., surrounded by a darkening horizon, and disillusioned into infinite *ennui* and chagrin; or Napoleon I., saying, "I regard life with horror," and contrasting his "abject misery" with the adored and beloved dominion of Christ, who was meek and lowly of heart. Napoleon confessed that, even in the zenith of his empire, and the fullest flush of his endless victories, his days were consumed in vanity and his years in trouble. The cry of one and all, finding that the soul, which is infinite, cannot be satisfied with the transient and hollow boons of earth, is, and ever must be, "Vanity of vanities, saith the Preacher, vanity of vanities; all is vanity." And this is one main lesson of the life of Solomon. Nothing is more certain than that, if earthly happiness is to be found at all, it can only be found in righteousness and truth; and if even these do not bring earthly *happiness* they securely give us a *blessedness* which is deeper and more eternal.

If the Book of Ecclesiastes, even traditionally, is the reflection and echo of Solomon's disenchantment, we see that in later years his soul had been sullied, his faith had grown dim, his fervour cold. All was emptiness. He stood horribly alone. His one son was not a wise man, but a fool. Gewgaws could no longer satisfy him. His wealth exhausted, his fame tarnished, his dominions reduced to insignificance, himself insulted by contemptible adversaries whom he could neither control nor punish, he entered on the long course of years "*plus pâles et moins couronnées.*" The peaceful is harried by petty raids; the magnificent is laden with debts; the builder of the Temple has sanctioned polytheism; the favourite of the nation has become a tyrant, scourging with whips an impatient people; the "darling of the Lord" has built shrines for Moloch and Astarte. The glamour of youth, of empire, of gorgeous tyranny was dispelled, and the splendid boy-king is the weary and lonely old man. Hiram of Tyre has turned in disgust from an ungenerous recompense. A new Pharaoh has dispossessed his Egyptian father-in-law and shelters his rebel servant. His shameful harem has given him neither a real home nor a true love; his commerce has proved to be an expensive failure; his politic alliances a hollow sham. In another and direr sense than after his youthful vision, "Solomon awoke, and behold it was a dream."[406]

The Talmudists show some insight amid their fantasies when they write: "At first, before he married strange wives, Solomon reigned over the angels (1 Chron. xxix. 23); then only over all kingdoms (1 Kings iv. 21); then only over Israel (Eccles. i. 12); then only over Jerusalem (Eccles. i. 1). At last he reigned only over his staff—as it is said, 'And this was the portion of my labour'; for by the word 'this,'" says Rav, "he meant that the only possession left to him was the staff which he held in his hand." The staff was not "the rod and staff" of the Good Shepherd, but the earthly staff of pride and pomp, and (as in the Arabian legend) the worm of selfishness and sensuality was gnawing at its base.

CHAPTER XXII
THE OLD AGE OF SOLOMON

1 Kings xi. 1-13

"That uxorious king, whose heart, though large,
Beguiled by fair idolatresses, fell
To idols foul."
Milton, *Paradise Lost.*

"Did not Solomon, king of Israel, sin by these things?" —
Neh. xiii. 26.

"That they might know, that wherewithal a man sinneth, by
the same also shall he be punished." —Wisdom xi. 16.

Solomon had endeavoured to give a one-sided development to Israelitish
nationality, and a development little in accord with the highest and purest
traditions of the people. What he did with one hand by building the Temple
he undid with the other by endowing and patronising the worship of heathen
deities.[407] In point of fact, Solomon was hardly a genuine off-shoot of
the stem of Jesse. It is at least doubtful whether Bathsheba was of Hebrew
race, and from her he may have derived an alien strain. It is at all events a
striking fact that, so far from being regarded as an ideal Hebrew king, he
was rather the reverse. The chronicler, indeed, exalts him as the supporter
and redintegrator of the Priestly-Levitic system, which it is the main object
of that writer to glorify; but this picture of theocratic purity, even if it be
not altogether an anachronism, is only obtained by the total suppression
of every incident in the story of Solomon which militates against it. In the
Book of Kings we are faithfully told of the disgust of Hiram at the reward
offered to him; of the alienation of a fertile district of the promised land; of
the apostasy, the idolatries, and the reverses which disgraced and darkened
his later years. The Book of Chronicles ignores every one of these disturbing
particulars. It does not tell us of the depths to which Solomon fell, though
it tells us of the extreme scrupulosity which regarded as a profanation the
residence of his Egyptian queen on the hill once hallowed as the resting-
place of Jehovah's Ark. Yet, if we understand in their simple sense the
statements of the editor of the Book of Kings, and the documents on which
he based his narrative, Solomon, even at the Dedication Festival, ignored

all distinction between the priesthood and the laity. Nay, more than this, he seems to have offered, with his own hands, both burnt offerings and peace offerings three times a year,[408] and, unchecked by priestly opposition or remonstrance, to have "burnt incense before the altar that was before the Lord," though, according to the chronicler, it was for daring to attempt this that Uzziah was smitten with the horrible scourge of leprosy.

The ideal of a good and great king is set before us in the Book of Proverbs, and in many respects Solomon fell very far short of it. Further than this, there are in Scripture two warning sketches of everything which a good king should *not* be and should *not* do, and these sketches exactly describe the very things which Solomon was and did. Those who take the view that the books of Scripture have undergone large later revision, see in each of these passages an unfavourable allusion to the king who raised Israel highest amongst the nations, only to precipitate her disintegration and ruin, and who combined the highest service to the centralisation of her religion with the deadliest insult to its supreme claim upon the reverence of the world.

1. The first of these pictures of selfish autocrats is found in 1 Sam. viii. 10-18:—

"And Samuel told all the words of the Lord unto the people that asked of Him a king. And he said, This will be the manner of the king that shall reign over you: He will take your sons, and appoint them for himself, for his chariots, and to be his horsemen; and some shall run before his chariots. And he will appoint his captains over thousands, and captains over fifties; and will set them to ear his ground, and to reap his harvest, and to make his instruments of war, and instruments of his chariots. And he will take your daughters to be perfumers, and to be cooks, and to be bakers. And he will take your fields, and your vineyards, and your oliveyards, even the best of them, and give them to his servants. And he will take the tenth of your seed, and of your vineyards, and give to his courtiers, and to his servants. And he will take your menservants and your maidservants, and your goodliest oxen, and your asses, and put them to his work. He will take the tenth of your sheep, and you shall be his servants. And ye shall cry out in that day because of your king which ye shall have chosen you; and the Lord will not hear you in that day."

2. The other, which is still more detailed and significant, was perhaps written with the express intention of warning Solomon's descendants from the example which Solomon had set.[409] It is found in Deut. xvii. 14-20. Thus, speaking of a king, the writer says:—

"Only he shall not multiply horses to himself, nor cause the people to return to Egypt, to the end that he should multiply horses: forasmuch as the Lord hath said unto you, Ye shall henceforth return no more that way. Neither shall he multiply wives to himself; that his heart turn not away; neither shall he greatly multiply to himself silver and gold. And it shall be that when he sitteth upon the throne of his kingdom, that he shall write him a copy of this law in a book ... that he may learn to fear the Lord his God, ... that his heart be not lifted up above his brethren, and that he turn not aside from the commandment, ... to the end that he may prolong his days in his kingdom, he, and his children, in the midst of Israel."

If Deuteronomy be of no older date than the days of Josiah, it is difficult not to see in this passage a distinct polemic against Solomon; for he did not do what he is here commanded, and he most conspicuously did every one of the things which is here forbidden.

It is quite clear that in his foreign alliances, in his commerce, in his cavalry, in his standing army, in his extravagant polygamy, in his exaggerated and exhausting magnificence, in his despotic autocracy, in his palatial architecture, and in his patronage of alien art, in his system of enforced labour, in his perilous religious syncretism, Solomon was by no means a king after the hearts of the old faithful and simple Israelites. They did not look with entire favour even on the centralisation of worship in a single Temple which interfered with local religious rites sanctioned by the example of their greatest prophets. His ideal differed entirely from that of the older patriarchs. He gave to the life of his people an alien development; he obliterated some of their best national characteristics; and the example which he set was at least as powerful for evil as for good.

When we read the lofty sentiments expressed by Solomon in his dedication prayer, we may well be amazed to hear that one who had aspirations so sublime could sink into idolatry so deplorable. If it was the object of the chronicler to present Solomon in unsullied splendour, he might well omit the deadly circumstance that when he was old, and prematurely old, "he loved many strange women, and *went after Ashtoreth the goddess of the Sidonians, and after Milcom the abomination of the Ammonites.*[410] *And Solomon did evil in the sight of the Lord, and went not fully after the Lord as did David his father. Then did Solomon build a high place for Chemosh the abomination of Moab, in the hill that is before Jerusalem, and for Molech the abomination of the children of Ammon.* [411] *And likewise did he for all his strange wives, which burnt incense and sacrificed unto their gods.*"[412]

The sacred historian not only records the shameful fact, but records its cause and origin. The heart of Solomon was perverted, his will was weakened, his ideal was dragged into the mire by the "strange wives" who crowded his seraglio. He went the way that destroys kings.[413] The polygamy of Solomon sprang naturally from the false position which he had created for himself. A king who puts a space of awful distance between himself and the mass of his subjects—a king whose will is so absolute that life is in his smile and death in his frown—is inevitably punished by the loneliest isolation. He may have favourites, he may have flatterers, but he can have no friends. A thronged harem becomes to him not only a matter of ostentation and luxury, but a necessary resource from the vacuity and *ennui* of a desolate heart. Tiberius was driven to the orgies of Capreæ by the intolerableness of his isolation. The weariness of the king who used to take his courtiers by the button-hole and say, "*Ennuyons-nous ensemble*," drove him to fill up his degraded leisure in the *Parc aux Cerfs*. Yet even Louis XV. had more possibilities of rational intercourse with human beings than a Solomon or a Xerxes. It was in the nature of things that Solomon, when he had imitated all the other surroundings of an Oriental despot, should sink, like other Oriental despots, from sensuousness into sensualism, from sensualism into religious degeneracy and dishonourable enervation.

Two facts, both full of warning, are indicated as the sources of his ruin: (1) the number of his wives; and (2) their heathen extraction.

1. "He had," we are told, "seven hundred wives, princesses, and three hundred concubines."[414]

The numbers make up a thousand, and are almost incredible. We are told indeed that in the monstrosities of Indian absolutism the Great Mogul had a thousand wives; but even Darius, "the king" *par excellence*, the awful autocrat of Persia, had only one wife and thirty-two concubines. [415] It is inconceivable that the monarch of a country so insignificant as Palestine could have maintained so exorbitant a household in a small city like Jerusalem. Moreover, there is, on every ground, reason to correct the statement. Saul, so far as we know, had only one wife, and one concubine; David, though he put so little restraint on himself, had only sixteen; no subsequent king of Israel or Judah appears to have had even a small fraction of the number which is here assigned to Solomon, either by the disease of exaggeration or by some corruption of the text. More probably we should read seventy wives, which at least partially assimilates the number to the "threescore queens" of whom we read in the Canticles.[416] Even then we have a household which must have led to miserable complications. The seraglio at Jerusalem must have been a burning fiery furnace of feuds, intrigues, jealousies, and discontent. It is this fact which gives additional meaning to the Song of Songs. That unique book of Scripture is a sweet idyll in honour of pure and holy love. It sets before us in glowing imagery and tender rhythms how the lovely maiden of Shunem, undazzled by all the splendours and luxuries of the great king's court, unseduced by his gifts and his persistence, remained absolutely faithful to her humble shepherd lover, and, amid the gold and purple of the palace at Jerusalem, sighed for her simple home amid the groves of Lebanon. Surely she was as wise as fair, and her chances of happiness would be a thousandfold greater, her immunities from intolerable conditions a thousandfold more certain, as she wandered hand in hand with her shepherd youth amid pure scenes and in the vernal air, than amid the heavy exotic perfumes of a sensual and pampered court.

Perhaps in the word "princesses" we see some sort of excuse for that effeminating self-indulgence which would make the exhortations to simplicity and chastity in the Book of Proverbs sound very hollow on the lips of Solomon. It may have been worldly policy which originally led him to multiply his wives. The alliance with Pharaoh was secured by a marriage with his daughter, and possibly that with Hiram by the espousal of a Tyrian princess. The friendliness of Edom on the south, of Moab and Ammon on the east, of Sidon and the Hittites and Syria on the north, might be enhanced by matrimonial connexions from which the greater potentates might profit and of which the smaller sheykhs were proud.[417] Yet if this were so, the policy, like all other worldly policy unsanctioned by the law of God, was very unsuccessful. Egypt as usual proved herself to be a broken reed. The Hittites only preserved a dream and legend of their olden power. Edom and Moab neither forgot nor abandoned their implacable and immemorial hatred. Syria became a dangerous rival awaiting the day of future triumphs. "It is better to trust in the Lord than to put any confidence in man; it is better to trust in the Lord than to put any confidence in princes."

2. But the heathen religion of these strange women from so many nations "turned away the heart of Solomon after other gods." It may be doubted whether Solomon had ever read the stern prohibitions against intermarriage with the Canaanite nations which now stand on the page of the Pentateuch. If so he broke them, for the Hittites and the Phœnicians were Canaanites. Marriages with Egyptians, Moabites, and Edomites had not been, in so many words, forbidden, but the feeling of later ages applied the rule analogously to them. The result proved how necessary the law was. When Solomon was old his heart was no longer proof against feminine wiles. He was not old in years, for this was some time before his death, and when he died he was little more than sixty. But a polygamous despot gets old before his time.

The attempt made by Ewald and others to gloss over Solomon's apostasy as a sign of a large-hearted tolerance is an astonishing misreading of history. Tolerance for harmless divergences of opinion there should always be, though it is only a growth of modern days; but tolerance for iniquity is a wrong to holiness.

The worship of these devils adored for deities was stained with the worst passions which degrade human nature. They were themselves the personification of perverted instincts. The main facts respecting them are collected in Selden's famous *De Dis Syris Syntagma*, and Milton has enshrined them in his stateliest verse: —

> "First Moloch, horrid king, besmeared with blood
> Of human sacrifice, and parents' tears: ...
> Next, Chemos, the obscene dread of Moab's sons,
> Peor his other name, when he enticed
> Israel in Sittim, on their march from Nile,
> To do him wanton rites, which cost them woe.
> Yet thence his lustful orgies he enlarged
> Even to that hill of scandal, by the Grove
> Of Moloch homicide; lust, hard by hate:
> Till good Josiah drove them thence to hell.
> ... With these in troop
> Came Ashtoreth, whom the Phœnicians call
> Astarte, queen of heaven, with crescent horns;
> To whose bright image nightly by the moon
> Sidonian virgins paid their vows and songs;
> In Sion also not unsung, where stood
> Her temple on the offensive mountain, built
> By that uxorious king, whose heart, though large,Beguiled
> by fair idolatresses, fell
> To idols foul."

What tolerance should there be for idols whose service was horrible infanticide and shameless lust? "What fellowship hath righteousness with unrighteousness? and what communion hath light with darkness? and what concord hath Christ with an infidel? and what agreement hath the temple of God with idols?" How vile the worship of Chemosh was, Israel had already experienced in the wilderness where he was called Peor.[418] What Moloch was they were to learn thereafter by many a horrible experience. Had Solomon never heard that the Lord God was a jealous God, and would not tolerate the rivalries of gods of fire and of lust? At least he was not afraid to desecrate one, if not two, of the summits of the Mount of Olives with shrines to these monstrous images, which seem to have been left "on that opprobrious mount" for many an age, so that they "durst abide"

> "Jehovah, thundering out of Sion, throned
> Between the cherubim; yea, often placed
> Within His sanctuary itself their shrines,
> Abominations, and with cursed things
> His holy rites and solemn feasts profaned,
> And with their darkness durst affront His light."

And, to crown all, Solomon not only showed this guilty complaisance to *all* his strange wives, but even, sinking into the lowest abyss of apostasy, "burnt incense and sacrificed unto their gods."

"He that built a temple for himself and for Israel in Sion," says Bishop Hall, "built a temple for Chemoch in the Mount of Scandal for his mistresses in the very face of God's house. Because Solomon feeds them in their superstition, he draws the sin home to himself, and is branded for what he should have forbidden."

CHAPTER XXIII
THE WIND AND THE WHIRLWIND

1 Kings xi. 14-41

"He that soweth to his flesh shall of the flesh reap
corruption." —Gal. vi. 8.

Such degeneracy could not show itself in the king without danger to
his people. "*Delirant reges, plectuntur Achivi.*" In the disintegration of
Solomon's power and the general disenchantment from the glamour of
his magnificence, the land became full of corruption and discontent. The
wisdom and experience of the aged were contemptuously hissed off the seat
of judgment by the irreverent folly of the young. The existence of a corrupt
aristocracy is always a bad symptom of national disease. These "lisping
hawthorn-buds" of fashion only bourgeon in tainted soil. The advice
given by the "young men" who had "grown up with Rehoboam and stood
before him" shows the insolence preceding doom which had been bred by
the idolism of tyranny in the hearts of silly youths who had ceased to care
for the wrongs of the people or to know anything about their condition.
Violence, oppression, and commercial dishonesty, as we see in the Book of
Proverbs, had been bred by the mad desire for gain; and even in the streets
of holy Jerusalem, and under the shadow of its Temple, "strange women,"
introduced by the commerce with heathen countries and the attendants on
heathen princesses, lured to their destruction the souls of simple and God-
forgetting youths.[419] The simple and joyous agricultural prosperity in
which the sons of the people grew up as young plants and their daughters
as the polished corners of the Temple was replaced by struggling discontent
and straining competition. And amid all these evils the voices of the courtly
priests were silent, and for a long time, under the menacing and irresponsible
dominance of an oracular royalty, there was no prophet more.

Early in Solomon's reign two adversaries had declared their existence,
but only became of much account in the darker and later days of its decline.
[420]

One of these was Hadad, Prince of Edom. Upon the Edomites in the
days of David the prowess of Joab had inflicted an overwhelming and all
but exterminating reverse. Joab had remained six months in the conquered

district to bury his comrades who had been slain in the terrible encounter, and to extirpate as far as possible the detested race. But the king's servants had been able to save Hadad, then but a little child, from the indiscriminate massacre, as the sole survivor of his house.[421] The young Edomite prince was conveyed by them through Midian and the desert of Paran into Egypt, and there, for political reasons, had been kindly received by the Pharaoh of the day, probably Pinotem I. of the Tanite dynasty, the father of Psinaces whose alliance Solomon had secured by marriage with his daughter. Pinotem not only welcomed the fugitive Edomite as the last scion of a kingly race, but even deigned to bestow on him the hand of the sister of Tahpenes, his own *Gebira* or queen-mother.[422] Their son Genubath was brought up among the Egyptian princes. But amid the luxurious splendours of Pharaoh's palace Hadad carried in his heart an undying thirst for vengeance on the destroyer of his family and race. The names of David and Joab inspired a terror which made rebellion impossible for a time; but when Hadad heard, with grim satisfaction, of Joab's judicial murder, and that David had been succeeded by a peaceful son, no charm of an Egyptian palace and royal bride could weigh in the balance against the fierce passion of an avenger of blood. Better the wild freedom of Idumea than the sluggish ease of Egypt. He asked the Pharaoh's leave to return to his own country, and, braving the reproach of ingratitude, made his way back to the desolated fields and cities of his unfortunate people.[423] He developed their resources, and nursed their hopes of the coming day of vengeance. If he could do nothing else he could at least act as a desperate marauder, and prove himself a "satan" to the successor of his foe.[424] Solomon was strong enough to keep open the road to Ezion-Gebir, but Hadad was probably master of Sela and Maon. [425]

Another enemy was Rezon, of whom but little is known. David had won a great victory, the most remarkable of all his successes, over Hadadezer, King of Zobah, and had then signalised his conquest by placing garrisons in Syria of Damascus. On this occasion Rezon, the son of Eli, who is perhaps identical with Hezion, the grandfather of Benhadad, King of Syria in the days of Asa, fled from the host of Hadadezer with some of the Syrian forces. With these and all whom he could collect about him, he became a guerilla captain. After a successful period of predatory warfare he found himself strong enough to seize Damascus, where, to all appearance, he founded a powerful hereditary kingdom. Thus with Hadad in the south to plunder his commercial caravans, and Rezon on the north to threaten his communication with Tiphsah, and alarm his excursions to his pleasances in Lebanon, Solomon was made keenly to feel that his power was rather an unsubstantial pageant than a solid dominion.

The enmity of these powerful Emirs of Edom and Syria was an hereditary legacy from the wars of David and the ruthless savagery of Joab. A third adversary was far more terrible, and he was called into existence by the conduct of Solomon himself. This was Jeroboam, the son of Nebat. In himself he was of no account, being a man of isolated position and obscure origin. He was the son of a widow named Zeruah,[426] who lived at Zarthan in the Jordan valley. The position of a widow in the ancient world was one of feebleness and difficulty; and if we may trust the apocryphal additions to the Septuagint, Zeruah was not only a widow but a harlot. But Jeroboam, whose name perhaps indicates that he was born in the golden days of Solomon's prosperity, was a youth of vigour and capacity. He made his way from the wretched clay fields of Zeredah to Jerusalem, and there became one of the vast undistinguished gang who were known as "slaves of Solomon." The *corvée* of many thousands from all parts of Palestine was then engaged in building the *Millo* and the huge walls and causeway in the valley between Zion and Moriah, which was afterwards known as the Valley of the Cheesemongers (*Tyropœon*). Here the unknown youth distinguished himself by his strenuousness, and by the influence which he rapidly acquired. Solomon knew the value of a man "diligent in his business," and therefore worthy to stand before kings. Untrammelled by any rules of seniority, and able to make and unmake as he thought fit, Solomon promoted him while still young, and at one bound, to a position of great rank and influence. Jeroboam was an Ephraimite, and Solomon therefore "gave him charge over all the compulsory levies (*Mas*) of the tribe of the house of Joseph" — that is, of the proud and powerful tribes of Ephraim and Manasseh, who practically represented all Israel except Judah, Benjamin, and the almost nominal Simeon.

The spark of ambition was now kindled in the youth's heart, and as he toiled among the workmen he became aware of two secrets of deadly import to the master who had lifted him out of the dust — secrets which he well knew how to use. One was that a deep undercurrent of tribal jealousy was setting in with the force of a tide. Solomon had unduly favoured his own tribe by exemptions from the general requisition, and Ephraim fretted under a sense of wrong. That proud tribe, the heir of Joseph's pre-eminence, had never acquiesced in the loss of the hegemony which it so long had held. From Ephraim had sprung Joshua, the mighty successor of Moses, the conqueror of the Promised Land, and his sepulchre was still among them at Timnath-Serah. From their kith had sprung the princely Gideon, the greatest of the judges, who might, had he so chosen, have anticipated the foundation of royalty in Israel. Shiloh, which God had chosen for His inheritance, was in their domains. It required very little at any time to make the Ephraimites second the cry of the insurgents who followed Sheba, the son of Bichri,—

"We have no part in David,
Neither have we inheritance in the son of Jesse.
Every man to his tents, O Israel."

Jeroboam, who was now by Solomon's favour a chief ruler over his fellow-tribesmen, had many opportunities to foment this jealousy, and to win for himself by personal graciousness the popularity of Solomon which had so long begun to wane.

But a yet deeper feeling was at work against Solomon. The men of Ephraim and all the northern tribes had not only begun to ask why Judah was to monopolise the king's partiality, but the much more dangerous question, What right has the king to enforce on us these dreary and interminable labours, in making a city of palaces and an impregnable fortress of a capital which is to overshadow our glory and command our subjection? With consummate astuteness, by a word here and a word there, Jeroboam was able to pose before Solomon as the enforcer of a stern yoke, and before his countrymen as one who hated the hard necessity and would fain be their deliverer from it.

And while he was already in heart a rebel against the House of David, he received what he regarded as a Divine sanction to his career of ambition.

The prophets, as we have seen, had sunk to silence before the oracular autocrat who so frequently impressed on the people that there is "a Divine sentence on the lips of kings." No special inspiration seemed to be needed either to correct or to corroborate so infallible a wisdom. But the heaven-enkindled spark of inspiration can never be permanently suffocated. Priests as a body have often proved amenable to royal seductions, but individual prophets are irrepressible.

What were the priests doing in the face of so fearful an apostasy? Apparently nothing. They seem to have sunk into comfortable acquiescence, satisfied with the augmentation of rank and revenue which the Temple and its offerings brought to them. They offered no opposition to the extravagances of the king, his violations of the theocratic ideal, or even his monstrous tolerance for the worship of idols. That prophets as a body existed in Judah during the early years of this reign there is no proof. The atmosphere was ill-suited to their vocation. Nathan probably had died long before Solomon reached his zenith.[427] Of Iddo we know almost nothing. Two prophets are mentioned, but only towards the close of the reign—Ahijah of Shiloh,[428] and Shemaiah; and there seems to have been some confusion in the *rôles* respectively assigned to them[429] by later tradition.

But the hour had now struck for a prophet to speak the word of the Lord. If the king, surrounded by formidable guards and a glittering court, was too exalted to be reached by a humble son of the people, it was time for Ahijah to follow the precedent of Samuel. He obeyed a divine intimation in selecting the successor who should punish the great king's rebellion against God, and inaugurate a rule of purer obedience than now existed under the upas-shadow of the throne. He was the *Mazkîr*, the annalist or historiographer of Solomon's court (2 Chron. ix. 29); but loyalty to a backsliding king had come to mean disloyalty to God. There was but one man who seemed marked out for the perilous honour of a throne. It was the brave, vigorous, ambitious youth of Ephraim who had risen to high promotion and had won the hearts of his people, though Solomon had made him the task-master of their forced labour. On one occasion Jeroboam left Jerusalem, perhaps to visit his native Zeredah and his widowed mother. [430] Ahijah intentionally met him on the road. He drew him aside from the public path into a solitary place. There, seen by none, he took off his own shoulders the new stately *abba* [431] in which he had clad himself, and proceeded to give to Jeroboam one of those object-lessons in the form of an acted parable, which to the Eastern mind are more effective than any words. [432] Rending the new garment into twelve pieces, he gave ten to Jeroboam, telling him that Jehovah would thus rend the kingdom from the hands of Solomon because of his unfaithfulness, leaving his son but one tribe[433] that the lamp of David might not be utterly extinguished. Jeroboam should be king over Israel; to the House of David should be left but an insignificant fragment. God would build a sure house for Jeroboam as He had done for David, if he would keep His commandments, though the House of David "should not be afflicted for ever."[434]

A scene so memorable, a prophecy of such grave significance, could hardly remain a secret. Ahijah may have hinted it among his sympathisers. Jeroboam would hardly be able to conceal from his friends the immense hopes which it excited; and as his position probably gave him the command of troops he became dangerous. His designs reached the ears of Solomon, and he sought to put Jeroboam to death. The young man, who had probably betrayed his secret ambition, and may even have attempted some premature and abortive insurrection, escaped from Jerusalem, and took refuge in Egypt. There the Bubastite dynasty had displaced the Tanite, and from Shishak I., the earliest Pharaoh whose individuality eclipsed the common dynastic name, he received so warm a welcome that, according to one story, Shishak gave him in marriage Ano, the elder sister of his Queen Tahpanes (or Thekemina, LXX.) and of Hadad's wife.[435] He stayed in Egypt till the death of Solomon, and then returned to Zeredah, either in consequence of the summons of his countrymen, or that he might be ready for any turn of events.

Under such melancholy circumstances the last great king of the united kingdom passed away. Of the circumstances of his death we are told nothing, but the clouds had gathered thickly round his declining years. "The power to which he had elevated Israel," says the Jewish historian Grätz, "resembled that of a magic world built up by spirits. The spell was broken at his death." It must not, however, be imagined that no abiding results had followed from so remarkable a rule. The nation which he left behind him at his death was very different from the nation to whose throne he had succeeded as a youth. It had sprung from immature boyhood to the full-grown stature of manhood. If the purity of its spiritual ideal had been somewhat corrupted, its intellectual growth and its material power had been immensely stimulated. It had tasted the sweets of commerce, and never forgot the richness of that intoxicating draught which was destined in later ages to transform its entire nature. Tribal distinctions, if not obliterated, had been subordinated to a central organisation. The knowledge of writing had been more widely spread, and this had led to the dawn of that literature which saved Israel from oblivion, and uplifted her to a place of supreme influence among the nations. Manners had been considerably softened from their old wild ferocity. The more childish forms of ancient superstition, such as the use of ephods and teraphim, had fallen into desuetude. The worship of Jehovah, and the sense of His unique supremacy over the whole world, was fostered in many hearts, and men began to feel the unfitness of giving to Him that name of "Baal" which began henceforth to be confined to the Syrian sun-god.[436] Amid many aberrations the sense of religion was deepened among the faithful of Israel, and the ground was prepared for the more spiritual religion which in later reigns found its immortal expositors in those Hebrew prophets who rank foremost among the teachers of mankind. [437]

But as for Solomon himself it is a melancholy thought that he is one of the three or four of whose salvation the Fathers and others have openly ventured to doubt.[438] The discussion of such a question is, indeed, wholly absurd and profitless, and is only here alluded to in order to illustrate the completeness of Solomon's fall. As the book of Ecclesiastes is certainly not by him it can throw no light on the moods of his latter days, unless it be conceivable that it represents some faint breath of olden tradition. The early commentators acquitted or condemned him as though they sat on the judgment-seat of the Almighty. They would have shown more wisdom if they had admitted that such decisions are—fortunately for all men—beyond the scope of human judges. Happily for us God, not man, is the judge, and He looks down on earth

> "With larger other eyes than ours
> To make allowance for us all."

Orcagna was wiser when, in his great picture in the Campo Santo at Pisa and in the Strozzi Chapel at Florence, he represented Solomon rising out of his sepulchre in robe and crown at the trump of the archangel, uncertain whether he is to turn to the right hand or to the left.

And Dante, as all men know, joins Solomon in Paradise with the Four Great Schoolmen. The great mediæval poet of Latin Christianity did not side with St. Augustine and the Latin Fathers against the wise king, but with St. Chrysostom and the Greek Fathers for him. He did so because he accepted St. Bernard's mystical interpretation of the Song of Songs:—

> "La quinta luce, ch'è tra noi più bella
> Spira di tale amor, che tutto il mondo
> Laggiù ne gola di saver novella.
> Entro v'è l'alta mente, u' sì profondo
> Saver fu messo, che si il vero è vero,
> A veder tanto non surse il secondo."[439]

There is a famous legend in the Qur'an about the death of Solomon. [440]

"Work ye righteousness O ye family of David; for I see that which ye do. And we made the wind subject unto Solomon.... And we made a fountain of molten brass to flow for him. And some of the genii were obliged to work in his presence by the will of his Lord. They made for him whatever he pleased of palaces, and statues, and large dishes like fishponds, and caldrons standing firm on their trivets; and we said, Work righteousness, O family of David, with thanksgiving; for few of my servants are thankful. And when we had decreed that Solomon should die, nothing discovered his death unto them, except the creeping thing of the earth that gnawed his staff. And when his body fell down, the genii plainly perceived that if they had known that which is secret they had not continued in a vile punishment."[441]

The legend briefly alluded to was that Solomon employed the genii to build his Temple, but, foreseeing that he would die before its completion, he prayed God to conceal his death from them, so that they might go on working. His prayer was heard, and the rest of the legend may best be told in the words of a poet:[442]—

"King Solomon stood in his crown of gold,
Between the pillars, before the altar In the House of the
Lord. And the king was old,
And his strength began to falter,
So that he leaned on his ebony staff,
Sealed with the seal of the Pentegraph.

And the king stood still as a carven king,
The carven cedar beams below,
In his purple robe, with his signet-ring,
And his beard as white as snow.
And his face to the Oracle, where the hymn
Dies under the wings of the cherubim.

And it came to pass as the king stood there,
And looked on the House he had built with pride,
That the hand of the Lord came unaware
And touched him, so that he died
In his purple robe and his signet ring
And the crown wherewith they had crowned him king.

And the stream of folk that came and went
To worship the Lord with prayer and praise,
Went softly ever in wonderment,
For the king stood there always;
And it was solemn and strange to behold
The dead king crowned with a crown of gold.

So King Solomon stood up dead in the House
Of the Lord, held there by the Pentegraph,
Until out from the pillar there ran a red mouse,
And gnawed through his ebony staff;
Then flat on his face the king fell down,
And they picked from the dust a golden crown."

The legends of the East describe Solomon as tormented indeed, yet not without hope. In the romance of Vathek he is described as listening earnestly to the roar of a cataract, because when it ceases to roar his anguish will be at an end.

"The king so renowned for his wisdom was on the loftiest elevation, and placed immediately beneath the Dome. 'The thunder,' he said, 'precipitated me hither, where, however, I do not remain totally destitute of hope; for an angel of light hath revealed that, in consideration of the piety of my early youth, my woes shall come to an end. Till then I am in torments, ineffable torments; an unrelenting fire preys on my heart.' The caliph was ready to sink with terror when he heard the groans of Solomon. Having uttered this exclamation, Solomon raised his hands towards heaven, in token of supplication; and the caliph discerned through his bosom, which was transparent as crystal, his heart enveloped in flames."

So Solomon passed away—the last king of all Palestine till another king arose a thousand years later, like him in his fondness for magnificence, like him in his tamperings with idolatry, like him in being the builder of the Temple, but in all other respects a far more grievous sinner and a far more inexcusable tyrant—Herod, falsely called "The Great."

And in the same age arose another King of Solomon's descendants, whose palace was the shop of the carpenter and His throne the cross, and whose mortal body was the true Temple of the Supreme—that King whose kingdom is an everlasting kingdom, and whose dominion endureth throughout all ages.

BOOK III
THE DIVIDED KINGDOM

b.c. 937-889

CHAPTER XXIV
A NEW REIGN

1 Kings xii. 1-5

"A foolish son is the calamity of his father." —Prov. xix. 13.

"He left behind him Roboam, even the foolishness of the people, and one that had no understanding." —Ecclus. xlvii. 23.

Rehoboam, who was Solomon's only son, succeeded in Jerusalem without opposition, b.c. 937.[443] But the northern tribes were in no mood to regard as final the prerogative acceptance of the son of Solomon by the rival tribe of Judah. David had won them by his vivid personality; Solomon had dazzled them by his royal magnificence. It did not follow that they were blindly to accept a king who emerged for the first time from the shadow of the harem, and was the son of an Ammonitess, who worshipped Chemosh. Instead of going to Rehoboam at Jerusalem as the tribes had gone to David at Hebron, they summoned an assembly at their ancient city of Shechem, on the site of the modern Nablus, between Mount Ebal and Gerizim. In this fortress-sanctuary they determined, as "men of Israel," to bring their grievances under the notice of the new sovereign before they formally ratified his succession. According to one view they summoned Jeroboam, who had already returned to Zeredah, to be their spokesman. [444] When the assembly met they told the king that they would accept him if he would lighten the grievous service which his father had put upon them.[445] Rehoboam, taken by surprise, said that they should receive his answer in "three days." In the interval he consulted the aged counsellors of his father. Their answer was astute in its insight into human nature.

It resembled the "long promises, short performance" which Guido da Montefeltro recommended to Pope Boniface VIII. in the case of the town of Penestrino.[446] They well understood the maxim of *"omnia serviliter pro imperio,"* which has paved the way to power of many a usurper from Otho to Bolingbroke. "Give the people a civil answer," they said; "tell them that *you* are *their* servant. Content with this they will be scattered to their homes, and you will bind them to your yoke for ever." In an answer so deceptive, but so immoral, the corrupting influence of the Solomonian autocracy is as conspicuous as in that of the malapert youths who made their appeal to the king's conceit.

"Who knoweth whether his son will be a wise man or a fool?" asks Solomon in the Book of Proverbs. Apparently he had done little or nothing to save his only son from being the latter. Despots in polygamous households, whether in Palestine or Zululand, live in perpetual dread of their own sons, and generally keep them in absolute subordination. If Rehoboam had received the least political training, or had been possessed of the smallest common sense, he would have been able to read the signs of the times sufficiently well to know that everything might be lost by blustering arrogance, and everything gained by temporising plausibility. Had Rehoboam been a man like David, or even like Saul in his better day, he might have grappled to himself the affections of his people as with hooks of steel by seizing the opportunity of abating their burdens, and offering them a sincere assurance that he would study their peace and welfare above all. Had he been a man of ordinary intelligence, he would have seen that the present was not the moment to exacerbate a discontent which was already dangerous. But the worldly-wise counsel of the "elders" of Solomon was utterly distasteful to a man who, after long insignificance, had just begun to feel the vertigo of autocracy. His sense of his right was strong in exact proportion to his own worthlessness. He turned to the young men who had grown up with him, and who stood before him—the *jeunesse dorée* of a luxurious and hypocritical epoch, the aristocratic idlers in whom the insolent self-indulgence of an enervated society had expelled the old spirit of simple faithfulness.[447] Their answer was the sort of answer which Buckingham and Sedley might have suggested to Charles II. in face of the demands of the Puritans; and it was founded on notions of inherent prerogative, and "the right Divine of kings to govern wrong," such as the Bishops might have instilled into James I. at the Hampton Court Conference, or Archbishop Laud into Charles I. in the days of "Thorough."

"Threaten this insolent canaille," they said, "with your royal severity. Tell them that you do not intend to give up your sacred right to enforced labour, such as your brother of Egypt has always enjoyed.[448] Tell them that your little finger shall be thicker than your father's loins,[449] and that instead of his whips you will chastise them with leaded thongs.[450] That is the way to show yourself every inch a king."

The insensate advice of these youths proved itself attractive to the empty and infatuated prince. He accepted it in the dementation which is a presage of ruin; for, as the pious historian says, "the cause was from the Lord."

The announcement of this incredibly foolish reply woke in the men of Israel an answering shout of rebellion. In the rhythmic war-cry of Sheba, the son of Bichri, which had become proverbial,[451] they cried:—

"What portion have we in David?
Neither have we inheritance in the son of Jesse.
To your tents, O Israel:
Now see to thine own house, David!"[452]

Unable to appease the wild tumult, Rehoboam again showed his want of sense by sending an officer to the people whose position and personality were most sure to be offensive to them. He sent "Adoram, who was over the tribute"—the man who stood, before the Ephraimites especially, as the representative of everything in monarchical government which was to them most entirely odious. Josephus says that he hoped to mollify the indignant people. But it was too late. They stoned the aged *Al-ham-Mas* with stones that he died; and when the foolish king witnessed or heard of the fate of a man who had grown grey as the chief agent of despotism he felt that it was high time to look after his own safety. Apparently he had come with no other escort than that of the men of Judah who formed a part of the national militia. Of Cherethites, Pelethites, and Gittites we hear no more. The princeling of a despoiled and humiliated kingdom was perhaps in no condition to provide the pay of these foreign mercenaries. The king found that the name of David was no longer potent, and that royalty had lost its awful glamour. He made an effort[453] to reach his chariot, and, barely succeeding, fled with headlong speed to Jerusalem. From that day for ever the unity of Israel was broken, and "the twelve tribes" became a name for two mutually antagonistic powers.[454] The men of Israel at once chose Jeroboam for their king, and an event was accomplished which had its effect on the history of all succeeding times. The only Israelites over whom the House of David continued to rule were those who, like the scattered remnant of Simeon, dwelt in the cities of Judah.[455]

Thus David's grandson found that his kingdom over a people had shrunk to the headship of a tribe, with a sort of nominal suzerainty over Edom and part of Philistia. He was reduced to the comparative insignificance of David's own position during his first seven years, when he was only king in Hebron. This disruption was the beginning of endless material disasters to both kingdoms; but it was the necessary condition of high spiritual blessings, for "it was of the Lord."

Politically it is easy to see that one cause of the revolt lay in the too great rapidity in which kings, who, as it was assumed, were to be elective, or at least to depend on the willing obedience of the people, had transformed themselves into hereditary despots. Judah might still accept the sway of a king of her own tribe; but the powerful and jealous Ephraimites, at the head of the Northern Confederation, refused to regard themselves as the destined footstool for a single family. As in the case of Saul and of David, they determined once more to accept no king who did not owe his sovereignty to their own free choice.

CHAPTER XXV
THE DISRUPTION

1 Kings xii. 6-20

"It was of the Lord." It is no small proof of the insight and courageous faithfulness of the historian that he accepts without question the verdict of ancient prophecy that the disruption was God's doing; for everything which happened in the four subsequent centuries, alike in Judah and in Israel, seemed to belie this pious conviction. We, in the light of later history, are now able to see that the disseverance of Israel's unity worked out results of eternal advantage to mankind; but in the sixth century before Christ no event could have seemed to be so absolutely disastrous. It must have worn the aspect of an extinction of the glory of the House of Jacob. It involved the obliteration of the great majority of the descendants of the patriarchs, and the reduction of the rest to national insignificance and apparently hopeless servitude. Throughout those centuries of troubled history, in the struggle for existence which was the lot of both kingdoms alike, it was difficult to say whether their antagonism or their friendship, their open wars or their matrimonial alliances, were productive of the greater ruin. Each section of the nation fatally hampered and counterpoised the other with a perpetual rivalry and menace. Ephraim envied Judah, and Judah vexed Ephraim. In extreme cases the south was ready to purchase the intervention of Syria, or even of Assyria, to check and overwhelm its northern rival, while the north could raise up Egypt or Edom to harass the southern kingdom with intolerable raids.

To us the Southern Kingdom, the kingdom of Judah, seems the more important and the more interesting division of the people. It became the heir of all the promises, the nurse of the Messianic hope, the mother of the four greater prophets, the continuer of all the subsequent history after the glory of Israel had been stamped out by Assyria for ever.

1. But such was not the aspect presented by the kingdom of Judah to contemporary observers. On the contrary, Judah seemed to be a paltry and accidental fragment—one tribe, dissevered from the magnificent unity of Israel. Nothing redeemed it from impotence and obliteration but the splendid possessions of Jerusalem and the Temple, which guaranteed the

often threatened perpetuity of the House of David. The future seemed to be wholly with Israel when men compared the relative size and population of the disunited tribes. Judah comprised little more than the environs of Jerusalem. Except Jerusalem, Mizpeh, Gibeon, and Hebron, it had no famous shrines and centres of national traditions. It could not even claim the southern town of Beersheba as a secure possession.[456] The tribe of Simeon had melted away into a shadow, if not into non-existence, amid the surrounding populations, and its territory was under the kings of Judah; but they did not even possess the whole of Benjamin, and if that little tribe was nominally reckoned with them, it was only because part of their capital city was in Benjamite territory, to which belonged the valley of Hinnom. To Israel, on the other hand, pertained all the old local sanctuaries and scenes of great events. On the east of Jordan they held Mahanaim; on the west Jericho, near as it was to Jerusalem, and Bethel with its sacred stone of Jacob, and Gilgal with its memorial of the conquest, and Shechem the national place of assembly, and Accho and Joppa on the sea shore. Israel, too, inherited all the predominance over Moab and Ammon, and the Philistines, which had been secured by conquest in the reign of David.[457]

2. Then, again, the greatest heroes of tradition had been sons of the northern tribes. The fame of Joshua was theirs, of Deborah and Barak, of fierce Jephthah, of kingly Gideon, and of bold Abimelech. Holy Samuel, the leader of the prophets, and heroic Saul, the first of the kings, had been of their kith and kin. Judah could only claim the bright personality of David, and the already tarnished glories of Solomon, which men did not yet see through the mirage of legend but in the prosaic light of every day.

3. Again, the Northern Kingdom was unhampered by the bad example and erroneous development of the preceding royalty. Jeroboam had not stained his career with crimes like David; nor had he sunk, as Solomon had done, into polygamy and idolatry. It seemed unlikely that he, with so fatal an example before his eyes, could be tempted into oppressive tyranny, futile commerce, or luxurious ostentation. He could found a new dynasty, free from the trammels of a bad commencement, and as fully built on Divine command as that of the House of Jesse.

4. Nor was it a small advantage that the new kingdom had an immense superiority over its southern compeer in richness of soil and beauty of scenery. To it belonged the fertile plain of Jezreel, rolling with harvests of golden grain. Its command of Accho gave it access to the treasures of the shore and of the sea. To it belonged the purple heights of Carmel, of which the very name meant "a garden of God"; and the silver Lake of Galilee, with its inexhaustible swarms of fish; and the fields of Gennesareth, which were a wonder of the world for their tropical luxuriance. Theirs also were

the lilied waters and paper-reeds of Merom, and the soft, green, park-like scenery of Gerizim, and the roses of Sharon, and the cedars of Lebanon, and the vines and fig trees and ancient terebinths of all the land of Ephraim, and the forest glades of Zebulon and Naphtali, and the wild uplands beyond the Jordan—which were all far different from the "awful barrenness" of Judah, with its monotony of rounded hills.[458]

5. Under these favourable conditions three great advantages were exceptionally developed in the Northern Kingdom.

(1) It evidently enjoyed a larger freedom as well as a greater prosperity. How gay and bright, how festive and musical, how worldly and luxurious, was the life of the wealthy and the noble in the ivory palaces and on the gorgeous divans of Samaria and Jezreel, as we read of it in the pages of the contemporary prophets![459] Naboth and Shemer show themselves as independent of tyranny as any sturdy dalesman or feudal noble, and "the great lady of Shunem, on the slopes of Esdraelom, in her well-known home, is a sample of Israelite life in the north as true as that of the reaper Boaz in the south. She leaves her home under the pressure of famine, and goes down to the plains of Philistia. When she returns and finds a stranger in her corn-fields, she insists on restitution, even at the hand of the king himself."[460]

(2) The Ten Tribes also developed a more brilliant literature. Some of the most glowing psalms are probably of northern origin, as well as the Song of Deborah, and the work of the writer who is now generally recognised by critics under the name of the Deuteronomist. The loveliest poem produced by Jewish literature—the Song of Songs—bears on every page the impress of the beautiful and imaginative north. The fair girl of Shunem loves her leopard-haunted hills, and the vernal freshness of her northern home, more than the perfumed chambers of Solomon's seraglic; and her poet is more charmed with the lustre and loveliness of Tirzah than with the palaces and Temple of Jerusalem. The Book of Job may have originated in the Northern Kingdom, from which also sprang the best historians of the Jewish race. [461]

(3) But the main endowment of the new kingdom consisted in the magnificent development and independence of the prophets.

It was not till after the overthrow of the Ten Tribes that the glory of prophecy migrated southwards, and Jerusalem produced the mighty triad of Isaiah, Jeremiah, and Ezekiel. For the two and a half centuries that the Northern Kingdom lasted scarcely one prophet is heard of in Judah except the scarcely known Hanani, and Eliezer, the son of Mareshah,[462] who is little more than a *nominis umbra*. To the north belongs the great herald-prophet of the Old Dispensation, the mighty Elijah; the softer spirit of the statesman-prophet Elisha; the undaunted Micaiah, son of Imlah; the picturesque Micah; the historic Jonah; the plaintive Hosea; and that bold and burning patriot, a fragment of whose prophecy now forms part of the Book of Zechariah. Amos, indeed, belonged by birth to Tekoa, which was in Judah, but his prophetic activity was confined to Bethel and Jezreel. The Schools of the Prophets at Ramah, Bethel, Jericho, and Gilgal were all in Israel. The passages in the third section of the Book of Zechariah are alone sufficient to show how vast was the influence in the affairs of the nation of the prophets of the north, and how fearless their intervention. Even when they were most fiercely persecuted, they were not afraid to beard the most powerful kings—an Ahab and a Jeroboam II.—in all their pride.[463] Samaria and Galilee were rich in prophetic lives; and they, too, were the destined scene of the life of Him of whom all the prophets prophesied, and from whose inspiration they drew their heavenly fire.

Against these advantages, however, must be set two serious and ultimately fatal drawbacks—germs of disease which lay in the very constitution of the kingdom, and from the first doomed it to death.

One of these was the image-worship, of which I shall speak in a later section; the other was the lack of one predominant and continuous dynasty.

The royalty of the north did not spring up through long years of gradual ascendency, and could not originally appeal to splendid services and heroic memories. Jeroboam was a man of humble, and, if tradition says truly, of tainted origin. He was not a usurper, for he was called to the throne by the voice of prophecy and the free spontaneous choice of his people; but in Solomon's days he had been a potential if not an actual rebel. He set the example of successful revolt, and it was eagerly followed by many a soldier and general of similar antecedents. In the short space of two hundred and forty-five years there were no less than nine changes of dynasty, of which those of Jeroboam, Baasha, Kobolam,[464] Menahem, consisted only of a father and son. There were at least four isolated or partial kings: Zimri, Tibni, Pekah, and Hosea. Only two dynasties, those of Omri and Jehu, succeeded in maintaining themselves for even four or five generations, and they, like the others, were at last quenched in blood. The close of the kingdom in its usurpations, massacres, and catastrophes reminds us of nothing so much as the disastrous later days of the Roman Empire, when the purple was so often rent by the dagger-thrust, and it was rare for emperors to die a natural death. The kingdom which had risen from a sea of blood set in the same red waves.

On the other hand, whatever may have been the drawback of the small and hampered Southern Kingdom, it had several conspicuous advantages.

It had a settled and incomparable capital, which could be rendered impregnable against all ordinary assaults; while the capital of the Northern Kingdom shifted from Shechem to Penuel[465] and Tirzah, and from Tirzah to Samaria and Jezreel. It had the blessing of a loyal people, and of the all-but-unbroken continuity of one loved and cherished dynasty for nearly four centuries. It had the yet greater blessing of producing not a few kings who more or less fully attained to the purity of the theocratic ideal. Asa, Jehoshaphat, Hezekiah, Josiah, were good and high-minded kings, and the two latter were religious reformers. Whatever may have been the sins and shortcomings of Judah—and they were often very heinous—still the prophets bear witness that her transgressions were less incurable than those of her sister Samaria. All good men began to look to Jerusalem as the nursing mother of the Promised Deliverer. "Out of Judah," said the later Zechariah, "shall come forth the corner stone, out of him the nail, out of him the battle bow, out of him every governor together."[466] Amos was born in Judah; Hoshea took refuge there; the later Zechariah laboured (ix., xi., xiii. 7-9) for the fusion of the two kingdoms. From the unknown, or little known, seers who endeavoured to watch over the infant destinies of Judah, to the mighty prophets who inspired her early resistance to Assyria, or menaced her apostasy with ruin at the hands of Babylon, she rarely lacked for any long period the inspired guidance of moral teachers. If Judah was for many years behindhand in power, in civilisation, in literature, even in the splendour of prophetic inspiration, she still managed on the whole to uplift to the nations the standard of righteousness. That standard was often fiercely assaulted, but the standard-bearers did not faint. The torn remnants of the old ideal were still upheld by faithful hands. Neither the heathen tendencies of princes nor the vapid ceremonialism of priests were allowed unchallenged to usurp the place of religion pure and undefiled. The later Judæan prophets, and especially the greatest of them, rose to a spirituality which had never yet been attained, and was never again equalled Till the rise of the Son of Righteousness with healing in His wings.

How clearly, then, do we see the truth of the prophetic announcement that the disruption of the kingdom was "of the Lord"! Out of apparent catastrophe was evolved infinite reparation. The abandonment of the Davidic dynasty of the Ten Tribes looked like earthly ruin. It did indeed hasten the final overthrow of all national autonomy; but that would have come in any case, humanly speaking, from Assyria, or Babylonia, Persia, or the Seleucids, or the Ptolemies, or Rome. On the other hand, it fostered a religious power and concentration which were of more value to the world than any other blessings. "On all the past greatness and glory of Israel," says Ewald,[467] "Judah cast its free and cheerful gaze. Before its kings floated the vision of great ancestors; before its prophets examples like those of Nathan and Gad; before the whole people the memory of its lofty days. And so it affords us no unworthy example of the honourable part which may be played for many centuries in the history of the world, and the rich blessings which may be imparted, even by a little kingdom, provided it adheres faithfully to the eternal truth. The gain to the higher life of humanity acquired under the earthly protection of this petty monarchy *far outweighs all that has been attempted or accomplished for the permanent good of man by many much larger states.*" "The people of Israel goes under," says Stade, "but the religion of Israel triumphs over the powers of the world, while it changes its character from the religion of a people into a religion of the world." This development of religion, as he proceeds to point out, was mainly due to the long, slow enfeeblement of the people through many centuries, until at last it had acquired a force which enabled it to survive the political annihilation of the nationality from which it sprang.

In reality both kingdoms gained under the appearance of total loss. "Every people called to high destinies," says Renan, "ought to be a small complete world, enclosing opposed poles within its bosom. Greece had at a few leagues from each other, Sparta and Athens, two antipodes to a superficial observer, but in reality rival sisters, necessary the one to the other. It was the same in Palestine."

The high merit of the historian of the two kingdoms appears in this, that, without entangling himself in details, and while he contents himself with sweeping and summary judgments, he established a moral view of history which has been ratified by the experience of the world. He shows us how the tottering and insignificant kingdom of Judah, secured by God's promise, and rising through many backslidings into higher spirituality and faithfulness, not only out-lasted for a century the overthrow of its far more powerful rival, but kept alive the torch of faith, and handed it on to the nations of many centuries across the dust and darkness of intervening generations. And in drawing this picture he helped to secure the fulfilment of his own ideal, for he inspired into many a patriot and many a reformer the indomitable faith in God which has enabled men, in age after age, to defy obloquy and opposition, to face the prison and the sword, secure in the ultimate victory of God's truth and God's righteousness amidst the most seemingly absolute failure, and against the most apparently overwhelming odds.

CHAPTER XXVI
"JEROBOAM THE SON OF NEBAT, WHO MADE ISRAEL TO SIN"

1 Kings xii. 21-23

"For from Israel is even this; the workman made it, and it is no god: yea, the calf of Samaria shall be broken in pieces." — Hosea viii. 6.

The condemnation of the first king of Israel sounds like a melancholy and menacing refrain through the whole history of the Northern Kingdom. [468] Let us consider the extent and nature of his crime; for though the condemnation is most true if we judge merely by the issue of Jeroboam's acts, a man's guilt cannot always be measured by the immensity of its unforeseen consequences, nor can his actions and intentions be always fairly judged after the lapse of centuries. The moral judgments recorded in the Book of Kings concerning legal and ritual offences are measured by the standard of men's consciences nearly a century after Josiah's Reformation in b.c. 623, not by that which prevailed in b.c. 937, when Jeroboam came to the throne. It seems clear that, even in the opinion of his contemporaries, Jeroboam was unfaithful to the duties of the call which he had received from God; but it would be an error to suppose that his sin was, in itself, so heinous as those of which both Solomon and Rehoboam and other kings of Judah were guilty. "Calf-worship," as it was contemptuously called in later days, did not present itself as "calf-worship" to Jeroboam or his people. To them it was only the more definite adoration of Jehovah under the guise of the cherubic emblem which Solomon had himself enshrined in the Temple and Moses himself had sanctioned in the Tabernacle. There is not a word to show that they were cognisant of the book which had narrated the fierce reprobation by Moses of Aaron's "golden calf" in the wilderness. Jeroboam's chief sin was not that as a king he tolerated, or even set up, a sort of idolatry, but that he induced the whole body of his subjects to share in his evil innovations.

The charge brought against him was threefold. First, he set up the golden calves at Dan and Bethel. Secondly, he "made priests from among all the people, which were not of the sons of Levi." Thirdly, he established his "harvest feast" not on the fifteenth day of the seventh month, which was the Feast of Tabernacles, but on the fifteenth day of the eighth month. In estimating these sins let us endeavour—for it is a sacred duty—to be just.

1. We read in the Authorised Version that "he made priests of *the lowest* of the people,"[469] and this tends to increase the prejudice against him. But to have done this wilfully would have been entirely against his own interests. The more honourable his priests were, the more was his new worship likely to succeed. The Hebrew only says that "he made priests of all classes of the people," or, as the Revised Version renders it, "from among all the people." No doubt this would appear to have been a heinous innovation, judged from the practice of later ages; it is not clear that it was equally so in the days of Jeroboam. If David, unrebuked, made his sons priests; if Ira the Ithrite was a priest; if Solomon, by his own fiat, altered the succession of the priesthood; if Solomon (no less than Jeroboam) arrogated to himself priestly functions on public occasions, the opinion as to priestly rights may not have existed in the days of Jeroboam, or may only have existed in an infinitely weaker form than in the days of the post-exilic chronicler. An incidental notice in another book shows us that in Dan, at any rate, he did *not* disturb the Levitic ministry. There the descendants of Jonathan, the son of Gershom, the grandson of Moses,[470] continued their priestly functions from the day when that unworthy descendant of the mighty lawgiver was seduced to conduct a grossly irregular cult for a few shillings a year, down to the day when the golden calf at Dan was carried away by Tiglath-Pileser, King of Assyria. If the Levites preferred to abide by the ministrations of Jerusalem, and migrated in large numbers to the south, Jeroboam may have held that necessity compelled him to appoint priests who were not of the House of Levi. Neither for this, nor for his new feast of Tabernacles, nor for the calf-worship, were the kings of Israel condemned (so far as is recorded) even by such mighty prophets as Elijah and Elisha.

In choosing Dan and Bethel as the seats for his new altars, the king was not actuated by purely arbitrary considerations. They were ancient and venerated shrines of pilgrimage and worship (Judg. xviii. 30, xx. 18, 26; 1 Sam. x. 3). He did not create any sacredness which was not already attached to them in the popular imagination.[471] In point of fact he would have served the ends of a worldly policy much better if he had chosen Shechem; for Dan and Bethel were the two farthest parts of his kingdom. Dan was in constant danger from the Syrians, and Bethel, which is only twelve miles from Jerusalem, more than once fell into the hands of the kings of Judah, though they neither retained possession of it, nor disturbed the shrines, nor threw down the "calf" of the new worship. Jeroboam could not have created the "calf-worship" if he had not found everything prepared for its acceptance. Dan had been, since the earliest days, the seat of a chapelry and ephod served by the lineal descendants of Moses in unbroken succession; Bethel was associated with some of the nation's holiest memories since the days of their forefather Israel.

2. Again, if in Jeroboam's day the Priestly Code was in existence, he was clearly guilty of unjustifiable wilfulness in altering the time for observing the Feast of Tabernacles from the seventh to the eighth month. But if there be little or no contemporary trace of any observation of the Feast of Tabernacles—if, as Nehemiah tells us, it had not once been *properly* observed from the days of Joshua to his own, or if Jeroboam was unaware of any sacred legislation on the subject—the writers of the tenth century may have judged too severely the fixing of a date for the Feast of Ingathering, which may have seemed more suitable to the conditions of the northern and western tribes. For in parts of that region the harvest ripens a month earlier than in Judah, and the festival was meant to be kept at the season of harvest.[472]

3. These, however, were but incidental and subordinate matters compared with the setting up of the golden calves.

Jeroboam felt that if his people flocked to do sacrifice at the new and gorgeous Temple in Jerusalem they would return to their old monarchy and put him to death. He wished to avoid the fate of Ishbosheth.[473] He believed that he should be doing both a popular and a politic act if he saved them from the burden of this long journey and again decentralised the cult which Solomon had so recently centralised. He determined, therefore, to furnish the Ten Tribes with high places, and temples of high places, and objects of worship which might rival the golden cherubim of Zion, and be honoured with festal music and royal pomp.

He never dreamed either of apostatising from Jehovah, or of establishing the worship of idols. He broke the Second Commandment under pretence of helping the people to keep the first. The images which he set up were not meant to be *substitutes* for the one God, the God of their fathers, the God who had brought them from the land of Egypt; they were regarded as figures of Jehovah under the well understood and universally adopted emblem of a young bull, the symbol of fertility and strength.[474] Some have fancied that he was influenced by his Egyptian reminiscences, and perhaps by Ano, his traditional Egyptian bride. That is an obvious error. In Egypt *living* bulls were worshipped under the names of Apis and Mnevis, not idol-figures. Egyptian gods would have been strange reminders of Him who delivered His people from Egyptian tyranny. It would have been insensate, by quoting the very words of Aaron, to recall to the minds of the people the disasters which had followed the worship of the golden calf in the wilderness.[475] Beyond all question, Jeroboam neither did nor would have dreamed of bidding his whole people to abandon their faith and worship Egyptian idols, which never found any favour among the Israelites. He only encouraged them to worship Jehovah under the form of the cherubim.[476] Whatever may have been the aspect of the cherubim in the Oracle of the Temple, cherubic emblems appeared profusely amid its ornamentation, and the most conspicuous object in its courts was the molten sea, supported on the backs of twelve bulls. It is true that later prophets and poets, like Hosea and the Psalmist, spoke in scorn of his images as mere "calves," and spoke of him as likening his Maker to "an ox that eateth hay."[477] They even came in due time to regard them as figures of Baal and Astarte,[478] but this view is falsified by the entire annals of the Northern Kingdom from its commencement to its close. Jeroboam was, and always regarded himself as, a worshipper of Jehovah. He named his son and destined successor Abijah ("Jehovah is my Father"). Rehoboam himself was a far worse offender than he was, so far as the sanction of idolatry was concerned.

And yet he sinned, and yet he made Israel to sin. It is true that he did not sin against the full extent of the light and knowledge vouchsafed to men in later days. The sin of which he was guilty was the sin of worldly policy. With professions of religion on his lips he pandered to the rude and sensuous instinct which makes materialism in worship so much more attractive to all weak minds than spirituality. Proclaiming as his motive the rights of the people, he accelerated their religious degeneracy. "The means to strengthen or ruin the civil power," says Lowth, "is either to establish or destroy the right worship of God. The way to destroy religion is to embase the dispenser of it.... This is to give the royal stamp to a piece of lead." If we may trust to Jewish tradition, there were some families in Israel who, though they clung to their old homes, and would not migrate to the south, yet refused to worship what is, not quite justly, called "the heifer Baal."[479] The legendary Tobit (i. 4-7) boasts that "when all the tribes of Naphthali fell from the house of Jerusalem and sacrificed to the heifer Baal I alone went often to Jerusalem at the feasts," and, in general, observed the provisions of the Levitic law.

There seems to have been but little religion in Jeroboam's temperament. In every other great national gathering at Shechem and other sacred places we read of religious rites.[480] No mention is made of them, no allusion occurs respecting them, in the assembly to which Jeroboam owed his throne. He might at least have consulted Ahijah, who had given him, when he was still a subject, the Divine promise and sanction of royalty. He might, had he chosen, have followed a higher and purer guidance than that of his own personal misgiving and his own arbitrary will. The error which he committed was this—he trusted in policy, not in the Living God. "It was," says Dean Stanley, "precisely the policy of Abder-Rahman, Caliph of Spain, when he arrested the movement of his subjects to Mecca, by the erection of a Holy Place of the Zeca at Cordova, and of Abd-el-Malik when he built the Dome of the Rock at Jerusalem, because of his quarrel with the authorities at Mecca." He was not guilty of revolt, for he acted under prophetic sanction; nor of idolatry, for he did not abandon the worship of Jehovah; but "he broke the unity and tampered with the spiritual conception of the national worship. From worshipping God under a gross material symbol, the Israelites gradually learnt to worship other gods altogether; and the venerable sanctuaries of Dan and Bethel prepared the way for the temples of Ashtaroth and Bethel at Samaria and Jezreel. The religion of the kingdom of Israel at last sank lower than that of the kingdom of Judah against which it had revolted. 'The sin of Jeroboam the son of Nebat, who made Israel to sin,' is the sin again and again repeated in the policy, half-worldly, half-religious, which has prevailed through large tracts of ecclesiastical history. Many are the forms of worship which, with high pretensions, have been nothing else but so many various and opposite ways of breaking the Second Commandment. Many a time has the end been held to justify the means, and the Divine character been degraded by the pretence, or even the sincere intention, of upholding His cause, for the sake of secular aggrandisement; for the sake of binding together good systems, which it was feared would otherwise fall to pieces; for the sake of supporting the faith of the multitude for fear they should otherwise fall away to rival sects, or lest the enemy should come and take away their place and nation. False arguments have been used in support of religious truths, false miracles promulgated or tolerated, false readings in the sacred text defended…. And so the faith of mankind has been undermined by the very means intended to preserve it. The whole subsequent history is a record of the mode by which, with the best intentions, Church and nation may be corrupted."

This view of Dean Stanley is confirmed by another wise teacher, Professor F. D. Maurice. Jeroboam, he says, "did not trust the Living God.

He thought, not that his kingdom stood upon a Divine *foundation*, but that it was to be upheld by certain Divine props and *sanctions*. The two doctrines seem closely akin. Many regard them as identical. In truth there is a whole heaven between them. The king who believes that his kingdom has a Divine foundation confesses his own subjection and responsibility to an actual living ruler. The king who desires to surround himself with Divine sanctions would fain make himself supreme, knows that he cannot, and would therefore seek help from the fear men have of an invisible power in which they have ceased to believe. He wants a God as the support of his authority. *What* God he cares very little."

And thus, to quote once more, "the departure from spiritual principles out of political motives surely leads to destruction, and is here portrayed for all times."[481]

CHAPTER XXVII
JEROBOAM, AND THE MAN OF GOD

1 Kings xiii. 1-34

"Beloved, believe not every spirit, but try the spirits whether they are of God." — 1 John iv. 1.

"Οὐ γὰρ ἔδει τὸν τῆς θείας ἀκηκοότα φωνῆς ἀνθρωπίνη πιστεύσαι τἀνάντια λεγούσῃ." — Theodoret.

We are told that Jeroboam, whose position probably made him restless and insecure, first built or fortified Shechem, and then went across the Jordan and established another palace and stronghold at Penuel. After this he shifted his residence once more to the beautiful town of Tirzah,[482] where he built for himself the palace which Zimri afterwards burnt over his own head. Although the prophet Shemaiah forbade Rehoboam's attempt to crush him in a great war, Jeroboam remained at war with him and Abijah all his life, till his reign of two-and-twenty troubled years ended apparently by a sudden death—for the chronicler says that "the Lord struck him, and he died."

Nearly all that we know of Jeroboam apart from these incidental notices is made up of two stories, both of which are believed by critics to date from a long subsequent age, but which the compiler of the Book of Kings introduced into his narrative from their intrinsic force and religious instructiveness.

The first of these stores tells us of the only spontaneous prophetic protest against his proceedings of which we read. So ancient is this curious narrative that tradition had entirely forgotten the names of the two prophets concerned in it. It probably assumed shape from the dim local reminiscences evoked in the days of Josiah's reformation, when the grave of a forgotten prophet of Judah was discovered among the tombs at Bethel, three hundred and twenty years after the events described.

A nameless man of God—Josephus calls him Jadon, and some have identified him with Iddo[483]—came out of Judah to atone for the silence of Israel, and to protest in God's name against the new worship. His protest, however, is against "the altar." He does not say a word about the golden calves. Jeroboam, perhaps, at his dedication festival of the king's shrine at Bethel, was standing on the altar-slope,[484] as Solomon had done in the Temple, to burn incense. Suddenly the man of God appeared, and threatened to the altar the destruction and desecration which subsequently fell upon it. We cannot be sure that some of the details are not later additions supplied from subsequent events. Josephus rationalises the story very absurdly in the style of Paulus. The sign of the destruction or rending of the altar, and the outpouring of the ashes,[485] may have been first fulfilled in that memorable earthquake which became a date in Israel.[486] The desecration which it received at the hands of Josiah reminded men of the threat of the unknown messenger.[487] Then we are told that Jeroboam raised his hand in anger, with the order to secure the bold offender, but that his arm at once "dried up," and was only restored by the man of God[488] at the king's entreaty. The king invites the prophet to go home and refresh himself and receive a reward; but he replies that not half Jeroboam's house could tempt him to break the command which he had received to eat no bread neither drink water at Bethel. An old Israelite prophet was living at Bethel, and his son told him what had occurred. Struck with admiration by the faithfulness of the southern man of God, he rode after him to bring him to his house. He found him seated under "the terebinth"—evidently some aged and famous tree. When he refused the renewed invitation, the old man lyingly said to him that he too was a man of God, and had been bidden by an angel to bring him back. Deceived, perhaps too easily deceived, the man of God from Judah went back. It would have been well for him if he had believed that even "an angel of God," or what may seem to wear such a semblance, may preach a false message, and may deserve nothing but an anathema.[489] With terrible swiftness the delusion was dispelled. While he was eating in Bethel, the old prophet, overcome by an impulse of inspiration, told him that for his disobedience he should perish and lie in a strange grave. Accordingly he had not gone far from Bethel when a lion met and killed him, not, however, mangling or devouring him, but standing still with the ass beside the carcase.[490] On hearing this the old prophet of Bethel went and brought back the corpse. He mourned over his victim with the cry, "Alas, my brother,"[491] and bade his sons that when he died they should bury him in the same sepulchre with the man of God, for all that he had prophesied should come to pass.

Josephus adds many idle touches to this story. If in a tale which assumed its present form so long after the events imaginative details were introduced, the incident of the lion subserves the moral aim of the narrative (2 Kings xvii. 25; Jer. xxv. 30, xlix. 19; Wisdom xi. 15-17, etc.). The significance of the story for us is happily neither historic nor evidential, but it is profoundly moral. It is the lesson not to linger in the neighbourhood of temptation, nor to be dilatory in the completion of duty.[492] It is the lesson to be ever on our guard against the tendency to assume inspired sanction for the conduct and opinions which coincide with our own secret wishes. Satan finds it easy to secure our credence when he answers us according to our idols, and can quote Scripture for our purpose as well as his own; and God sometimes punishes men by granting them their own desires, and sending leanness withal into their bones. The man of God from Judah had received a distinct injunction from which the invitation of a king had been insufficient to shake him. If the old prophet wilfully lied, his victim was willingly seduced. We may think his sin venial, his punishment excessive. It will not seem so unless we unduly extenuate his sin and unduly exaggerate the nature of his penalty.

His sin consisted in his ready acceptance of a sham inspiration which came to him from a tainted source, and which he ought to have suspected because it conceded what he desired. God's indisputable intimations to our individual souls are not to be set aside except by intimations no less indisputable. There had been an obvious reason for the command which God had given. The reason still existed; the prohibition had not been withdrawn. The sham revelation furnished him with an excuse; it did not give him a justification. Doubtless Jadon's first thought was that

"He lied in every word,
That hoary prophet, with malicious eye,
Askance to watch the working of his lie."

Why did he yield so readily? It was for the same reason which causes so many to sin. "The tempting opportunity" did but meet, as sooner or later it always *will* meet, "the susceptible disposition."

Yet his punishment does not justify us in branding him as a weak or a vicious man. We must judge him and all men, at his best, not at his worst; in his hours of faithfulness and splendid courage, not in his moment of unworthy acquiescence.

And his speedy punishment was his best blessing. Who knows what might not have happened to him if the speck of conventionality and corruption had been allowed to spread? Who can tell whether in due time he might not have sunk into something no better than his miserable tempter? Rather than that we should be in any respect false to our loftiest ideals, or less noble than our better selves, let the lion meet us, let the tower of Siloam fall on us, let our blood be mingled with our sacrifices. Better physical death than spiritual degeneracy.

CHAPTER XXVIII
DOOM OF THE HOUSE OF NEBAT

1 Kings xiv. 1-20.[493]

"Whom the gods love die young."

"Τὸ παιδίον ἀπέθανεν; ἀπεδόθη."—Epictet.

The other story about Jeroboam is full of pathos; and though here, too, there are obvious signs that, in its present form, it could hardly have come from a contemporary source, it doubtless records an historic tradition. It is missing in the Septuagint, though in some copies the blank is supplied from Aquila's version.

Jeroboam was living with his queen at Tirzah when, as a judgment on him for his neglect of the Divine warning, his eldest and much loved son, Abijah, fell sick. Torn with anxiety the king asked his wife to disguise herself that she might not be recognised on her journey, and to go to Shiloh, where Ahijah the prophet lived,[494] to inquire about the dear youth's fate. "Take with you," he said, "as a present to the prophet ten loaves, and some little cakes for the prophet's children,[495] and a cruse of honey."

Jeroboam remembered that Ahijah's former prophecy had been fulfilled, and believed that he would again be able to reveal the future, and say whether the heir to the throne would recover. The queen obeyed; and if she were indeed the Egyptian princess Ano, it must have been for her a strange experience. Through the winding valley, she reached the home of the aged prophet unrecognised. But he had received a Divine intimation of her errand; and though his eyes were now blind with the *gutta serena*,[496] he at once addressed her by name when he heard the sound of her approaching footsteps. The message which he was bidden to pronounce was utterly terrible; it was unrelieved by a single gleam of mitigation or a single expression of pity. It reproached and denounced Jeroboam for faithless ingratitude in that he had cast God behind his back;[497] it threatened hopeless and shameful extermination to all his house.[498] His dynasty should be swept away like dung. The corpses of his children should be left unburied and be devoured by vultures and wild dogs.[499] The moment the feet of the queen reached her house the youth should die, and this bereavement, heavy as it was, should be the sole act of mercy in the tragedy, for it should take away Abijah from the dreadful days to come, because in him alone of the House of Jeroboam had God seen something good. The avenger should be a new king, and all this should come to pass "even now."[500]

This speech of the prophet is given in a rhythmical form, and has probably been mingled with later touches. It falls into two strophes (7-11, 12-16) of 3+2 and 2+3 verses.[501] The expressions "thou hast done above *all that were before thee*, for thou hast gone and made thee *other gods*" (verse 9) hardly suits the case of Jeroboam; and the omission by the LXX. of the prophecy of Israel's ultimate captivity, together with the treatment of the prophecy by Josephus, throw some doubt on verses 9, 15, and 16.[502] They seem to charge Jeroboam with sanctioning *Asherim*, or wooden images of the Nature-goddess Asherah, of which we read in the history of Judah, but which are never mentioned in the acts of Jeroboam, and do not accord with his avowed policy. These may possibly be due to the forms which the tradition assumed in later days.

The awful prophecy was fulfilled. As the hapless mother set foot on the threshold of her palace at beautiful Tirzah the young prince died, and she heard the wail of the mourners for him.[503] He alone was buried in the grave of his fathers, and Israel mourned for him. He was evidently a prince of much hope and promise, and the deaths of such princes have always peculiarly affected the sympathy of nations. We know in Roman history the sigh which arose at the early death of Marcellus: —

"Ostendent terris hunc tantum fata neque ultra
Esse sinent. Nimium vobis, Romana propago,
Visa potens, superi, propria hæc si dona fuissent,
Heu miserande puer, si qua fata aspera rumpas
Tu Marcellus eris."[504]

We know the remark of Tacitus as he contemplates the deaths of Germanicus, Caius, and Drusus, Piso Licinianus, Britannicus, and Titus, *"breves atque infaustos Populi Romani amores."* We know how, when Prince William was drowned in the *White Ship*, Henry of England never smiled again; and how the nation mourned the deaths of Prince Alfonso, of the Black Prince, of Prince Arthur, of Prince Henry, of the Princess Charlotte, of the Duke of Clarence and Avondale. But these untimely deaths of youths in their early bloom, before their day,

"Impositique rogis juvenes ante ora parentum,"

are not half so deplorable as the case of those who have grown up like Nero to blight every hope which has been formed of them. When Louis le *Bien-Aimé* lay ill of the fever at Metz which seemed likely to be fatal, all France wept and prayed for him. He recovered, and grew up to be that portent of selfish boredom and callous sensuality, Louis XV. It was better that Abijah should die than that he should live to be overwhelmed in the shameful ruin which soon overtook his house. It was better far that he should die than that he should grow up to frustrate the promise of his youth. He was beckoned by the hand of God "because in him was found some good thing towards the Lord God of Israel." We are not told wherein the goodness consisted, but Rabbinic tradition guessed that in opposition to his father he discountenanced the calf-worship and encouraged and helped the people to continue their visits to Jerusalem. Such a king might indeed have recovered the whole kingdom, and have dispossessed David's degenerate line. But it was not to be. The fiat against Israel had gone forth, though a long space was to intervene before it was fulfilled. And God's fiats are irrevocable, because with Him there is no changeableness neither shadow of turning.

> "The moving finger writes, and, having writ,
> Moves on; nor all thy piety nor wit
> Shall lure it back to cancel half a line,
> Nor all thy tears wash out a word of it."

But the passage about Abijah has a unique preciousness, because it stands alone in Scripture as an expression of the truth that early death is no sign at all of the Divine anger, and that the length or brevity of life are matters of little significance to God, seeing that, at the best, the longest life is but as one tick of the clock in the eternal silence. The promise to filial obedience, "that thy days may be long," in the Fifth Commandment is primarily national; and although undoubtedly "length of days" then, as now, was regarded as a blessing,[505] yet the blessing is purely relative, and wholly incommensurate with others which affect the character and the life to come. This passage may be the consolation of many thousands of hearts that ache for some dear lost child. "Is it well with the child?" "It is well!" The story of Cleobis and Biton shows how fully the wisest of the ancients had recognised the truth that early death may be a boon of God to save His children from being snared in the evil days. "Honourable age," says the Book of Wisdom, "is not that which standeth in length of time, nor that is measured by number of years. But wisdom is the grey hair unto men, and an unspotted life is old age. He pleased God, and was beloved of Him: so that living among sinners he was translated. Yea, speedily was he taken away, lest that wickedness should alter his understanding, or deceit beguile his soul.... He, being made perfect in a short time, fulfilled a long time: for his soul pleased the Lord: therefore He hastens to take him away from among the wicked."[506] It is the truth so beautifully expressed by Seneca: "*Vita non quam diu sed quam bene acta refert*"; by St. Ambrose: "*Perfecta est ætas, ubi perfecta est virtus*"; by Shakspeare:—

> "The good die early,
> And they whose hearts are dry as summer dust
> Burn to the socket;"

and by Ben Jonson:—

> "It is not growing like a tree
> In bulk, doth make man better be:
> Or standing long an oak, three hundred year,
> To fall, a log at last, dry, bald, and sere:
> A lily of a day
> Is fairer far in May,
> Although it fall and die that night—
> It was the plant and flower of Light.
> In small proportions we just beauties see,
> And in short measures life may perfect be."

It is recorded also on the tomb of a gallant youth, in Westminster Abbey, "Francis Holles, who died at eighteen years of age after noble deeds":—

> "Man's life is measured by the work, not days;
> Not aged sloth, but active youth, hath praise."

CHAPTER XXIX
NADAB; BAASHA; ELAH

1 Kings xv. 25-xvi. 10

"Wheresoever the carcase is, there will the vultures be gathered together."—Matt. xxiv. 28.

Jeroboam slept with his fathers and went to his own place, leaving behind him his dreadful epitaph upon the sacred page. His son Nadab succeeded him. In his reign of twenty-two years the first king of Israel had outlived Rehoboam and his son Abijah. Asa, the great grandson of Solomon, was already on the throne of Judah. Of Nadab we are told next to nothing. The appreciation of the kings of Israel tends to drift into the meagre formula that they did that which was evil in the sight of the Lord, and walked in the way of Jeroboam, the son of Nebat, and in his sin wherewith he caused Israel to sin. In the second year of his reign Nadab was engaged in a wearisome military expedition against Gibbethon in the Shephelah, which belonged to the Philistines. It was a Levitical city in the tribe of Dan, which had been assigned to the Kohathites, and its siege continued for twenty-seven years with no apparent result.[507] That the Philistines, who had been so utterly crushed by David and who were an insignificant power, should have thus been able to assert themselves once more, is a proof of the weakness to which Israel had been reduced. While Nadab was thus occupied, an obscure conspirator, Baasha, son of Ahijah, of the tribe of Issachar,[508] actuated perhaps by tribal jealousy, or stirred up as Jeroboam had been before him and as Jehu was after him by some prophetic message, conspired against him, and slew him.[509] As soon as this military revolt had placed Baasha on the throne he fulfilled the frightful curse which Ahijah had uttered against the House of Jeroboam. He absolutely exterminated the family of Nebat, and left him neither kinsman nor friend to avenge his death. He seems to have been a powerful soldier, and he inflicted severe humiliation on the Southern Kingdom until Asa bribed Benhadad to invade his territory. He reigned at Tirzah for twenty-four years, of which nothing is recorded but the ordinary formula. Towards the close of his reign he received from the prophet Jehu, the son of Hanani, the message of his doom. Jehu must have been at this time a young prophet. According to the Chronicles his father Hanani rebuked Asa for the alliance which (as we shall see) he made with the Syrian against Baasha;[510] and he himself rebuked Jehoshaphat for his alliance with Ahab, and lived to be his annalist.[511] Like Amos, he lived in Judah, but prophesied also against a king of Israel. He told Baasha that God, who had exalted him out of the dust to be king of Israel. should inflict on his family the same terrible extirpation which He had inflicted on the House of Jeroboam, whose sins he had, nevertheless, followed.

Baasha "slept with his fathers," and his son Elah succeeded him. Elah seems to have been an incapable drunkard, and reigned in Tirzah for less than two years. While he was drinking himself drunk, not even secretly in his own palace, but in the house of his chamberlain Arza—a shamelessness which was regarded as an aggravation of his offence[512]—he was murdered by Zimri, the captain of half of his chariots, and the revolting tragedy of massacre was enacted once again.[513] The fact that Baasha was a man of no distinction, but "exalted *out of the dust*" (1 Kings xvi. 2), probably added to the weakness of his dynasty.

From such meagre records of horror there is not much to learn beyond the general truth of the Nemesis which dogs the heels of crime; but there is one significant clause which throws great light on the judgment which we are asked to form of these events. The prophet Jehu rebukes Baasha for showing himself false to the destiny to which God had summoned him. He implies, therefore, that Baasha had some Divine sanction for the revolution which he headed; and certainly in his slaughter of the House of Jeroboam he was the instrument of a Divine decree. Yet we are expressly told that "he provoked the Lord to anger with the work of his hands, in being like the House of Jeroboam, *and because he killed him*," or, as it is rendered in the Revised Version margin, "*because he smote it*." This is not the only place where we find that a man may be in *one sense* commissioned to do a deed of blood, yet in another sense may be held guilty for fulfilment of the commission.[514] The prophecy of extirpation had been passed, but the cruel agent of its accomplishment was not thereby condoned. God's decrees are carried out as part of the vast scheme of Providence, and He may use guilty hands to fulfil His purposes. King Jehu is His minister of vengeance, but the tiger-like ferocity with which he carried out his work awoke God's anger and received God's punishment. The King of Babylon fulfils the purpose for which he had been appointed, but his ruthlessness receives its just recompense. The wrath of man may accomplish the decrees of God, but it worketh not His righteousness. Herod and Pontius Pilate, Jews and Gentiles, priests and Pharisees, rulers and the mob may rage against Christ, but all they can accomplish is "whatsoever God's hand and God's counsel determine before to be done."

CHAPTER XXX
THE EARLIER KINGS OF JUDAH

1 Kings xiv. 21-31, xv. 1-24

The history of *"the Jews"* begins, properly speaking, from the reign of Rehoboam, and for four centuries it is mainly the history of the Davidic dynasty.

The only records of the son of Solomon are meagre records of disaster and disgrace. He reigned seventeen years, and his mother, the Ammonitess Naamah, occupied the position of queen-mother.[515] She was, doubtless, a worshipper in the shrine which Solomon had built for her national god, Molech of Ammon, who was the same as the Ashtar-Chemosh of the Moabite stone—the male form of Ashtoreth.[516] Whether her son was twenty-one or forty-one when he succeeded to the throne we do not know.[517] His attempted expedition against Jeroboam was forbidden by Shemaiah;[518] but ineffectual and distressing war smouldered on between the Northern and Southern Kingdoms. If Jeroboam sinned by the erection in the old sanctuaries of the two golden calves, Rehoboam surely sinned far more heinously. He not only sanctioned the high places—which in him may have been very venial, since they held their own unchallenged till the days of Hezekiah—but he allowed stone obelisks (*Matstseboth*) in honour of Baal, and pillars (*Chammanim*) of the Nature-goddess (*Asherah*) to be set up on every high hill and under every green tree.[519] Worse than this, and a proof of the abyss of corruption into which the evil example of Solomon had beguiled the nation, there were found in the land the *Kedeshim*, the infamous eunuch-ministers of a most foul worship.[520] In spite of Temple and priesthood, "they did according to all the abominations of the nations which the Lord drave out before the children of Israel."[521] Since Rehoboam thus sinned so much more heinously than his northern compeer we can hardly admire the conduct of the Levites, who, according to the chronicler, fled southward in swarms from the innovations of the son of Nebat. The Scylla of calf-worship was incomparably less shameful than the Charybdis of these heathen abominations.

Such atrocities could not be left unpunished. Where the carcase is the eagles will gather. In the fifth year of Rehoboam, Shishak, King of

Egypt,[522] put an end to the shortlived glories of the age of Solomon. Of his reason for invading Palestine we know nothing. It was probably mere ambition and the love of plunder, stimulated by stories which Jeroboam may have brought to him about the inexhaustible riches of Jerusalem. He is the first Pharaoh whose individuality was so marked as to transcend and replace the common dynastic name.[523] He was astute enough to seize the opportunity of self-aggrandisement which offered itself when Jeroboam took refuge at his court; but the conjecture that former friendly relations induced Jeroboam to invite the services of Shishak for the destruction of his rival, is rendered impossible if Egyptologists have correctly deciphered the splendid memorial of his achievements which he twice carved on the great Temple of Amon at Karnak. There the most conspicuous figure is the colossal likeness of the king. His right hand holds a sword;[524] his left grasps by the hair a long line which passes round the necks of a troop of thirty-eight mean and diminutive Jewish captives. The smaller figure of the god Amon leads other strings of one hundred and thirty-three captives, and the third king from his left hand bears a name which Champollion deciphered *Yudeh-Malk*, which he took to mean King of Judah.[525] If the interpretation were correct, we should here have a picture of the son of Solomon. On the other figures are the names of the cities of which they were kings or sheykhs. Among these are not only the names of southern towns, like Ibleam, Gibeon, Bethhoron, Ajalon, Mahanaim, but even of Canaanite and Levitic cities in the Northern Kingdom, including Taanach and Megiddo.[526] Shashonq (as the monuments call him) came with a huge and motley army of many nationalities, among whom were Libyans, Troglodytes, and Ethiopians. This host was composed of twelve hundred chariots, sixty thousand horsemen, and a numberless infantry of mercenaries. Such an invasion, though it was little more than an insulting military parade and predatory incursion, rendered resistance impossible, especially to a people enervated by luxury. Shishak came, saw,—and plundered. His chief spoil was taken from the poor dishonoured Temple and the king's palace.[527] Judah specially grieved for the loss of the shields of gold which hung on the cedar pillars of the house of the forest of Lebanon,[528]—apparently both those which Solomon had made, and those which David had consecrated from the spoils of Hadadezer, King of Zobah.[529] Perhaps a great soul would hardly have been consoled by putting mean substitutes in their place. Rehoboam, however, made bronze imitations of them in the guard-room,[530] and marched in pomp to the Temple preceded by his meanly armed runners,[531] "as though everything was the same as before." "The bitter irony with which the sacred historian records the parade of these counterfeits," says Stanley, "may be considered as the keynote to this whole period. They well represent the 'brazen shields' by which fallen churches and kingdoms have endeavoured to conceal from their own and their neighbours' eyes that the golden shields of Solomon have passed away from them."[532] The age of pinchbeck follows the age of gold, and a Louis XV. succeeds Le Grand Monarque.[533]

Rehoboam had many sons, and he "wisely" (2 Chron. xi. 23) gave them, by way of maintenance, the governorship of his fenced cities. That "he sought for them a multitude of wives" was perhaps a stroke of worldly policy, but an unwise and unworthy one. But their little courts and their little harems may have helped to keep them out of mischief. They might otherwise have destroyed each other by mutual jealousies.

Rehoboam was succeeded by his son Abijam. There is a little doubt as to the exact name of this king. The Book of Chronicles calls him Abijah,[534] but in 1 Kings xv. 1, 7, 8, he is called Abijam.[535] As the curious form Abijam seems to be unmeaning, it has been precariously conjectured that dislike to his idolatries led the Jews to alter a name which means "Jehovah is my Father."[536] Some doubt also rests on the name of his mother. She is here called "Maacha, the daughter of Abishalom," but in Chronicles "Michaiah, the daughter of Uriel of Gibeah." Maachah was perhaps the *granddaughter* of Absalom, whose beautiful daughter Tamar (named after his dishonoured sister) may have been the wife of Uriel. In that case her name, Maachah, was a name given her in reminiscence of her royal descent as a great-granddaughter of the princess of Geshur, who was mother of Absalom. All sorts of secrets, however, sometimes lie behind these changes of names. She was the second, but favourite wife of Rehoboam; and Abijam, who was not the eldest son, owed his throne to his father's preference for her.[537]

All that we are here told of Abijam is that "his heart was not perfect with Jehovah his God," and that "he walked in all the sins of his father"; though "for David's sake his God gave him a lamp in Jerusalem";[538] and that, after a brief reign of three years—*i.e.*, of one year and parts of two others—he slept with his fathers. For "the rest of his acts and all that he did," the historian refers us to the Chronicles of the Kings of Judah: he does not trouble himself with military details. The chronicler, referring to the Commentary of Iddo,[539] adds a great deal more. Jeroboam, he says, went out against him with eight hundred thousand men. Abijam, who had only half the number, stood on Mount Zemaraim in the hill country of Ephraim,[540] and made a speech to Jeroboam and his army. He reproached him with rebellion against his father when he was "young and tender-hearted," and with his golden calves, and his non-Levitical priests. He vaunted the superiority of the Temple priests with their holocausts and sweet incense and shewbread and golden candlestick, which priests were now with the army. Jeroboam sets an ambuscade, but at the shout of the men of Judah is routed with a loss of five hundred thousand men, after which Abijah recovers "Bethel with the towns thereof,"[541] and Jeshanah and Ephron (or "Ephraim"), completely humbling the northern king until "the Lord smote him and he died." After this Abijah waxes mighty, has fourteen wives, twenty-two sons, and sixteen daughters.

If we had read two accounts so different, and presenting such insuperable difficulties to the harmonist, in secular historians, we should have made no attempt to reconcile them, but merely have endeavoured to find which record was the more trustworthy. If the pious Levitical king of 2 Chron. xiii. be a true picture of the idolater of 1 Kings xv. 3, it is clear that the accounts are difficult to reconcile, unless we resort to incessant and arbitrary hypotheses. But the earlier authority is clearly to be preferred when the two obviously conflict with each other. As it is we can only say that the kings of whom the chronicler approves are, as it were, clericalised, and seen "through a cloud of incense," all their faults being omitted. The edifying speech of Abijah, and his boast about purity of worship, sounds most strange on the lips of a king who—if he "walked in all the sins of his father"—suffered his people to be guilty of a worship grossly idolatrous, including the toleration of *Bamoth, Chammanim,* and *Asherim* on every high hill and under every green tree; and of all the abominations of the neighbouring idolaters,[542]—a state of things infinitely worse than the symbolic Jehovah-worship which Jeroboam had set up. Yet such was the strange syncretism of religion in Jerusalem, of which Solomon had set the fatal example, that (as we learn quite incidentally) Abijah seems to have dedicated certain vessels—part of his warlike spoils—to the service of the Temple.[543] They were perhaps intended to supply the gaps left by the plundering raid of Shishak.

After this brief and perplexing, but apparently eventful reign, Abijah was succeeded by his son Asa, whose long reign of forty-one years was contemporary with the reigns of no less than seven kings of Israel—Nadab, Baasha, Elah, Zimri, Omri, Tibni, and Ahab.

We are told that—aided perhaps by such prophets as Hanani and Azariah, son of Oded[544] (or Iddo)—"he did that which was right in the sight of the Lord." Of this he gave an early, decisive, and courageous proof.

When he succeeded to the throne at an early age his grandmother Maachah still held the high position of queen-mother.[545] This great lady inherited the fame and popularity of Absalom, and was a princess both of the line of David and of Tolmai, King of Geshur. She was, and always had been, an open idolatress.[546] Asa began his reign with a reformation. He took away the contemptible idols (*Gilloolim*) which his fathers had made, and suppressed the odious *Kedeshim*; or he at least made a serious, if an unsuccessful, effort to do so.[547] As to the high places we have a direct verbal contradiction. Here we are told that "they were not removed," whereas the chronicler says that "he took them away out of all the cities of Judah," but afterwards that "the high places were not taken away out of Israel," in spite of Asa's heart being perfect all his days. The explanation would seem to be that he made a partial attempt to anticipate the subsequent reformation of Hezekiah, but was defeated by the inveteracy of popular custom. He did, however, take the great step of branding with infamy the impure idolatry of the queen-mother, and he degraded her from her rank. She had made an idol, which is significantly called "a fright" or "a horror" (*Miphletzeth*),[548] to serve as an emblem of the Nature-goddess. It was probably a phallic symbol which he indignantly cut down, and burnt it, where all pollutions were destroyed, in the dry wady of the Kidron.[549] In the fifteenth year of his reign he dedicated in the Temple "silver and gold and vessels," consecrated by his father and himself for this purpose. He also restored the great altar in the porch of the Temple, which in the course of more than sixty years had fallen into neglect and disrepair.

For ten years the land had rest under this pious king, though war was always smouldering between him and Baasha. In the eleventh year, however, according to the chronicler, "Zerach the Ethiopian"[550] attacked him with an army of *a million* Sushim and Lubim and three hundred chariots, and suffered an immense defeat in the valley of Zephathah, "the watch-tower" at Mareshah.[551] It was the sole occasion in sacred history in which an Israelite army met and defeated one of the great world powers in open battle, and it was deemed so remarkable a proof of Divine interposition that Asa, encouraged by the prophet Azariah, invited his people to renew their covenant with God.

More alarming to Asa was the action of Baasha in fortifying Ramah[552] in the thirty-sixth year of Asa's reign. This was a veritable ἐπιτειχισμὸς of the most dangerous kind, for Ramah, in the heart of Benjamin, was only five miles north of Jerusalem. If Abijah's signal defeat of Jeroboam and capture of Bethel, Jeshanah, and Ephron be historical, these towns must not only have been speedily recovered, but Baasha had even pushed towards Jerusalem, five miles south of Bethel. Had Ramah been left undisturbed it would have been a thorn in the side of Judah, as Deceleia was in Attica, and Pylos in Messenia. Asa saw that the demolition of this fortress was a positive necessity. Since he was too weak to effect this, he stripped both his own palace and the Temple of the treasures with which he had himself enriched them, and sent them as a vast bribe to Benhadad I., King of Damascus, begging him to renew the treaty which had existed between their fathers, and to invade the kingdom of Baasha. This step shows to what a depth of weakness Judah had fallen, for Benhadad was a son of Tabrimmon, the son of Hezion (probably Rezon) of Damascus;[553] so that here we have the great-grandson of Solomon stripping Solomon's Temple of its consecrated vessels wherewith to bribe the grandson of the petty rebel freebooter, whose whole present kingdom had once been a part of Solomon's dominions! The policy was successful. It is easy for us now to condemn it as unpatriotic and short-sighted, but to Asa it seemed a matter of life or death. Benhadad invaded Israel, and mastered its territory in the tribe of Naphtali, from Ijon and Abel-beth-maachah on the waters of Merom[554] down to Chinnereth or the Lake of Gennesareth.[555] Baasha in alarm abandoned his attempt to blockade Jerusalem, and retired to Tirzah for the protection of his own kingdom. Thereupon Asa proclaimed a levy of all Judah to seize and dismantle Ramah, and with the ample materials which Baasha had amassed he fortified Geba to the north of Ramah[556] and Mizpah (probably Neby Samwyl, to the north of the Mount of Olives), where he also sank a deep well for the use of the garrison.[557] He thus effectually protected the frontier of Benjamin. He built, as Bossuet says, "the fortresses of Judah out of the ruins of those of Samaria," and thus set us the example of making holy use of hostile and heretical materials. We should have thought that the invitation of Benhadad was, in a worldly point of view, brilliantly successful, and that it saved the kingdom of Judah from utter ruin. It involved, however, a dangerous precedent, and Hanani rebuked Asa for having done foolishly.

After a powerful and useful reign Asa was attacked with gout in his feet two years before his death. The chronicler reproaches him for seeking "not to Jehovah but to the physicians" in his "exceeding great disease." If this was a sin, it is one of which we are unable to estimate the sinfulness from this meagre notice. It has been conjectured that it may have some reference to the name Asa, which, if written Asjah, might mean "whom Jehovah heals."[558] It belongs, however, to the theocratic standpoint of the chronicler, who condemns everything which bears the aspect of a worldly policy. He slept with his fathers in a tomb which he had built for himself, and was buried with unusual magnificence, amid the burning of many spices.

We are not surprised that the historian should not mention the invasion of Zerah, since he refers us for the wars f Asa to the Judæan annals. It is much more remarkable that he wholly omits all reference to the prophetic activity of which the chronicler speaks as exercised in this reign. He had evidently formed a very high estimate of Asa, with none of the shadows and drawbacks which in the later annalist seemed to point to a marked degeneracy of character in his later days. On the favourable side the historian does not mention the high and eulogistic encouragement which the king received from Azariah, the son of Oded; nor the multitude which joined him out of Israel; nor the cities which he took from the hill country of Ephraim; nor his restoration of the altar. He even passes over the solemn league and covenant which he made with Judah and Benjamin and many members of the Ten Tribes in his fifteenth year, at a festival celebrated with an immense sacrifice, and with shouting and trumpets and cornets and a great exultant oath.[559] On the unfavourable side he does not tell us that Hanani the Seer rebuked him for summoning the help of the Syrians instead of relying on Jehovah; and that Asa "was in a rage because of this thing, and shut up Hanani in the House of the Stocks," and "oppressed some of the people at the same time," apparently because they took part with the prophet.[560] For none of these events does the chronicler refer us to any ancient authority. They came from separate records, perhaps written in prophetic commentaries and unknown to the compiler of the Kings. But whatever may have been the failings or shortcomings of Asa it is clear that he must be ranked among the more eminent and righteous sovereigns of Judah.

CHAPTER XXXI
JEHOSHAPHAT

1 Kings xxii. 41-50

Before we leave the House of David we must speak of Jehoshaphat, the last king of Judah whose reign is narrated in the First Book of Kings. He was abler, more powerful, and more faithful to Jehovah than any of his predecessors, and was alone counted worthy in later ages to rank with Hezekiah and Josiah among the most pious rulers of the Davidic line. The annals of his reign are found chiefly in the Second Book of Chronicles, where his story occupies four long chapters. The First Book of Kings compresses all record of him into nine verses, except so far as his fortunes are commingled with the history of Ahab. But both accounts show us a reign which contributed as greatly to the prosperity of Judah as that of Jeroboam II. contributed to the prosperity of Israel.

He ascended the throne at the age of thirty-five. He was apparently the only son of Asa, by Azubah, the daughter of Shilhi; for Asa, greatly to his credit, seems to have been the first king of Judah who set his face against the monstrous polygamy of his predecessors, and, so far as we know, contented himself with a single wife. He received the high eulogy that "he turned not aside from doing that which was right in the eyes of the Lord," with the customary qualification that, nevertheless, the people still burnt incense and offerings at the *Bamoth*, which were not taken away. The chronicler says that he *did* take them away. This stock contradiction between the two authorities must be accounted for either by a contrast between the effort and its failure, or by a distinction between idolatrous *Bamoth* and those dedicated to the worship of Jehovah to which the people clung with the deep affection which local sanctuaries inspire.

To the historians of the Book of Kings the central fact of Jehoshaphat's history is that "he made peace with the King of Israel." As a piece of ordinary statesmanship no step could have been more praiseworthy. The sixty-eight years or more which had elapsed since the divinely-suggested choice of Jeroboam by the Northern Kingdom had tended to soften old exasperations. The kingdom of Israel was now an established fact, and nothing had become more obvious than that the past could not be undone.

Meanwhile the threatening spectre of Syria, under the dynasty of Benhadad, was beginning to throw a dark shadow over both kingdoms. It had become certain that, if they continued to destroy each other by internecine warfare, both would succumb to the foreign invader. Wisely, therefore, and kindly Jehoshaphat determined to make peace with Ahab, in about the eighth year after his accession; and this policy he consistently maintained to the close of his twenty-five years' reign.

No one surely could blame him for putting an end to an exhaustive civil war between brethren. Indeed, in so doing he was but carrying out the policy which had been dictated to Rehoboam by the prophet Shemaiah, when he forbade him to attempt the immense expedition which he had prepared to annihilate Jeroboam. Peace was necessary to the development and happiness of both kingdoms, but even more so to the smaller and weaker, threatened as it was not only by the more distant menace of Syria, but by the might of Egypt on the south and the dangerous predatory warfare of Edom and Moab on the east.

But Jehoshaphat went further than this. He cemented the new peace by an alliance between his young son Jehoram and Athaliah, daughter of Ahab and Jezebel, who was then perhaps under fifteen years of age.

Later chroniclers formed their moral estimates by a standard which did not exist so many centuries before the date at which they wrote. If we are to judge the conduct of these kings truthfully we must take an unbiassed view of their conduct. We adopt this principle when we try to understand the characters of saints and patriarchs like Abraham, Isaac, and Jacob, or judges and prophets like Gideon, Deborah, and Samuel; and in general we must not sweepingly condemn the holy men of old because they lacked the full illumination of the gospel. We must be guided by a spirit of fairness if we desire to form a true conception of the kings who lived in the ninth century before Christ. It is probable that the religious gulf between the kings of Judah and Israel was not so immense as on a superficial view it might appear to be; indeed, the balance seems to be in favour of Jeroboam as against Abijam, Rehoboam, or even Solomon. The worship of the golden symbols at Dan and Bethel did not appear half so heinous to the people of Judah as it does to us. Even in the Temple they had cherubim and oxen. The *Bamoth* to Chemosh, Milcom, and Astarte glittered before them undisturbed on the summit of Olivet, and abominations which they either tolerated or could not remove sheltered themselves in the very precincts of the Temple, under the shadows of its desecrated trees. To the pious Jehoshaphat the tolerance of Baal-worship by Ahab could hardly appear more deadly than the tolerance of Chemosh-worship by his great-great-grandfather, and the permission of *Asherim* and *Chammanim* by his grandfather, to say nothing of the phallic horror openly patronised by the queen-mother who was a granddaughter of David. That Ahab himself was a worshipper of Jehovah is sufficiently proved by the fact that he had given the name of Athaliah to the young princess whose hand Jehoshaphat sought for his son, and the name of Ahaziah ("Jehovah taketh hold") to the prince who was to be his heir. Jehoshaphat acted from policy; but so has every king done who has ever reigned. He could neither be expected to see these things with the illumination of a prophet, nor to read—as later writers could do in the light of history—the awful issues involved in an alliance which looked to him so necessary and so advantageous.

At the time of the proposed alliance there seems to have been no protest—at any rate, none of which we read. Micaiah alone among the prophets uttered his stern warning when the expedition to Ramoth Gilead was actually on foot, and Jehu, son of Hanani, went out to rebuke Jehoshaphat at the close of that disastrous enterprise. It is to the history attributed to this seer and embodied in the annals of Israel that the chronicler refers. "Shouldst thou help the wicked," asked the bold prophet, "and love them that hate the Lord? For this thing wrath is upon thee from the Lord. Nevertheless, there are good things found in thee, in that thou hast put away the Asheroth out of the land, and hast set thy heart to seek God."

The moral principle which Jehu, son of Hanani, here enunciated is profoundly true. It was terribly emphasised by the subsequent events. A just and wise forecast may have sanctioned the restoration of peace, but Jehoshaphat might at least have learnt enough to avoid affinity with a queen who, like Jezebel, had introduced frightful and tyrannous iniquities into the House of Ahab. Faithful as the King of Judah evidently intended to be to the law of Jehovah, he should have hesitated before forming such close bonds of connexion with the cruel daughter of the usurping Tyrian priest. His error hardly diminished the warmth of that glowing eulogy which even the chronicler pronounces upon him; but it brought upon his kingdom, and upon the whole family of his grandchildren, overwhelming misery and all but total extermination. The rules of God's moral government are written large on the story of nations, and the consequences of our actions come upon us not arbitrarily, but in accordance with universal laws. When we err, even though our error be leniently judged and fully pardoned, the human consequences of the deeds which we have done may still come flowing over us with the resistless march of the ocean tides.

> "You little fancy what rude shocks apprise us.
> We sin: God's intimations rather fail
> In clearness than in energy."

Jehoshaphat did not live to see the ultimate issues of massacre and despotism which came in the train of his son Jehoram's marriage.[561] Perhaps to him it wore the golden aspect which it wears in the forty-fifth Psalm, which, as some have imagined, was composed on this occasion. But he had abundant proof that close relationship for mutual offence and defence with the kings of Israel brought no blessing in its train. In the expedition against Ramoth Gilead when Ahab was slain, he too very nearly lost his life. Even this did not disturb his alliance with Ahab's son Ahaziah, with whom he joined in a maritime enterprise which, like its predecessors, turned out to be a total failure.

Jehoshaphat in his successful wars had established the supremacy over Edom which had been all but lost in the days of Solomon. The Edomite Hadad and his successors had not been able to hold their own, and the present kings of Edom were deputies or vassals under the suzerainty of Judæa.[562] This once more opened the path to Elath and Ezion-Geber on the gulf of Akaba. Jehoshaphat, in his prosperity, felt a desire to revive the old costly commerce of Solomon with Ophir for gold, sandal wood, and curious animals. For this purpose he built "ships of Tarshish," i.e., merchant ships, like those used for the Phœnician trade between Tyre and Tartessus, to go this long voyage. The ships, however, were wrecked on the reefs of Ezion-Geber, for the Jews were timid and inexperienced mariners. Hearing of this disaster, according to the Book of Kings, Ahaziah made an offer to Jehoshaphat to make the enterprise a joint one,—thinking, apparently, that the Israelites, who, perhaps, held Joppa and some of the ports on the coast, would bring more skill and knowledge to bear on the result. But Jehoshaphat had had enough of an attempt which was so dangerous and which offered no solid advantages. He declined Ahaziah's offer. The story of these circumstances in the chronicler is different. He speaks as if from the first it was a joint experiment of the two kings, and says that, after the wreck of the fleet, a prophet of whom we know nothing, "Eliezer, the son of Dodavahu of Mareshah,"[563] prophesied against Jehoshaphat, saying, "Because thou hast joined thyself with Ahaziah, Jehovah hath made a breach in thy works." The passage shows that the word "prophesied" was constantly used in the sense of "preached," and did not necessarily imply any prediction of events yet future. The chronicler, however, apparently makes the mistake of supposing that ships were built at Ezion-Geber on the Red Sea to sail to Tartessus in Spain![564] The earlier and better authority says correctly that these merchantmen were built to trade with Ophir, in India, or Arabia. The chronicler seems to have been unaware that "ships of Tarshish," like our "Indiamen," was a general title for vessels of a special build.[565]

We see enough in the Book of Kings to show the greatness and goodness of Jehoshaphat, and later on we shall hear details of his military expeditions. [566] The chronicler, glorifying him still more, says that he sent princes and Levites and priests to teach the Book of the Law throughout all the cities of Judah; that he received large presents and tribute from neighbouring peoples; that he built castles and stone cities; and that he had a stupendous army of 160,000 troops under four great generals. He also narrates that when an immense host of Moabites, Ammonites, and Meunim came against him to Hazezon-Tamar or Engedi, he took his stand before the people in the Temple in front of the new court and prayed. Thereupon the Spirit of the Lord came upon "Jahaziel the son of Zechariah, the son of Benaiah, the son of Jeiel, the son of Mattaniah the Levite. of the sons of Asaph," who told them that the next day they should go against the invader, but that they need not strike a blow. The battle was God's, not theirs. All they had to do was to stand still and see the salvation of Jehovah. On hearing this the king and all his people prostrated themselves, and the Levites stood up to praise God. Next morning Jehoshaphat told his people to believe God and His prophets and they should prosper, and bade them chant the verse, "Give thanks unto the Lord, for His mercy endureth for ever," which now forms the refrain of Psalm cxxxvi.[567] On this Jehovah "set liers in wait against the children of Ammon, Moab, and Mount Seir." Intestine struggles arose among the invaders. The inhabitants of Mount Seir were first destroyed, and the rest then turned their swords against each other until they were all "dead bodies fallen to the earth." The soldiers of Jehoshaphat despoiled these corpses for three days, and on the fourth assembled themselves in the valley of Beracah ("Blessing"), which received its name from their tumultuous rejoicings. [568] After this they returned to Jerusalem with psalteries and harps and trumpets, and God gave Jehoshaphat rest from all his enemies round about. Of all this the historian of the Kings tells us nothing. Jehoshaphat died full of years and honours, leaving seven sons, of whom the eldest was Jehoram.[569] His reign marks a decisive triumph of the prophetic party. The prophets not only felt a fiercely just abhorrence of the abominations of Canaanite idolatry, but wished to establish a theocracy to the exclusion on the one hand of all local and symbolic worship, and on the other of all reliance on worldly policy. Up to this time, as Dean Stanley says in his usual strikingly picturesque manner, "if there was a 'holy city,' there was also an 'unholy city' within the walls of Sion. It was like a seething caldron of blood and froth 'whose scum is therein and whose scum has not gone out of it.' The Temple was hemmed in by dark idolatries on every side. Mount Olivet was covered with heathen sanctuaries, monumental stones, and pillars of Baal. Wooden images of Astarte under the sacred trees, huge images of Molech appeared at every turn in the walks around Jerusalem."[570] Jehoshaphat introduced a decisive improvement into the conditions which prevailed under Rehoboam and Abijah, but practically the conflict between light and darkness goes on for ever. It was in days when Jerusalem had come to be regarded by herself and by all nations as exceptionally holy, that she, who had been for centuries the murderess of the prophets, became under her priestly religionists the murderess of the Christ, and—far different in God's eyes from what she was in her own—deserved the dreadful stigma of being "the great city which spiritually is called Sodom and Egypt."

CHAPTER XXXII
THE KINGS OF ISRAEL FROM ZIMRI TO AHAB

b.c. 889-877

1 Kings xvi. 11-34

As far as we can understand from our meagre authorities—and we have no independent source of information—we infer that Elah, son of the powerful Baasha, was a self-indulgent weakling. The army of Israel was encamped against Gibbethon—originally a Levitical town of the Kohathites, in the territory of Dan—which they hoped to wrest from the Philistines. It was during the interminable and intermittent siege of this town that Nadab, the son of Jeroboam, had been murdered. Whatever may have been his sins, he was in his proper place leading the armies of Israel. Elah was not there, but in his beautiful palace at Tirzah. It was probably contempt for his incapacity and the bad example of Baasha's successful revolt, that tempted Zimri to murder him as he was drinking himself drunk in the house of his chamberlain Arza. Zimri was a commander of half the chariots, and probably thinking that he could secure the throne by a *coup de main* he slew not only Elah, but every male member of his family. To extinguish any possibility of vengeance, he even massacred all who were known to be friends of the royal house.

It was a consummate crime, and it was followed by swift and condign judgment. Through that sea of blood Zimri only succeeded in wading to one week's royalty, followed by a shameful and agonising death. We are told that he did evil in the sight of the Lord by following the sin of Jeroboam's calf-worship. The phrase must be here something of a formula, for in seven days he could hardly have achieved a religious revolution, and every other king of Israel, some of whom have long and prosperous reigns, maintained the unauthorised worship. But Zimri's atrocious revolt had been so ill-considered that it furnished a proverb of the terrible fate of rebels.[571] He had not even attempted to secure the assent of the army at Gibbethon. No sooner did the news reach the camp than the soldiers tumultuously refused to accept Zimri as king, and elected Omri their captain. Omri instantly broke up the camp, and led them to besiege the new king in Tirzah. Zimri saw that his cause was hopeless, and took refuge in the fortress (*birah*) attached to the palace.[572] When he saw that even there he could not maintain himself, he preferred speedy death to slow starvation or falling into the hands of his rival. He set fire to the palace, and, like Sardanapalus, perished in the flames.[573]

The swift suppression of his treason did not save the unhappy kingdom from anarchy and civil war. However popular Omri might be with the army, he was unacceptable to a large part of the people. They chose as their king a certain Tibni, son of Ginath, who was supported by a powerful brother named Joram. For four years the contest was continued. At the end of that time Tibni and Joram were conquered and killed,[574] and Omri began his sole reign, which lasted eight years longer.

He founded the most conspicuous dynasty of Israel, and so completely identified his name with the Northern Kingdom that it was known to the Assyrians as Beit-Khumri, or "the House of Omri."[575] They even speak of Jehu the destroyer of Omri's dynasty, as "the son of Omri."

Incidental allusions in the annals of his son show that Omri was engaged in incessant wars against Syria. He was unsuccessful, and Benhadad robbed him of Ramoth Gilead and other cities, enforcing the right of Syrians to have streets of their own even in his new capital of Samaria.[576] On the other hand, he was greatly successful on the south-east against the Moabites and their warrior-king Chemosh-Gad, the father of Mesha.

Few details of either war have come down to us.[577] We learn, however, from the famous Moabite stone that he began his assault on Moab by the capture of Mediba, several miles south of Heshbon, overran the country, made the king a vassal, and imposed on Moab the enormous annual tribute of 100,000 sheep and 100,000 rams.[578] Mesha in his inscription records that Omri "oppressed Moab many days," and attributed this to the fact that Chemosh was angry with his chosen people.

He stamped his impress deep upon his subjects. It must have been to him that the alliance with the Tyrians was due, which in his son's reign produced consequences so momentous. He "did worse we are told than all the kings that were before him."[579] Although he is only charged with walking in the way of Jeroboam, the indignant manner in which the prophet Micah speaks of "the statutes of Omri" as still being kept,[580] seems to prove that his influence on religion was condemned by the prophetic order on special grounds. It is clear that he was a sovereign of far greater eminence and importance than we might suppose from the meagreness of his annals as here preserved; indeed, for thirty-four years after his accession the history of the Southern Kingdom becomes a mere appendix to that of the Northern.

One conspicuous service he rendered to his subjects by providing them with the city which became their permanent and famous capital. This he did in the sixth year of his reign. The burning of the fortress-palace of Tirzah, and the rapidity with which the town had succumbed to its besiegers, may have led him to look out for a site, which was central, strong, and beautiful. His choice was so prescient that the new royal residence superseded not only Penuel and Tirzah, but even Shechem. It was, says Dean Stanley, "as though Versailles had taken the place of Paris, or Windsor of London." He fixed his eye on an oblong hill, with long flat summit, which rose in the midst of a wide valley encircled with hills, near the edge of the plain of Sharon, and six miles north-west of Shechem. Its beauty is still the admiration of the traveller in Palestine. It gave point to the apostrophe of Isaiah: "Woe to the crown of pride, to the drunkards of Ephraim, whose glorious beauty is a fading flower, which is on the head of the fat valleys of them that are overcome with wine!... The crown of pride, the drunkards of Ephraim, shall be trodden under foot: and the fading flower of his glorious adornment, which is on the head of the fat valley, shall become as a fading flower and as an early fig."[581] All around it the low hills and rich ravines were clothed with fertility. They recall more nearly than any other scene in Palestine the green fields and parks of England.

It commanded a full view of the sea and the plain of Sharon on the one hand, and of the vale of Shechem on the other. The town sloped down from the summit of this hill; a broad wall with a terraced top ran round it. "In front of the gates was a wide open space or threshing floor, where the kings of Samaria sat on great occasions. The inferior houses were built of white brick, with rafters of sycomore, the grandeur of hewn stones and cedar (Isa. ix. 9, 10). Its soft, rounded, oblong platform was, as it were, a vast luxurious couch, in which the nobles securely rested, propped and cushioned up on both sides, as in the cherished corner of a rich divan."[582]

Far more important in the eyes of Omri than its beauty was the natural strength of its position. It did not possess the impregnable majesty of Jerusalem, but its height and isolation, permitting of strong fortifications, enabled it to baffle the besieging hosts of the Aramæans in b.c. 901 and in b.c. 892. For three long years it held out against the mighty Assyrians under Sargon and Shalmanezer. Its capture in b.c. 721 involved the ruin of the whole kingdom in its fall.[583] Nebuchadnezzar took it in b.c. 554, after a siege of thirteen years. In later centuries it partially recovered. Alexander the Great took it, and massacred many of its inhabitants, b.c. 332. John Hyrcanus, who took it after a year's siege, tried to demolish it in b.c. 129. After various fortunes it was splendidly rebuilt by Herod the Great, who called it Sebaste, in honour of Augustus. It still exists under the name of Sebastïyeh.[584]

When Omri chose it for his residence it belonged to a certain Shemer, who, according to Epiphanius, was a descendant of the ancient Perizzites or Girgashites. The king paid for this hill the large sum of two talents of silver,[585] and called it Shomeron. The name means "a watch tower," and was appropriate both from its commanding position and because it echoed the name of its old possessor.[586]

The new capital marked a new epoch. It superseded as completely as Jerusalem had done the old local shrines endeared by the immemorial sanctity of their traditions; but as its origin was purely political it acted unfavourably on the religion of the people. It became a city of idolatry and of luxurious wealth; a city in which Baal-worship with its ritual pomp threw into the shade the worship of Jehovah; a city in which corrupted nobles, lolling at wine feasts on rich divans in their palaces inlaid with ivory, sold the righteous for silver and the needy for a pair of shoes. Of Omri we are told no more. After a reign of twelve years he slept with his fathers, and was buried in the city which was to be for so many centuries a memorial of his fame.

The name of Omri marks a new epoch. He is the first Jewish king whose name is alluded to in Assyrian inscriptions. Assyria had emerged into importance in the twelfth century before Christ under Tiglath-Pileser I., but during the eleventh and down to the middle of the tenth century it had sunk into inactivity. Assurbanipal, the father of Shalmanezer II. (884-860), enlarged his dominions to the Mediterranean westwards and to Lebanon southwards. In 870, when Ahab was king, the Assyrian warriors had exacted tribute from Tyre, Sidon, and Biblos.[587] It is not impossible that Omri also had paid tribute, and it has even been conjectured that it was to Assyrian help that he owed his throne. The Book of Kings only alludes to the valour of this warrior-king in the one word "his might";[588] but it is evident from other indications that he had a stormy and chequered reign.

BOOK IV
AHAB AND ELIJAH

b.c. 877-855

CHAPTER XXXIII
KING AHAB AND QUEEN JEZEBEL

"Besides what that grim wolf with privy paw
Daily devours apace, and nothing said."
Lycidas.

1 Kings xvi. 29-34

Omri was succeeded by his son Ahab, whose eventful reign of upwards of twenty years[589] occupies so large a space even in these fragmentary records. His name means "brother-father," and has probably some sacred reference. He is stigmatised by the historians as a king more wicked than his father, though Omri had "done worse than all who were before him.". That he was a brave warrior, and showed some great qualities during a long and on the whole prosperous career; that he built cities, and added to Israel yet another royal residence; that he advanced the wealth and prosperity of his subjects; that he was highly successful in some of his wars against Syria, and died in battle against those dangerous enemies of his country; that he maintained unbroken, and strengthened by yet closer affinity, the recent alliance with the Southern Kingdom,—all this goes for nothing with the prophetic annalists. They have no word of eulogy for the king who added Baal-worship to the sin of Jeroboam. The prominence of Ahab in their record is only due to the fact that he came into dreadful collision with the prophetic order, and with Elijah, the greatest prophet who had yet arisen. The glory and the sins of the warrior-king interested the young prophets of the schools solely because they were interwoven with the grand and sombre traditions of their mightiest reformer.

The historian traces all his ignominy and ruin to a disastrous alliance. The kings of Judah had followed the bad example of David and had been polygamists. Up to this time the kings of Israel seem to have been contented with a single wife. The wealth and power of Ahab led him to adopt the costly luxury of a harem, and he had seventy sons.[590] This, however, would have been regarded in those days as a venial offence, or as no offence at all; but just as the growing power of Solomon had been enhanced by marriage with a princess of Egypt, so Ahab was now of sufficient importance to wed a daughter of the King of Tyre. "As though it had been a light thing for him to walk in the sins of Jeroboam the son of Nebat, he took to wife Jezebel, the daughter of Ethbaal, King of the Zidonians."

It was an act of policy in which religious considerations went for nothing. There is little doubt that it flattered his pride and the pride of his people, and that Jezebel brought riches with her and pomp and the prestige of luxurious royalty.[591] The Phœnicians were of the old race of Canaan, with whom all affinity was so strongly forbidden. Ethbaal—more accurately, perhaps, Itto-baal (Baal is with him)[592]—though he ruled all Phœnicia, both Tyre and Sidon, was a usurper, and had been the high priest of the great Temple of Ashtoreth in Tyre. Hiram, the friend of Solomon, had now been dead for half a century. The last king of his dynasty was the fratricide Phelles, whom in his turn his brother Ethbaal slew. He reigned for thirty-two years, and founded a dynasty which lasted for sixty-two years more. He was the seventh successor to the throne of Tyre in the fifty years which had elapsed since the death of Hiram. Menander of Ephesus, as quoted by Josephus, shows us that in the history of this family we find an interesting point of contact between sacred and classic history. Jezebel was the aunt of Virgil's Belus, and great-aunt of Pygmalion, and of Dido, the famous foundress of Carthage.[593]

A king named after Baal, and who had named his daughter after Baal—a king whose descendants down to Maherbal and Hasdrubal and Hannibal bore the name of the Sun-god[594]—a king who had himself been at the head of the cult of Ashtoreth, the female deity who was worshipped with Baal—was not likely to rest content until he had founded the worship of his god in the realm of his son-in-law. Ahab, we are told, "went and served Baal and worshipped him." We must discount by recorded facts the impression which might *primâ facie* be left by these sweeping denunciations. It is certain that to his death Ahab continued to recognise Jehovah. He enshrined the name of Jehovah in the names of his children.[595] He consulted the prophets of Jehovah, and his continuance of the calf-worship met with no recorded reproof from the many true prophets who were active during his reign. The worship of Baal was due to nothing more than the unwise eclecticism which had induced Solomon to establish the *Bamoth* to heathen deities on the mount of offence. It is exceedingly probable that the permission of Baal-worship had been one of the articles of the treaty between Tyre and Israel, which, as we know from Amos, had been made at this time. It had probably been the condition on which the fanatical Phœnician usurper had conceded to his far less powerful neighbour the hand of his daughter. It was, as we see, alike in sacred and secular history a time of treaties. The menacing spectre of Assyria was beginning to terrify the nations. Hamath, Syria, and the Hittites had formed a league of defence against the northern power, and similar motives induced the kings of Israel to seek alliance with Phœnicia. Perhaps neither Omri nor Ahab grasped all the consequences of their concession to the Sidonian princess.[596] But such compacts were against the very essence of the religion of Israel, which was "Yahveh Israel's God, and Israel Yahveh's people."

The new queen inherited the fanaticism as she inherited the ferocity of her father. She acquired from the first a paramount sway over the weak and uxorious mind of her husband. Under her influence Ahab built in Samaria a splendid temple and altar to Baal, in which no less than four hundred orgiastic priests served the Phœnician idol in splendid vestments, and with the same pompous ritual as in the shrines at Tyre. In front of this temple, to the disgust and horror of all faithful worshippers of Jehovah, stood an *Asherah* in honour of the Nature-goddess, and *Matstseboth* pillars or obelisks which represented either sunbeams or the reproductive powers of nature. In these ways Ahab "did more to provoke the Lord God to anger than all the kings of Israel that were before him."[597] When we learn what Baal was, and how he was worshipped, we are not surprised at so stern a condemnation. Half Sun-god, half Bacchus, half Hercules, Baal was worshipped under the image of a bull, "the symbol of the male power of generation." In the wantonness of his rites he was akin to Peor; in their cruel atrocity to the kindred Moloch; in the demand for victims to be sacrificed to the horrible consecration of lust and blood he resembled the Minotaur, the wallowing "infamy of Crete," with its yearly tribute of youths and maidens. What the combined worship of Baal and Asherah was like—and by Jezebel with Ahab's connivance they were now countenanced in Samaria—we may learn from the description of their temple at Apheka.[598] It confirms what we are incidentally told of Jezebel's devotions. It abounded in wealthy gifts, and its multitude of priests, women, and mutilated ministers—of whom Lucian counted three hundred at one sacrifice—were clad in splendid vestments. Children were sacrificed by being put in a leathern bag and flung down from the top of the temple, with the shocking expression that "they were calves, not children." In the forecourt stood two gigantic phalli. The *Galli* were maddened into a tumult of excitement by the uproar of drums, shrill pipes, and clanging cymbals, gashed themselves with knives and potsherds, and often ran through the city in women's dress.[599] Such was the new worship with which the dark murderess insulted the faith in Jehovah. Could any condemnation be too stern for the folly and faithlessness of the king who sanctioned it?

A consequence of this tolerance of polluted forms of worship seems to have shown itself in defiant contempt for sacred traditions. At any rate, it is in this connexion that we are told how Hiel of Bethel set at naught an ancient curse. After the fall of Jericho Joshua had pronounced a curse upon the site of the city. It was never to be rebuilt, but to remain under the ban of God. The site, indeed, had not been absolutely uninhabited, for its importance near the fords of Jordan necessitated the existence of some sort of caravanserai in or near the spot.[600] At this time it belonged to the kingdom of Israel, though it was in the district of Benjamin and afterwards reverted to Judah.[601] Hiel, struck by the opportunities afforded by its position, laughed the old *cherem* to scorn, and determined to rebuild Jericho into a fortified and important city. But men remarked with a shudder that the curse had not been uttered in vain. The laying of the foundation was marked by the death of his firstborn Abiram, the completion of the gates by the death of Segub, his youngest son.[602]

The shadow of Queen Jezebel falls dark for many years over the history of Israel and Judah. She was one of those masterful, indomitable, implacable women who, when fate places them in exalted power, leave a terrible mark on the annals of nations. What the Empress Irene was in the history of Constantinople, or the "She-wolf of France" in that of England, or Catherine de Medicis in that of France, that Jezebel was in the history of Palestine. The unhappy Juana of Spain left a physical trace upon her descendants in the perpetuation of the huge jaw which had gained her the soubriquet of *Maultascr*; but the trace left by Jezebel was marked in blood in the fortunes of the children born to her. Already three of the six kings of Israel had been murdered, or had come to evil ends; but the fate of Ahab and his house was most disastrous of all, and it became so through the "whoredoms and witchcrafts" of his Sidonian wife. A thousand years later the name of Jezebel was still ominous as that of one who seduced others into fornication and idolatry.[603] If no king so completely "sold himself to work wickedness" as Ahab, it was because "Jezebel his wife stirred him up."[604]

Yet, however guilty may have been the uxorious apostasies of Ahab, he can hardly be held to be responsible for the marriage itself. The dates and ages recorded for us show decisively that the alliance must have been negotiated by Omri, for it took place in his reign and when Ahab was too young to have much voice in the administration of the kingdom. He is only responsible for abdicating his proper authority over Jezebel, and for permitting her a free hand in the corruption of worship, while he gave himself up to his schemes of worldly aggrandisement. Absorbed in the strengthening of his cities and the embellishment of his ivory palaces, he became neglectful of the worship of Jehovah, and careless of the more solemn and sacred duties of a theocratic king.

The temple to Baal at Samaria was built; the hateful Asherah in front of it offended the eyes of all whose hearts abhorred an impure idolatry. Its priests and the priests of Astarte were the favourites of the court. Eight hundred and fifty of them fed in splendour at Jezebel's table, and the pomp of their sensuous cult threw wholly into the shade the worship of the God of Israel. Hitherto there had been no protest against, no interference with the course of evil. It had been suffered to reach its meridian unchecked, and it seemed only a question of time that the service of Jehovah would yield to that of Baal, to whose favour the queen probably believed that her priestly father had owed his throne. There are indications that Jezebel had gone further still, and that Ahab, however much he may secretly have disapproved, had not interfered to prevent her. For although we do not know the exact period at which Jezebel began to exercise violence against the worshippers of Jehovah, it is certain that she did so. This crime took place before the great famine which was appointed for its punishment, and which roused from cowardly torpor the supine conscience of the king and of the nation. Jezebel stands out on the page of sacred history as the first supporter of *religious persecution*. We learn from incidental notices that, not content with insulting the religion of the nation by the burdensome magnificence of her idolatrous establishments, she made an attempt to crush Jehovah-worship altogether. Such fanaticism is a frequent concomitant of guilt. She is the authentic authoress of priestly inquisitions.

The Borgian monster, Pope Alexander VI., who founded the Spanish Inquisition, is the lineal inheritor of the traditions of Jezebel. Had Ahab done no more than Solomon had done in Judah, the followers of the true faith in Israel would have been as deeply offended as those of the Southern Kingdom. They would have hated a toleration which they regarded as wicked, because it involved moral corruption as well as the danger of national apostasy. Their feelings would have been even more wrathful than were stirred in the hearts of English Puritans when they heard of the Masses in the chapel of Henrietta Maria, or saw Father Petre gliding about the corridors of Whitehall. But their opposition was crushed with a hand of iron. Jezebel, strong in her *entourage* of no less than eight hundred and fifty priests, to say nothing of her other attendants, audaciously broke down the altars of Jehovah—even the lonely one on Mount Carmel—and endeavoured so completely to extirpate all the prophets of Jehovah that Elijah regarded himself as the sole prophet that was left. Those who escaped her fury had to wander about in destitution, and to hide in dens and caves of the earth.

The apostasy of Churches always creeps on apace, when priests and prophets, afraid of malediction, and afraid of imperilling their worldly interests become cowards, opportunists, and time-servers, and not daring to speak out the truth that is in them, suffer the cause of spirituality and righteousness to go by default. But "when Iniquity hath played her part, Vengeance, leaps upon the stage. The comedy is short, but the tragedy is long. The black guard shall attend upon you: you shall eat at the table of sorrow, and the crown of death shall be upon your heads, many glittering faces looking upon you."[605]

CHAPTER XXXIV
ELIJAH

1 Kings xvii. 1-7

"And Elias the prophet stood up as fire, and his word was burning as a torch."—Ecclus. xlviii. 1.

"But that two-handed engine at the door
Stands ready to smite once, and smite no more."
Lycidas.

Many chapters are now occupied with narratives of the deeds of two great prophets, Elijah and Elisha, remarkable for the blaze and profusion of miracles and for similarity in many details. For thirty-four years we hear but little of Judah, and the kings of Israel are overshadowed by the "men of God." Both narratives, of which the later in sequence seems to be the earlier in date, originated in the Schools of the Prophets. Both are evidently drawn from documentary sources apart from the ordinary annals of the Kings.

Doubtless something of their fragmentariness is due to the abbreviation of the prophetic annals by the historians.

Suddenly, with abrupt impetuosity, the mighty figure of Elijah the Prophet bursts upon the scene like lightning on the midnight. So far as the sacred page is concerned, he, like Melchizedek, is "without father, without mother, without descent." He appears before us unannounced as "Elijah the Tishbite of the inhabitants of Gilead." Such a phenomenon as Jezebel ~ explains and necessitates such a phenomenon as Elijah. "The loftiest and sternest spirit of the true faith is raised up," says Dean Stanley, "face to face with the proudest and fiercest spirit of the old Asiatic Paganism."

The name Elijah, or, in its fuller and more sonorous Hebrew form, Elijahu, means "Jehovah is my God." Who he was is entirely unknown. So completely is all previous trace of him lost in mystery that Talmudic legends confounded him with Phinehas, the son of Aaron, the avenging and fiercely zealous priest; and even identified him with the angel or messenger of Jehovah who appeared to Gideon and ascended in the altar flame.

The name "Tishbite" tells us nothing. No town of Tishbi occurs in Scripture, and though a Thisbe in the tribe of Naphtali is mentioned as the birthplace of Tobit,[606] the existence of such a place is as doubtful as that of "Thesbon of the Gileadite district" to which Josephus assigns his birth. [607] The Hebrew may mean "the Tishbite from Tishbi of Gilead," or "*The sojourner from the sojourners of Gilead*"; and we know no more. Elijah's grandeur is in himself alone. Perhaps he was by birth an Ishmaelite. When the wild Highlander in Rob Roy says of himself "I am a man," "A man!" repeated Frank Osbaldistone; "that is a very brief description." "It will serve," answered the outlaw, "for one who has no other to give. He who is without name, without friends, without coin, without country, is still at least a man: and he that has all these is no more." So Elijah stands alone in the towering height of his fearless manhood.

Some clue to the swift mysterious movements, the rough asceticism, the sheepskin robe, the unbending sternness of the Prophet may lie in the notice that he was a Gileadite, or at any rate among the sojourners of Gilead, and therefore akin to them. It might even be conjectured that he was of Kenite origin, like Jonadab, the son of Rechab, in the days of Jehu.[608] The Gileadites were the Highlanders of Palestine, and the name of their land implies its barren ruggedness.[609] They, like the modern Druses, were

"Fierce, hardy, proud, in conscious freedom bold."

We catch a glimpse of these characteristics in the notice of the four hundred Gadites who swam the Jordan in Palestine to join the freebooters of David in the cave of Adullam, "whose faces were like the faces of lions, and who were as swift as the roes upon the mountains." Though of Israelitish origin they were closely akin to the Bedawin, swift, strong, temperate, fond of the great solitudes of nature, haters of cities, scorners of the softnesses of civilisation. Elijah shared these characteristics. Like the forerunner of Christ, in whom his spirit reappeared nine centuries later, he had lived alone with God in the glowing deserts and the mountain fastnesses. He found Jehovah's presence, not in the

"Gay religions, full of pomp and gold,"

which he misdoubted and despised, but in the barren hills and wild ravines and bleak uplands where only here and there roamed a shepherd with his flock. In such hallowed loneliness he had learnt to fear man little, because he feared God much, and to dwell familiarly on the sterner aspects of religion and morality. The one conscious fact of his mission, the sufficient authentication of his most imperious mandates, was that "he stood before Jehovah." So unexpected were his appearances and disappearances, that in the popular view he only seemed to flash to and fro, or to be swept hither and thither, by the Spirit of the Lord. We may say of him as was said of John the Baptist, that "in his manifestation and agency he was like a burning torch; his public life was quite an earthquake; the whole man was a sermon, the voice of one crying in the wilderness." And, like the Baptist, he had been "in the deserts, till the day of his showing unto Israel."

Somewhere—perhaps at Samaria, perhaps in the lovely summer palace at Jezreel—he suddenly strode into the presence of Ahab. Coming to him as the messenger of the King of kings he does not deign to approach him with the genuflexions and sounding titles which Nathan used to the aged David. With scanted courtesy to one whom he does not respect or dread—knowing that he is in God's hands, and has no time to waste over courtly periphrases or personal fears—he comes before Ahab unknown, unintroduced. What manner of man was it by whom the king in his crown and Tyrian purple was thus rudely confronted? He was, tradition tells us, a man of short stature, of rugged countenance. He was "a lord of hair"—the thick black locks of the Nazarite (for such he probably was) streamed over his shoulders like a lion's mane, giving him a fierce and unkempt aspect. They that wear soft clothing are in king's houses, and doubtless under a queen who, even in old age, painted her face and tired her head, and was given to Sidonian luxuries, Ahab was accustomed to see men about him in bright apparel. But Elijah had not stooped to alter his ordinary dress, which was the dress of the desert by which he was always known. His brown limbs, otherwise bare, were covered with a heavy mantle, the skin of a camel or a sheep worn with the rough wool outside, and tightened round his loins by a leathern girdle. So unusual was his aspect in the cities east of Jordan, accustomed since the days of Solomon to all the refinements of Egyptian and Phœnician culture, that it impressed and haunted the imagination of his own and of subsequent ages. The dress of Elijah became so normally the dress of prophets who would fain have assumed his authority without one spark of his inspiration, that the later Zechariah has to warn his people against sham prophets who appeared with hairy garments, and who wounded their own hands for no other purpose than to deceive.[610] The robe of skin, after the long interspace of centuries, was still the natural garb of "the glorious eremite," who in his spirit and power made straight in the deserts a highway for our God.

Such was the man who delivered to Ahab in one sentence his tremendous message: "As Jehovah, God of Israel, liveth, before whom I stand"— such was the introductory formula, which became proverbial, and which authenticated the prophecy—"There shall not be dew[611] nor rain these years but according to my word." The phrase "to stand before Jehovah" was used of priests: it was applicable to a prophet in a far deeper and less external sense.[612] Drought was one of the recognised Divine punishments for idolatrous apostasy. If Israel should fall into disobedience, we read in Deuteronomy, "the Lord shall make the rain of thy land powder and dust;

from heaven shall it come down upon thee—until thou be destroyed"; and in Leviticus we read, "If ye will not hearken, I will make your heaven as iron and your earth as brass." The threat was too significant to need any explanation. The conscience of Ahab could interpret only too readily that prophetic menace.

The message of Elijah marked the beginning of a three, or three and a half years' famine. This historic drought is also mentioned by Menander of Tyre, who says that after a year, at the prayer of Ethbaal, the priest and king, there came abundant thunder showers. St. James represents the famine as well as its termination as having been caused by Elijah's prayer.[613] But the expression of the historian is general. Elijah might pray for rain, but no prophet could, *proprio motu*, have offered up a prayer for so awful a curse upon an entire country as a famine, in which thousands of the innocent would suffer no less severely than the guilty. Three years' famine was a recognised penalty for apostasy. It was one of the sore plagues of God. It had befallen Judah "because of Saul and his bloody house,"[614] and had been offered to guilty David as an alternative for three days' pestilence, or three years' flight before his enemies.[615] We are not here told that Elijah prayed for it, but that he announced its commencement, and declared that only in accordance with his announcement should it close.

He delivered his message, and what followed we do not know. Ahab's tolerance was great; and, however fierce may have been his displeasure, he seems in most cases to have personally respected the sacredness and dignity of the prophets. The king's wrath might provoke an outburst of sullenness, but he contented himself with menacing and reproachful words. It was otherwise with Jezebel. A genuine idolatress, she hated the servants of Jehovah with implacable hatred, and did her utmost to suppress them by violence. It was probably to save Elijah from her fury that he was bidden to fly into safe hiding, while her foiled rage expended itself in the endeavour to extirpate the whole body of the prophets of the Lord. But, just as the child Christ was saved when Herod massacred the infants of Bethlehem, so Elijah, at whom Jezebel's blow was chiefly aimed, had escaped beyond her reach. A hundred other imperilled prophets were hidden in a cave by the faithfulness of Obadiah, the king's vizier.

The word of the Lord bade Elijah to fly eastward and hide himself "in the brook Cherith,[616] that is before Jordan." The site of this ravine—which Josephus only calls "a certain torrent bed"—has not been identified. It was doubtless one of the many wadies which run into the deep Ghôr or cleft of the Jordan on its eastern side. If it belonged to his native Gilead, Elijah would be in little fear of being discovered by the emissaries whom Ahab sent in every direction to seek for him. Whether it was the Wady Kelt,[617] or the

Wady el Jabis,[618] or the Ain Fusail,[619] we know the exact characteristics of the scene. On either side, deep, winding and precipitous, rise the steep walls of rock, full of tropic foliage, among which are conspicuous the small dark green leaves and stiff thorns of the nubk. Far below the summit of the ravine, marking its almost imperceptible thread of water by the brighter green of the herbage, and protected by masses of dewy leaves from the fierce power of evaporation, the hidden torrent preserves its life in all but the most long-continued periods of drought. In such a scene Elijah was absolutely safe. Whenever danger approached he could hide himself in some fissure or cavern of the beetling crags where the wild birds have their nest, or sit motionless under the dense screen of interlacing boughs. The wildness and almost terror of his surroundings harmonised with his stern and fearless spirit. A spirit like his would rejoice in the unapproachable solitude, communing with God alike when the sun flamed in the zenith and when the midnight hung over him with all its stars.

The needs of an Oriental—particularly of an ascetic Bedawy prophet—are small as those of the simplest hermit. Water and a few dates often suffice him for days together. Elijah drank of the brook, and God "had commanded the ravens to feed him there." The shy, wild, unclean birds[620] "brought him"—so the old prophetic narrative tells us—"bread and flesh in the morning, and bread and flesh in the evening." We may remark in passing, that flesh twice a day or even once a day, if with Josephus we read "bread in the morning and flesh in the evening," is no part of an Arab's ordinary food. It is regarded by him as wholly needless, and indeed as an exceptional indulgence. The double meal of flesh does not resemble the simple diet of bread and water on which the Prophet lived afterwards at Sarepta. Are we or are we not to take this as a literal fact? Here we are face to face with a plain question to which I should deem it infamous to give a false or a prevaricating answer.

Before giving it, let us clear the ground. First of all, it is a question which can only be answered by serious criticism. Assertion can add nothing to it, and is not worth the breath with which it is uttered. The anathemas of obsolete and *a priori* dogmatism against those who cannot take the statement as simple fact do not weigh so much as a dead autumn leaf in the minds of any thoughtful men.

Some holy but uninstructed soul may say, "It stands on the sacred page: why should you not understand it literally?" It might be sufficient to answer, Because there are many utterances on the sacred page which are purely poetic or metaphorical. "The eye that mocketh at his father, and despiseth to obey his mother, the ravens of the brook shall pick it out, and the young vultures shall eat it."[621] The statement looks prosaic and positive enough, but what human being ever took it literally? "Curse not the king—for a bird of the air shall carry the voice, and that which hath wings shall tell the matter." Who does not see at once that the words are poetic and metaphorical? "Where their worm dieth not, and their fire is not quenched." How many educated Christians can assert that they believe that the unredeemed will be eaten for ever by literal worms in endless flames? The man who pretends that he is obliged to understand literally the countless Scriptural metaphors involved in an Eastern language of which nearly every word is a pictorial metaphor, only shows himself incompetent to pronounce an opinion on subjects connected with history, literature, or religious criticism.

Is it then out of dislike to the supernatural, or disbelief in its occurrence, that the best critics decline to take the statement literally?

Not at all. Most Christians have not the smallest difficulty in accepting the supernatural. If they believe in the stupendous miracles of the Incarnation and the Resurrection, what possible difficulty could they have in accepting any other event merely on the ground that it is miraculous? To many Christians all life seems to be one incessant miracle. Disbelieving that any force less than the fiat of God could have thrilled into inorganic matter the germs of vegetable and still more of animal life; believing that their own life is supernatural, and that they are preserved as they were created by endless cycles of ever-recurrent miracles; believing that the whole spiritual life is supernatural in its every characteristic; they have not the slightest unwillingness to believe a miracle when any real evidence can be adduced for it. They accept, without the smallest misgiving, the miracles of Jesus Christ our Lord, radiating as ordinary works from His Divine nature, performed in the full blaze of history, attested by hundredfold contemporary evidence, leading to results of world-wide and eternal significance—miracles which were, so to speak, natural, normal, and necessary, and of which each revealed some deep moral or spiritual truth. But if miracles can only rest on evidence, the dullest and least instructed mind can see that the evidence for this and for some other miracles in this narrative stands on a wholly different footing. Taken apart from dogmatic assertions which are themselves unproven or disproved, the evidence that ravens daily fed Elijah is wholly inadequate to sustain the burden laid upon it.

In the first place, the story occurs in a book compiled some centuries after the event which it attests; in a book solemn indeed and sacred, but composite, and in some of its details not exempt from the accidents which have always affected all human literature.

And this incident is unattested by any other evidence. It is, so to speak, isolated. It is quite separable from the historic features of the narrative, and is out of accordance with what is truly called the Divine economy of miracles. No miracle was wrought to supply Elijah with water; and if a miracle was needed to supply him with bread and flesh, it is easy to imagine hundreds of forms of such direct interposition which would be more normal and more in accordance with all other Scripture miracles than the continuous overruling of the natural instincts of ravenous birds. It has been said that this particular form of miracle was needed for its evidential value; but there is nothing in the narrative to imply that it had the smallest evidential value for any one of Elijah's contemporaries, or even that they knew of it at all.

Further, we find it, not in a plain prose narrative, but in a narrative differing entirely from the prosaic setting in which it occurs—a narrative which rises in many parts to the height of poetic and imaginative splendour. There is nothing to show that it was not intended to be a touch of imaginative poetry and nothing more. Part of the greatness of Hebrew literature lies in its power of conveying eternal truth, as, for instance, in the Book of Job and in many passages of the prophets, in the form of imaginative narration. The stories of Elijah and Elisha come from the Schools of the Prophets. If room was left in them for the touch of poetic fiction, or for the embellishment of history with moral truth, conveyed in the form of parable or apologue, we can at once account for the sudden multitude of miracles. They were founded no doubt in many instances on actual events, but in the form into which the narrative is thrown they were recorded to enhance the greatness of the heroic chiefs of the Schools of the Prophets. It is therefore uncertain whether the original narrator believed, or meant his readers literally to believe, such a statement as that Elijah was fed morning and evening by actual ravens. It cannot be proved that he intended more than a touch of poetry, by which he could convey the lesson that the prophet was maintained by marked interventions of that providence of God which is itself in all its workings supernatural. God's feeding of the ravens in their nest was often alluded to in Hebrew poetry; and if the marvellous support of the Prophet in his lonely hiding-place was to be represented in an imaginative form, this way of representing it would naturally occur to the writer's thoughts. Similarly, when Jerome wrote the purely fictitious life of Paul the Hermit, which was taken for fact even by his contemporaries, he thinks it quite natural to say that Paul and Antony saw a raven sitting on a tree, who flew gently down to them and placed a loaf on the table before them. Ravens haunt the lonely, inaccessible cliffs among which Elijah found his place of refuge. It needed but a touch of metaphor to transform them into ministers of Heaven's beneficence.

But besides all this, the word rendered ravens (*Orebim*, מִיבְרֹעַ) only has that meaning if it be written with the vowel points. But the vowel points are confessedly not "inspired" in any sense, but are a late Massoretic invention. Without the change of a letter the word may equally well mean people of the city Orbo,[622] or of the rock Oreb (as was suggested even in the Bereshith Rabba by Rabbi Judah); or "merchants," as in Ezek. xxvii. 27; or Arabians. No doubt difficulties might be suggested about any of these interpretations; but which would be most reasonable, the acceptance of such small difficulties, or the literal acceptance of a stupendous miracle, unlike any other in the Bible, by which we are to believe on the isolated authority of a nameless and long subsequent writer, that, for months or weeks together, voracious and unclean birds brought bread and flesh to the Prophet twice a day? The old naturalistic attempts to explain the miracle are on the face of them absurd; but it is as perfectly open to any one who chooses to say that "Arabians," or "Orbites," or "merchants," or "people of the rock Oreb" fed Elijah, as to say that the "ravens" did so. The explanation now universally accepted by the Higher Criticism is different. It is to accept the meaning "ravens," but not with wooden literalness to interpret didactic and poetic symbolism as though it were bald and matter-of-fact prose. The imagery of a grand religious *Haggada* is not to be understood, nor was it ever meant to be understood, like the page of a dull annalist. Analogous stories are found abundantly alike in early pagan and early Christian literature and in mediæval hagiology. They are true in essence though not in fact, and the intention of them is often analogous to this; but no story is found so noble as this in its pure and quiet simplicity.

Let this then suffice and render it needless to recur to similar discussions. If any think themselves bound to interpret this and all the other facts in these narratives in their most literal sense; if they hold that the mere mention of such things by unknown writers in unknown time—possibly centuries afterwards, when the event may have become magnified by the refraction of tradition—is sufficient to substantiate them, let them hold their own opinion as long as it can satisfy them. But *proof* of such an opinion they neither have nor can have; and let them beware of priding themselves on the vaunt of their "faith," when such "faith" may haply prove to be no more than a distortion of the truer faith which proves all things and only holds fast that which will stand the test. A belief based on some *a priori* opinion about "verbal dictation" is not necessarily meritorious. It may be quite the reverse. Such a dogma has never been laid down by the Church in general. It has very rarely been insisted upon by any branch of the Church in any age. A belief which prides itself on ignorance of the vast horizon opened to us by the study of many forms of literature, by the advance of criticism, by the science of comparative religion—so far from being religious or spiritual may only be a sign of ignorance, or of a defective love of truth. A dogmatism which heaps upon intelligent faith burdens at once needless and intolerable may spring from sources which should tend to self-humiliation rather than to spiritual pride.[623] *Abundet quisque in sensu suo.* But such beliefs have not the smallest connexion with true faith or sincere Christianity. God is a God of truth, and he who tries to force himself into a view which history and literature, no less than the faithful following of the Divine light within him, convince him to be untenable, does not rise into faith, but sins and does mischief by feebleness and *lack* of faith.[624]

CHAPTER XXXV
ELIJAH AT SAREPTA

1 Kings xvii. 7, xviii. 19

"The rain is God's compassion." — Mohammed.

The fierce drought continued, and "at the end of days"[625] even the thin trickling of the stream in the clefts of Cherith was dried up. In the language of Job it felt the glare and vanished.[626] No miracle was wrought to supply the Prophet with water, but once more the providence of God intervened to save his life for the mighty work which still awaited him. He was sent to the region where, nearly a millennium later, the feet of his Lord followed him on a mission of mercy to those other sheep of His flock who were not of the Judæan fold.

The word of the Lord bade him make his way to the Sidonian city of Zarephath. Zarephath, the Sarepta of St. Luke, the modern Surafend, lay between Tyre and Sidon, and there the waters would not be wholly dried up, for the fountains of Lebanon were not yet exhausted. The drought had extended to Phœnicia,[627] but Elijah was told that there a widow woman would sustain him. The Baal-worshipping queen who had hunted for his life would be least of all likely to search for him in a city of Baal-worshippers in the midst of her own people. He is sent among these Baal-worshippers to do them kindness, to receive kindness from them — perhaps to learn a wider tolerance, and to find that idolaters also are human beings, children, like the orthodox, of the same heavenly Father. He had been taught the lesson of "dependence upon God": he was now to learn the lesson of "fellowship with man." Travelling probably by night both for coolness and for safety, Elijah went that long journey to the heathen district. He arrived there faint with hunger and thirst. Seeing a woman gathering sticks near the city gate he asked her for some water, and as she was going to fetch it he called to her and asked her also to bring him a morsel of bread. The answer revealed the condition of extreme want to which she was reduced. Recognising that Elijah was an Israelite, and therefore a worshipper of Jehovah, she said, "As Jehovah thy God liveth, I have not a cake, but (only) a handful of meal in the barrel, and a little oil in the cruse." She was gathering a couple of sticks to make one last meal for herself and her son, and then to lie down and die.[628] For drought did not only mean universal anguish, but much actual starvation. It meant, as Joel says, speaking of the desolation caused by locusts, that the cattle groan and perish, and the corn withers, and the seeds rot under their clods.

Strong in faith Elijah told her not to fear, but first to supply his own more urgent needs, and then to make a meal for herself and her son. Till Jehovah sent rain, the barrel of meal should not waste, nor the cruse of oil fail. She believed the promise, and for many days, perhaps for two whole years, the Prophet continued to be her guest.

But after a time her boy fell grievously sick, and at last died, or seemed to die.[629] So dread a calamity—the smiting of the stay of her home, and the son of her widowhood—filled the woman with terror. She longed to get rid of the presence of this terrible "man of God."[630] He must have come, she thought, to bring her sin to remembrance before God, and so to cause Him to slay her son. The Prophet was touched by the pathos of her appeal, and could not bear that she should look upon him as the cause of her bereavement. "Give me thy son," he said. Taking the dead boy from her arms, he carried him to the chamber which she had set apart for him, and laid him on his own bed. Then, after an earnest cry to God, he stretched himself three times over the body of the youth, as though to breathe into his lungs and restore his vital warmth, at the same time praying intensely that "his soul might come into him again."[631] His prayer was heard; the boy revived. Carrying him down from the chamber, Elijah had the happiness of restoring him to his widowed mother with the words, "See, thy son liveth." So remarkable an event not only convinced the woman that Elijah was indeed what she had called him, "a man of God," but also that Jehovah was the true God. It was not unnatural that tradition should interest itself in the boy thus strangely snatched from the jaws of death. The Jews fancied that he grew up to be servant of Elijah, and afterwards to be the prophet Jonah. The tradition at least shows an insight into the fact that Elijah was the first missionary sent from among the Jews to the heathen, and that Jonah became the second.

We are not to suppose that during his stay at Zarephath Elijah remained immured in his chamber. Safe and unsuspected, he might, at least by night, make his way to other places, and it is reasonable to believe that he then began to haunt the glades and heights of beautiful and deserted Carmel, which was at no great distance, and where he could mourn over the ruined altar of Jehovah and take refuge in any of its "more than two thousand tortuous caves." But what was the object of his being sent to Zarephath? That it was not for his own sake alone, that it had in it a purpose of conversion, is distinctly implied by our Lord when He says that in those days there were many widows in Israel, yet Elijah was not sent to them, but to this Sidonian idolatress. The prophets and saints of God do not always understand the meaning of Providence or the lessons of their Divine training. Francis of Assisi at first entirely misunderstood the real drift and meaning of the Divine intimations that he was to rebuild the ruined Church of God, which he afterwards so gloriously fulfilled. The thoughts of God are not as man's thoughts, nor His ways as man's ways, nor does He make all His servants as it were "fusile apostles," as He made St. Paul. The education of Elijah was far from complete even long afterwards. To the very last, if we are to accept the records of him as historically literal, amid the revelations vouchsafed to him he had not grasped the truth that the Elijah-spirit, however needful it may seem to be, differs very widely from the Spirit of the Lord of Life. Yet may it not have been that Elijah was sent to learn from the kind ministrations of a Sidonian widow, to whose care his life was due, some inkling of those truths which Christ revealed so many centuries afterwards, when He visited the coasts of Tyre and Sidon, and extended His mercy to the great faith of the Syro-Phœnician woman? May not Elijah have been meant to learn what had to be taught by experience to the two great Apostles of the Circumcision and the Uncircumcision, that not every Baal-worshipper was necessarily corrupt or wholly insincere? St. Peter was thus taught that God is no respecter of persons, and that whether their religious belief be false or true, in every nation he that feareth Him and doeth righteousness is accepted of Him. St. Paul learnt at Damascus and taught at Athens that God made of one every nation of men to dwell on the face of the earth, that they should seek God if haply they might feel after Him and find Him, though He be not far from every one of us.

CHAPTER XXXVI
ELIJAH AND AHAB

1 Kings, xviii. 1-19

"Return, oh backsliding children, and I will heal your backslidings. Behold, we come unto thee; for Thou art Jehovah our God. Truly in vain is salvation hoped for from the tumult (of votaries) upon the mountains. Truly in Jehovah our God is the salvation cf Israel. And the Shame (*i.e.*, Baal) hath devoured the labour of our fathers." —Jer. iii. 22-24.

Elijah stayed long with the Sidonian widow, safe in that obscure concealment, and with his simple wants supplied. But at last the word of the Lord came to him with the conviction that the drought had accomplished its appointed end in impressing the souls of king and people, and that the time was come for some immense and decisive demonstration against the prevalent apostasy. All his sudden movements, all his stern incisive utterances were swayed by his allegiance to Jehovah before whom he stood, and he now received the command, "Go, show thyself unto Ahab; and I will send rain upon the earth."

To obey such a mandate showed the strength of his faith. It is clear that even before the menace of the thought he had been known, and unfavourably known, to Ahab. The king saw in him a prophet who fearlessly opposed all the idolatrous tendencies into which he had led his easy and faithless people. How terribly must Ahab's hatred have been now intensified! We see from all the books of the prophets that they were personally identified with their predictions; that they were held responsible for them, were even regarded in popular apprehension as having actually brought about the things which they predicted. "See," says Jehovah to the timid boy Jeremiah, "I have this day set thee over the nations and over the kingdoms to root out, and to pull down, and to destroy, and to throw down, to build, and to plant." The Prophet is addressed as though he personally effected the ruin he denounced. Elijah, then, would be regarded by Ahab as in one sense the author of the three years' famine. It would be held—not indeed with perfect accuracy, yet with a not unnatural confusion—that it was *he* who had shut up the windows of heaven and caused the misery and starvation of the suffering multitudes. With what wrath would a great and powerful king like Ahab look on this bold intruder, this skin-clad alien of Gilead, who had frustrated his policy, defied his power, and stamped his reign with so overwhelming a disaster. Yet he is bidden, "Go, show thyself unto Ahab"; and perhaps his immediate safety was only secured by the additional message, "and I will send rain upon the earth."

Things had, indeed, come to their worst. The "sore famine" in Samaria had reached a point which, if it had not been alleviated, would have led to the utter ruin of the miserable kingdom.

In this crisis Ahab did all that a king could do. Most of the cattle had perished, but it was essential to save if possible some of the horses and mules. No grass was left on the scorched plains and bare brown hills except where there were fountains and brooks which had not entirely vanished under that copper sky. To these places it was necessary to drive such a remnant of the cattle as it might be still possible to preserve alive. But who could be trusted to rise entirely superior to individual selfishness in such a search? Ahab thought it best to trust no one but himself and his vizier Obadiah. The very name of this high official, Obadjahu, like the common Mohammedan names Abdallah, Abderrahnan, and others, implied that he was "a servant of Jehovah." His conduct answered to his name, for on Jezebel's persecuting attempt to exterminate Jehovah's prophets in their schools or communities, he, "the Sebastian of the Jewish Diocletian," had, at the peril of his own life, taken a hundred of them, concealed them in two of the great limestone caves of Palestine—perhaps in the recesses of Mount Carmel,[632] and fed them with bread and water. It is to Ahab's credit that he retained such a man in office, though the touch of timidity which we trace in Obadiah may have concealed the full faithfulness of his personal allegiance to the old worship. Yet that such a man should still hold the post of chamberlain (*al-hab-baith*) furnishes a fresh proof that Ahab was not himself a worshipper of Baal.

The king and his vizier went in opposite directions, each of them unaccompanied, and Obadiah was on his way when he was startled by the sudden appearance of Elijah. He had not previously seen him, but recognising him by his shaggy locks, his robe of skin, and the awful sternness of his swarthy countenance, he was almost abjectly terrified. Apart from the awe-inspiring aspect and manner of the Prophet, this seemed no mere man who stood before him, but the representative of the Eternal, and the wielder of His power. To his contemporaries he appeared like the incarnate vengeance of Jehovah against guilty times, a flash as it were of God's consuming fire. To the Moslem of to-day he is still *El Khudr*, "the eternal wanderer." Springing from his chariot, Obadiah fell flat on his face and cried, "Is it thou, my lord Elijah?" "It is I," answered the Prophet, not wasting words over his terror and astonishment. "Go, tell thy lord, Behold, Elijah is here."

The message enhanced the vizier's alarm. Why had not Elijah showed himself at once to Ahab? Did some terrible vindictive purpose lurk behind his message? Did Elijah confuse the aims and deeds of the minister with those of the king? Why did he despatch him on an errand which might move Ahab to kill him? Was not Elijah aware, he asks, with Eastern hyperbole, that Ahab had sent "to every nation and kingdom" to ask if Elijah was there, and when told that he was not there he made them confirm the statement by an oath?[633] What would come of such a message if Obadiah conveyed it? No sooner would it be delivered than the wind of the Lord would sweep Elijah away into some new and unknown solitude,[634] and Ahab, thinking that he had only been befooled, would in his angry disappointment, put Obadiah to death. Had he deserved such a fate? Had not Elijah heard of his reverence for Jehovah from his youth, and of his saving the hundred prophets at the peril of his life? Why then send him on so dangerous a mission? To these agitated appeals Elijah answered by his customary oath, "As Jehovah of hosts liveth, before whom I stand,[635] I will show myself unto him to-day." Then Obadiah went and told Ahab, and Ahab with impetuous haste hastened to meet Elijah, knowing that on him depended the fate of his kingdom.

Yet when they met he could not check the burst of anger which sprang to his lips.

"Is it thou, thou troubler of Israel?" he fiercely exclaimed.[636] Elijah was not the man to quail before the *vultus instantis tyranni.* "I have not troubled Israel," was the undaunted answer, "but thou and thy father's house." The cause of the drought was not the menace of Elijah, but the apostasy to Baalim. It was time that the fatal controversy should be decided. There must be an appeal to the people. Elijah was in a position to dictate, and he did dictate. "Let all Israel," he said, "be summoned to Mount Carmel;" and there he would singly meet in their presence the four hundred and fifty prophets of Baal, and the four hundred prophets of the Asherah, all of whom ate at Jezebel's table.[637] Then and there a great challenge should take place, and the question should be settled for ever, whether Baal or Jehovah was to be the national god of Israel. What challenge could be fairer, seeing that Baal was the Sun-god, the god of fire?

CHAPTER XXXVII
ELIJAH ON MOUNT CARMEL

1 Kings xviii. 20-40

"O for a sculptor's hand,
That thou might'st take thy stand,
Thy wild hair floating in the eastern breeze!"
Keble.

It never occurred to Ahab to refuse the challenge, or to arrest the hated messenger. The hermit and the dervish are sacrosanct; they stand before kings and are not ashamed. Having nothing to desire, they have nothing to fear. So Antony stalked into the streets of Alexandria to denounce its prefect; so Athanasius fearlessly seized the bridle of Constantine in his new city; so a ragged and dwarfish old man—Macedonius the Barley-eater—descended from his mountain cave at Antioch to stop the horses of the avenging commissioners of Thedosius, and bade them go back and rebuke the fury of their Emperor,—and so far from punishing him they alighted, and fell on their knees, and begged his blessing.

The vast assembly was gathered by royal proclamation. There could have been no scene in the land of Israel more strikingly suitable for the purpose than Mount Carmel. It is a ridge of upper oolite, or Jura limestone, which at the eastern extremity rises more than sixteen hundred feet above the sea, sinking down to six hundred feet at the western extremity. The "excellency of Carmel" of which the prophet speaks[638] consists in the fruitfulness which to this day makes it rich in flowers of all hues, and clothes it with the impenetrable foliage of oak, pine, walnut, olive, laurel, dense brushwood, and evergreen shrubberies thicker than in any other part in Central Palestine. The name means "Garden of God," and travellers, delighted with the rocky dells and blossoming glades, describe Carmel as "still the fragrant lovely mountain that it was of old."[639] It "forms the southern extremity of the Gulf of Khaifa, and separates the great western plain of Philistia from the plain of Esdraelon, and the plain of Phœnicia." "It is difficult," says Sir G. Grove, "to find another site in which every particular is so minutely fulfilled as in this." The whole mountain is now called *Mar Elias* from the Prophet's name.

The actual spot of the range near which took place this most memorable event in the history of Israel was almost undoubtedly a little below the eastern summit of the ridge. It is "a terrace of natural rock," which commands a fine view of the plains and lakes and the hills of Galilee, and the windings of the Kishon, with Jezreel glimmering in the far distance under the heights of Gilboa. The remains of an old and massive square structure are here visible, called *El-Muhrakkah*, "the burning," or "the sacrifice," perhaps the site of Elijah's altar. Under the ancient olives still remains the round well of perennial water from which, even in the drought, the Prophet could fill the barrels which he poured over his sacrifice. Elijah's grotto is pointed out in the Church of the Convent, and another near the sea. In the region known as "the garden of Elijah" are found the *geodes* and *septaria*—stones and fossils which assume the aspect, sometimes of loaves of bread, sometimes of water-melons and olives, and are still known as "Elijah's fruits." The whole mountain murmurs with his name.[640] He became in local legend the oracular god Carmelus, whose "altar and devotion" drew visitors no less illustrious than Pythagoras and Vespasian to visit the sacred hill.[641]

Here, then, at early dawn the Prophet of Jehovah, in his solitary grandeur, met the four hundred and fifty idolatrous priests and their rabble of attendant fanatics in the presence of the half-curious king and the half-apostate people. He presented the oft-repeated type of God's servant alone against the world.[642] Most rarely is it otherwise. They who speak smooth things and prophesy deceits may always live at ease in amicable compromise with the world, the flesh, and the devil. But the Prophet has ever to set his face as a flint against tyrants, and mobs and false prophets, and intriguing priests, and all who daub tottering walls with untempered mortar, and all who, in days smooth and perilous, softly murmur, "Peace, peace, when there is no peace." So it was with Noah in the days of the deluge; so with Amos and Hosea and the later Zechariah; so with Micaiah, the son of Imlah; so with Isaiah, mocked as a babbler by the priests at Jerusalem, and at last sawn asunder; so with Jeremiah, struck in the face by the priest Pashur, and thrust into the miry dungeon, and at last murdered in exile; so with Zechariah, the son of Jehoiada, whom they slew between the porch and the altar. Nor has it been less so since the earliest dawn of the New Dispensation. Of John the Baptist the priests and Pharisees said, "He has a devil," and Herod slew him in prison. All, perhaps, of the twelve Apostles were martyred. Paul, like the rest, was intrigued against, thwarted, hated, mobbed, imprisoned, hunted from place to place by the world, the Jews, and the false Christians. Treated as the offscouring of all things, he was at last contemptuously beheaded in utter obscurity. Similar fates befell many of the best and greatest of the Fathers. Ignatius, Polycarp, Justin, were slain by wild beasts and by fire. Origen's life was one long martyrdom, mostly at the hands of his fellow-Christians. Did not Athanasius stand against the world? What needs it to summon from the prison or the stake the mighty shades of Savonarola, of Huss, of Jerome of Prague, of the Albigenses and Waldenses, of the myriad victims of the Inquisition, of those who were burnt at Smithfield and Oxford, of Luther, of Whitfield? Did Christ mean nothing when he said, among His first beatitudes, "Blessed are ye when all men shall revile you, and persecute you, and say all manner of evil against you falsely for My sake and the gospel's"? Was it mere accident and metaphor when He said, "Ye are of the world, and therefore the world cannot hate you; but Me it hateth"; and, "If they have called the Master of the house Beelzebub, much more them of His household"? Which of His best and purest sons, from the first Good Friday down to this day, has ever passed through life unpersecuted of slanderous tongues? Has the nominal Church ever shown any more mercy to saints than the sneering and furious world? What has sustained Christ's hated ones? What but that confidence towards God which lives among those whose heart condemns them not? What but the fact that "they could turn from the storm without to the approving sunshine within"? "See," it has been said, "he who builds on the general esteem of the world builds, not on the sand, but, which is worse, upon the wind, and writes the title-deeds of his hope upon the face of a river." But when a man knows that "one with God is always in a majority," then his loneliness is changed into the confidence that all the ten thousand times ten thousand of Heaven are with him. "His banishment becomes his preferment, his rags his trophies, his nakedness his ornament; and, so long as his innocence is his repast, he feasts and banquets upon bread and water."

And so,

"Among the faithless, faithful only he;
Among innumerable false, unmoved,
Unshaken, unseduced, unterrified,"

Elijah fearlessly stood alone, while all the world confronted him with frowning menace. The coward sympathies of the neutrals who face both ways may have been with him, but the multitude of such Laodiceans wink at wrong, and from love of their own ease do not, and dare not, speak. God only was the protector of Elijah, and in himself alone was all his state, as in his garment of hair he approached the people and confronted the idolatrous priests in all the gorgeousness of Baal's vestry. He, like his great predecessor Moses, was the champion of moral purity, of the national faith, of religious freedom and simplicity, of the immediate access of man to God; they were the champions of fanatical and unhallowed religionism, of usurping priestcraft, of unnatural self-abasements, of persecuting despotism, of licentious and cruel rites. Elijah was the deliverer of his people from a hideous and polluted apostasy which, had he not prevailed that day, would have obliterated their name and their memory from the annals of the nations. That he was a genuine historic character—a prophet of Divine commission and marvellous power—cannot for a moment be doubted, however impossible it may now be in every incident to disentangle the literal historic facts from the poetic and legendary emblazonment which those facts not unnaturally received in the ordinary recollection of the prophetic schools. Throughout the great scene which followed, his spirit was that of the Psalmist: "Though an host of men should encamp against me, yet will not my heart be afraid"; that of the "servant of the Lord" in Isaiah: "He hath made my mouth like a sharp sword, and in His quiver hath He hid me."[643]

His first challenge was to the people. "How long," he asked, "do ye totter between two opinions?[644] If Jehovah be God, follow Him; but if Baal, follow him."

Awestruck and ashamed the multitude kept unbroken silence. Doubtless it was, in part, the silence of guilt. They knew that they had followed Jezebel into the cruelties of Baal-worship, and the forbidden lusts which polluted the temples of the Asherah. Puritanism simplicity, spirituality of worship involves a strain too great and too lofty for the multitude. Like all Orientals, like the negroes of America, like most weak minds, they loved to rely on a pompous ritual and a sensuous worship. It is so easy to let these stand for the deeper requirements which lie in the truth that "God is a Spirit, and they that worship Him must worship Him in spirit and in truth."

Receiving no answer to his stern question, Elijah laid down the conditions of the contest. "The prophets of Baal," he said, "are four hundred and fifty: I stand alone as a prophet of Jehovah. Let two bullocks be provided for us; they shall slay and dress one, and lay it on wood, but—for there shall be no priestly trickeries to-day—they shall put no fire under. I, though I be no priest, will slay and dress the other, and lay it on wood, and put no fire under. Then let all of you, Baal-priests and people if you will, cry to your idols; I will call on the name of Jehovah. The god that answereth by fire let *him* be God."

No challenge could be fairer, for Baal was the Sun-god; and what god could be more likely to answer by fire from that blazing sky? The deep murmur of the people expressed their assent. The Baal priests were caught as in a snare. Their hearts must have sunk within them; his did not. Perhaps some of them believed sufficiently in their idol to hope that, were he demon or deity, he might save himself and his votaries from humiliation and defeat; but most of them must have been seized with terrible misgiving, as they saw the assembled people prepared to wait with Oriental patience, seated on their abbas on the sides of that natural amphitheatre, till the descending flame should prove that Baal had heard the weird invocation of his worshippers. But, since they could not escape the proposed ordeal, they chose, and slew, and dressed their victim. From morning till noon—many of them with wildly waving arms, others with their foreheads in the dust— they upraised the wild chant of their monotonous invocation, "Baal, hear us! Baal, hear us!" In vain the cry rose and fell, now uttered in soft appealing murmurs, now rising into passionate entreaties. All was silent. There lay the dead bullock putrescing under the burning orb which was at once their deity and the visible sign of his presence. No consuming lightning fell, even when the sun flamed in the zenith of that cloudless sky. There was no voice nor any that answered.

Then they tried still more potent incantations. They began to circle round the altar they had made in one of their solemn dances to the shrill strains of pipe and flute. The rhythmic movements ended in giddy whirls and orgiastic leapings which were a common feature of sensuous heathen worship; dances in which, like modern dervishes, they bounded and yelled and spun round and round till they fell foaming and senseless to the ground. [645] The people looked on expectant, but it was all in vain.

Hitherto the Prophet had remained silent, but now when noon came, and still no fire descended, he mocked them. Now, surely, if ever, was their time! They had been crying for six long hours in their vain repetitions and incantations. Surely they had not shouted loud enough! Baal was a god; some strange accident must have prevented him from hearing the prayer of his miserable priests. Perhaps he was in deep meditation, so that he did not notice those frantic appeals; perhaps he was too busy talking to some one else,[646] or was on a journey somewhere; or was asleep and must be awaked; or, he added with yet more mordant sarcasm, and in a gibe which would have sounded coarse to modern ears, perhaps he has gone aside for a private purpose. He must be called, he must be aroused; he must be made to hear.[647]

Such taunts, addressed to this multitude of priests in the hearing of the people, whom they desired to dupe or to convince, drove them to fiercer frenzy. Already the westering sun began to warn them that their hour was past, and failure imminent. They would not succumb without trying the darker sorceries of blood and self-mutilation, which were only resorted to at the most dread extremities. With renewed and redoubled yells they offered on their altar the blood of human sacrifice, stabbing and gashing themselves with swords and lances, till they presented a horrid spectacle. Their vestments and their naked bodies were besmeared with gore[648] as they whirled round and round with shriller and more frenzied screams. [649] They raved in vain. The shadows began to lengthen. The hour for the evening *Minchah*, the evening meal-offering, and oblation of flour and meal, salt and frankincense, drew near.[650] It was already "between the two evenings." They had continued their weird invocations all through the burning day, but there was not any that regarded There lay the dead bullock on the still fireless altar; and now their Tyrian Sun-god, like the fabled "Hercules," was but burning himself to death on the flaming pyre of sunset amid the unavailing agony of his worshippers.

Then Elijah bade the sullen and baffled fanatics to stand aside, and summoned the people to throng round him. There was nothing tumultuous or orgiastic in his proceedings. In striking contrast with the four hundred and fifty frantic sun-worshippers, he proceeded in the calmest and most deliberate way. First, in the name of Jehovah, he repaired the old *bamah*— the mountain-altar, which probably Jezebel had broken down. This he did with twelve stones, one for each of the tribes of Israel. Then he dug a broad trench.[651] Then, when he had prepared his bullock, in order to show the people the impossibility of any deception, such as are common among priests, he bade them drench it three times over with four barrels of water,[652] from the still-existent spring, and, not content with that, he filled the trench also with water.[653] Lastly at the time of the evening oblation he briefly offered up one prayer that Jehovah would make it known this day to His backsliding people that He, not Baal, was the Elohim of Israel. He used no "much speaking"; he did not adopt the dervish yells and dances and gashings which were abhorrent to God, though they appealed so powerfully to the sensuous imaginations of the multitude. He only raised his eyes to heaven,[654] and cried aloud in the hush of expectant stillness:—

"Jehovah, God of Abraham, of Isaac, and of Israel,
Let it be known this day that Thou art God in Israel,
And that I am Thy servant,
And that I have done all these things at Thy word.
Hear me, Jehovah, hear me.
That this people may know that Thou, Jehovah, art God,
And that Thou hast turned their heart back again."

The prayer, with its triple invocation of Jehovah's name, and its seven rhythmic lines, was no sooner ended than down streamed the lightning, and consumed the bullock and the wood, and shattered the stones, and burnt up the dust, and licked up the water in the trenches;[655] and, with one terror-stricken impulse, the people all prostrated themselves on their faces with the cry, "*Yahweh—hoo—ha—Elohim, Yahweh—hoo—ha—Elohim!*" "The

Lord, He is God; the Lord, He is God!"—a cry which was almost identical with the name of the victorious prophet Elijahu—"Yah, He is my God."[656]

The magnificent narrative in which the interest has been wound up to so high a pitch, and expressed in so lofty a strain of imaginative and dramatic force, ends in a deed of blood. According to Josephus, the people, by a spontaneous movement, "seized and slew the prophets of Baal, Elijah exhorting them to do so." According to the earlier narrative, Elijah said to the people: "Take the prophets of Baal; let not one of them escape. And they took them: and Elijah brought them down to the brook Kishon, and slew them there with the sword."[657] It is not necessarily meant that he slew them with his own hand, though indeed he may have done so, as Phinehas sacrificed Jephthah's daughter, and Samuel hewed Agag in pieces before the Lord. His moral responsibility was precisely the same in either case. We are not told that he had any commission from Jehovah to do this, or was bidden thereto by any voice of the Lord. Yet in those wild days—days of ungovernable passions and imperfect laws, days of ignorance which God winked at—it is not only perfectly probable that Elijah would have acted thus, but most unlikely that his conscience reproached him for doing so, or that it otherwise than approved the sanguinary vengeance. It was the frightful *lex talionis*, which was spoken "to them of old time," and which inflicted on the defeated what they would certainly have inflicted on Elijah had he not been the conqueror. The prophets of Baal indirectly, if not directly, had been the cause of Jezebel's persecution of the prophets of the Lord. The thought of pity would not occur to Elijah any more than it did to the writer, or writers, of Deuteronomy, perhaps, long afterwards, who commanded the stoning of idolaters, whether men or women (Deut. xiii. 6-9, xvii. 2-4). The massacre of the priests accorded with the whole spirit of those half-anarchic times. It accords with that Elijah-spirit of orthodox fanaticism, which, as Christ Himself had to teach to the sons of thunder, is not His spirit, but utterly alien from it. If, perhaps two centuries later, the savage deed could be recorded, and recorded with approval, by this narrator from the School of the Prophets in these superb eulogies of his hero; if so many centuries later the disciple whom Jesus loved, and the first martyr-apostle could deem it an exemplary deed; if, centuries later, it could be appealed to as a precedent by Inquisitors with hearts made hard as the nether millstone by bigoted and hateful superstition; if even Puritans could be animated by the same false hallowing of ferocity; how can we judge Elijah if, in dark, unilluminated early days, he had not learnt to rise to a purer standpoint? To this day the names about Carmel shudder, as it were, with reminiscence of this religious massacre. There is *El-Muhrakkah*, "the place of burning"; there is *Tel-el-Kusis*, "the hill of the priests"; and that ancient river, the river Kishon, which had once been choked with the corpses of the host of Sisera, and has since then been incarnadined by the slain of many a battle, is—perhaps in memory of this bloodshed most of all—still known as the *Nahr-el-Mokatta*, or "the stream of slaughter." What wonder that the Eastern Christians in their pictures of Elijah still surround him with the decapitated heads of these his enemies? To this day the Moslim regard him as one who terrifies and slays.[658]

But though the deed of vengeance stands recorded, and recorded with no censure, in the sacred history, we must—without condemning Elijah, and without measuring his days by the meting-rod of Christian mercy—still unhesitatingly hold fast the sound principle of early and as yet uncontaminated Christianity, and say, as said the early Fathers, Βία ἐχθρὸν Θεῷ. Violence is a thing hateful to the God of love.

Even Christians, and that down to our own day, have abused the example of Elijah, and asked, "Did not Elijah slaughter the priests of Baal?" as a proof that it is always the duty of States to suppress false religion by violence. Stahl asked that question when he preached before the Prussian court at the Evangelical Conference at Berlin in 1855, adding the dreadful misrepresentation that "Christianity is the religion of intolerance, and its kernel is exclusiveness." Did these hard spirits never consider Christ's own warning? Did they wholly forget the prophecy that "He shall not strive nor cry, neither shall His voice be heard in the streets. A bruised reed shall He not break, and smoking flax shall He not quench, till He send forth judgment unto victory, and in His name shall the Gentiles hope"?[659] Calvin reproved Réné, Duchess of Ferrara, for not approving of the spirit of the imprecatory psalms. He said that this was "to set ourselves up as superior to Christ in sweetness and humility"; and that "David even in his hatreds is an example and type of Christ." When Cartwright argued for the execution of the heretics he said: "If this be thought savage and intolerant, I am content to be so with the Holy Ghost." Far wiser is the humble minister in *Old Mortality*, when he withstood Balfour of Burleigh, in the decision to put to the sword all the inhabitants of Tillietudlem Castle. "By what law," asks Henry Morton, "would you justify the atrocity you would commit?" "If thou art ignorant of it," said Balfour, "thy companion is well aware of the law which gave the men of Jericho to the sword of Joshua, the son of Nun." "Yes," answered the divine, "but we live under a better dispensation, which instructeth us to return good for evil, and to pray for those who despitefully use us and persecute us."

CHAPTER XXXVIII
THE RAIN

1 Kings xviii. 41-46

"Are there any of the vanities of the nations that can cause rain?"—Jer. xiv. 22.

But the terrible excitement of the day was not yet over, nor was the victory completely won. The fire had flashed from heaven, but the long-desired rain on which depended the salvation of land and people still showed no signs of falling. And Elijah was pledged to this result. Not until the drought ended could he reach the culmination of his victory over the Sun-god of Jezebel's worship.

But his faith did not fail him. "Get thee up," he said to Ahab, "eat and drink, for there is a sound of the feet of the rain-storm."[660] Doubtless through all that day of feverish anxiety, neither king, nor people, nor prophet had eaten. As for the Prophet, but little sufficed him at any time, and the slaughter of the defeated priests would not prevent either king or people from breaking their long fast. Doubtless the king's tent was pitched on one of the slopes over the plain. But Elijah did not join him. He heard, indeed, with prophetic ear the rush of the coming rain, but he had still to wrestle in prayer with Jehovah for the fulfilment of His promise. So he ascended towards the summit of the promontory where the purple peak of Carmel—still called Jebel Mar Elias ("the hill of Lord Elijah")—overlooks the sea, and there he crouched low on the ground in intense prayer, putting his face between his knees. After his first intensity of supplication had spent itself, he said to his boy attendant,[661] traditionally believed to have been the son of the widow of Zarephath whom he had plucked from death:—

"Go up now, look towards the sea."

The youth went up, and gazed out long and intently, for he well knew that if rain came it would sweep inland from the waters of the Mediterranean, and to an experienced eye the signals of coming storm are patent long before they are noticed by others. But all was as it had been for so many weary and dreadful months. The sea a sheet of unruffled gold glared under the setting sun, which still sank through an unclouded sky. Can we not imagine the accent of misgiving and disappointment with which he brought back the one word:—

"Nothing."

Once more the Prophet bowed his face between his knees in prayer, and sent the youth; and again, and yet again, seven times. And each time had come to him the chilling answer, "Nothing." But the seventh time he called out from the mountain summit his joyous cry: "Behold, there ariseth a cloud out of the sea, as small as a man's hand."

And now, indeed, Elijah knew that his triumph was completed. He bade his servant fly with winged speed to Ahab, and tell him to make ready his chariot at once, lest the burst of the coming rain should flood the river and the road, and prevent him from getting over the rough ground which lay between him and his palace at Jezreel.

Then the blessed storm burst on the parched soil with a sense of infinite refreshfulness which only an Eastern in a thirsty land can fully comprehend. And Ahab mounted his chariot. He had not driven far before the heaven, which had for so long been like brass over an iron globe, was one black mass of clouds driven by the wind, and the drenching rain poured down in sheets. And through the storm the chariot swept, and Elijah girded up his loins, and, filled with a Divine impulse of exultation, ran before it, keeping pace with the king's steeds for all those fifteen miles, even after the overwhelming strain of all he had gone through, apparently without food, that day. And as through the rifts of rain the king saw his wild dark figure outrunning his swift steeds, and seeming "to dilate and conspire" with the rushing storm, can we wonder that the tears of remorse and gratitude streamed down his face?[662]

The chariot reached Jezreel, and at the city gate Elijah stopped. Like his antitype, the great forerunner, Elijah was a voice in the wilderness; like his Lord that was to be, he loved not cities. The instinct of the Bedawin kept him far from the abodes of men, and his home was never among them. He needed no roof to shelter him, nor change of raiment. The hollows of Mount Gilboa were his sufficient resting-place, and he could find a sleeping-place in the caves near its abundant Eastern spring. Nor was he secure of safety. He knew, in spite of his superhuman victory, that a dark hour awaited Ahab when he would have to tell Jezebel that the people had repudiated her idol, and that Elijah had slain her four hundred and fifty priests. He knew "that axe-like edge unturnable" which always smote and feared not. Ahab was but as plastic clay in the strong hands of his queen, and for her there existed neither mystery nor miracle except in the worship of the insulted Baal. Was not Baal, she said, the real sender of the rain, on whose priests this fanatic from rude Gilead had wrought his dreadful sacrifice? Oh that she could have been for one hour on Carmel in the place of her vacillating and easily daunted husband! For was she not convinced, and did not the pagan historian afterwards relate, that the ending of the drought was due to the prayers and sacrifices, not of Elijah, but of her own father who was Baal's priest and king?[663] Yet, for all her spirit of defiance, we can hardly doubt that the feelings of Jezebel towards Elijah had much of dread mingled with her hatred. She must have felt towards him much as Mary Queen of Scots felt towards John Knox—of whom she said that she feared his prayers more than an army of one hundred thousand men.[664]

"May we really venture," asks Canon Cheyne, "to *look* out for answer to prayer? Did not Elijah live in the *heroic* ages of faith? No; God still works miracles. Take an instance from the early history of Christian Europe. You know the terror excited by the Huns, who in the sixth century after Christ penetrated into the very heart of Christian France. Already they had occupied the suburbs of Orleans, and the people who were incapable of bearing arms lay prostrate in prayer. The governor sent a message to observe from the ramparts. Twice he looked in vain, but the third time he reported a small cloud on the horizon. 'It is the aid of God,' cried the Bishop of Orleans. It was the dust raised by the advancing squadrons of Christian troops."[665]

A much nearer parallel, and that a very remarkable one, may be quoted.[666] It records—and the fact itself, explain it how men will, seems to be unquestionable—how a storm of rain came to answer the prayer of a good leader of the Evangelical Revival—Grimshaw, rector of Haworth. Distressed at the horrible immoralities introduced among his parishioners by some local races, and wholly failing to get them stopped, he went to the racecourse, and, flinging himself on his knees in an agony of supplication, entreated God to interpose and save his people from their moral danger. He had scarcely ceased his prayer when down rushed a storm of rain so violent as to turn the racecourse into a swamp, and render the projected races a matter of impossibility.

CHAPTER XXXIX
ELIJAH'S FLIGHT

1 Kings xix. 1-4

"A still small voice comes through the wild,
Like a father consoling his fretful child,
Which banisheth bitterness, wrath and fear,
Saying, 'Man is distant, but God is near.'"
Temple.

The misgiving which, joined to his ascetic dislike of cities, made Elijah stop his swift race at the entrance of Jezreel was more than justified. Ahab's narrative of the splendid contest at Carmel produced no effect upon Jezebel whatever, and we can imagine the bitter objurgations which she poured upon her cowering husband for having stood quietly by while *her* prophets and Baal's prophets were being massacred by this dark fanatic, aided by a rebellious people. Had *she* been there all should have been otherwise! In contemptuous defiance of Ahab's fears or wishes, she then and there—and it must now have been after nightfall—despatched a messenger to find Elijah, wherever he might be hiding himself, and say to him in her name: "As sure as thou art Elijah, and I am Jezebel,[667] may my gods avenge it upon me if on the morrow by this time I have not made thy life like the life of one of my own murdered priests." In the furious impetuosity of the message we see the determination of the sorceress-queen. In her way she was as much in deadly earnest as Elijah was. Whether Baal had been defeated or not, *she* was not defeated, and Elijah should not escape her vengeance. The oath shows the intensity of her rage, like that of the forty Jews who bound themselves by the *cherem* that they would not eat or drink till they had slain Paul; and the fixity of her purpose as when Richard III. declared that he would not dine till the head of Buckingham had fallen on the block. We cannot but notice the insignificance to which she reduced her husband, and the contempt with which she treated the voice of her people. She presents the spectacle, so often reproduced in history and reflected in literature, of a strong fierce woman—a Clytemnestra, a Brunhault, a Lady Macbeth, an Isabella of France, a Margaret of Anjou, a Joan of Naples, a Catherine de Medicis—completely dominating a feebler consort.

The burst of rage which led her to send the message defeated her own object. The awfulness which invested Elijah, and the supernatural powers on which he relied, when he was engaged in the battles of the Lord, belonged to him only in his public and prophetic capacity. As a man he was but a poor, feeble, lonely subject, whose blood might be shed at any moment. He knew that God works no miracles for the supersession of ordinary human precautions. It was no part of his duty to throw away his life, and give a counter triumph to the Baal-worshippers whom he had so signally humiliated. He fled, and went for his life.

Swift flight was easy to that hardy frame and that trained endurance, even after the fearful day on Carmel and the wild race of fifteen miles from Carmel to Jezreel. It was still night, and cool, and the haunts and byways of the land were known to the solitary and hunted wanderer. "He feared, and he rose, and he went for his life," ninety-five miles to Beersheba, once a town of Simeon, now the southern limit of the kingdom of Judah, thirty-one miles south of Hebron.[668] But in the tumult of his feelings and the peril of his position he could not stay in any town. At Beersheba he left his servant—perhaps, as legend says, the boy of Zarephath, who became the prophet Jonah—but, in any case, not so much a servant as a youth in training for the prophetic office. It was necessary for him to spend his dark hour alone; for, if there are hours in which human sympathy is all but indispensable, there are also hours in which the soul can tolerate no communion save that with God.[669] So, leaving all civilisation behind him, he plunged a day's journey into that great and terrible wilderness of Paran, where he too was alone with the wild beasts. And then, utterly worn out, he flung himself down under the woody stem of a solitary rhotem plant.[670] The plant is the wild broom with "its cloud of pink blossoms" which often afford the only shadow under the glaring sun in the waste and weary land, and beneath the slight but grateful shade of which the Arab to this day is glad to pitch his tent. And there the pent-up emotions of his spirit, which had gone through so tremendous a strain, broke up as in one terrible sob, when the strong man, like a tired child, "requested for himself that he might die."[671]

Of what use was life any longer? He had fought for Jehovah, and won, and after all been humiliatingly defeated. He had prophesied the drought, and it had withered and scorched up the erring, afflicted land. He had prayed for the rain, and it had come in a rush of blessing on the reviving fields. In the Wady Cherith, in the house of the Phœnician widow, he had been divinely supported and sheltered from hot pursuit. He had snatched her boy from death. He had stood before kings, and not been ashamed. He had stretched forth his hands to a disobedient and gainsaying people, and not in vain. He had confounded the rich-vested and royally maintained band of Baal's priests, and in spite of their orgiastic leapings and self-mutilations had put to shame their Sun-god under his own burning sun. He had kept pace with Ahab's chariot-steeds as he conducted him, as it were in triumph, through the streaming downpour of that sweeping storm, to his summer capital. Of what use was it all? Was it anything but a splendid and deplorable failure? And he said: "It is enough; now, O Lord, take away my life; for I am not better than my fathers." He could have cried with the poet: —

> "Let the heavens burst, and drown with deluging rain
> The feeble vassals of lust, and anger, and wine,
> The little hearts that know not how to forgive;
> Arise, O God, and strike, for we count Thee just, —
> We are not worthy to live."

Who does not know something of this feeling of utter overwhelming despondency, of bitter disillusionment concerning life and our fellow-men? Some great writer has said, with truth, "that there is probably no man with a soul above that of the brutes that perish, to whom a time has not come in his life, when, were you to tell him that he would not wake to see another day, he would receive the message with something like gladness." There are some whose lives have been so saddened by some special calamity that for long years together they have not valued them. F. W. Robertson, troubled by various sorrows, and worried (as the best men are sure to be) by the petty ecclesiastical persecutions of priests and formalists, wrote in a letter on a friend's death: "How often have I thought of the evening when he left Tours, when, in our boyish friendship, we set our little silver watches exactly together, and made a compact to look at the moon exactly at the same moment that night and think of each other. *I do not remember a single hour in life since then which I would have arrested, and said, 'Let this stay.'*" Melancholy so deep as this is morbid and unnatural, and he himself wrote in a brighter mood: "Positively I will not walk with any one in these tenebrous avenues of cypress and yew. I like sunny rooms and sunny truth. When I had more of spring and warmth I could afford to be prodigal of happiness; but now I want sunlight and sunshine. I desire to enter into those regions where cheerfulness and truth and health of heart and mind reside." Life has its real happiness for those who have deserved, and taken the right method to attain it; but it can never escape its hours of impenetrable gloom, and they sometimes seem to be darkest for the noblest souls. Petty souls are irritated by little annoyances, and the purely selfish disappointments which avenge the exaggerated claims of our "shivering egotism." But while little mean spirits are tormented by the insect-swarm of little mean worries, great souls are liable to be beaten down by the waves and storms of immense calamities—the calamities which affect nations and churches, the "desperate currents" of whose sins and miseries seem to be sometimes driven through the channels of their single hearts. Only such a man as an Elijah can measure the colossal despondency of an Elijah's heart. In the apparently absolute failure, the seemingly final frustration of such men as these there is something nobler than in the highest personal exaltations of ignobler souls.

"Now, O Lord, take away my life!" The prayer, however natural, however excusable, is never right. It is a sign of insufficient faith, of human imperfection; but it is breathed by different persons in a spirit so different that in some it almost rises to nobleness, as in others it sinks quite beneath contempt.

Scripture gives us several specimens of both moods. If Jonah was, indeed, the servant-pupil of Elijah, the legendary story of that meanest-minded of all the prophets—the meanest-minded and paltriest, not perhaps as he was in reality—for of him, historically, we know scarcely anything—but as he is represented in the profound and noble allegory which bears his name—might almost seem to have been written in tacit antithesis to the story of Elijah. Elijah flies only when he has done the mighty work of God, and only when the life is in deadly peril which he would fain save for future emergencies of service; Jonah flies that he may escape, out of timid selfishness, the work of God. Elijah wishes himself dead because he thinks that the glorious purpose of his life has been thwarted, and that the effort undertaken for the deliverance of his people has failed; Jonah wishes himself dead, first, because he repines at God's mercy, and would prefer that his personal credit should be saved and his personal importance secured than that God should spare the mighty city of Nineveh with its one hundred and twenty thousand little children; and then because the poor little castor-oil plant has withered, which gave him shelter from the noon. Considering the traditional connexion between them, it seems to me impossible to overlook an allusive contrast between the noble and mighty Elijah under his solitary rhotem plant in the wilderness wishing for death in the anguish of a heart "which nobly loathing strongly broke," and the selfish splenetic Jonah wishing himself dead in pettish vexation under his *palma Christi* because Nineveh is forgiven and the sun is hot.

There are indeed times when humanity is tried beyond its capacity, when the cry for restful death is wrung from souls crushed under accumulations of quite intolerable anguish and calamity. In the fret of long-continued sleeplessness, in sick and desolate and half-starved age, in attacks of disease incurable, long-continued, and full of torture, God will surely look with pardoning tenderness on those whose faith is unequal to so terrible a strain. It was pardonable surely of Job to curse the day of his birth when—smitten with elephantiasis, a horror, a hissing, an astonishment, bereaved of all his children, and vexed by the obtrusive orthodoxies of his petty Pharisaic friends; unconscious, too, that it was God's hand which was all the while leading him through the valley of the shadow into the land of righteousness—he cried: "Wherefore is light given to him that is in misery, and life to the bitter in soul?" In those who have no hope and are without God in the world, this mood—not when expressed in passing passion as by the saintly man of Uz, but when brooded on and indulged—leads to suicide, and in the one instance recorded in each Testament, an Ahithophel and a Judas, the despairing souls of the guilty:—

> "Into the presence of their God
> Rushed in with insult rude."

But Elijah's mood, little as it was justifiable in this its extreme form, was but the last infirmity of a noble mind. It has often recurred among those grandest of the servants of God who may sink into the deepest dejection from contrast with the spiritual altitudes to which they have soared. It is with them as with the lark which floods the blue air with its passion of almost delirious rapture, yet suddenly, as though exhausted, drops down silent into its lowly nest in the brown furrows. There is but one man in the Old Testament who, as a prophet, stands on the same level as Elijah,—he who stood with Elijah on the snowy heights of Hermon when their Lord was transfigured into celestial brightness, and they spake together of His decease at Jerusalem. And Moses had passed through the same dark hour as that through which Elijah was passing now, when he saw the tears, and heard the murmurs of the greedy, selfish, ungrateful people, who hated their heavenly manna, and lusted for the leeks and fleshpots of their Egyptian bondage. Revolted by this obtrusion upon him of human nature in its lowest meanness, he cried to God under his intolerable burden: "Have I conceived all this people?... I am not able to bear all this people alone.... And if Thou deal thus with me, kill me, I pray Thee, out of hand; and let me not see my wretchedness." In Moses, as doubtless in Elijah, so far from being the clamour of whining selfishness, his anguish was part of the same mood which made him offer his life for the redemption of the people; which made St. Paul ready to wish himself anathema from Jesus Christ if thereby he could save his brethren after the flesh. Danton rose into heroism when he exclaimed, "*Que mon nom soit flétri, pourvu que la France soit libre*"; and Whitefield, when he cried, "Perish George Whitefield, so God's work be done"; and the Duke of Wellington when—remonstrated with for joining in the last charge at Waterloo, with the shot whistling round his head—he said,

"Never mind; the victory is won, and now my life is of no consequence."
In great souls the thought of others, completely dominating the base man's
concentration in self, may create a despondency which makes them ready
to give up their life, not because it is a burden to themselves, but because it
seems to them as if their work was over, and it was beyond their power to
do more for others.

Tender natures as well as strong natures are liable to this inrush of
hopelessness; and if it sometimes kills them by its violence, this is only a
part of God's training of them into perfection.

"So unaffected, so composed a mind,
So firm, yet soft, so strong, yet so refined,
Heaven, as its purest gold, by tortures tried:—
The saint sustained it, but the woman died."![672]

The cherubim of the sanctuary had to be made of the gold of Uphaz, the
finest and purest gold. It was only the purest gold which could be tortured
by workmanship into forms of exquisite beauty. The mind of Jeremiah
was as unlike that of Elijah's as can possibly be conceived. He was a man
of shrinking and delicate temperament, and his life is the most pathetic
tragedy among the biographies of Scripture. The mind of Elijah, like those
of Dante or Luther or Milton, was all ardour and battle brunt; the mind of
Jeremiah, like that of Melancthon, was timid as that of a gentle boy. A man
like Dante or Milton, when he stands alone, hated by princes and priests
and people, retorts scorn for scorn, and refuses to change his voice to hoarse
or mute. Yet even Dante died of a broken heart, and in Milton's mighty
autobiographical wail of Samson Agonistes, amid all its trumpet-blast of
stern defiance, we read the sad notes:—

"Nor am I in the list of them that hope;
Hopeless all my evils, all remediless;
This one prayer yet remains, might I be heard,
No long petition, speedy death,
The close of all my miseries, and the balm."

When the insolent priest Pashur smote Jeremiah in the face, and put him
for a night and a day in the common stocks, the prophet—after telling Pashur
that, for this awful insult to God's messenger, his name, which meant "joy
far and wide," should be changed into Magormissa-bib, "terror on every
side"—utterly broke down, and passionately cursed the day of his birth.
[673] And yet his trials were very far from ended then. Homeless, wifeless,
childless, slandered, intrigued against, undermined—protesting apparently
in vain against the hollow shams of a self-vaunting reformation—the object
of special hatred to all the self-satisfied religionists of his day, the lonely

persecuted servant of the Lord ended only in exile and martyrdom the long trouble of his eternally blessed but seemingly unfruitful life.

I dwell on this incident in the life of Elijah because it is full of instructiveness. Scripture is not all on a dead level. There are many pages of it which belong indeed to the connected history, and therefore carry on the general lessons of the history, but which are, in themselves, almost empty of any spiritual profit. Only a fantastic and artificial method of sermonising can extract from them, taken alone, any Divine lessons. In these Books of Kings many of the records are simply historical, and in themselves, apart from their place in the whole, have no more religious significance than any other historic facts; but because these annals are the annals of a chosen people, and because these books are written for our learning, we find in them again and again, and particularly in their more connected and elevated narratives, facts and incidents which place Scripture incomparably above all secular literature, and are rich in eternal truth for all time, and for a life beyond life.

It is with such an experience that we are dealing here, and therefore it is worth while, if we can, to see something of its meaning. We may, therefore, be permitted to linger for a brief space over the causes of Elijah's despair, and the method in which God dealt with it.

CHAPTER XL
ELIJAH'S DESPAIR

1 Kings xix. 4-8

"So much I feel my genial spirits droop,
My hopes all flat, nature within me seems
In all her functions weary of herself,
My race of glory run, and race of shame,
And I shall shortly be with them that rest."
Samson Agonistes.

What are the causes which may drive even a saint of God into a mood of momentary despair as he is forced to face the semblance of final failure?

1. Even the lowest element of such despair has its instructiveness. It was due in part, doubtless, to mere physical exhaustion. Elijah had just gone through the most tremendous conflict of his life. During all that long and most exhausting day at Carmel he had had little or no food, and at the close of it he had run across all the plain with the king's chariot. In the dead of that night, with his life in his hand, he had fled towards Beersheba, and now he had wandered for a whole day in the glare of the famishing wilderness. It does not do to despise the body. If we *are* spirits, yet we *have* bodies; and the body wreaks a stern and humiliating vengeance on those who neglect or despise it. The body reacts upon the mind. "If you rumple the jerkin, you rumple the jerkin's lining." If we weaken the body too much, we do not make it the slave of the spirit, but rather make the spirit its slave. Even moderate fasting, as a simple physiological fact—if it be *fasting* at all, as distinguished from healthful moderation and wise temperance—tends to increase, and not by any means to decrease, the temptations which come to us from the appetites of the body. Extreme self-maceration—as all ascetics have found from the days of St. Jerome to those of Cardinal Newman—only adds new fury to the lusts of the flesh. Many a hermit and stylite and fasting monk, many half-dazed, hysterical, high-wrought men have found, sometimes without knowing the reason of it, that by wilful and artificial devices of self-chosen saintliness, they have made the path of purity and holiness not easier, but more hard. The body is a temple, not a tomb. It is not permitted

us to think ourselves wiser than God who made it, nor to fancy that we can mend His purposes by torturing and crushing it. By violating the laws of physical righteousness we only make moral and spiritual righteousness more difficult to attain.

2. Elijah's dejection was also due to forced inactivity. "What *doest* thou here, Elijah?" said the voice of God to him in the heart of man. Alas! he was doing nothing: there was nothing left for him to do! It was different when he hid by the brook Cherith, or in Zarephath, or in the glades of Carmel. Then a glorious endeavour lay before him, and there was hope. But

> "Life without hope draws nectar in a sieve,
> And hope without an object cannot live."

The mighty vindication of Jehovah in which all the struggle of his life culminated, had been crowned with triumph, and had failed. It had blazed up like fire, and had sunk back into ashes. To such a spirit as his nothing is so fatal as to have nothing to do and nothing to hope for. "What did the Maréchal die of?" asked a distinguished Frenchman of one of his comrades. "He died of having nothing to do." "Ah!" was the reply; "that is enough to kill the best General of us all."

3. Again, Elijah was suffering from mental reaction. The bow had been bent too long, and was somewhat strained; the tense string needed to have been relaxed before. It is a common experience that some great duty or mastering emotion uplifts us for a time above ourselves, makes us even forget the body and its needs. We remember Jeremy Taylor's description of what he had noticed in the Civil Wars,—that a wounded soldier, amid the heat and fury of the fight, was wholly unconscious of his wounds, and only began to feel the smart of them when the battle had ended and its fierce passion was entirely spent.

Men, even strong men, after hours of terrible excitement, have been known to break down and weep like children. Macaulay, in describing the emotions which succeeded the announcement that the Reform Bill had passed, says that not a few, after the first outburst of wild enthusiasm, were bathed in tears.

And any one who has seen some great orator after a supreme effort of eloquence, when his strength seems drained away, and the passion is exhausted, and the flame has sunk down into its embers, is aware how painful a reaction often follows, and how differently the man looks and feels if you see him when he has passed into his retirement. pale and weak, and often very sad. After a time the mind can do no more.

4. Further, Elijah felt his loneliness. At that moment indeed he could not bear the presence of any one, but none the less his sense that none sympathised with him, that all hated him, that no voice was raised to cheer him, that no finger was uplifted to help him, weighed like lead upon his spirit. "I only am left." There was awful desolation in that thought. He was alone among an apostatising people. It is the same kind of cry which we hear so often in the life of God's saints. It is the Psalmist crying: "I am become like a pelican in the wilderness, and like an owl that is in the desert. Mine enemies reproach me all the day long, and they that are mad upon me are sworn together against me";[674] or, "My lovers and my neighbours did stand looking upon my trouble, and my kinsmen stood afar off. They also that sought after my life laid snares for me."[675] It is Job so smitten and afflicted that he is half tempted for the moment to curse God and die. It is Isaiah saying of the hopeless wickedness of his people, "The whole head is sick, and the whole heart faint." It is Jeremiah complaining, "The prophets prophesy falsely, and the priests bear rule by their means; and my people love to have it so: and what will ye do in the end thereof?"[676] It is St. Paul wailing so sadly, "All they of Asia have turned from me. Only Luke is with me." It is the pathos of desolation which breathes through the sad sentence of the Gospels, "Then all the disciples forsook Him, and fled." The anticipation of desertion had wrung from the Lord Jesus the sad prophesy, "Behold, the hour cometh, yea, is now come, when ye shall be scattered, every man to his own, and shall leave Me alone: and yet I am not alone, because the Father is with Me."[677] And this heart-anguish of loneliness is, to this day, a common experience of the best men. Any man whose duty has ever called him to strike out against the stream of popular opinion, to rebuke the pleasant vices of the world, to plead for causes too righteous to be popular, to deny the existence of vested interests in the causes of human ruin, to tell a corrupt society that it is corrupt, and a lying Church that it lies;—any man who has had to defy mere plausible conventions of veiled wrong-doing, to give bold utterance to forgotten truths, to awake sodden and slumbering consciences, to annul agreements with death and covenants with hell; every man who rises above the trimmers and the facing-both-ways, and those who try to serve two masters—they who swept away the rotting superstitions of a tyrannous ecclesiasticism, they who purified prisons, they who struck the fetters off the slave—every saint, reformer, philanthropist, and faithful preacher in the past, and those now living saints, who, walking in the shining steps of these, endeavour to rescue the miserable out of the gutter, and to preach the gospel to the poor, know the

anguish of isolation, when, because they have been benefactors, they are cursed as though they were felons, and when, for the efforts of their noble self-sacrifice, the contempt of the world, and its pedantry, and its malice can find for them no words too contemptuous or too bitterly false.

5. But there was even a deeper sorrow than these which made Elijah long for death. It was the sense of utter and seemingly irretrievable failure. It happens often to the worldling as well as to the saint. Many a man, weary of life's inexorable emptiness, has exclaimed in different ways:—

> "Know that whatever thou hast been,
> 'Tis something better not to be."

That sentiment is not in the least peculiar to Byron. We find it again and again in the Greek tragedians. We find it alike in the legendary revelation of the god Pan, and in the Book of Ecclesiastes, and in Schopenhauer and Von Hartmann. No true Christian, no believer in the mercy and justice of God, can share that sentiment, but will to the last thank God for His creation and preservation and all the blessings of this life, as well as for the inestimable gift of His redemption, for the means of grace, and for the hope of glory. Nevertheless, it is part of God's discipline that He often requires His saints as well as His sinners to face what looks like hopeless discomfiture, and to perish, as it were,

> "In the lost battle
> Borne down by the flying,
> Where mingles war's rattle
> With groans of the dying."

Such was the fate of all the Prophets. They were tortured; they had trials of cruel mockings and scourgings, yea, moreover of bonds and imprisonment; they were stoned, were sawn asunder, were tempted, were slain with the sword; they wandered about in sheepskins and goatskins, they hid in caves and dens of the earth, being destitute, afflicted, tormented, though of them the world was not worthy. Such, too, was the fate of all the Apostles—set forth last of all as men doomed to death; made a spectacle to the world, to angels, and to men. They were hungry, thirsty, naked, buffeted; they had no certain dwelling-place; they were treated as fools and weak, were dishonoured, defamed, treated as the filth of the world and the offscouring of all things. Such was conspicuously the case of St. Paul in that death, so lonely and forsaken, that the French sceptic thinks he must have awakened with infinite regret from the disillusionment of a futile life. Nay, it was the earthly lot of Him who was the prototype, and consolation, known or unknown, of all these:—it was the lot of Him who, from that which seemed the infinite collapse and immeasurable abandonment of His cross of shame, cried out: "My God, My God, why hast Thou forsaken Me?" He warned His true followers that they, too, would have to face the same finality of earthly catastrophes, to die without the knowledge, without even the probable hope, that they have accomplished anything, in utter forsakenment, in a monotony of execration, often in dejection and apparent hiding of God's countenance. The olden saints who prepared the way for Christ, and those who since His coming have followed His footsteps, have had to learn that true life involves a bearing of the cross.

Take but one or two out of countless instances. Look at that humble brown figure, kneeling drowned with tears to think of the disorders which had already begun to creep into the holy order which he had designed. It is sweet St. Francis of Assisi, to whom God said in visions: "Poor little man: thinkest thou that I, who rule the universe, cannot direct in My own way thy little order?" Look at that monk in his friars' dress, racked, tortured, gibbeted in fetters over the flaming pyre in the great square at Florence, stripped by guilty priests of his priestly robe, degraded from a guilty Church by its guilty representatives, pelted by wanton boys, dying amid a roar of execration from the brutal and fickle multitude whose hearts he once had moved. It is Savonarola, the prophet of Florence. Look at that poor preacher dragged from his dungeon to the stake at Basle, wearing the yellow cap and sanbenito painted with flames and devils. It is John Huss, the preacher of Bohemia. Look at the lion-hearted reformer feeling how much he had striven, not knowing as yet how much he had achieved, appealing to God to govern His world, saying that he was but a powerless man, and would be "the veriest ass alive" if he thought that he could meddle with the intricacies of Divine Providence. It is Luther. Look at the youth, starving in an ink-stained garret, hunted through the streets by an infuriated mob, thrust into the city prison as the only way to save his life from those who hated his exposure of their iniquities. It is William Lloyd Garrison. Look at that missionary, deserted, starving, fever-stricken, in the midst of savages, dying on his knees, in daily sufferings, amid frustrated hopes. It is David Livingstone, the pioneer of Africa. They, and thousands like them, have borne squalors and shames and tragedies, while they looked not at the things that are seen, but at the things that are not seen; for the things that are seen are temporal, but the things which are not seen are eternal. Might not they all have said with the disappointed Apostles, "Master, we have toiled all the night and have taken nothing"? Might not their lives and deaths—the lives which fools thought madness, and their end to be without honour—be described as one poet has described that of his disenchanted king:—

"He walked with dreams and darkness, and he found
A doom that ever poised itself to fall,
An ever-moaning battle in the mist,
Death in all life, and lying in all love,
The meanest having power upon the highest,
And the high purpose broken by the worm."

"Yes; the smelter of Israel had now to go down himself into the crucible."[678]

CHAPTER XLI
HOW GOD DEALS WITH DESPONDENCY

1 Kings xix. 5-8

"Why art thou so vexed, O my soul? and why art thou so disquieted within me? O put thy trust in God; for I will yet praise Him who is the health of my countenance, and my God."—Psalm xlii. 11.

"It is enough; now, O Lord, take away my life; for I am not better than my fathers."

The despondency was deeper than personal. It was despair of the world; despair of the fate of the true worship; despair about the future of faith and righteousness; despair of everything. Elijah, in his condition of pitiable weariness, felt himself reduced to entire uncertainty about all God's dealings with him and with mankind. "I am not better than my fathers": *they* failed one by one, and died, and entered the darkness; and I have failed likewise. To what end did Moses lead this people through the wilderness? Why did the Judges fight and deliver them? Of what use was the wise guidance of Samuel? What has come of David's harp, and Solomon's temple and magnificence, and Jeroboam's heaven-directed rebellion? It ends, and my work ends, in the despotism of Jezebel, and a nation of apostates!

God pitied His poor suffering servant, and gently led him back to hope and happiness, and restored him to his true self, and to the natural elasticity of his free spirit.

1. First, he gave His beloved sleep. Elijah lay down and slept. Perhaps this was what he needed most of all. When we lose that dear oblivion of "nature's soft nurse, and sweet restorer, balmy sleep," then nerve and brain give way. So God sent him

"The innocent sleep,
Sleep that knits up the ravelled sleeve of care,
Balm of hurt minds, great nature's second course,
Chief nourisher in life's feast."

And doubtless, while he slept, "his sleeping mind," as the Greek tragedian says, "was bright with eyes," and He, who had thus "steeped his senses in forgetfulness," spoke peace to his troubled heart, or breathed into it the rest over which hope might brood with her halcyon wings.

2. Next, God provided him with food. When he awoke he saw that at his head, under the rhotem-plant, God had spread him a table in the wilderness. It was a provision, simple indeed, but for his moderate wants more than sufficient—a cake baked on the coals[679] and a cruse of water. A *Maleakh*—a "messenger"—"some one," as the Septuagint and as Josephus both render it,[680] some one who was, to him at any rate, an angel of God—touched him, and said, "Arise and eat." He ate and drank, and thus refreshed lay down again to make up, perhaps, for long arrears of unrest. And again God's messenger, human or angelic, touched him, and bade him rise and eat once more, or his strength would fail in the journey which lay before him. For he meant to plunge yet farther into the wilderness. In the language of the narrator, "He arose, and did eat and drink, and went in the strength of that food forty days and forty nights."

3. Next God sent him on a hallowed pilgrimage to bathe his weary spirit in the memories of a brighter past.

It does not require forty days and forty nights, nor anything like so long a period, to get from one day's journey in the wilderness to Horeb, the Mount of God, which was Elijah's destination. The distance does not exceed one hundred and eighty miles even from Beersheba. But, as in the case of Moses and of our Lord, "forty days"—a number connected by many associations with the idea of penance and temptation—symbolises the period of Elijah's retirement and wanderings. No doubt, too, the number has an allusive significance, pointing back to the forty years' wanderings of Israel in the wilderness. The Septuagint omits the words "of God," but there can be little doubt that Sinai was selected for the goal of Elijah's pilgrimage with reference to the awful scenes connected with the promulgation of the law. It is well known that the Mount of the Commandments is as a rule called Sinai in Exodus, Leviticus, and Numbers, though the name Horeb occurs in Exod. iii. 1, xxxiii. 6. To account for the double usage there have been, since the Middle Ages, two theories: (1) that Horeb is the name of the range, and Sinai of the mountain; (2) that Horeb properly means the northern part of the range, and Sinai the southern, especially Jebel Mousa. Horeb is the prevalent name for the mountain in Deuteronomy; Sinai is the ordinary name, and occurs thirty-one times in the Old Testament.

After his wanderings Elijah reached Mount Sinai, and came to "the cave," and took shelter there. The use of the article shows that a particular cave is meant, and there can be little reason to discredit the almost immemorial tradition that it is the hollow still pointed out to hundreds of pilgrims as the scene of the theophany which was here granted to Elijah. Perhaps in the same cave the vision had been granted to Moses, in the scene to which this narrative looks back. It is not so much a cave as, what it is called in Exodus, a "cleft of the rock."[681] From the foot of the mountain, the level space on which now stands the monastery of Saint Katherine, a steep and narrow pathway through the rocks leads up to Jebel Mousa, the southernmost peak of Sinai, which is seven thousand feet high. Half-way up this mountain is a little secluded plain in the inmost heart of the granite precipice, in which is an enclosed garden, and a solitary cypress, and a spring and pool of water, and a little chapel. Inside the chapel is shown a hole, barely large enough to contain the body of a man. "It is," says Dr. Allon, "a temple not made with hands, into which, through a stupendous granite screen, which shuts out even the Bedouin world, God's priests may enter to commune with Him."[682]

If, indeed, Elijah had heard by tradition the vision of Moses of which this was the scene, he must have been filled with awful thoughts as he rested in the same narrow fissure, and recalled what had been handed down respecting the manifestation of Jehovah to his mighty predecessor.

4. And as God had pointed out to him the way to restore his bodily strength by sleep and food, so now He opened before the Prophet the remedy of renewed activity. The question of the Lord came to him—it was re-echoed by the voice of his own conscience—"What doest thou here, Elijah?"

"What doest thou?" He was doing nothing! He had, indeed, fled for his life; but was all the rest of his life to be so different from its beginning? Was there, indeed, no more work to be done in Israel or in Judah, and was he tamely to allow Jezebel to be the final mistress of the situation? Was one alien and idolatrous woman to overawe God's people Israel, and to snatch from God's prophet all the fruits of his righteous labours? "What doest *thou* here, Elijah?" Is not the very significance of thy name "Jehovah, He is my God"? Is He to be the God but of one fugitive? "What doest thou *here*?" This is the wilderness. There are no idolaters or murderers, or breakers of God's commandments here; but are there not multitudes in the crowded cities where Baal's temple towers over Samaria, and his sun-pillars cast their offensive shadows? Are there not multitudes in Jezreel, where the queen's Asherah-shrine amid its guilt-shrouding trees flings its dark protection over unhallowed orgies committed in the name of religion? Should there not have been inspiration as well as reproof in the mere question? Should it not mean to him, "Why art thou cast down, O my soul? and why art thou so disquieted within me? Put thy trust in God, for I will yet praise Him, who is the health of my countenance, and my God"?

5. The question stirred the heart of Elijah, but did not yet dispel his sense of hopelessness and frustration, nor did it restore his confidence that God would govern the world aright. As yet it only called forth the heavy murmur of his grief. "I have been very jealous for Jehovah the God of Hosts": I, alone among my people; "for the children of Israel" —not the wicked queen only, with her abominations and witchcrafts, but the renegade people with her— "have forsaken Thy covenant," which forbids them to have any God but Thee, and have "thrown down Thine altars,[683] and slain Thy prophets with the sword; and I, even I only, am left; and they seek my life, to take it away." It was as it were an appeal to Jehovah before whom he stood, if not almost a reproach to Him. It was as though he said, "I have done my utmost; I have failed: wilt not Thou put forth Thy power and reign? I am but one poor hunted prophet alone against the world. There is no prophet more: not one is there among them that understandeth any more. I can do no more. Of what use is my life? Carest Thou not that Thy people have revolted from Thee? Behold they perish; they perish, they all perish! Of what use is my life? My work has failed: let me die!"

6. God dealt with this mood as He has done in all ages, as He had done before to Jacob, as He did afterwards to David and to Hezekiah, and to Isaiah and Jeremiah; and as the Son of God did to the antitype of Elijah—the great forerunner—when his faith failed him. He let the conviction steal into his mind that the ways of God are wider than men, and His thoughts greater than men's. He unteaches His prophet the delusion that everything depends on *him*. He shows him that though He works for men by men, and though

> "God cannot make best man's best
> Without best men to help Him,"

still no living man is necessary, nor can any man, however great, either hasten or understand the purposes of God.

Elijah had need to be taught that man is nothing—that God is all in all. Instead of answering his complaint, the voice said to him: "Go forth to-morrow, and stand upon the mount before the Lord. Behold, the Lord is passing by."[684]

CHAPTER XLII
THE THEOPHANY AND ITS SIGNIFICANCE

1 Kings xix. 9-15

"Who heardest the rebuke of the Lord in Sinai, and in Horeb the judgment of vengeance." — Ecclus. xlviii. 7.

Throughout the Scriptures infinite care is taken to preclude every notion that the Most High God can be represented in visible form. He manifested Himself at Sinai to the children of Israel, but though the mount burned with fire, and there were clouds and thick darkness, and the voice of a trumpet speaking long and loud, the people were reminded with the utmost solemnity that "they saw no manner of similitude."[685] Indeed, in later times, when there was a keener jealousy of every anthropomorphic expression, the giving of the law is rather represented as a part of the ministry of angels. The word *Makom*, or "Place," is substituted for Jehovah, so that Moses and the elders and the Israelites do not see God but only His *Makom*, the space which He fills;[686] the delivery of the law is ascribed to angelic ministers. At times the angels are almost identified with the careering flames and rushing winds which a modern theologian describes to us as being "the skirts of their garments, the waving of their robes"; for is it not written, "He that maketh the winds His angels and the flaming fires His ministers"?[687] And in the daring description of Jehovah's visible manifestation of Himself to Moses, when He hid him in that fissure of the rock with the hollow of His hand, Moses only observes as it were the fringe and evanishment of His glory, "dark with excessive light."

It was natural that Jehovah should reveal Himself to Elijah under the aspect of those awful elemental forces with which his solitary life had made him familiar. No spot in the world is more suitable for those powers in all their fire and magnificence than the knot of mountains which crowd the Sinaitic peninsula with their entangled cliffs. Travellers have borne witness to the overwhelming violence and majesty of the storms which rush and reverberate through the granite gorges of those everlasting hills. It was in such surroundings that Jehovah spoke to the heart of his servant.

First "a great and strong wind rent the mountains, and brake in pieces the rocks, before the Lord."[688] The winds of God, which blow where they list, and we know not whence they come nor whither they go, have in them so awful and irresistible a strength, that man and the works of man, are reduced to impotence before them. And when they rush and roar through the gullies of innumerable hills in tropic lands where the intense heat has rarefied the air, the sound of them is beyond all comparison weird and terrific. We cannot wonder that this roar of the hurricane was regarded as the trump of the archangel and the voice of God at Sinai; or that the Lord answered Job out of the whirlwind;[689] and appeared to Ezekiel in a great cloud and a whirlwind out of the north;[690] or that Jeremiah compared His anger to a whirling and sweeping storm;[691] or that the Psalmist describes Him as bowing the heavens and coming down and casting darkness under His feet, and flying upon a cherub, and walking upon the wings of the wind;[692] or that Nahum says, "The Lord hath His way in the whirlwind and the storm, and the clouds are the dust of His feet, ... and the mountains quake at Him."[693]

And Elijah felt the terror of the scene, as the storm dislodged huge masses of the mountain granite, and sent them rolling and crashing down the hills. But it did not speak to his inmost heart: for

"The Lord was not in the wind."

And after the wind an earthquake shook the solid bases of the Sinaitic range. The mountain saw God and trembled. The Lord, in the language of the Psalmist, shook the wilderness of Kadesh, the mountains skipped like rams and the little hills like young sheep.[694] And man never feels so abjectly helpless, he is never reduced to such absolute insignificance, as when the solid earth beneath him, the very emblem of stability, trembles as with a palsy, and cleaves beneath his feet; and shakes his towers to the earth, and swallows up his cities. Once more the soul of Elijah shuddered at the terrific impression of this sign of Jehovah's power. But it had no message for his inmost heart: for

"The Lord was not in the earthquake."

And after the earthquake a fire. Jehovah overwhelmed the Prophet's senses with the dread magnificence of one of those lurid thunderstorms of which the terrors are never so tremendous as in such mountain scenes, where travellers tell us that the burning air seems transfused into sheets of flame. In that awful muttering and roar of the lurid clouds, that millionfold reverberation of what the Psalmist calls "the voice of the Lord," when the lightnings "light the world, and run along the ground," and, in the language of Habakkuk, "God sends abroad His arrows, and the light of His glittering spear, and burning coals go forth under His feet, the lips of man quiver at the voice, and his heart sinks, and he trembles where he stands." And this, too, Elijah must have felt as "the hiding-place of God's power:"[695] and yet it did not speak to his inmost heart; for

"The Lord was not in the fire."

"And after the fire a still small voice."

However the rendering may be altered into "a gentle murmuring sound," or, as in the Revised Version, "a sound of gentle stillness," no expression is more full of the awe and mystery of the original than the phrase "a still small voice."[696] It was the shock of awful stillness which succeeded the sudden cessation of the earthquake and hurricane and thunderstorm, and instantly, in it appalling hush and gentleness, Elijah felt that God was there; and he no sooner heard that voiceful silence speaking within him than he was filled with fear and self-abasement. He wrapped his face in his mantle, even as Moses "was afraid to look upon God." He came from the hollow of the rock which had sheltered him amidst that turbulence of material forces, and stood in the entering in of the cave.

At once the silence became articulate to his conscience, and repeated to him the reproachful question, "What doest thou here, Elijah?"

Amazed and overwhelmed as he is, he has not yet grasped the meaning of the vision. Something of it perhaps he saw and felt. It breathed something of peace into the despair and tumult of his heart, but he still can only answer as before:—

"I have been very jealous for the Lord God of hosts: because the children of Israel have forsaken Thy covenant, thrown down Thine altars, and slain Thy prophets with the sword; and I, I only, am left; and they seek my life, to take it away."

Whatever that theophany had taught him, it had not yet fully removed his perplexity. But now God, in tender forbearance, unfolds at any rate the practical issue of the vision. Elijah is to be inactive no longer. He is to find in faithfulness and work the removal of all doubts, and is to learn that man may not abandon his duties, even when they are irksome, even when they seem hopeless, even when they have become intolerable and full of peril. He has to learn that it is only when men have finished their day's work that God sends them sleep, and that his own day's work was as yet unfinished. He is no longer to linger in the wilderness apart from the ways of guilty and suffering men. He is one with them: he may not separate his destiny from theirs; he has to feel that God has no favourites and is no respecter of persons, but that all men are His children, and that each child of His must work for all. "Go," the Lord said unto him, "return on thy way by the wilderness to Damascus." Did the return involve unknown dangers? Still he must commit his way unto the Lord, and simply be doing good, regardless of all consequences. The saints of the Old Dispensation no less than of the New had to go forth bearing their cross, and on their way to Golgotha.

Three missions still awaited him.

First, he is to supersede the old dynasty of Benhadad, King of Syria, founded by Solomon's enemy, and to anoint Hazael to be king over Syria.

Next, he is to abolish the dynasty of Omri, and to anoint Jehu, the son of Nimshi, to be king over Israel.[697]

Thirdly—and there was deep significance in this behest, and one which must have humiliated to the dust the risings of pride and the half-reproach, so to speak, for inadequate support which had underlain his appeal to Jehovah—he is to anoint Elisha, the son of Shaphat, of Abel-meholah, to be prophet in his room.

Elijah had thought himself necessary—an indispensable agent for the task of delivering Israel from the guilty and demoralising apostasy of Baal-worship. God teaches him that there is no such thing as a necessary man; that man at his best estate is altogether vanity; that God is all in all; that "God buries His workmen, but continues His work."

And something of the meaning of these tasks is explained to him. The people of Israel are not yet converted. They still needed the hand of chastisement. The three years' drought had been ineffectual to wean them from their backslidings, and turn their hearts again to the Lord. On the royal house and on the worshippers of Baal should fall the remorseless sword of Jehu. On the whole nation the ruthless invasions of Hazael should press with terrible penalty. And him that escaped from their avenging missions should Elisha slay. The last clause is enigmatical. Elisha can hardly be said directly to have slain any. He lived, on the whole, in friendship with the kings both of Israel and of Aram, and in peace and honour in the cities. But the general idea seems to be that he would carry on the mission of Elijah alike for the guidance and the heaven-directed punishments of kings and nations, and that the famines, raids, and humiliations which rendered his nation miserable under the sons of Ahab should be elements of his sacred mission.[698]

One more revelation remained to lift the Prophet above his lower self. His cry had been, again and again: "I, I only, am left; and they seek my life, to take it away." He must not indulge the mistaken fancy that the worship of the true God would die with him, or that God needed his advice, or that God was slack concerning His promise as some men count slackness. He was not the only faithful person left, nor would truth perish when he was called away. Nor is he to judge only by outward appearances, nor to suppose that the arm of God can be measured by the finger of man. A new prophet is soon to take his place, but God has not been so neglectful as he supposes,—"Yet," in spite of all thy murmurings of failure and a frustrated purpose—"yet will I leave Me"—not *thee, thee only*—"but *seven thousand* in Israel, all the knees which have not bowed unto Baal, and every mouth which has not kissed him."[699]

It has been regarded as a difficulty that Elijah fulfilled but one of the three behests. But Scripture does not narrate events with the finical and pragmatic accuracy of modern annals. Elisha, directly or indirectly, caused both Jehu to be anointed and Hazael to ascend the throne of Syria, and we are left to infer that in these deeds he carried out the instructions of his Master.

It is a more serious question, What was the exact meaning of the theophany granted to Elijah on the Mount of God?

Here, too, we are left to large and liberal applications. The greatest utterances of men, the loftiest works of human genius, often admit of manifold interpretations, and lend themselves to "springing and germinal developments." Far more is this the case in the revelations of God to the spirit of man. We can see the main truths which were involved in that mighty scene, even if the narrator of it leaves unexplained its central significance.

It is usually interpreted as a reproof to the spirit which led Elijah to regard the tempestuous manifestations of wrath and vengeance as the normal methods of the interposition of God. He was fresh from the stern challenge of Carmel; his hands were yet red with the blood of those four hundred and fifty priests. It was perhaps needful for him to learn that God's gentler agencies are more effectual and more expressive of His inmost nature, and that God is Love even though He can by no means clear the guilty. Something of this lesson has been at all times learnt from the narrative.[700]

> "The raging fire, the roaring wind,
> Thy boundless power display;
> But in the gentler breeze we find
> Thy Spirit's viewless way.

> "The dew of heaven is like Thy grace,
> It steals in silence down;
> But where it lights, the favoured place
> By richest fruits is known."

Quite naturally men have always seen in the storm, the earthquake, and the fire, the presence of God as manifested in His wrath. "Then the earth shook and trembled," says the Psalmist; "the foundations also of the hills moved and were shaken, because He was wroth. There went up a smoke in His nostrils, and fire out of His mouth devoured: coals burnt forth from it. He bowed the heavens also, and came down: and darkness was under His feet. And He rode upon a cherub, and swooped down: yea, He did fly upon the wings of the wind."[701] "I will shake the heavens, and the earth shall remove out of her place, at the wrath of the Lord."[702] "Thou shalt be visited," says Isaiah, "of the Lord of Hosts with thunder, and with earthquake, and great noise, with storm and tempest, and the flame of devouring fire."[703] On the other hand, in His mercy God "maketh the storm a calm." When He reveals Himself in a vision of the night to Eliphaz the Temanite "a wind passed before my face, so that the hair of my head stood up, and there was silence, and I heard a voice saying, Shall mortal man be great before God? shall a man be pure before his Maker?" These passages in no small measure explain the symbolism of Elijah's vision, and point to its essential significance. Who can measure (asks Mr. Ruskin) the total effect produced upon the minds of men by the phenomenon of a single thunderstorm?—"the questioning of the forest leaves together in their terrified stillness which way the wind shall come—the murmuring together of the Angels of Destruction as they draw in the distance their swords of flame—the rattling of the dome of heaven under the chariot wheels of death?" Yet it is not the thunderstorms nor the hurricanes that have been most powerful in altering the face or moulding the structure of the world, but rather the long continuance of Nature's most gentle influences.

Viewing the vision thus, we may say that it pointed forward to that transcendently greater than Elijah who did not strive, nor cry, nor was His voice heard in the streets. "There is already a gospel of Elijah. He, the farthest removed of all the Prophets from the evangelical spirit and character, had yet enshrined in the heart of his story the most forcible of all protests against the hardness of Judaism, the noblest anticipation of the breadth and depth of Christianity." This view of the passage is taken, with slight modifications, by many, from Irenæus down to Grotius and Calvin, and modern commentators.

Similarly it is a universal law of history that, while some mighty and tumultuous energy may be needed to initiate the first movement or upheaval, the greatest work is done by gentler agencies. As in the old fable, the quiet shining of the sun effects more than the bluster of the storm. Love is stronger than force, and persuasion than compulsion. Mr. J. S. Mill treats it not only as a platitude but as a falsity to assert that truth cannot be suppressed by violence. He says that (for instance) the truths brought into prominence by the Reformation had been again and again suppressed by the brutal tyrannies of the Papacy. But in all these instances has not the truth ultimately prevailed? Is it not a fact of experience that

> "Truth, pressed to earth shall rise again,
> The eternal years of God are hers;
> But error, wounded, writhes in pain
> And dies among her worshippers"?

The truth prevails and the error dies under the slow light of knowledge and by the long results of time.

Nor is it any answer to this view of the revelation to Elijah on the Mount of God that there is not the slightest proof of his having learnt any such lesson, or of such a lesson having been deduced from it by the narrator himself. Neither Elijah, it has been said, nor the writer of the Book of Kings, felt the smallest regret for the avenging deed of Carmel. Their consciences approved of it. They looked on it with pride, not with compunction. This is shown by the subsequently recorded story of Elijah's calling down fire from heaven on the unfortunate captains and soldiers of Ahaziah, in whatever light we regard that story which was evidently current in the Schools of the Prophets. If the massacre of the priests cannot be regarded as morally excusable, the destruction of these royal emissaries by consuming fire was certainly much less so. The vision may have had a deeper significance than Elijah or the Schools of the Prophets understood, just as the words of Jesus often had a deeper significance than was dreamt of even by the Apostles when they heard them. The foolishness of God is wiser than men, and the weakness of God is stronger than men. Neither Elijah nor the sacred historian may have grasped all that was meant by the wind, and earthquake, and fire, and still small voice.

> "As little children sleep and dream of heaven,
> So thoughts beyond their thoughts to those high bards
> were given."

It is scarcely more than another aspect of the many-sided truth that love is more potent and more Divine than violence, if we also see in this incident a foreshadowing of the truth, so necessary for the impatient souls of men that God neither hasteth nor resteth; that He is patient because Eternal; that a thousand years in His sight are but as yesterday, seeing that it is past as a dream in the night. Something of this we learn from the study of nature. It used to be thought that the upheaval of the continents and the rearing of the great mountains was due to cataclysms and conflagrations and vast explosions of volcanic force. It has long been known that they are due, on the contrary, to the inconceivably slow modifications produced by the most insignificant causes. It is the age-long accumulation of mica-flakes which has built up the mighty bastions of the Alps. It is the toil of the ephemeral coral insect which has reared whole leagues of the American Continent and filled the Pacific Ocean with those unnumbered isles

"Which, like to rich and various gems, inlay
The unadorned bosom of the deep."

It is the slow silting up of the rivers which has created vast deltas for the home of man. It has required the calcareous deposit of millions of animalculæ to produce even one inch of the height of the white cliffs along the shores. Even so the thoughts of man have been made more merciful in the slow course of ages, and quiet, incommensurable influences have caused all those advances in civilisation and humanity which elevate our race. The "bright invisible air" has produced effects incomparably more stupendous than the wild tornadoes. "That air, so gentle, so imperceptible, is more powerful, not only than all the creatures that breathe and live by it, not only than all the oaks of the forest which it rears in an age and shatters in a moment, not only than the monsters of the sea, but than the sea itself, which it tosses up with foam and breaks upon every rock in its vast circumference; for it carries in its bosom all perfect calm, and compresses the incontrollable ocean and the peopled earth, like an atom of a feather."[704]

"Thus regarded," says Professor Van Oort, "the picture of Elijah at Mount Horeb is full of consolation to all lovers of the truth. Sometimes they cry, All is lost! and are ready to despair. But God answers, Never lose heart. Storms in which God is not, in which the power of darkness seems to sweep unbridled and unconquered o'er the earth, come before the whispering of the cooling breeze, but the kingdom of peace and blessedness is ever drawing nigh. Let all who love God truly, work for its 'approach.'"

Let us then cling to the lesson that mercy is better than sacrifice, and is transcendently to be preferred to holocausts of human sacrifice, even when the victims are polluted and cruel idolaters. Scripture never hides from us the imperfections of its heroes, and St. James tells us that Elijah was but a man of like passions with ourselves. The progress of the generations, the slow shining of the light of God, has not been in vain, and we can see truths and read the meaning of theophanies by the experience of three subsequent millenniums, of which two have followed the incarnation of the Son of God.

CHAPTER XLIII
THE CALL OF ELISHA

1 Kings xix. 19-21.

"The one remains, the many change and pass;
Heaven's light alone remains, earth's shadows flee."
Shelley.

Whether Elijah saw or saw not all that God had meant by the revelation at Horeb, much at any rate was abundantly clear to him, and the path of new duties lay straight before him.

The first of those duties—the only one immediately possible—was to anoint Elisha as prophet in his room, and so prepare for the continuation of the task which he had been chosen to inaugurate. He had been bidden to return across the wilderness in the direction of Damascus. Whether he traversed the eastern side of Jordan among his own familiar hills of Gilead, and then crossed over at Bethshean, where there was a ford, or whether, braving an danger from Jezebel and her emissaries, he passed through the territories of the western tribes, it is certain that we find him next at Abel-meholah, "the meadow of the dance," which was not far from Bethshean. [705] This, as he knew, was the home of Elisha, his future successor.

The position of Elisha was wholly unlike his own. He himself was a homeless Bedawy, bound to earth by no ties of family, coming like the wind and vanishing like the lightning. Elisha, on the other hand, whose history was to be so different and so far less stormy—Elisha, whose work and whose residence was mainly to be in cities—was a child of civilisation. But the civilisation was still that of a society in which anarchic forces were by no means tamed. Dean Stanley, in his sketch of Elisha, seems to dwell too much on his gentleness of spirit. He, too, had to carry out the anointing of Hazael and Jehu. "He was still less capable than Elijah," says Ewald, "of inaugurating a purely benign and constructive mode of action, since at that time the whole spirit of the ancient religion was still unprepared for it."

Elijah found him in the heritage of his fathers, ploughing the rich level land with twelve yoke of oxen. Eleven were with his servants, and he himself guided the twelfth.[706] Elijah must have felt that the youth would have to make a great earthly sacrifice, if he left all this—father and mother and home and lands—to become the disciple and attendant of a wild, wandering, and persecuted prophet. He would say nothing to him. He merely left the high road, and "passed over unto him," as he plowed his fields.[707] Reaching him he took off his shaggy garment of skin, which, in imitation of him, became in after years the normal garb of prophets, and flung it over Elisha's shoulders. This apparently was all the "anointing" requisite, save such as came from the Spirit of God. The act had a twofold symbolism: it meant the adoption of Elisha by Elijah to be his "*mantelkind*," his spiritual son; and it meant a distinct call to the prophetic office.

At first Elisha seems to have stood still—amazed almost stupefied, by the sudden necessity for so tremendous a decision. The thought of resigning all the hopes and comforts of ordinary life and of severing so many dear and lifelong ties, could not be unmixed with anguish. Again and again we see in the call of the prophets this natural shrinking, the human reluctance born of humility, frailty, and misgiving. It was so that Moses at the burning bush had at first fought to the utmost against the conviction of his destiny. It was so that Gideon had pleaded that he was but the least of the children of Abiezer. It was thus that, in later days, Jonah fled from the face of the Lord to Tarshish; and Isaiah cried, "Woe is me, for I am a man of unclean lips"; and Jeremiah wailed, "Ah, Lord God! behold, I cannot speak, for I am a child!" And if we may allude to modern instances we know the shrinking hesitations of Luther; and how Cromwell affirmed that he had prayed to God not to put him to his terrible work; and how Wesley hesitated long before he "made himself vile" by preaching in the open air to the Kingswood colliers; and how Father Matthew shrank from his great temperance efforts, till one day, rising from long prayer, and at last convinced of his destined task, he uttered the homely resolve, "In the name of God here goes!"

Elisha did not hesitate long. The mysterious Prophet of Carmel— he whose voice was believed to have shut up the heavens, he who had confounded king and priest and people at Carmel—had spoken no word. He had only flung over Elisha the garment of hair, and then stridden back to the road, and gone on his way without once looking back. Soon he would have vanished beyond recall. Elisha decided that he would obey the call of God; that he would not make "the great refusal." He ran after Elijah, and overtook him, and, accepting the position to which he had been elevated, made but the one human natural request that he might be suffered first to kiss—that is, to bid final farewell to—his father and mother, and then he would follow Elijah.

The request has often been compared to that of the young scribe who said to Jesus, "Lord, suffer me first to bury my father"; to whom Jesus replied, "Let the dead bury their dead: follow thou Me." But the two petitions are not really analogous. The scribe practically asked that he might stay at home till his father died; and as that was an uncertain term, and the ministry of Christ was very brief, the delay was incompatible with such discipleship as Christ then required. There was no such indefinite postponement in Elisha's petition. It showed in him a tender heart, not a reluctant purpose or a wavering will.

"Go back again," answered Elijah; "for what have I done to thee?"

The words are often explained as a veiled yet severe rebuke, as though Elijah had meant to say with scorn, "Go back; perhaps you are not fit for the high call; you do not understand the significance of what I have done;" or, at any rate, "Go back; yet beware of being softly led away from the path of duty; for consider how deep is the meaning of what I have done to thee."

The words involve no such disapprobation, nor does the context agree with that view of them. I can detect no accent of reproof in the words. Elijah, as is shown by several incidents in his career, had room for tenderness and human affection in his rugged lonely heart. I understand his reply to mean, "Go back; it is right, it is natural that thou shouldst thus bid a last farewell before leaving thy home. Thy coming to me must be purely voluntary; I have but cast my mantle over thee, nothing more. Thine own conscience alone can interpret the full meaning of the act, and God will make thy way clear before thy face."

Such, I believe, was Elijah's free permission. He was no hard Stoic, unnaturally trampling on the sweet affections of the soul. He was no despotic spiritual guide full of gloomy superstition, like the grim Spaniard, Ignatius Loyola, who seemed to hold that God liked even our needless anguish, and our voluntary self-tortures as an acceptable sacrifice to Himself. When St. Francis Xavier, on the journey of the first Jesuits to Rome, passed quite near the castle of his parents and ancestors, the teachings of Loyola would not suffer the young noble to turn aside to print one last kiss upon his mother's cheek. Such hard exactions belong to that sphere of will-worship and voluntary humility which St. Paul condemns. Excessive violence needlessly inflicted on our innocent affections finds no sanction either in ancient Judaism or genuine Christianity.

And it was thus that Elisha understood the Prophet. He went back, and kissed his father and mother, and, like Matthew when he left his toll-booth to follow Christ, he made a great feast to his dependents, kinsfolk, and friends. To mark his complete severance from the happy past he unyoked his pair of oxen, slew them, used the plough and goad and wooden yokes as fuel, boiled the flesh of the oxen, and invited the people to his farewell feast. Then he arose, and went after Elijah, and ministered unto him. He was thenceforth recognised as a son of the prophetic schools, and as their future head. For the present he became known as "Elisha, who poured water on the hands of Elijah." His subsequent career belongs entirely to the Second Book of Kings.

CHAPTER XLIV
AHAB AND BENHADAD

1 Kings xx. 1-30

In the Septuagint and in Josephus the events narrated in the twentieth chapter of the Book of Kings are placed after the meeting of Elijah with Ahab at the door of Naboth's vineyard, which occupies the twenty-first chapter in our version. This order of events seems the more probable, but no chronological data are given us in the long but fragmentary details of Ahab's reign. They are, in fact, composed of different sets of records, partly historical, partly prophetic, and partly taken from some special monograph on the career of Elijah. Here, too, we may observe that some most important details are altogether omitted, and that we only learn them (1) from the inscription of King Mesha, and (2) from the clay tablets of Assyria.

1. As regards King Mesha, the monument containing his very interesting annals is generally known as The Moabite Stone. It is a stele of black basalt, 3 feet 10 inches high, 2 feet broad, 14½ inches thick, rounded at the top and bottom almost into a semicircle. The Phœnician inscription is of capital importance both for philology and history. It was first discovered by Mr. Klein, the German missionary of an English society at Dibon, east of the Dead Sea, and it is now at the Louvre. Dibon is now Dibbân.

Mr. Klein in 1868, at Jerusalem, informed Professor Petermann of Berlin of the existence of this ancient relic, and from a few letters of the thirty-four lines which he had copied the Professor at once pronounced that the language employed was Phœnician. When M. Clermont Ganneau, the French consul at Jerusalem, endeavoured to get possession of it, the Bedawin discovered that it was regarded with deep interest by European scholars. They immediately began to quarrel over its possession, and the Arab who had been sent to copy it barely escaped with his life. In their greed and jealousy these modern Moabites "sooner than give it up, put a fire under it, and threw cold water on it, and so broke it, and then distributed the bits among the different families to be placed in the granaries and to serve as blessings upon the corn; for they said that without the stone (or its equivalent in hard cash) a blight would fall upon their crops." Squeezes had been previously taken from it by M. Ganneau and Captain Warren, from which the text has been restored.[708]

It records three great events in the reign of Mesha.

(1) Lines 1-21. Wars of Mesha with Omri and his successors.

(2) Lines 21-31. Public works of Mesha after his deliverance from his Jewish oppressors.

(3) Lines 31-34. His successful wars against the Edomites (or a people of Horonaim), undertaken by command of his god Chemosh. The date of the erection of the monolith is about b.c. 890.

It begins thus:—

"(1) I, Mesha, am son of Chemosh-Gad,[709] King of Moab, (2) the Dibonite. My father reigned over Moab 30 years, and I reigned (3) after my father. And I erected this Stone to Chemosh (a stone of salvation),[710] (4) for he saved me from all despoilers, and let me see my desire upon all my enemies. (5) Now Omri, King of Israel, he oppressed Moab many days, for Chemosh was angry with his (6) land. His son succeeded him, and he also said, I will oppress Moab. In my days he said (Let us go) (7) and I will see my desire on him and his house, and Israel said, I shall destroy it for ever. Now Omri took the land (8) Medeba, and (the enemy) occupied it (in his days and in) the days of his sons, forty years. And Chemosh (had mercy) (9) on it in my days."

He goes on to tell how he built Bael Meon and Kirjathaim; captured Ataroth, and killed all its warriors, and devoted its spoil to Chemosh. "And Chemosh said to me, Go take Nebo against Israel." He took it, slew seven thousand men, devoted the women and maidens to Ashtar-Chemosh, and offered Jehovah's vessels to Chemosh. Then he took Jahas which the king of Israel had fortified, and annexed it to Dibon; built Korcha, its palaces, prisons, etc., Aroer, Bethbamoth, and other towns which he colonised with poor Moabites; and took Horonaim by assault.

There the inscription ends, but not until it has given us some details of a series of bloody wars about which the Scripture narrative is almost entirely silent, though in 2 Kings iii. 4-27 it narrates Mesha's desperate resistance of Israel, Judah, and Edom (b.c. 896).

On this inscription we may briefly remark that for Chemosh-Gad, Dr. Neubauer reads Chemosh-melech, and makes various other changes and suggestions.

2. From the annals of Assyria we learn the altogether unexpected fact that *Ahabu Sirlai, i.e.,* "Ahab of Israel," was acting as one of the allies, or

more probably as one of the vassals, of Syria in the great battle fought at Karkar, b.c. 854, against Shalmanezer II., by Hittites, Hamathites, and Syrians. Whether this was before the invasion of Benhadad, or after his defeat, is uncertain.

The twentieth chapter of the Book of Kings tells us that Benhadad, the Aramæan king, accompanied by thirty-two feudatory princes of Hittites, Hamathites, and others, gathered together all his host with his horses and chariots, and proclaimed war against Israel. Unable to meet this vast army in the field, Ahab shut himself up in Samaria, and Benhadad went up and besieged it. We do not know which Benhadad this was. It could not have been the grandson of Rezon, whom, fourteen years earlier, King Asa had bribed to attack Baasha in order to divert him from building Ramah.[711] It may have been his son or grandson bearing the same religious dynastic name. In any case the policy of attacking Israel was suicidal. If the kings had possessed the prescient glance of the prophets they could not have failed to see on the northern horizon the cloud of Assyrian power, which menaced them all with cruel extinction at the hands of that atrocious people. Their true policy would have been to form an offensive and defensive league, instead of coveting one another's dominions. Although Assyria had not yet risen to the zenith of her empire, she was already formidable enough to convince the King of Damascus that he would never be able single-handed to prevent Syria from being crushed before her. Instead of inflicting ruinous losses and humiliations on the tribes of Israel, the dynasty of Rezon, if it had been wise in its day, would have insured their friendly aid against the horrible common enemy of the nations.

When Benhadad had succeeded in reducing Ahab to hopeless straits, he sent him a herald to demand the admission of ambassadors. Their ultimatum was couched in language of the deadliest insult. Benhadad laid insolent claim to everything which Ahab possessed—his silver, his gold, his wives, and the fairest of his children. To save his people from ruin, Ahab— it is strange that throughout the narrative we do not hear one word either about Jezebel or Elijah—sent an answer of the humblest submission. Tyre gave him no help, nor did Judah. He seems at this time to have been entirely isolated and to have sunk to the nadir of his degradation. "It is true," he said, "my lord, and king; I, and all that I possess, is thine." The depth of humiliation involved in such a concession is the measure of the utter straits to which Ahab was reduced. When an Eastern king had to give up to his conqueror even his seraglio—yes, even his queen—all his power must have been humbled to the very dust. And at the head of Ahab's seraglio was Jezebel. How frenzied must have been the thoughts of that terrible woman, when she saw that her Baal, and the Astarte to whom her father was a priest, in spite of the temple which she had built, and her eight hundred and fifty priests of Baal and Asherah with all their vestments and pompous ceremonies and blood-stained invocations, had wholly failed to save her—a great king's daughter and a great king's wife—from drinking to the very dregs this cup of shame!

Encouraged by this abject demeanour into yet more outrageous insolence, Benhadad sent back his ambassadors with the further menace that he would himself send his messengers next day into Samaria, who should search and rifle not only the palace of Ahab, but the houses of all his servants, from which they should take away everything that was pleasant in their eyes.

The merciless demand kindled in the breast of the wretched king one last spark of the courage of despair. Nothing could be worse than such a pillage. Death itself seemed preferable. He summoned together all the elders of the land to a great council, to which the people also were invited, and he set the state of things before them. The fact gives us an interesting glimpse into the constitution of the kingdom of Israel. It greatly resembled that of the little Greek states in the days of the *Iliad*. Under ordinary circumstances of prosperity the king was within certain limits despotic; but he might easily be reduced to the necessity of consulting a sort of senate (γερουσία), composed of his greatest subjects,[712] and at these open-air deliberations the people were present as assessors on whose will depended the ultimate decision.

Ahab put before his council the desperate condition to which he had been reduced by the Syrian leaguer. He recounted the cruel terms to which he had submitted in order to save his people from destruction. From the second embassage of Benhadad it was clear that the first demand had only been made in the hope that its refusal would give the Syrians an excuse for pressing on the siege, and delivering the city to ravage and slaughter. Was it their will that the insolent foreign tyrant should have his way, and be permitted without let or hindrance to rifle their houses, and carry away their goodliest sons as eunuchs and their fairest wives as concubines? He asked their advice how to overcome this dire calamity;

> "What reinforcement we may gain from hope,
> If not what resolution from despair."

The elders saw that even massacre and pillage could hardly be worse than a tame submission to such demands. They plucked up courage and said to Ahab, "Hearken not to him, nor consent"; and the people shouted their applause to the heroic refusal.[713] The king seems in this instance to have been more despondent than his subjects, perhaps because he was better able than they to gauge the immense military superiority of his invader. Even his second message, though it rejected Benhadad's demand, was almost pusillanimous in its submission. With bated breath and whispering humbleness Ahab said to the Syrian ambassadors, quite in the tone of a vassal: "Tell my lord the king, I *will* submit to his first demands; I *may* not consent to his final ones."

The ambassadors went to Benhadad, and returned with the fierce menace that in the name of his god[714] their king would shatter Samaria into dust, of which the handfuls would not suffice for each of his soldiers. [715] Ahab replied firmly in a happy proverb, "Let not him that girdeth on his armour boast himself as he that putteth it off."[716]

The warning proverb was reported to the Aramæan king, whilst in the insolent confidence of victory he was drinking himself drunk in his war-booths.[717] It nettled him to fury. "Plant the engines," he exclaimed. The catapults and battering-rams,[718] with all the engines which constituted the siege-train of the day, were at once set in motion, the scaling ladders brought up, and the archers set in position, just as we see in the Assyrian Kouyunjik sculptures of the siege of Lachish and other cities by Sennacherib. [719]

Ahab's heart must have sunk within him, for he knew his impotence, and he knew also the horrors which befell a city taken after desperate resistance. But he was not left unencouraged. The characteristic of the prophets was that dauntless confidence in Jehovah which so often made a prophet the Tyrtæus of his native land, unless the land had sunk into utter apostasy. In this extreme of peril a nameless prophet—the Rabbis, who always guess at a name when they can, say it was Micaiah ben Imlah—came to Ahab. As though to emphasise the supernatural character of his communication, he pointed to the chariots and archers and the Syrian host—which, if the subsequent numbers be accurate, must have reached the astounding total of one hundred and thirty thousand men—and said, in the name of Jehovah:—

"Hast thou seen all this great multitude?
Lo! I will deliver it into thine hand to-day:
And thou shalt know that I am the Lord."

"By whom?" was the astonished and half-despairing question of the king; and the strange answer was:—

"By the young servants[720] of the provincial governors."

It was to be made clear that this was a victory due to the intervention of God, and not won by the power nor the might of man, lest the warriors of Israel should be able to boast of the arm of flesh.

"Who shall lead the assault?" asked the king.

"Thou!" answered the prophet.

Nothing could be wiser than this counsel, now that the nation was brought to the extreme edge of hazard. The veterans, perhaps, were intimidated. They would see more clearly the hopelessness of attempting to cope with that colossal host under its five-and-thirty kings. But now the nation, whose veterans had been driven back, evoked the battle-brunt of its youths. The two hundred and thirty-two pages of the district governors were ready to obey orders, ready, like an army of Decii to devote their lives to the cause of their country. They were put in the forefront of the battle, and so pitiable was the depression of the capital that Ahab could only number a paltry army of seven thousand soldiers to stand behind their desperate undertaking.[721]

Their plan was well laid. They went out at noon. At that burning hour, under the intolerable glare and heat of the Syrian sun—and campaigns were only undertaken in spring and summer—it is almost impossible to bear the weight of armour, or to sit on horseback, or to endure the fierce heat of iron chariots. The first little army which issued from the gates of Samaria might rely on the effects of a surprise. Thousands of the Syrian soldiers expecting nothing less than a battle would be unarmed, and taking their siesta. Their chariots and war steeds would be unharnessed and unprepared.

Benhadad was still continuing his heavy drinking bout with his vassal princes, and not one of them was in a condition to give coherent commands. A messenger announced to the band of royal drunkards that "men" were come out of Samaria. They were too few to call them "an army," and the notion of an attack from that poor handful seemed ridiculous. Benhadad thought they were coming to sue for peace, but whether peace or war were their object he gave the contemptuous order to "take them alive."

It was easier said than done. Led by the king at the head of his valorous youths the little host clashed into the midst of the unwieldly, unprepared, ill-handled Syrian host, and by their first slaughter created one of those fearful panics which have often been the destruction of Eastern hosts. The Syrians, whose army was made up of heterogeneous forces, and which could not be managed by thirty-four half-intoxicated feudatories of differing interests and insecure allegiance, was doubtless afraid that internal treachery must have been at work. Like the Midianites, like Zerah's Ethiopian host, like the Edomites in the Valley of Salt, like the Ammonites and Moabites in the wilderness of Tekoa, like the army of Sennacherib, like the enormous and motley hosts of Persia at Marathon, at Platæa, and at Arbela, they were instantly flung into irremediable confusion which tended every moment to be more fatal to itself. The little band of the youths and horses of Israel had nothing to do but to slay, and slay, and slay.[722] No effective resistance was even attempted. Long before evening the hundred and thirty thousand Syrians, with the entangled mass of their chariots and horsemen, were in headlong flight, while Ahab and the people of Israel slaughtered their flying rear. The defeat became an absolute rout. Benhadad himself had a most narrow escape. He could not even wait for his war chariot. He had to fly with a few of his horsemen, and apparently, so the words may imply, on an inferior horse.[723]

What effect was produced on the national mind and on the social religion by this immense deliverance we are not told. Never, certainly, had any nation deeper cause for gratitude to its religious teachers, who alone had not despaired of the commonwealth when everything seemed lost. We would fain know where was Elijah at this crisis, and whether he took any part in it. We cannot tell, but we know that as a rule the sons of the prophets acted together under their chiefs, and that individual impulses were rarely encouraged. The very meaning of the "Schools of the Prophets" was that they were all trained to adopt the same principles and to move together as one body.

The service rendered by this prophet, whose very name has been buried in undeserved oblivion, did not end here. Perhaps he saw signs of carelessness and undue exultation. He went again to the king, and warned him that his victory, immense as it had been, was not final. It was no time for him to settle on his lees. The Syrians would assuredly return the following year,[724] probably with increased resources, and with the burning determination to avenge their defeat. Let Ahab look well to his army and his fortresses, and prepare himself for the coming shock!

CHAPTER XLV
AHAB'S INFATUATION

1 Kings xx. 31-43

"Quem vult Deus perire dementat prius."

The courtiers of Benhadad found it easy to flatter his pride by furnishing reasons to account for such an alarming overthrow. They had attacked the Israelites on their hills, and the gods of Israel were hill-gods. Next time they would take Israel at a disadvantage by fighting only on the plain. Further, the vassal kings were only an element of dissension and weakness. They prevented the handling of the army as one strong machine worked by a single supreme will. Let Benhadad depose from command these incapable weaklings, and put in their place dependent civil officers (*pachoth*) who would have no thought but to obey orders.[725] And so, with good heart, let the king collect a fresh army with horses and chariots as powerful as the last. The issue would be certain conquest and dear revenge.

Benhadad followed this advice. The next year he went with his new host and encamped near Aphek. There is an Aphek (now Fîk) which lay on the road between Damascus on the east of Jordan on a little plain south-east of the Sea of Galilee. This may have been the town of Issachar, in the valley of Jezreel, where Saul was defeated by the Philistines (1 Sam. xxix. 1). Israel went out to meet them duly provisioned.[726] The Syrian host spread over the whole country; the Israelite army looked only like two little flocks of kids.[727]

To strengthen the misgivings of the anxious king of Israel, another nameless prophet—probably, like Elijah, a Gileadite—came to promise him the victory. Jehovah would convince the Syrians that He was something more than a mere local god of the hills as they had blasphemously said, and Israel would once more be shown that He was indeed the Lord.

For seven days the vast army and the little band of patriots gazed at each other, as the Israelites and Philistines had done in the days of Saul and Goliath. On the seventh day they joined battle. In what special way the aid of Jehovah seconded the desperate valour of His people who were fighting for their all we do not know, but the result was, once more, their stupendous victory. The army of the Syrians was not only defeated, but practically annihilated. In round numbers 100,000 Syrians fell in the slaughter of that day, and when the remnant took refuge in Aphek, which they had captured, they perished in a sudden crash—perhaps of earthquake—which buried them in the ruins of its fortifications.[728] Rescued, we know not how, from this disaster, Benhadad fled from chamber to chamber[729] to hide himself from the victors in some innermost recess.

But it was impossible that he should not be discovered, and therefore his servants persuaded him to throw himself on the mercy of his conqueror. "The kings of Israel," they said, "are, as we have heard, compassionate kings; let us go before the king with sackcloth on our loins, and ropes round our necks, and ask if he will save thy life."

So they went, as the burghers of Calais went before Edward I.; and then Ahab heard from the ambassadors of the king who had once dictated terms to him with such infinite contempt, the message: "Thy slave Benhadad saith, I pray thee, let me live."

The incident that followed is eminently characteristic of Eastern customs. In *rencontres* between Orientals everything depends on the first words which are exchanged. It is believed that superior powers wield the utterances of the tongue amid the chances which are really destiny, so that the most casual expression is caught up superstitiously as a sort of Bath Kol, or "the daughter of a voice," which not only indicates but even helps to bring about the purposes of Heaven. A chance friendly greeting may become the termination of a blood feud, because something more than chance is supposed to be behind it![730] Once when a group of doomed gladiators gathered themselves under the Imperial *podium* of the amphitheatre with their sublimely monotonous chant, "*Ave Cæsar, morituri te salutamus*," the half-dazed emperor inadvertently answered, "*Avete vos!*" "He has bidden us, 'Hail!'" shouted the gladiators: "the contest is remitted; we are free!" Had the Romans been Orientals the twenty thousand assembled spectators would have felt the force of the appeal. Even as it was the significance of the omen was felt to be so great that the gladiators threw down their arms, and it was only by whips and violence that they were finally driven to the combat in which they perished.[731]

So with intense eagerness the ambassadors, in their sackcloth and their halters, awaited the Bath Kol. It came far more favourably than they had dared to hope. Surprised, and perhaps half-touched with pity for so immense a reverse of misfortune, "Is he yet alive?" exclaimed the careless king: "he is my brother!"

The Syrians snatched at the expression as a decisive omen.[732] It constituted an absolute end of the feud. It became an implicit promise of that sacred *dakheel*, that "protection" to which the slightest and most accidental expression constitutes a recognised claim.[733] "Thy *brother* Benhadad," they earnestly and emphatically repeated. In accordance with Eastern custom and augury their whole end was gained. As far as Benhadad was concerned he was now safe; as far as Ahab was concerned, the mischief, if mischief it were, was irreparably done.

Ahab could hardly have drawn back even if he wished to do so, but perhaps he was swayed by a fellow feeling for a king. This strange uxorious monarch, with his easily swayed impulses, his fits of schoolboy sullenness and swift repentance, his want of insight into existing conditions, his—if the expression may be excused—happy-go-lucky way of letting questions settle themselves, was, no doubt, a brave warrior, but he was a most incapable statesman. His conduct was perfectly infatuated. Pity is one thing, but the security of a nation has also to be considered. It would have been a worse than insensate piece of pseudo-chivalry if the Congress of Vienna had not sent Napoleon to Elba, and if England had not confined him in St. Helena. To set free a man endowed with passionate hatred, with immense ambitions, with boundless capacities for mischief—or only to bind him with the packthread of insecure promises—was the conduct of a fool.[734] If it was compassion which induced Ahab to give Benhadad his life, it showed either gross incapacity or treachery against his own nation not to clip his wings, and hamper him from the future injuries which the burden of gratitude was little likely to prevent. The sequel shows that Benhadad's resentment against his royal "brother" only became more hopelessly implacable, and in all probability it was largely mingled with contempt.

And Ahab's conduct, besides being foolish, was guilty. It showed a frivolous non-recognition of his duties as a theocratic king. It flung away the national advantages, and even the national security, which had not been vouchsafed to any power or worth of his, but only to Jehovah's direct interposition to save the destinies of his people from premature extinction.

When Benhadad came out of his hiding-place, Ahab, not content with sparing the life of this furious and merciless aggressor, took him up into his chariot, which was the highest honour he could have paid him, and accepted the excessively easy terms which Benhadad himself proposed. The Syrians were not required to pay any indemnity for the immense expenditure and unutterable misery which their wanton invasions had inflicted upon Israel! They simply proposed to restore the cities which Benhadad's father had taken from Omri, and to allow the Israelites to have a protected bazaar in

Damascus similar to the one which the Syrians enjoyed in Samaria.[735] On this covenant Benhadad was sent home scatheless, and with a supineness which was not so much magnanimous as fatuous, Ahab neglected to take hostages of any kind to secure the fulfilment even of these ridiculously inadequate terms of peace.

Benhadad was not likely to throw away the chance which gave him such an easy-going and improvident adversary. It is certain that he did not keep the covenant. He probably never even intended to keep it. If he condescended to any excuse for breaking it, he would probably have affected to regard it as extorted by violence, and therefore invalid, as Francis I. defended the forfeiture of his parole after the battle of Pavia. The recklessness with which Ahab had reposed in Benhadad a confidence, not only undeserved, but rendered reckless by all the antecedents of the Syrian king, cost him very dear. He had to pay the penalty of his dementation three years later in a new and disastrous war, in the loss of his life, and the overthrow of his dynasty. The fact that, after so many exertions, and so much success in war, in commerce, and in worldly policy, he and his house fell unpitied, and no one raised a finger in his defence, was doubtless due in part to the alienation of his army by a carelessness which flung away in a moment all the fruits of their hard-won victories.[736]

There was one aspect in which Ahab's conduct assumed an aspect more supremely culpable. To whom had he owed the courage and inspiration which had rescued him from ruin, and led to the triumphs which had delivered him and his people from the depths of despair? Not in the least to himself, or to Jezebel, or to Baal's priests, or to any of his captains or counsellors. In both instances the heroism had been inspired and the success promised by a prophet of Jehovah. What would convince him, if this would not, that in God only was his strength? Did not the most ordinary gratitude as well as the most ordinary wisdom require that he should recognise the source of these unhoped-for blessings? There is not the least trace that he did so. We read of no word of gratitude to Jehovah, no desire to follow the guidance of the prophets to whom he was so deeply indebted, and who had proved their right to be regarded as interpreters of God's will. Had he done this he would not have suffered the clannishness of royalty to plunge him into a step which was the chief cause of his final destruction.

He might ignore guidance, but he could not escape reproof. Again an unknown monitor from the sons of the prophets was commissioned to bring home to him his error. He did so by an acted parable, which gave concrete force and vividness to the lesson which he desired to convey. Speaking "by the word of the Lord"—*i.e.*, as a part of the prophetic inspiration which dictated his acts—he went to one of his fellows in the school of which the members are here first called "the sons of the prophets," and bade him to wound him. His comrade, not unnaturally, shrank from obeying so strange a command. It must be borne in mind that the mere appeal to an inspiration from Jehovah did not always authenticate itself. Over and over again in the prophetic books, and in these histories which the Jews call "the earlier prophets," we find that men could profess to act in Jehovah's name, and even perhaps to be sincere in so doing, who were mere dupes of their own wills and fancies. It was, in fact, possible for them to become false prophets, without always meaning to be so; and these chances of hallucination—of being misled by a lying spirit—led to fierce contentions in the prophetic communities. "Since you have not obeyed Jehovah's voice," said the man, "the lion shall immediately slay you." "And as soon as he was departed from him the lion found him and slew him." There is nothing impossible in the incident, for in those days lions were common in Palestine, and they multiplied when the country had been depopulated by war. But we can never feel certain how far the ethical and didactic and parabolic elements were allowed, for purposes of edification, to play a part in these ancient yet not contemporaneous *Acta Prophetarum*, and at any rate to dictate the interpretation of things which may have actually occurred.

The prophet then bade another comrade to smite him, and he did so effectually, inflicting a serious wound.[737] This was a part of the intended scene in which the prophet meant for a moment to play the *rôle* of a soldier who had been wounded in the Syrian war. So he bound up his head with a bandage,[738] and waited for the king to pass by. An Eastern king is liable at any time to be appealed to by the humblest of his subjects, and the prophet stopped Ahab and stated his imaginary case. "A captain," he said, "brought me one of his war captives,[739] and ordered me to keep him safe. If I failed to do so, I was to pay the forfeit of my life, or to pay as a fine a silver talent. [740] But as I was looking here and there the captive escaped." "Be it so," answered Ahab; "you are bound by your own bargain." Thus Ahab, like David, was led to condemn himself out of his own mouth. Then the prophet tore the bandage from his face, and said to Ahab: "Thou art the man! Thus saith Jehovah, I entrusted to thee the man under my ban (*cherem*),[741] and thou hast let him escape. Thou shalt pay the forfeit. Thy life shall go for his life, thy people for his people."

Anger and indignation filled the heart of the king; he went to his house "heavy and displeased." The phrase, twice applied to him and never used of another, shows that he was liable to characteristic moods of overwhelming sullenness, the result of an uneasy conscience, and of a rage which was compelled to remain impotent. It is evident that he did not dare to chastise the audacious offender, though the Jews say that the prophet was Micaiah, the son of Imlah, and that he was imprisoned for this offence.[742] As a rule the prophets—like Samuel and Nathan, and Gad and Shemaiah, and Jehu the son of Hanani—were protected by their sacrosanct position. Now and then an Urijah, a Jeremiah, a Zechariah son of Berechiah, paid the penalty of bold denunciation, not only by hatred and persecution, but with his life. This, however, was the exception. As a rule the prophets felt themselves safe under the wing of a Divine protector. Not only Elijah in his sheepskin mantle, but even the humblest of his imitators in the prophetic schools might fearlessly stride up to a king, seize his steed by the bridle, as Athanasius did to Constantine, and compel him to listen to his rebuke or his appeal.

CHAPTER XLVI
NABOTH'S VINEYARD

1 Kings xxi. 1-29

"The triumphing of the wicked is short, and the joy of the godless is but for a moment." —Job xx. 5.

"If weakness may excuse,
What murderer, what traitor, parricide,
Incestuous, sacrilegious, but may plead it?
All wickedness is weakness."
Samson Agonistes.

The chief glory of the institution of prophecy was that it rightly estimated the supremacy of the moral law. The prophets saw that the enforcement of one precept of righteousness involved more true religion than hundreds of pages of Levitic ritual. It is the temptation of priests and Pharisees to sink into formalism; to warp the conceptions of the Almighty into that of a Deity who is jealous about inconceivable pettinesses of ceremonial; to think that the Eternal cares about niceties of rubric, rules of ablutions, varieties of nomenclature or organisation. In their solicitude about these nullities they often forget, as they did in the days of Christ, the weightier matters of the law, mercy, judgment, and truth. When religion has been dwarfed into these inanities the men who deem themselves its only orthodox votaries, and scorn all others as "lax" and "latitudinarian," are not only ready to persecute every genuine teacher of righteousness, but even to murder the Christ Himself. They come to think that falsehood and cruelty cease to be criminal when practised in the cause of religious intolerance.

Against all such dwarfing perversion of the conceptions of the essential service which man owes to God the prophets were called forth to be in age after age the energetic remonstrants. It is true that they also had their own special temptations; they, too, might become the slaves of shibboleths; they might sink into a sort of automatic or mechanical form of prophecy which contented itself with the wearing of garbs and the repetition of formulæ long after they had become evacuated of their meaning.[743] They might distort the message "Thus saith Jehovah" to serve their own ends.[744] They might yield to the temptations both of individual and of corporate ambition. They might assume the hairy garb and rough locks of Elijah for the sake of the awe they inspired while their heart "was not but for their own covetousness."[745] They might abuse their prestige to promote their own party or their own interests. They were assailed by the same perils to which in after days so many monks, hermits, and religious societies succumbed. Many a man became a nominal prophet, as many a man became a monk, because the office secured to him a maintenance—

> "'Twas not for nothing the good belly-ful,
> The warm serge and the rope that goes all round,
> And day long blessed idleness besides;"

and also because it surrounded him with a halo of imaginary sanctity. The monks, we know, by their turbulence and partisanship, became the terror of the fourth century after Christ, and no men more emphatically denounce their mendicancy and their impostures than the very fathers who, like St. Jerome and St. Augustine, were most enamoured of their ideal. [746] As for the hermits, if one of them securely established a reputation for abnormal austerities he became in his way as powerful as a king. In the stories even of such a man as St. Martin of Tours[747] we detect now and then a gleam of hauteur, of which traces are not lacking in the stories of these nameless or famous prophets in the Book of Kings.

No human institution, even if it be avowedly religious, is safe from the perilous seductions of the world, the flesh, and the devil. Perpetually

> "The old order changeth, giving place to new,
> And God fulfils Himself in many ways
> Lest one good custom should corrupt the world."

Mendicant brotherhoods and ascetic communities were soon able, by legal fictions, to revel in opulence, to steep themselves in luxury, and yet to wield a religious authority which princes envied. When we read what the Benedictines and the Minorites and the Carthusians often became, we are the less surprised to find that even the Schools of the Prophets, while Elijah and Elisha yet lived, could abdicate as a body their best functions, and, deceiving and deceived, could learn to answer erring kings according to their idols.

But the greatest and truest prophets rose superior to the influences which tended to debase the vulgar herd of their followers, in days when prophecy grew into an institution and the world became content to side with a church which gave it no trouble and mainly spoke in its own tones. True prophecy cannot be made a matter of education, or "tamed out of its splendid passion." The greatest prophets, like Amos and Isaiah, did not come out of the Schools of the Prophets. Inspiration cannot be cultivated, or trained to grow up a wall. "Much learning," says Heraclitus very profoundly, "does not teach; but the Sibyl with maddening lips, uttering things unbeautified, unperfumed, and unadorned, reaches through myriads of years because of God." The man whom God has summoned forth to speak the true word or do the heroic deed, at the cost of all hatred, or of death itself, has normally to protest not only against priests, but against his fellow-prophets also when they immorally acquiesced in oppression and wrong which custom sanctioned.[748] It was by such true prophets that the Hebrews and through them the world were taught the ideal of righteousness. Their greatest service was to uphold against idolatry, formalism, and worldliness, the simple standard of the moral law.

It was owing to such teaching that the Israelites formed a true judgment of Ahab's culpability. The act which was held to have outweighed all his other crimes, and to have precipitated his final doom, was an isolated act of high-handed injustice to an ordinary citizen.

Ahab was a builder. He had built cities and palaces, and was specially attached to his palace at Jezreel, which he wished to make the most delightful of summer residences. It was unique in its splendour as the first palace inlaid with ivory. The nation had heard of Solomon's ivory throne, but never till this time of an "ivory palace." But a palace is nothing without pleasant gardens. The neighbourhood of Jezreel, as is still shown by the ancient winepresses cut out of the rock in the neighbourhood of its ruins, was enriched by vineyards, and one of these vineyards adjoining the palace belonged to a citizen named Naboth.[749] It happened that no other ground would so well have served the purpose of Ahab to make a garden near his palace, and he made Naboth a fair offer for it. "I will give you," he said, "a better vineyard for it, or I will pay you its full value in ingots of silver."[750]

Naboth, however, was perfectly within his rights[751] in rejecting the offer. It was the inheritance of his fathers, and considerations nothing short of sacred—considerations which then or afterwards found a place in the written statutes of the nation—made it wrong in his judgment to sell it. He sturdily refused the offer of the king. His case was different from that of the Jebusite prince Araunah, who had sold his threshing floor to David, and that of Shemer, who sold the Hill of Samaria to Omri.[752]

A sensible man would have accepted the inevitable, and done the best he could to find a garden elsewhere. But Ahab, who could not bear to be thwarted, came into his house "heavy and displeased." Like an overgrown, sullen boy he flung himself on his divan, turned his face to the wall, and would not eat.

News came to Jezebel in her seraglio of her lord's ill-humour, and she came to ask him, "What mutiny in his spirit made him decline to take food?"[753]

He told her the sturdy refusal of Naboth, and she broke into a scornful laugh. "Are you King of Israel?" she asked. "Why this is playing at kinghood![754] It is not the way we do things in Tyre. Arise, eat bread, be merry. *I* will give thee the vineyard of Naboth the Jezreelite."

Did he admire the mannish spirit of the Syrian princess, or did he secretly shrink from it? At any rate he let Jezebel take her own course. With intrepid insolence she at once wrote a letter in Ahab's name from Samaria, and sent it sealed with his signet to the elders of Jezreel.[755] She ordered them to proclaim a fast as though to avert some public calamity, and—with a touch of dreadful malice as though to aggravate the horror of his ruin—to exalt Naboth to a conspicuous position in the assembly.[756] They were to get hold of two "sons of worthlessness," professional perjurers, and to accuse Naboth of blasphemy against God and the king.[757] His mode of refusing the vineyard might give some colourable pretext to the charge. On the testimony of those two false witnesses Naboth must be condemned, and then they must drag him outside the city to the pool or tank with his sons and stone them all.

Everything was done by the subservient elders of Jezreel exactly as she had directed. Their fawning readiness to carry out her vile commands is the deadliest incidental proof of the corruption which she and her crew of alien idolaters had wrought in Israel. On that very evening Jezebel received the message, "Naboth is stoned and is dead." By the savage law of those days his innocent sons were involved in his overthrow,[758] and his property, left without heirs, reverted by confiscation to the crown.[759] "Arise," said the triumphant sorceress, "and take possession of the vineyard you wished for. I have given it to you as I promised. Its owner and his sons have died the deaths of blasphemers, and he crushed under the stones outside Jezreel."

Caring only for the gratification of his wish, heedless of the means employed, hastily and joyously at early dawn the king arose to seize the coveted vineyard. The dark deed had been done at night, the king was alert with the morning light.[760] He rode in his chariot from Samaria to Jezreel, which is but seven miles distant, and he rode in something of military state, for in separate chariots, or else riding in the same chariot, behind him were two war-like youths, Jehu and Bidkar, who were destined to remember the events of that day, and to refer to them four years afterwards, when one had become king and the other his chief commander.[761]

But the king's joy was shortlived!

News of the black crime had come to Elijah, probably in his lonely retreat in some cave at Carmel. He was a man who, though he flamed out on great occasions like a meteor portending ruin to the guilty, yet lived in general a hidden life. Six years had elapsed since the calling of Elisha, and we have not once been reminded of his existence. But now he was instantly inspired to protest against the atrocious act of robbery and oppression, and to denounce upon it an awful retribution which not even Baal-worship had called forth.

Ahab was at the summit of his hopes. He was about to complete his summer palace and to grasp the fruits of the crime which he had allowed the ἀνδϱόβουλον κεὰϱ of his wife to commit. But at the gate of Naboth's vineyard stood the swart figure of the Prophet in his hairy garb. We can imagine the revulsion of feeling which drove the blood to the king's heart as he instantly felt that he had sinned in vain. The advantage of his crime was snatched from him at the instant of fruition. Half in anger, half in anguish, he cried, "Hast thou found me, O mine enemy?"

"I have found thee," said the Prophet, speaking in Jehovah's name. "Thou hast sold thyself to work evil before me, and I will requite it and extinguish thee before me. Surely the Lord saw yesternight the blood of Naboth and the blood of his sons.[762] Thy dynasty shall be cut off to the last man, like that of Jeroboam, like that of Baasha. Where the dogs licked the blood of Naboth, the dogs shall lick thine. The harlots shall wash themselves in the water which thy blood has stained. Him that dieth of thee in the city the dogs shall eat, and him that dieth in the field shall the vultures rend, and the dogs shall eat Jezebel also in the moat of Jezreel."[763]

It is the duty of prophets to stand before kings and not be ashamed. So had Abraham stood before Nimrod, and Moses before Pharaoh, and Samuel before Saul, and Nathan before David, and Iddo before Jeroboam. So was Isaiah to stand hereafter before Ahaz, and Jeremiah before Jehoiachin, and John the Baptist before Herod, and Paul before Nero. Nor has it been at all otherwise in modern days. So did St. Ignatius confront Trajan, and St. Ambrose brave the Empress Justina, and St. Martin the Usurper Maximus, and St. Chrysostom the fierce Eudoxia, and St. Basil the heretic Valens, and St. Columban the savage Thierry, and St. Dunstan our half-barbarous Edgar. So, too, in later days, Savonarola could speak the bare bold truth to Lorenzo the Magnificent, and Knox to Mary Queen of Scots, and Bishop Ken to Charles II. But never was any king confronted by so awful a denunciation of doom. Probably the moment that Elijah had uttered it he disappeared; but could not a swift arrow have reached him from Jehu's or Bidkar's bow? We know how they remembered two reigns later the thunder of those awful words, but they would hardly have disobeyed the mandate of their king had he bidden them to seize or slay the Prophet. Nothing was further from their thoughts. Elijah had become to Ahab the incarnation of his own awakened conscience, and it spoke to him in the thunders of Sinai. He quailed before the tremendous imprecation. We may well doubt whether he even so much as entered again the vineyard of Naboth; never certainly could he have enjoyed it. He had indeed sold himself to do evil, and, as always happens to such colossal criminals, he had sold himself for naught—as Achan did for a buried robe and a useless ingot, and Judas for the thirty pieces of silver which he could only dash down on the Temple floor. Ahab turned away from the vineyard, which might well seem to him haunted by the ghosts of his murdered victims and its clusters full of blood. He rent his clothes, and clad himself in sackcloth, and slept in sackcloth, and went about barefooted with slow steps[764] and bent brow, a stricken man. Thenceforward as long as he lived he kept in penitence and humiliation the anniversary of Naboth's death,[765] as James IV. of Scotland kept the anniversary of the death of the father against whom he had rebelled.

This penitence, though it does not seem to have been lasting, was not wholly in vain. Elijah received a Divine intimation that, because the king troubled himself, the threatened evil should in part be postponed to the days of his sons. The sun of the unfortunate and miserable dynasty set in blood. But though it is recorded that, incited by his Tyrian wife, he did very abominably in worshipping "idol-blocks," and following the ways of the old Canaanite inhabitants of the land, none of his crimes left a deeper brand upon his memory than the judicial seizure of the vineyard which he had coveted and the judicial murder of Naboth and his sons.

How adamantine, how irreversible is the law of retribution! With what normal and natural development, apart from every arbitrary infliction, is the irrevocable prophecy fulfilled: "Be sure your sin will find you out."

> "Yea, he loved cursing, and it came unto him;
> Yea, he delighted not in blessing, and it is far from him;
> Yea, he clothed himself with cursing like as with his
> garment,
> And it came into his bowels like water, like oil into his
> bones."[766]

Ahab had to be taught by adversity since he refused the lesson of prosperity.

> "Daughter of Jove, relentless power,
> Thou tamer of the human breast,
> Whose iron scourge and torturing hour

The bad affright, afflict the best,
Bound in thine adamantine chain
The proud are taught to taste of pain,
And purple tyrants vainly groan
With woes unfelt before, unpitied and alone."

But as for Elijah himself, he once more vanished into the solitude of his own life, and we do not hear of him again till four years later, when he sent to Ahaziah, the son of Ahab, the message of his doom.

CHAPTER XLVII
ALONE AGAINST THE WORLD

1 Kings xxii. 1-40

"I have not sent these prophets, yet they ran: I have not spoken to them, yet they prophesied.... I have heard what the prophets said who prophesied lies in My name."—Jer. xxiii. 21-25.

"Μάντι κακῶν οὐ πώποτέ μοι τὸ κρήγυον εἶπας
Αἰεί τοι τὰ κάκ' ἐστὶ φίλα φρεσὶ μαντεύεσθαι
Ἐσθλὸν δ' οὐδε τί πω εἶπας ἔπος οὐδ' ἐτέλεσσας."
Hom., *Iliad*, i. 106.

We now come to the last scene of Ahab's troubled and eventful life. His two immense victories over the Syrians had secured for his harassed kingdom three years of peace, but at the end of that time he began to be convinced that the insecure conditions upon which he had weakly set Benhadad free would never be ratified. The town of Ramoth in Gilead, which was one of great importance as a frontier town of Israel, had, in express defiance of the covenant, been retained by the Syrians, who still refused to give it up. A favourable opportunity, he thought, had now occurred to demand its cession.

This was the friendly visit of Jehoshaphat, King of Judah. It was the first time that a king of Judah had visited the capital of the kings who had revolted from the dynasty of David. It was the first acknowledged close of the old blood-feuds, and the beginning of a friendship and affinity which policy seemed to dictate. After all Ephraim and Judah were brothers, though Ephraim had vexed Judah, and Judah hated Ephraim. Jehoshaphat was rich, prosperous, successful in war. No king since Solomon had attained to anything like his greatness—the reward, it was believed, of his piety and faithfulness. Ahab, too, had proved himself a successful warrior, and the valour of Israel's hosts had, with Jehovah's blessing, extricated their afflicted land from the terrible aggressions of Syria. But how could the little kingdom of Israel hope to hold out against Syria, and to keep Moab in subjection? How could the still smaller and weaker kingdom of Judah keep itself from vassalage to Egypt and from the encroachments of Philistines on the west and Moabites on the east? Could anything but ruin be imminent, if these two nations of Israel and Judah—one in land, one in blood, one in language, in tradition, and in interests—were perpetually to destroy each other with internecine strife? The kings determined to make a league with one another, and to bind it by mutual affinity. It was proposed that Athaliah, daughter of Ahab and Jezebel, should marry Jehoram, the son of Jehoshaphat.

The dates are uncertain, but it was probably in connexion with the marriage contract that Jehoshaphat now paid a ceremonial visit to Ahab. The King of Israel received him with splendid entertainments to all the people.[767] Ahab had already broached to his captains the subject of recovering Ramoth Gilead, and he now took occasion of the King of Judah's visit to invite his co-operation. What advantages and compensations he offered are not stated. It may have been enough to point out that, if Syria once succeeded in crushing Israel, the fate of Judah would not be long postponed. Jehoshaphat, who seems to have been too ready to yield to pressure, answered in a sort of set phrase: "I am as thou art; my people as thy people; my horses as thy horses."[768]

But it is probable that his heart misgave him. He was a truly pious king. He had swept the Asherahs out of Judah, and endeavoured to train his people in the principles of righteousness and the worship of Jehovah. In joining Ahab there must have been in his conscience some unformulated murmur of the reproof which on his return to Jerusalem was addressed to him by Jehu, the son of Hanani, "Shouldst thou help the ungodly, and love them that hate the Lord? Therefore is wrath upon thee from the Lord." But at the beginning of a momentous undertaking he would not be likely to imitate the godless indifference which had led Ahab to take the most fatal steps without seeking the guidance of God. He therefore said to Ahab, "Inquire, I pray thee, of the word of the Lord to-day."

Ahab could not refuse, and apparently the professional prophets of the schools had been pretty well cajoled or drilled into accordance with his wishes. A great and solemn assembly was summoned. The kings had clothed themselves in their royal robes striped with laticlaves of Tyrian purple,[769] and sat on thrones in an open space before the gate of Samaria. No less than four hundred prophets of Jehovah were summoned to prophesy before them. Ahab propounded for their decision the formal and important question, "Shall I go up to Ramoth Gilead to battle, or shall I forbear?"

With one voice the prophets "philippised." They answered the king according to his idols. Had the gold of Ahab or of Jezebel been at work among them? Had they been in king's houses, and succumbed to courtly influences? Or were they carried away by the interested enthusiasm of one or two of their leaders who saw their own account in the matter? Certain it is that on this occasion they became false prophets. They used their formula "Thus saith Jehovah" without authority, and promised Jehovah's aid in vain.[770] Conspicuous in his evil ardour was one of them named Zedekiah, son of Chenaanah. To illustrate and emphasise his jubilant prophecies he had made and affixed to his head a pair of iron horns; and as though to symbolise the bull of the House of Ephraim, he said to Ahab, "Thus saith Jehovah. With these shalt thou push the Assyrians until thou have consumed them."[771] And all the prophets prophesied so.

What could be more encouraging? Here was a patriot-king, the hero-victor in great battles, bound by fresh ties of kinship and league with the pious descendant of David, meditating a just raid against a dangerous enemy to recover a frontier-fortress which was his by right; and here were four hundred prophets—not Asherah-prophets or Baal-prophets, but genuine prophets of Jehovah—unanimous, and even enthusiastic, in approving his design and promising him the victory! The Church and the world were—as they so often have been—delightfully at one.

"One with God" is the better majority. These loud-voiced majorities and unanimities are rarely to be trusted. Truth and righteousness are far more often to be found in the causes which they denounce and at which they sneer. They silence opposition, but they produce no conviction. They can torture, but they cannot refute. There is something unmistakable in the accent of sincerity, and it was lacking in the voice of these prophets on the popular side. If Ahab was deceived and even carried away by the unwonted approval of so many messengers of Jehovah, Jehoshaphat was not. These four hundred prophets who seemed superfluously sufficient to Ahab by no means satisfied the King of Judah.

"Is there not," he asked, with uneasy misgiving, "one prophet of the Lord besides, that we might inquire of him?"

One prophet of the Lord besides?[772] Were not, then, *four hundred* prophets of the Lord enough? They must have felt themselves cruelly slighted when they heard the pious king's inquiry, and doubtless a murmur of disapproval arose amongst them.

And the King of Israel said, "There is yet one man." Had Jehoshaphat been secretly thinking of Elijah? Where was Elijah? He was living, certainly, for he survived even into the reign (apparently) of Jehoram. But where was Elijah? If Jehoshaphat had thought of him, Ahab at any rate did not care to mention him. Perhaps he was inaccessible, in some lonely unknown retreat of Carmel or of Gilead. Since his fearful message to Ahab he had not been heard of; but why did he not appear at a national crisis so tremendous as this?

"There is yet one man," said Ahab. "Micaiah, the son of Imlah, by whom we may inquire of the Lord; but"—such was the king's most singular comment—"I hate him; for he doth not prophesy good concerning me, but evil."[773]

It was a weak confession that he was aware of one man who was indisputably a true prophet of Jehovah, but whom he had purposely excluded from this gathering because he knew that his was an undaunted spirit which would not consent to shout with the many in favour of the king. Indeed, it seems probable that he was, at this moment, in prison. Jewish legend says that he had been put there because he was the prophet who had reproved Ahab for his folly in suffering Benhadad to escape with the mere breath of a general promise. Till then he had been unknown. He was not like Elijah, and might safely be suppressed. And Ahab, as was universally the case in ancient days, thought that the prophet could practically prophesy as he liked, and not merely prophesy, but bring about his own vaticinations. Hence, if a prophet said anything which he disliked, he regarded him as a personal enemy, and, if he dared, he punished him—just as Agamemnon punished Calchas.

Jehoshaphat, however, was still dissatisfied; he wanted further confirmation. "Let not the king say so," he said. If he is a genuine prophet, the king should not hate him, or fancy that he prophesies evil out of malice prepense. Would it not be more satisfactory to hear what he might have to say?

However reluctantly, Ahab saw that he should have to send for Micaiah, and he despatched a eunuch to hurry him to the scene with all speed.[774]

The mention of a eunuch as the messenger is significant. Ahab had become the first polygamist among the kings of Israel, and a seraglio so large as his[775] could never be maintained without the presence of these degraded and odious officials, who here first appear in the hardier annals of the Northern Kingdom.

This eunuch, however, seems to have had a kindly disposition. He was good-naturedly anxious that Micaiah should not get into trouble. He advised him, with prudential regard for his own interest, to swim with the stream. "See now," he said, "all the prophets with one mouth are prophesying good to the king. Pray agree with them. Do not spoil everything."

How often has the same base advice been given! How often has it been followed! How certain is its rejection to lead to bitter animosity! One of the most difficult lessons of life is to learn to stand alone when all the prophets are prophesying falsely to please the rulers of the world. Micaiah rose superior to the eunuch's temptation. "By Jehovah," he said, "I will speak only what He bids me speak."

He stood before the kings, the eager multitude, the unanimous and passionate prophets; and there was deep silence when Ahab put to him the question to which the four hundred had already shouted an affirmative.

His answer was precisely the same as theirs: "Go up to Ramoth Gilead and prosper, for the Lord shall deliver it into the hand of the king!" Every one must have been astonished. But Ahab detected the tone of scorn which rang through the assenting words, and angrily adjured Micaiah to give a true answer in Jehovah's name. "How many times," he cried, "shall I adjure thee that thou tell me nothing but that which is true in Jehovah's name." The "how many times" shows how faithfully Micaiah must have fulfilled his duty of speaking messages of God to his erring king.

So adjured, Micaiah could not be silent, however much the answer might cost him, or however useless it might be.

"I saw all Israel,"[776] he said, "scattered on the mountain like sheep without a shepherd. And Jehovah said, These have no master, let every man return to his house in peace."

The vision seemed to hint at the death of the king, and Ahab turned triumphantly to his ally, "Did I not tell you that he would prophesy evil?"

Micaiah justified himself by a daringly anthropomorphic apologue which startles us, but would not at all have startled those who regarded everything as coming from the immediate action of God, and who could ask, "Shall there be evil in a city, and the Lord hath not done it?"[777] The prophets were self-deceived, but this would be expressed by saying that Jehovah deceived them. Pharaoh hardens his heart, and God is said to have done it.

He had seen Jehovah on His throne, he said, surrounded by the host of heaven, and asking who would entice Ahab to his fall at Ramoth Gilead. After various answers the spirit[778] said, "I will go and be a lying spirit in the mouths of all his prophets, and will entice him." Then Jehovah sent him, so that they all spoke good to the king though Jehovah had spoken evil. God had sent to them all—king, people, prophets—strong delusion that they should believe a lie.

This stern reproof to all the prophets was more than their coryphæus Zedekiah could endure. Having recourse to "the syllogism of violence" he strode up to Micaiah and smote the defenceless, isolated, hated man on the cheek,[779] with the contemptuous question, "Which way went the spirit of the Lord from me, to speak unto thee?"

"Behold thou shalt know," was the answer, "on the day when thou shalt flee from chamber to chamber to hide thyself." If the hands of the prophet were bound as he came from the prison, there would have been an infinite dignity in that calm rebuke.

But as though the case was self-evident, and Micaiah's opposition to the four hundred prophets proved his guilt, Ahab sent him back to prison. "Issue orders," he said, "to Amon, governor of the city, and Joash, the king's son, to feed him scantily on bread and water till the king's return in peace."

"If thou return at all in peace," said Micaiah, "Jehovah hath not spoken by me."[780]

It is a sign of the extreme fragmentariness of the narrative that of Micaiah and Zedekiah we hear nothing further, though the sequel respecting them must have been told in the original record. But the prophecy of Micaiah came true, and the unanimous four hundred had prophesied lies. There are times when "the Catholic Church" dwindles down to the one man and the small handful of those who speak the truth. The expedition was altogether disastrous. Ahab, perhaps knowing by spies how bitterly the Syrians were incensed against him, told Jehoshaphat that he would disguise himself and go into the battle, but begged his ally to wear his robes as was usual with kings.[781] Benhadad, with the implacable hatred of one who had received a benefit, was so eager to be avenged on Ahab that he had told his thirty-two captains to make his capture their special aim.[782] Seeing a king in his robes they made a fierce onset on Jehoshaphat and surrounded his chariot. His cries for rescue showed them that he was not Ahab, and they turned away.[783] But Ahab's disguise did not save him. A Syrian—the Jews say that it was Naaman[784]—drew a bow with no particular aim,[785] and the arrow smote Ahab in the place between the upper and lower armour.[786] Feeling that the wound was deadly he ordered his charioteer to turn his hands and drive him out of the increasing roar of the *mêlée*. But he would not wholly leave the fight, and with heroic fortitude remained standing in his chariot in spite of agony. All day the blood kept flowing down into the hollow of the chariot. At evening the Syrians had to retire in defeat, but Ahab died. The news of the king's death was proclaimed at sunset by the herald, and the cry was raised which bade the host disband and return home.[787]

They carried the king's body back to Samaria, and they buried it. They washed the blood-stained chariot in the pool outside the city, and there the dogs licked the king's blood, and the harlot-votaries of Asherah bathed in the blood-dyed waters, as Elijah had prophesied.[788]

So ended the reign of a king who built cities and ivory palaces,[789] and fought like a hero against the foes of his country, but who had never known how to rule his own house. He had winked at the atrocities committed in his name by his Tyrian queen, had connived at her idolatrous innovations, and put no obstacle in the way of her persecutions. The people who might have forgotten or condoned all else never forgot the stoning and spoliation of Naboth and his sons, and his death was regarded as a retribution on this crime.

CHAPTER XLVIII
CONCLUSION

It will have been seen that there are two main heroes of the First Book of Kings—Solomon and Elijah. How vast is the gulf which separates those two ideals! In Solomon we see man in all the adventitious splendour which he can derive from magnificent surroundings and from exaltation to a dizzy height above his fellows. Everything that the earth can give him he possesses from earliest youth, yet all turns to dust and ashes under his touch. Wealth, rank, power, splendour cannot ever, or under any circumstances, satisfy the soul. The soul can only be sustained by heavenly food, by the manna which God sends it from heaven in the wilderness. Its divineness can only be maintained by feeding on the Divine. If we think of Solomon, even in his most dazzling hour, we see no element of happiness or of reality in his lonely splendour or loveless home. It is nothing but a miserable pageant. The Book of Ecclesiastes, though written centuries after he had passed away, yet shows sufficiently, as the Eastern legends also show, that mankind was not misled by the glamour which surrounded him into the supposition that he was to be envied. It was felt, whether he uttered it or not, that "Vanity of vanities, vanity of vanities, all is vanity," is the real echo of his weariness. In the famous fiction the Khaliph sees him with the other giant shades on his golden throne at the banquet; but each and all have on their faces an expression of solemn agony, and under the folds of their purple a little flame is ever burning at their hearts.

How different is the rough Prophet of Gilead, the ascetic, in his sheepskin mantle and leathern girdle, who can live for months on a little water and meal baked with oil![790] In him we see the grandeur of manhood reduced to its simplest elements; we see the dignity of man as simply man towering over all the adventitious circumstance of royalty. One who, like Elijah, has no earthly desires, has no real fears. If he flies from Jezebel to save his life, it is only because he is not justified in flinging it away; otherwise he is as dauntless before the *vultus instantis tyranni* as before the *civium ardor prava jubentium*. Hence, Elijah in his absolute poverty, in his despised isolation—Elijah, hunted and persecuted, and living in dens and caves of the earth—is immeasurably greater than Solomon, because he is the messenger of the living God before whom he stands. And his work is immeasurably more permanent and more valuable for humanity than that of all the kings and great men among whom he moved. He believed in God, he fought for righteousness, and therefore he left behind him an unperishable memorial, showing that he who would live for eternity rather than for time is he who best achieves the high ends of his destiny. He may err as Elijah erred, but with the blessing of the Lord he shall not miscarry. Though he go forth weeping, he shall come again with joy, bringing his sheaves with him. Solomon, after his death, almost vanished from the history of Israel into the legends of Arabia. In the New Testament he is but barely mentioned. But Elijah still lives in, and haunts, the memory of his nation. A chair is placed for his invisible presence at every circumcision. A cup is set aside for him at sacred banquets, and all dubious questions are postponed for solution "until the day when Elijah comes." He shone with Moses on the Mount of Transfiguration; and St. James, the Lord's brother, appeals to him as the most striking example of the power of that prayer which

"Moves the arm of Him who moves the world."

NOTE ON THE CHRONOLOGY OF THE FIRST BOOK OF KINGS

I have not thought it worth while to trouble the reader with conjectures or corrections of the text, intended to remove the numerous and obvious discrepancies which the redactor of the Book of Kings leaves uncorrected in his references to the synchronism of the reigns.[791] Many of them are removed or modified when we bear in mind that, *e.g.,* Nadab and Elah and Ahaziah are described as reigning "two years" each (xv. 25, xvi. 8, xxii. 51), whereas the reign of each may not have exceeded a year, or even a few months, if these months came at the end of one year and the beginning of another. Periods of anarchic interregnum, or of association of a son with his father on the throne, may account for other confusions and contradictions; but they are purely conjectural, and in some cases far from probable. Jerome, as is well known, gave up all attempts to harmonise the chronologic data as a hopeless problem. "Relege," he says, "omnes et veteris et novi Testamenti libros, et tantam annorum reperies dissonantiam *ut hujuscemodi hærere quæstionibus non tam studiosi quam otiosi hominis esse videatur.*"

The Assyrians were, for the most part (though, as Schrader shows, not *always*), as scrupulously exact in their chronological details as the Jews were careless in theirs. The cuneiform inscriptions give us the following data, which may be regarded as *points de repère*, and which are not reconcilable with the received dates:—

	b.c.
Battle of Karkar, in which Ahab and Benhadad were defeated	854
Jehu pays tribute to Shalmanezer II.	842
Menahem tributary to Assyria	738
Fall of Samaria	722
Sennacherib's Invasion	701

These dates do not accord with those which we should derive from the Book of Kings in the ordinary system of chronology, which seem to fix the Fall of Samaria in 737.

The dates of the later Kings of Assyria seem to be as follows:—

	b.c.
Rimmon-Nirari III.	810
Shalmanezer III.	781
Assur-dân IV.	771
Tiglath-Pileser III. (Pul, a usurper)	745
Shalmanezer IV.	727
Sargon	722
Sennacherib	705
Esar-haddon I.	681
Assur-bani-pal	668
Destruction of Nineveh	606

Adding up the separate data of this book for the kings of Israel we have from Jeroboam to the death of Joram ninety-eight years seven days; and for the same period of the kings of Judah from Rehoboam to Ahaziah we have ninety-five years. Supposing that some such errors as we have indicated have crept into the computation, the dates of the reigns may be, as reckoned by Kittel:—

	b.c.
Saul	1037-1017
David	1017-977
Solomon	977-937
Jeroboam I.	937-915
Nadab	915-914
Baasha	914-890
Elah	890-889
Zimri	889
Omri	889-877
Ahab	877-855
Ahaziah	855-854
Jehoram	854-842
Rehoboam	937-920
Abijah	920-917
Asa	917-876
Jehoshaphat	876-851

| Joram | 851-843 |
| Ahaziah | 843-342 |

From Phœnician inscriptions (recorded in the *Corpus Inscriptionum Semiticarum*) little of *historical* importance has hitherto been reaped.

In the Egyptian monuments there is nothing which illustrates the period of the Kings except the inscription of Sheshonk recording his invasion in the days of Rehoboam, of which I have given some account.

The Assyrian inscriptions, to which allusion is made in their place, are of extreme importance and interest, and from the lists of kings we have good details of chronology. The best book on their bearing upon Hebrew history is that of Schrader, *Die Keilinschriften und d. Alte Testament*, 1883.

On the datum of four hundred and eighty years from the Exodus to the building of the Temple, I have already touched. It does not agree with Acts xiii. 20, nor with the Book of Judges. The LXX. reads "four hundred and forty." It is almost certainly a late and erroneous chronological gloss derived in very simple fashion, thus:—The wanderings forty years, Joshua forty years, Othniel forty years, Ehud eighty years, Jabin twenty years, Barak forty years, Gideon forty years, the Philistines forty years, Samson twenty years, Samuel forty years, Saul forty years, David forty years = four hundred and eighty, or twelve generations of forty years.

But the same result was arrived at with equal empiricism by omitting the episodes of heathen dominations (Jabin and the Philistines), and only adding up the years assigned to the Judges, and the four years of Solomon's reign before he began to build the Temple, thus:—Othniel forty years, Ehud eighty years, Barak forty years, Gideon forty years, Tola twenty-three years, Jair twenty-two years, Jephthah six years, Ibzan seven years, Elom ten years, Abdon eight years, Samson twenty years = two hundred and ninety-six.

Eli forty years, Samuel twenty years (1 Sam. vii. 15), David forty years, Solomon four = one hundred and four. Add to the four hundred the two generations of the wanderings and Joshua, and we again have four hundred and eighty; but quite as arbitrarily, for the period of Saul is omitted.[792]

The problems of early Hebrew chronology cannot yet be regarded as even approximately solved.

FOOTNOTES:

[1] "Scriptura est sensus Scripturæ." — St. Augustine.

[2] For a decisive proof of these statements I refer to my Bampton Lectures on the *History of Interpretation* (Macmillan, 1890).

[3] Bacon.

[4] How closely these documents are transcribed is shown by the recurrence of *"unto this day,"* though the phrase had long ceased to be true when the book appeared.

[5] It is inferred from 1 Kings viii. 12, 13, which have a poetic tinge, and to which the LXX. add "Behold they are written in the Book of the Song," that in this section the "Book of Jashar" has been utilised, and that the reading רשיה has been confused with רישה (Driver, p. 182).

[6] 2 Chron. xx. 34, R.V., "The history of Jehu, the son of Hanani, which *is inserted in the Book of the Kings of Israel"* (not "who is mentioned," A.V., which, however, gives in the margin the literal meaning "was made to ascend").

[7] Movers, *Krit. Untersuch.*, p. 185 (Bonn, 1836). The use of older documents explains the phrase "till this day," and the passages which speak of the Temple as still standing (1 Kings viii. 8, ix. 21, xii. 19; 2 Kings x. 27, xiii. 23). Sometimes the traces of earlier and later date are curiously juxtaposed, as in 2 Kings xvii. 18, 21 and 19, 20.

[8] Difference of sources is marked by the different designations of the months, which are called sometimes by their numbers, as in the Priestly Codex (1 Kings xii. 32, 33), sometimes by the old Hebrew names Zif (*"blossom,"* April, May, 1 Kings vi. 1), Ethanim (*"fruit,"* Sept., Oct., 1 Kings viii. 2), and Bul (*"rain,"* 1 Kings vi. 38).

[9] הַנָּהָר־זֶמ (compare הָרֲהַנ־רֲבֵע). *Lit.*, *"Beyond* the river," *i.e.*, from the Persian standpoint. It becomes a fixed geographical phrase. Traces of the editor's hand occur in 1 Kings xiii. 32 ("the cities of Samaria"); 2 Kings xiii. 23 ("as yet").

[10] Comp. 2 Kings viii. 25 with ix. 29.

[11] See 2 Kings xv. 30 and 33, viii. 25 and ix. 29.

[12] As, perhaps, the clause "In the thirty and first year of Asa king of Judah" in 1 Kings xvi. 23; and the much more serious "in the 480th year after the children of Israel were come out of the land of Egypt," which are omitted by Origen (*comm. in Johannem*, ii. 20), and create many difficulties. The only narratives which critics have suggested as possible interpolations, from the occurrence of unusual grammatical forms, are 2 Kings viii. 1-6 and iv. 1-37 (in the story of Elisha); but these forms are perhaps northern provincialisms.

[13] *Speaker's Commentary*, ii. 475. Instances will be found in 1 Kings xiv. 21, xvi. 23, 29; 2 Kings iii. 1, xiii. 10, xv. 1, 30, 33, xiv. 23, xvi. 2, xvii. 1, xviii. 2.

[14] Stade, p. 79; Kalisch, *Exodus*, p. 495.

[15] See Keil, pp. 9, 10.

[16] R. F. Horton, *Inspiration*, p. 843.

[17] He was not the author of the Book of Samuel, for the standpoint and style are quite different. In the First and Second Books of Samuel the high places are never condemned, as they are incessantly in Kings (1 Kings iii. 2, xiii. 32, xiv. 23, xv. 14, xxii. 43, etc.).

[18] Baba Bathra, 15 a.

[19] *Seder Olam Rabba*, 20.

[20] Even then he would have been ninety years old.

[21] There are, however, some *differences* between 2 Kings xxv. and Jer. lii. (see Keil, p. 12), though the manner is the same, Carpzov, *Introd.*, i. 262-64 (Hävernick, *Einleit.*, ii. 171). Jer. li. (verse 64) ends with "Thus far are the words of Jeremiah," excluding him from the authorship of chap. lii. (Driver, *Introd.*, p. 109). The last chapter of Jeremiah was perhaps added to his volume by a later editor.

[22] "The Old Testament does not furnish a history of Israel, though it supplies the materials from which such a history can be constructed. For example, the narrative of Kings gives but the merest outline of the events that preceded the fall of Samaria. To understand the inner history of the time we must fill up this outline with the aid of the prophets Amos and Hoshea." —Robertson Smith's *Preface* to translation of Wellhausen, p. vii.

[23] "In der Chronik," on the other hand, "ist es der Pentateuch, d.h. vor Allem der *Priestercodex*, nach dessen Muster die Geschichte des alten Israels dargestellt wird" (Wellhausen, *Prolegom.*, p. 309). It has been said that the Book of Kings reflects the political and prophetic view, and the Book of Chronicles the priestly view of Jewish history. It is about the Pentateuch,

its date and composition, that the battle of the Higher Criticism chiefly rages. With that we are but indirectly concerned in considering the Book of Kings; but it is noticeable that the ablest and most competent defender of the more conservative criticism, Professor James Robertson, D.D., both in his contribution to *Book by Book* and in his *Early Religion of Israel*, makes large concessions. Thus he says, "It is particularly to be noticed that in the Book of the Pentateuch itself the Mosaic origin is not claimed" (*Book by Book*, p. 5). "The anonymous character of all the historical writings of the Old Testament would lead us to conclude that the ancient Hebrews had not the idea of literary property which we attach to authorship". "It is long since the composite character of the Pentateuch was observed". "There may remain doubts as to when the various parts of the Pentateuch were actually written down; it may be admitted that the later writers wrote in the light of the events and circumstances of their own times".

[24] Driver, p. 189. Comp. Professor Robertson Smith: "The most notable feature in the extant redactions of the book is the strong interest shown in the Deuteronomic law of Moses, and especially in the centralisation of worship in the Temple on Zion, as pre-supposed in Deuteronomy and enforced by Josiah. This interest did not exist in ancient Israel, and is quite foreign to the older memories incorporated in the book."

[25] Driver, p. 192.

[26] Delitzsch, *Genesis*, 6th ed., p. 567.

[27] *Geschichte des Volkes Israel*, i. 73.

[28] Even the First Book of Maccabees begins with καὶ ἐγένετο.

[29] Stade thinks that this is confirmed by viii. 46-49.

[30] Stade, pp. 32 ff. Thus, in 1 Kings viii. 14-53, verses 12, 13 are in the Septuagint placed *after* verse 53, are incomplete in the Hebrew text, and have a remarkable reading in the Targum. Professor Robertson Smith infers that a Deuteronomic insertion has misplaced them in one text, and mutilated them in another. The order of the LXX. differs in 1 Kings iv. 19-27; and it omits 1 Kings vi. 11-14; ix. 15-26. It transposes the story of Naboth, and omits the story of Ahijah and Abijah, which is added from Aquila's version to the Alexandrian MS. See Wellhausen-Bleek, *Einleitung*, §§ 114, 134.

[31] See Appendix on the Chronology .

[32] See Wellhausen, *Prolegomena*, pp. 285-87; Robertson Smith, *Journ. of Philology*, x. 209-13.

[33] *Encycl. Brit.*, s.v. Kings (W.R.S.).

[34] See Stade, i. 88-99; W. R. Smith, *l. c.*; Kreuz, *Zeitschr. f. Wiss. Theol.*, 1877, p. 404. Some of the dates, as Dr. W. R. Smith shows, are "traditional," and are probably taken from Temple records (*e.g.*, the invasion of Shishak, and the change of the revenue system in the twenty-third year of Joash). Taking these as data, we have (roughly) 160 years to the twenty-third year of Joash, 160 to the death of Hezekiah, 160 years to the return from the Exile = 480. He infers that "the existing scheme was obtained by setting down a few fixed dates, and filling up the intervals with figures in which 20 and 40 were the main units."

[35] *Speaker's Commentary*, ii. 477.

[36] 1 Kings xiii. 1-32, xx. 13-15, 28, 35, 42; 2 Kings xxi. 10-15.

[37] 2 Kings xvii. 7-23, 32, 41, xxiii. 26, 27.

[38] מִינְוֹשֵׁאר מִיאִיכְבֶן. The three greater and twelve minor prophets are called *prophetæ posteriores* (מִינְוֹרֶחֹא). Daniel is classed among the Hagiographa (מִיבוּתְכֹ). This title of "former prophets" was, however, given by the Jews to the historic books from the mistaken fancy that they were all *written* by prophets.

[39] Martensen, *Dogmatics*, p. 363.

[40] 2 Sam. vii. 12-16; 1 Kings xi. 36, xv. 4; 2 Kings viii. 19, xxv. 27-30. "His object evidently was," says Professor Robertson, "to exhibit the bloom and decay of the Kingdom of Israel, and to trace the influences which marked its varying destiny. He proceeds on the fixed idea that the promise given to David of a sure house remained in force during all the vicissitudes of the divided kingdom, and was not even frustrated by the fall of the kingdom of Judah."

[41] 1 Kings xi. 9-13.

[42] Amos ix. 11, 12.

[43] Psalm lxxxix. 48-50.

[44] 2 Kings xx. 16-18, xxii. 16-20.

[45] Isa. xxx. 16.

[46] *Queen of the Air*, p. 87.

[47] Tac., *Hist.*, 1, 2: "Opus aggredior opimum casibus, atrox prœliis, discors seditionibus, ipsa etiam pace sævum."

[48] Wellhausen, *History of Israel*, p. 432; Stade, *Gesch. des Volkes Israel*, i., p. 12; Robinson, *Ancient History of Israel*, p. 15.

[49] *Od.*, ix. 51, 52.

[50] Acts iv. 27, 28.

[51] 1 Cor. i. 26-28.

[52] *Id.*, v. 25.

[53] Deut. xxvi. 5.

[54] Isa. xxxviii. 17 (Heb.).

[55] See Stade, i. 1-8.

[56] 1 Chron. xxiii. 1.

[57] 2 Sam. v. 5.

[58] It is mentioned by Galen, vii.; Valesius, *De Sacr. Philos.*, xxix., p. 187; Bacon, *Hist. Vitæ et Mortis*, ix. 25; Reinhard, *Bibel-Krankheiten*, p. 171. See Josephus, *Antt.*, VII. xv. 3.

[59] Now Solam, near *Zerin* (Jezreel), five miles south of Tabor (Robinson, *Researches*, iii. 462), on the south-west of Jebel el-Duhy (Little Hermon), Josh. xix. 18; 1 Sam. xxviii. 4.

[60] Æsch., *Sept. c. Theb.*, 690.

[61] See Psalm cxxii. 3-5.

[62] See Kittel, ii. 147.

[63] The same word is rendered "worship" in Psalm xlv. 11. Comp. 2 Sam. ix. 6; Esth. iii. 2-5. In 1 Chron. xxix. 20 we are told that the people *"worshipped"* the Lord and the king.

[64]

> "Μηδὲ βαρβάρου φωτὸς δίκην
> Χαμαιπετὲς βόαμα προσχανῆς ἐμοί."
> Æsch., *Agam.*, 887.

[65] Ecclus. xvi. 1-3. He must have had at least twenty sons, and at least one daughter (2 Sam. iii. 1-5, v. 14-16; 1 Chron. iii. 1-9, xiv. 3-7). Josephus again (*Antt.*, VII. iii. 3) has a different list.

[66] *Kohanim.*

[67] From the fact that his son Eliada (2 Sam. v. 16) is called Beeliada (*i.e.*, "Baal knows") in 1 Chron. xiv. 7, it is surely a precarious inference that "now and then he paid his homage to some Baal, perhaps to please one of his foreign wives" (Van Oort, *Bible for Young People*, iii. 84). The true explanation seems to be that at one time Baal, "Lord," was not regarded as an unauthorised title for Jehovah. The fact that David once had *teraphim*

in his house (1 Sam. xix. 13, 16) shows that his advance in knowledge was gradual.

[68] Chileab was either dead, or was of no significance.

[69] 2 Sam. xiii. 39. "The soul of king David longed to go forth unto Absalom."

[70] Max. Tyr., *Dissert.*, 9 (Keil, *ad loc.*).

[71] In 2 Sam. xv. 7 we should certainly alter "forty" into four.

[72] Rephaim seems a more probable reading than Ephraim in 2 Sam. xviii. 6; see Josh. xvii. 15, 18. Yet the name "Ephraim" may have been given to this transjordanic wood. The notion that he *hung by his hair* is only a conjecture, and not a probable one.

[73] His three sons had pre-deceased him; his beautiful daughter Tamar (2 Sam. xiv. 27) became the wife of Rehoboam. She is called Maachah in 1 Kings xv. 2, and the LXX. addition to 2 Sam. xiv. 27 says that she bore both names. The so-called tomb of Absalom in the Valley of Hebron is of Asmonæan and Herodian origin.

[74] Morier tells us that in Persia "runners" before the king's horses are an indispensable adjunct of his state.

[75] The Stone of Zoheleth, probably a sacred stone—one of the numerous isolated rocks of Palestine; is not mentioned elsewhere. The Fuller's Fountain is mentioned in Josh. xv. 7, xviii. 16; 2 Sam. xvii. 17. It was south-east of Jerusalem, and is perhaps identical with "Job's Fountain," where the wadies of Kedron and Hinnom meet (*Palestine Exploration Fund*, 1874, p. 80).

[76] Comp. 1 Kings i. 9-25.

[77] The same phrase is used of Rehoboam (2 Chron. xii. 13, xiii. 7) when he was twenty-one, reading אך for מ, forty-one.

[78] 2 Sam. xii. 25: "And he sent by the hand of Nathan, the prophet; he called his name Jedidiah, because of the Lord" (A.V.). The verse is somewhat obscure. It either means that David sent the child to Nathan to be brought up under his guardianship, or sent Nathan to ask of the oracle the favour of some well-omened name (Ewald, iii. 168). Nathan was perhaps akin to David. The Rabbis absurdly identify him with Jonathan (1 Chron. xxvii. 32; 2 Sam. xxi. 21), nephew of David, son of Shimmeah.

[79] 1 Chron. xxii. 6-9.

[80] LXX., Σαλωμών, and in Ecclus. xlvii. 13. Comp. Shelōmith (Lev. xxiv. 11), Shelōmi (Num. xxxiv. 27). But it became Σαλόμων in the New

Testament, Josephus, the Sibylline verses, etc. The long vowel is retained in Salōme and in the Arabic Sūleyman, etc.

[81] Among Solomon's adherents are mentioned "Shimei and Rei" (1 Kings i. 8), whom Ewald supposes to stand for two of David's brothers, Shimma and Raddai, and Stade to be two officers of the Gibborim. Thenius adopts a reading partly suggested by Josephus, "Hushai, the friend of David." Others identify Rei with Ira; a Shimei, the son of Elah, is mentioned among Solomon's governors (*Nitzabim*, 1 Kings iv. 18); and there was a Shimei of Ramah over David's vineyards (1 Chron. xxvii. 27). The name was common, and meant "famous."

[82] Duncker, Meyer, Wellhausen, Stade, regard Solomon's accession as due to a mere palace intrigue of Nathan and Bathsheba, and David's dying injunctions as only intended to excuse Solomon. They treat 1 Kings ii. 1-12 as a Deuteronomic interpolation. Dillmann, Kittel, Kuenen, Budde, rightly reject this view. Stade says, "Nach menschlichen Gefühl, ein Unrecht war die Salbung Salomos." He thinks that "the aged David was over-influenced by the intrigues of the harem and the court" (i. 292).

[83] She said that they would be counted as "offenders" (*chattaim*) Comp. 1 Kings i. 12, where Nathan assumes that they will both be put to death. Thus Cassander put to death Roxana, the widow of Alexander the Great, and her son Alexander (Justin., xv. 2).

[84] Reuss, *Hist. des Israelites*, i. 409.

[85] Comp. 2 Sam. iv. 9; Psalm xix. 14.

[86] "The servants of your Lord." Comp. 2 Sam. xx. 6, 7.

[87] Comp. Gen. xli. 43; 1 Kings i. 33; Esth. vi. 8.

[88] 2 Chron. xxxii. 30, xxxiii. 14. It was apparently "the Virgin's Fountain," east of Jerusalem, in the Valley of Jehoshaphat.

[89] Comp. 2 Kings ix. 13.

[90] 1 Chron. xxvii. 5, where the true rendering is not "Benaiah the chief priest," as in A.V., nor "principal officer," as in the margin: but "Benaiah the priest, as chief."

[91] 1 Sam. xxx. 14; Josephus, σωματοφύλακες. The Targum calls them "archers and slingers" (which is unlikely), or "nobles and common soldiers." This body-guard is also said to be composed of Gittites (2 Sam. xv. 18, xviii. 2); but some suppose that they were so called not by nationality, but because they had served under David at Gath. The question is further complicated by the appearance of "Carians" (A.V., captains) in 2 Kings xi. 4, 15, and also

in 2 Sam. xx. 23 (Heb.). The Carians were universal mercenaries (Herod., ii. 152; Liv., xxxvii. 40). That there was an early intercourse between Palestine and the West is shown by the fact that such words as peribolory, machaera, macaina, lesche, pellex, have found their way into Hebrew (see Renan, *Hist. du Peuple Israel*, ii. 33).

[92] 2 Sam. xxiii. 8-39; 1 Chron. xi. 10-47; 1 Kings i. 8. The Gibborim are by some supposed to be a different body from the Krêthi and Plêthi (2 Sam. xv. 18, xx. 7); but from 1 Kings i. 8, 10, 38 they seem to be the same (Stade, i. 275). The thirty heroes at their head furnish, as Renan says, the first germ of a sort of "Legion of Honour."

[93] Saul (1 Sam. x. 1), David (1 Sam. xvi. 13, and twice afterwards, 2 Sam. ii. 4, v. 3), Jehu (1 Kings xix. 16), Joash (2 Chron. xxiii. 11).

[94] 1 Kings i. 39. "Tent," not "tabernacle," as in A.V. It has generally been supposed that Zadok took it from the tabernacle at Gibeon (1 Chron. xvi. 39), but there would have been no time to send so far. Zadok is called a "Seer" in the A.V. (2 Sam. xv. 27); but the true version may be "Seeth thou?" The LXX. and Vulgate omit the words.

[95] Morier, quoted by Stanley, p. 172, says that the Mustched, or chief priest, and the Munajem, or prophet, are always present at a Persian coronation.

[96] LXX., ἐῤῥάγη, ἤχησεν; Vulg., insonuit. Comp. Josephus, *Antt.*, VII. xiv. 3, 5.

[97] 2 Sam. xv. 27, xvii. 17.

[98] 2 Sam. xviii. 27. Heb., אִישׁ־חַיִל; LXX., ἀνὴρ δυνάμεως; Vulg., vir fortis. It is rather "virtuous," as in Prov. xii. 4.

[99] It is true that Solomon's adherents had wasted no time over a feast.

[100] 1 Kings i. 50.

[101] Psalm cxviii. 27, and Exod. xxvii. 2 ff., xxix. 12, xxx. 10. Comp. Exod. xxi. 14.

[102] Exod. xxi. 14. It protected the homicide, but not the wilful murderer.

[103] 1 Kings i. 51. The words "this day" should be "first of all," *i.e.*, before I leave the sanctuary. Many must have been reminded of this scene when Eutropius, the eunuch-minister of Arcadius, under the protection of St. Chrysostom, cowered in front of the high altar at Constantinople.

[104] "There shall not a hair of him fall." Comp. 1 Sam. xiv. 45; 2 Sam. xiv. 11.

[105] "Bowed himself." Comp. 1 Kings i. 47.

[106] Grätz, i. 138 (E. T.).

[107] 2 Sam. xxiii. 1-7. It is no part of my duty here to enter into the extent of David's share in the Psalms; but I think that it is an exaggerated inference (of Wellhausen and others) from Amos vi. 5, 6 to suppose that he only wrote festal and warlike songs.

[108] Apparently an allusion to Deut. xvii. 18-20. We read of no such exhortation having been addressed to Saul, or to David.

[109] Chimham accompanied David to Jerusalem (2 Sam. xvii. 27, xix. 37-40), and perhaps inherited his property at Bethlehem, where he founded the Khan (Jer. xli. 17), in the cavern stable of which it may be that Christ was born.

[110] Wellhausen, Stade, and others venture on the conjecture that David never gave these injunctions at all, but that they were invented afterwards to excuse Solomon for his acts of severity towards Adonijah's conspirators. I cannot see any valid ground for such arbitrary re-writing of the history. Shimei had taken no part in Adonijah's rebellion.

[111] Zeruiah was "a sister of the sons of Jesse" (1 Chron. ii. 16), and was therefore a sister of Abigail, mother of Amasa; but she is called "the daughter of *Nahash*" (2 Sam. xvii. 25).

[112] 1 Chron. ii. 17. "Jether (*i.e.*, Jethro, 'pre-eminence') the Ishmaelite" has been altered in 2 Sam. xvii. 25 into Ithra, an *Israelite* (see 2 Sam. xix. 13). The way in which names have been tampered with is an interesting study, and often conceals Masoretic secrets.

[113] David's enemies thought but little of the fact that David had spared Mephibosheth. They may have supposed that David spared him, not only because he was the son of the beloved Jonathan, but because being lame he could never become king. David's relations to him do not seem to have been very cordial.

[114] 2 Sam. xvi. 14 (Heb.). For Bahurim, see 2 Sam. xvi. 5, xvii. 18.

[115] Acts xvii. 30.

[116] Matt. v. 43, 44.

[117] There is something analogous to protection *granted only for a lifetime* in the fact that the homicide at a refuge city could not be slain there while the high priest lived. See Num. xxxv. 28.

[118] Comp. Josh. xxiii. 14; Keil, *ad loc.*

[119] Acts ii. 29. Josephus says that both Hyrcanus and Herod opened it to find the treasures which legend asserted to have been buried there (*Antt.*, VII. xv. 3. Comp. XIII. viii. 4, XVI. vii.). The kings alone were buried in Jerusalem; but legend says that an exception was made in favour of Huldah the prophetess.

[120] These events—like almost everything derogatory to David and Solomon—are omitted by the chronicler.

[121] Luke iii. 31. Salathiel, son of Neri (Luke iii. 27), of Nathan's house, was probably adopted by Jeconiah, who was childless; or if he had a son Assir (captive), the son had died. 1 Chron. iii. 17; Isa. xxii. 3.

[122] 2 Sam. xii. 8. Comp. 1 Kings xx. 7; 2 Kings xxiv. 15. We only know, however, of one wife of Saul, and one concubine.

[123] Herod., iii. 68; Justin., x. 2.

[124] Comp. 1 Kings xv. 13; 2 Kings xi. 1. The queen-mother, like the Sultana Walidé, is always more powerful than even the favourite wife.

[125] Cant. iii. 11.

[126] Psalm xlv. 9. Some little mystery evidently hangs over the name of Bathsheba. In 2 Sam. xi. 3 she is called "Bathsheba, the daughter of Eliam, the wife of Uriah the Hittite"; but in 1 Chron. iii. 5 she is called "*Bathshua*, the daughter of *Ammiel*." Now Shua was a Canaanite name (Gen. xxxviii. 12; 1 Chron. ii. 3), and it is at least remarkable that Bathsheba should be married to a Hittite. Further, the chronicler disguises "Ahithophel the Gilonite (the father of Eliam) into Ahijah the Pelonite," who is one of David's Gibborim in 1 Chron. xi. 36. Pelonite means *nescio qius*; in Spanish, Don Fulano,—Signor So-and-so. And how are we to account for the strange name Ahithophel ("brother of foolishness?")?

[127] Comp. Cant. vii. 1. It has been assumed that Solomon had already married Naamah the Ammonitess, and that Rehoboam was already born (see 1 Kings xiv. 21), but this is uncertain. Rehoboam, if he had reached the age of forty-one, could hardly have been called "young and tender-hearted" (2 Chron. xiii. 7).

[128] Shunem (Sulem, Euseb., *Jer.*) is now *Solam* (Robinson, *Researches*, iii. 402).

[129] 1 Sam. xxii. 23.

[130] 2 Sam. xv. 18 (LXX.).

[131] *Anata*, Robinson, *Researches*, ii, 319; Josh. xxi. 18; 1 Chron. vi. 60. It was the native town of Jeremiah (Jer. i. 1).

[132] It should be remembered that, as Ewald points out, imprisonment for life was a thing unknown.

[133] This interesting addition is found in the Septuagint version.

[134] 2 Sam. xxiii. 20. Ewald, Thenius, and most other critics, followed by the R.V., adopt the LXX. reading, "Slew the two sons of Ariel of Moab."

[135] Comp. 2 Kings xi. 15.

[136] See Deut. xix. 13.

[137] 2 Sam. iii. 28, 29.

[138] הַנָּאָו הֲנָא (1 Kings ii. 36).

[139] It should be remembered that when Shimei came to meet David on his return, he managed to muster one thousand of his Benjamite kinsmen. Such local influence might prove troublesome.

[140] Achish seems to have been the dynastic name of the kings of Gath (1 Sam. xxi. 10, xxvii. 2). If this was the Achish, son of Maoch, with whom David had taken refuge fifty years before, he must now have been a very old man.

[141] Esth. ii. 5.

[142] Prov. xix. 11, xx. 2, 8, 26.

[143] 1 Kings ii. 7; Jer. xli. 17.

[144] Lev. x. 1-20; Num. iii. 4, xxvi. 61. This has been not unnaturally inferred from the prohibition to the priests to drink wine while serving the tabernacle lest they die, which occurs immediately after the catastrophe of the two priests (Lev. x. 9-11).

[145] 1 Chron. vii. 4-15. In David's time there were only eight descendants of Ithamar, but sixteen of Eleazar (1 Chron. xxiv. 4). For full discussion of these priestly genealogies, see Lord A. Hervey, *On the Genealogies*, pp. 277-306. It is true that they are not free from elements of difficulty, but I am unable to find any valid ground for the suspicion of some critics that Zadok was not even a priest, or of the priestly house at all. All the evidence we have points in the opposite direction.

[146] Num. xxv. 13.

[147] 2 Chron. xxxiii. 6; 2 Kings xxi. 6. "His children."

[148] 2 Chron. xxviii. 3; 2 Kings xvi. 3. "His son."

[149] 1 Sam. ii. 27-36. For eight centuries there was no other instance of a high priest's deposition.

[150] Isa. iii. 10.

[151] See 1 Sam. xxi. 6, compared with 1 Chron. xvi. 39, 40; 2 Chron. i. 3.

[152] An old Hivite capital (Josh. xviii. 21-25), now El Jib. Josephus alters it to "Hebron."

[153] See 1 Chron. xvi. 39, 40, xxi. 29; 2 Chron. i. 3. The annals of Solomon fall into three divisions: first, his secure establishment upon the throne (1 Kings i, ii.); next, his wisdom, wealth, glory, and great buildings, especially the building of the Temple (iii.-x.); lastly, his fall and death (xi.).

[154] It was sufficiently sanctioned by Exod. xx. 24, and Jerusalem was not yet chosen (Deut. xii. 13, 14). See Judg. vi. 24, xiii. 19; 1 Sam. ix. 12, etc. This seems to have been the last great sacrifice there. In 1 Kings iii. 5-15 the sacrifice is regarded with approval; in verses 2, 3 it is condemned, but excused by circumstances; in the verses inserted by the chronicler (2 Chron. i. 3-6) it is said that the Tabernacle was there.

[155] See 1 Sam. xxii. 17-19.

[156] Herod., vii. 43. Xerxes offered one thousand at Troy, and Crœsus three thousand at Delphi (*Id.*, i. 50).

[157] Hence, perhaps, the LXX. rendering of Δήλωσις καὶ Ἀλήθεια. This view is accepted by Hengstenberg (*Egypt and the Five Books of Moses*, chap. vi.), and Kalisch (on Exod. xxviii. 31).

[158] Arist., *Eth. Nic.*, i. 13: "βελτίω τὰ φαντάσματα τῶν ἐπιεικῶν ἢ τῶν τυχόντων."

[159] Bishop Hall.

[160] "Εὕδουσα γὰρ φρὴν ὄμμασιν λαμπρύνεται."—Æsch., *Eum.*, 104.

[161] Ecclus. xv. 16, 17.

[162] Emerson.

[163] The phrase "a little child" (comp. Jer. i. 6) hardly bears on his actual age. See Gen. xliii. 8; Exod. xxxiii. 11. It is proverbial like the subsequent phrase, for which see Deut. xxviii. 6; Psalm cxxi. 8, etc.

[164] Heb., "A hearing heart." LXX., "A heart to hear and judge Thy people in righteousness." In 2 Chron. i. 10, "Wisdom and knowledge."

[165] Matt. vi. 33.

[166] Josephus (*Antt.*, VIII. vii. 8) makes him die at ninety-four, and become king at fourteen. Perhaps he mistook μ′ for π′ in the LXX.

[167] Psalm cxxvii. 2 (uncertain).

[168] 1 Sam. viii. 6, 20; 2 Sam. xv. 4. "To rule was with the ancients the synonym of to judge." Artemidorus, *Oneirocr.*, ii. 14. (Bähr, *ad loc.*).

[169] Compare the Phœnician's *Suffetes* (Liv.).

[170] As instances of the lower sense in which the term "wisdom" was applied, see 2 Sam. xiii. 3 (Jonadab); xiv. 2 (the woman of Tekoa); xx. 16 (the woman of Abel of Beth-maachah).

[171] The Rabbis call them "innkeepers," as they call Rahab.

[172] I follow the not improbable additional details given by Josephus from tradition.

[173] יֶלֶד. LXX., παιδίον.

[174] So the Greek version, which represents the clause rightly. Tradition narrates a yet earlier specimen of Solomon's wisdom. Some sheep had strayed into a pasture. The owner of the land demanded reparation. David said that to repay his loss he might keep the sheep. "No," said Solomon, who was but eleven years old, "let him keep them only till their wool, milk, and lambs have repaid the damage; then let him restore them to their owner." David admitted that this was the more equitable judgment, and he adopted it. See The Qur'an, *Sura* xxi. 79 (Palmer's Qur'an, ii. 52).

[175] The parallel is adduced by Grotius.

[176] Quoted by Bähr.

[177] Suet., *Claud.*, 15.

[178] For references to animals, etc., see Prov. vi. 6, xxiv. 30-34, xxx. 15-19, 24-31; Josephus, *Antt.*, VIII. ii. 5; Ecclus. xlvii. 17.

[179] See Isa. xix. 11, xxxi. 2; Acts vii. 22; Herod., ii. 160; Josephus, *Antt.*, VIII. ii. 5 (Keil).

[180] See 1 Chron. ii. 6, vi. 44, xv. 17, 19, xxv. 5. Titles of Psalms xviii., lxxxviii., lxxxix. "Ezrahite," perhaps, is a transposition of Zerahite.

[181] 1 Chron. ii. 6. In *Seder Olam* they are called "prophets who prophesied in Egypt."

[182] "Sons of Mahol" (comp. Eccles. xii. 4).

[183] Psalms lxxii., cxxvii. The so-called "Psalms of Solomon," fifteen in number, are of the Maccabean age; Josephus calls his songs βίβλια περὶ ᾠδῶν καὶ μελῶν, and his proverbs βίβλους παραβολῶν καὶ εἰκόνων.

[184] See Euseb., *Præp. Evang.*, ix. 34, § 19.

[185] Prov. xi. 22, xxiv. 30-34, xxv. 25, xxvi. 8, xxx. 15.

[186] *E.g.*, Prov. vi. 10.

[187] 1 Kings x. 1; LXX., ἐν αἰνίγμασι. See Wünsche, *Die Räthselweisheit*, 1883; Grätz, *Hist. of the Jews*, i. 162. For specimens of her traditional puzzles see the author's *Solomon*, p. 135 (Men of the Bible).

[188] "And Solomon was David's heir, and said, Ye folk! we have been taught the speech of birds, and we have been given everything: verily this is a Divine grace" (Qur'an, *Sura* xxvii. 15). For the legend of Solomon and the hoopoes, see *Sura* 27.

[189] According to Suidas (s.v., Ἐζεκίας) Hezekiah found his (magic?) formulæ for the cure of diseases engraved on the posts of the Temple. See Targum on Esth. i. 2; Eccles. ii. 8.

[190] Job xxviii. 23, 28.

[191] Prov. i. 7.

[192] Ecclus. xlvii. 13-18.

[193] Josephus, *Antt.*, VIII. vii. 8. According to one tradition he lived to fifty-three (Ewald, iii. 208), and was only twelve when he succeeded David.

[194] 2 Chron. viii. 3. Ewald thinks it is confirmed by 2 Kings xiv. 28, where, however, the Hebrew is obscure.

[195] 1 Kings x. 26.

[196] 1 Kings ix. 18. Here the "Q'rî," the marginal, or "read" text, has Tadmor (*i.e.*, Palmyra), as also in 2 Chron. viii. 4. But this Tamar (Ezek. xlvii. 19, xlviii. 28) is *"in the land"* on the south border. In the Chronicles Tadmor is the right reading, for the chronicler is speaking of Hamath-Zobah and the north. It is not at all unlikely that Solomon also built Tadmor (Josephus, *Antt.*, VIII. vi. 1) to protect his commerce on the route to the Euphrates.

[197] The forty-fifth psalm is supposed by old interpreters to have been an epithalamium on this occasion, but was probably much later. Perhaps notices like 1 Kings iii. 1-3 (the Egyptian alliance), the admonition in 1 Kings ix. 1-9 and the luxury described in x. 14-29, are meant as warning notes of what follows in xi. 1-8 (the apostasy), 9-13 (the prophecy of disruption), and 14-43 (the concluding disaster).

[198] Gezer is Abu-Shusheh, or Tell-el-Gezer, between Ramleh and Jerusalem (Oliphant, *Haifa*, p. 253), on the lower border of Ephraim. Ewald identifies it with Geshur, the town of Talmai, Absalom's grandfather. See

Lenormant, *Hist. anc. de l'Orient.*, i. 337-43. The genealogy of this dynasty is thus given by Brugsch-Bey (Gen. Table iv.), *Hist. of Egypt*, vol. ii.:—

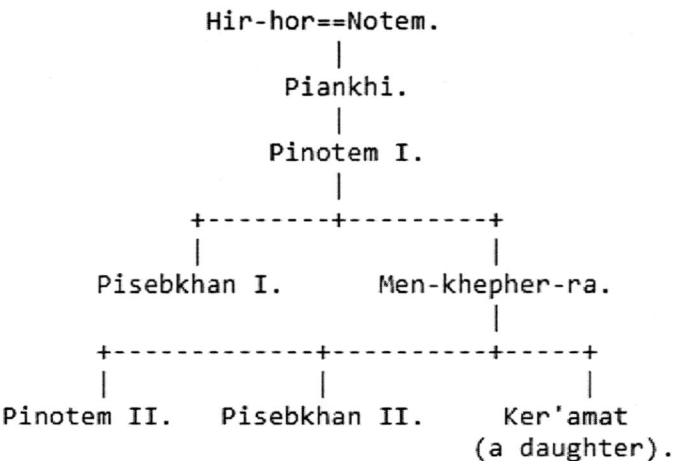

```
              Hir-hor==Notem.
                    |
                 Piankhi.
                    |
                Pinotem I.
                    |
        +--------+--------+
        |                 |
   Pisebkhan I.     Men-khepher-ra.
                          |
        +------------+---------+-----+
        |            |               |
  Pinotem II.   Pisebkhan II.    Ker'amat
                                (a daughter).
```

[199] See Deut. xxiii. 7, 8.

[200] Schwab's *Berakhoth*, p. 252; Hershon, *Treasures of the Talmud*, p. 25. In Sanhedrin, ff. 21, 22, there is another trace of the dislike with which the marriage (though not forbidden, Deut. xxiii. 7, 8) was regarded: "When Solomon married the daughter of Pharaoh, Gabriel descended and fixed a reed in the sea. A sandbank formed around it on which *Rome* was subsequently built." In Shabbath, ff. 51, 52, we are told that "the princess brought with her one thousand different kinds of musical instruments, and *taught Solomon the chants to his various idols.*"

[201] No trace of any such misgiving is found in the Book of Kings.

[202] "Seine Liebhaberei sind kostbare Bauten, fremde Weiber, reiche Prachtentfaltung" (Kittel, ii. 160).

[203] Perhaps rather "the grandson." He was the son of Ahimaaz (comp. Gen. xxix. 5; Ezra v. 1, where *son = grandson*).

[204] Shisha and Shavsha are perhaps corruptions of Seraiah (2 Sam. viii. 17).

[205] Comp. Esth. vi. 1. LXX., Isa. xxxvi. 3, ὁ ὑπομνηματογράφος 2 Sam. viii. 17, ὁ ἐπὶ τῶν ὑπομνημάτων. Jerome, "*a commentariis.*" Comp. Suet., *Aug.* 79, "*qui e memoria Augusti.*"

[206] It is a somewhat ominous fact that *netsib* means properly an ἐπιτειχισμός, a garrison in a hostile country.

[207] The king's friend (2 Sam. xv. 37) seems to have been a sort of confidential privy councillor (Prov. xxii. 11).

[208] Isa. xxii. 21.

[209] 2 Sam. xx. 24.

[210] Possibly this clause is an interpolation.

[211] 2 Sam. viii. 18. Even "Ira the Jairite" is called "a priest" (2 Sam. xx. 26). An attempt has been made to explain the word away because it obviously clashes with Levitic ordinances; but the word "priest" could not be used in two different senses in two consecutive lines. Dogmatic considerations have tampered with the obvious meaning of the word. The LXX. omits it, and in the case of David's sons calls them αὐλάρχαι. The A.V. renders it "chief officer." The Vulgate wrongly refers it to Zadok (filius Sadoc *sacerdotis*). Movers (*Krit. Unters.*, 301 ff.) renders it "court chaplains." Already in 1 Chron. xviii. 17 we find that the title gave offence, and we read instead, "And the sons of David *were at the hand of the king*" (see Ewald, *Alterthumsk*, p. 276). Compare the title "Bishop of Osnaburg," borne by Frederick, Duke of York, son of George III.

[212] 2 Sam. v. 14; Zech. xii. 12; Luke iii. 31.

[213] The degraded and ominous apparitions of *Sarisim* (eunuchs) probably began at the court of Solomon on a large scale, though the name occurs in the days of David (1 Sam. viii. 15; 1 Chron. xxviii. 1). In the Northern Kingdom we first hear of them in the harem of the polygamous Ahab.

[214] 2 Kings xviii. 18; Isa. xxii. 15.

[215] 2 Sam. xx. 24. He is not mentioned in 1 Chron. xxvii. 25-31.

[216] This use of patronymics only is common among the Arabs, but not in Scripture (Reuss, *Hist. d. Isr.*, i. 423).

[217] If he was the son of David's elder brother (1 Sam. xvi. 8, xvii. 13) he was Solomon's first cousin. The materialistic or non-religious element in Solomon seems to come out in the names of his only known children. The element "Jehovah," afterwards so universal, does not occur in them. Basmath, characteristically, means "fragrant"; Taphath is perhaps connected with טפף, to go mincingly; Rehoboam means "enlarger of the people."

[218] The LXX. indeed reads καὶ νασεο εἰς ἐν γῇ Ἰούδα ("and he was the only officer in the land of Judah"). But this would make thirteen fiscal overseers. The Targum, adopting the same reading, says that the thirteenth *nitzab* was to maintain the king in the intercalary month.

[219] Taking the *cor* at a low estimate this would amount to eighteen thousand pounds of bread a day.

[220] 1 Kings iv. 23, סיֻרְבָּב. Vulg., *Avium altilium.*

[221] Athen., *Deipnos.*, iv. 146.

[222] 2 Sam. iv. 6 (LXX.).

[223] This description of *agricultural* felicity soon became an anachronism.

[224] Not "dromedaries" (A.V.). The ruins of his stables are still pointed out at Jerusalem. He traded with Egypt for horses and chariots which his merchants brought to Tekoa, and he then sold them at a profit to the Hittite princes. The forty thousand stalls of 1 Kings iv. 26 should doubtless be four thousand (2 Chron. ix. 25), as Solomon only had fourteen hundred chariots (1 Kings x. 26). In 1 Kings x. 28 the meaning and reading is "as for the export of horses, which Solomon got from Egypt *even from Tekoa*" (LXX., καὶ ἐκ Θεκουὲ), "the royal merchants used to fetch a troop of horses at a price." The "linen yarn" of the A.V. is a mistranslation.

[225] Cant. i. 9.

[226] 1 Kings v. 6, ix. 19, x. 26, 28. Two of those passages are omitted in the LXX. Comp. 1 Kings xvi. 9.

[227] Deut. xvii. 16.

[228] Josh. xi. 9; 1 Sam. viii. 11, 12; 2 Sam. viii. 4.

[229] The energetic dislike to the importation or use of horses is also found in Isa. ii. 7, xxx. 16, 17, xxxi. 1-3; Micah v. 10-14; Zech. ix. 10, x. 5, xii. 4.

[230] Psalm xxxiii. 17, lxxvi. 6, cxlvii. 10.

[231] Compare Poludemos, Eurudemos.

[232] Xen., *Anab.*, i. 4, 11; Arrian, ii. 13, iii. 7. For the phrase "on *this* side of the river," see *ante*, p. 18 .

[233] Psalm lxxviii. 58-64.

[234] According to 2 Chron. i. 3.

[235] David's suggestion does not seem to have been received favourably at first (2 Sam. vii. 1-17). The chronicler (1 Chron. xxviii. 19) indulges in the amazing hyperbole that David had been made to understand all the works of the pattern of the Temple *"in writing* from the hand of the Lord."

[236] The ancient Israelites named their months from the seasons, as did the Canaanites. Only four of those old names are preserved in the Bible:

Zif, "brightness" (comp. *Floreal*, *Lenz*); *Bul*, "rain-month" (*Pluviose*); *Abib*, "corn-ear month"; *Ethanim*, "fruit-month" (*Fructidor*).

[237] In 1 Kings vi. 1 we read "in the 480th year after the children of Israel were come out of the land of Egypt." This may possibly be a later gloss. The LXX., Origen, Josephus, etc., omit the words, and the Old Testament does not, as a rule, date events by epochs. Further, the date is full of difficulties, though our received chronology is based on it. It was perhaps arrived at after the Exile, by counting backwards from the Decree of Cyrus, b.c. 535. See note at the end of the volume.

[238] 1 Chron. xxii. 14 says that David (comp. xxviii., xxix.) "with much labour" (A.V., "in my trouble," 1 Chron. xxii. 14) bequeathed to Solomon 100,000 talents of gold and 100,000 talents of silver! This impossible number is very considerably reduced in 1 Chron. xxix. 4, where the mention of *darics* shows an author living in the captivity.

[239] Comp. Ezek. xxvii. 17; Acts xii. 20.

[240] According to Tatian, *Orat. ad Græc.*, p. 171, Solomon married a daughter of Hiram. Hiram, like the Queen of Sheba, acknowledges Jehovah as the (local) God of Israel. He was the son of Abibaal, and, according to Menander (a Greek historian of Ephesus about b.c. 300, who consulted Tyrian records), he began to reign at nineteen, and reigned thirty-four years. Josephus thinks that there were two successive Hirams.

[241] *Giblim*, 1 Kings v. 18, where "and the stone-squarers" should be "and especially the men of Gebal." LXX., Alex., οἱ Βίβλιοι; Vulg., *Giblii*, Comp. Ezek. xxvii. 9, Psalm lxxxiii. 7, "The ancients of Gebal and the wise thereof were in thee." It is now Jebeil, between Beyrout and Tripoli. The Phœnician and Sidonian artisans were famous from the earliest antiquity for metal-work, embroidery, dyes, ship-building, and the fine arts (Hom., *Il.*, xxiii. 743; *Od.*, iv. 614-18, xv. 425; Herod., iii. 19, vii. 23, 96, etc.).

[242] 2 Chron. ii. 13, iv. 16, where "a cunning man of Huram my father's" should be "even Huram, my father," *i.e.*, master-workman or deviser (comp. Gen. xlv. 8). In Chronicles he is called the son of a Danite mother. Here we have another of the manipulations used by later Jewish tradition to get rid of what they disliked; for in Eupolemos (Euseb., *Præp. Evang.*, ix. 34) Hiram is said to belong to the family of David. "Quite a little romance," as Wellhausen says, "has been constructed out of the fact that the chronicler assigns his mother to the tribe of Dan; but it is not worth repeating, being a mass of hypotheses." To the dislike of Sidonian and semi-Sidonian influence, we perhaps owe the notion that David had already received a design from the hand of God Himself (1 Chron. xxviii. 11-19)

(Ewald, iii. 227). Jerome mentions the Jewish fable that the artist Hiram was of the family of Aholiab, the artist of the wilderness.

[243] "Araunah the king" (2 Sam. xxiv. 23). The Temple Mount was usually called the "Mount of the House." It is only called Mount Moriah in 2 Chron. iii. 1. It cannot be regarded as certain that "the land of Moriah" (Gen. xxii. 2) is identical with it.

[244] "The present platform is 1521 feet long on the east, 940 on the south, 1617 on the west, 1020 on the north." Bartlett, *Walks about Jerusalem,* pp. 161-70; Williams, *The Holy City,* pp. 315-62. Kugle, *Gesch. der Baukunst,* p. 125. The excellent stone was supplied by quarries at Jerusalem itself. Comp. "Cavati sub terra montes." (Tac., *Hist.,* v. 12). It may have been extended by Justinian when he built his church. See Ewald, iii. 232, "The Mount of the Temple was 500 yards square"; *Middoth,* c. 2. Comp. Ezek. xiii. 15-20, xlv. 2; Josephus, *Antt.,* XV. xi. 3.

[245] Exod. i., ii.

[246] 1 Kings iv. 6, v. 13, 14, 17, 18, ix. 15, 21, xii. 18.

[247] Ewald thinks that it was only "at the beginning" that Solomon, like Sesostris (Diod. Sic., *Hist.,* i. 56), could boast that his work was done without exacting bitter labour from his own countrymen. But 1 Kings ix. 22 shows that the king's opinion on this subject differed widely from that of his people (1 Kings xi. 28, xii. 3); for we are told that he did not make *servants* of the children of Israel, but used them as military officers (*Sarim*) and chariot-warriors (*Shalishim,* τριστάται) and knights. It required a little euphemism to gild the real state of affairs. The details of numbers in the Books of Chronicles differ from those in the Kings.

[248] 1 Kings v. 13, ix. 22; 2 Chron. viii. 9. (Omitted in the LXX.)

[249] In token of this defeat of Solomon he was represented in a statue outside the church leaning his hand on his cheek with a gesture of sorrow.

[250] Professor Williams, *Prolus. Architectonicæ.*

[251] Professor Hoskins (*Enc. Brit.*); Canina, *Jewish Antiquities;* Thrupp, *Ancient Jerusalem;* Count de Vogüé, *Le Temple de Jérusalem.*

[252] Fergusson, *Temples of the Jews;* E. Robbins, *Temple of Solomon.*

[253] Eupolemos (Euseb., *Præp. Evang.,* ix. 30) and Alex. Polyhistor (Clem. Alex., *Strom.,* i. 21) idly talk of help furnished to Solomon in building the Temple by an Egyptian King Vaphres, and of letters interchanged between them. Vaphres seems to be a mere anachronism for Hophra.

[254] The Phœnician style may, however, have been borrowed in part from Egypt.

[255] I have spoken of the Temple in *Solomon and his Times* (Men of the Bible), and have there furnished some illustrations. The following special authorities may be referred to. Stade, i. 311-57, Friederich, *Tempel und Palast Salomo's* (Innsbruck, 1887); Chipiez et Perrot, *Le Temple de Jérusalem* (Paris, 1889); Warren, *Underground Jerusalem*; Wilson and Warren, *Recov. of Jerusalem* (1871).

[256] *Parbarim* (2 Kings xxiii. 11). Comp. 1 Chron. xxvi. 18 (A.V., "suburbs"; R.V., "precincts" and "Parbar"). Descriptions of the Temple, imperfect, and not always accordant with each other, are found in 1 Kings v.-vii.; 2 Chron. ii.-v.; Josephus, *Antt.*, VIII. iii. 7, 8.

[257] As we infer from Psalms lii. 8, lxxxiv. 3, lxxvi. 2 (where "tabernacle" should be "covert"). Eupolemos (*ap.* Euseb., *Præp. Evang.*, etc.). Scattered passages of the Talmud which refer mainly to Herod's Temple are full of extravagances.

[258] Jer. xxxvi. 10.

[259] 2 Chron. iv. 1. This could not have been the brazen altar of the wilderness, the fate of which we do not know. It was far larger, but probably on the same model, except that steps were forbidden as an approach to the altar of the Tabernacle (Exod. xx. 24-26). It is difficult to reconcile the description of the brazen altar with the distinct prohibition of that passage. Comp. Ezek. xliii. 17.

[260] The huge stone vase of Amathus was borne on a bull (Duncker, ii. 184). Josephus says that in making these oxen Solomon broke the law (*Antt.*, VIII. vii. 5), as well as by the lions on his throne. The Romans called huge vases *lacus*.

[261] The descriptions of these lavers, whether in the Hebrew, the LXX., or Josephus, are not intelligible, and are wholly unimportant.

[262] Like the palace of Ecbatana (Polyb., x. 27, 10; Herod., i. 98), and possibly the upper stories of the great temple of Bel at Birs-Nimrud (Borsippa).

[263] In 1 Kings x. 12 "pillars" should be "a rail" or "balustrade." Heb., מסעד; LXX., ὑποστηρίγματα; Vulg., *fulcra*.

[264] Lilies symbolised beauty and innocence; pomegranates good works (so the Chaldee in Cant. iv. 13, vi. 11. Bähr, *Symbol.*, ii. 122). Raphael crowns his Theology with pomegranates, Giotto places a pomegranate in

the hand of his youthful Dante, and Giovanni Bellini in the hand of the Virgin Mary.

[265] Some suppose that the words imply "He will establish" (Jachin) "in strength" (Boaz). "After some favourite persons of the time, perhaps young sons of Solomon," says Ewald, very improbably. LXX. (2 Chron. iii. 17), Κατόρθωσις and Ἰσχύς. See a description of these pillars in Jer. lii. 21-23.

[266] Some writers have supplied the Temple with a porch 180 feet high, misled by the astounding method of the chronicler of adding the four sides into the total. Thus, he tells us that the wings of the cherubim were 30 feet long, meaning that each single wing was 7½ feet long (2 Chron. iii. 11). Josephus does the same in telling us the height of the Temple wall.

[267] The ground plans of most ancient temples were alike.

[268] 2 Sam. viii. 7; 1 Chron. xviii. 7.

[269] So 2 Chron. iv. 8. But it would seem from 1 Kings vii. 48; 2 Chron. xiii. 11, xxix. 18 that only one table and one candlestick were ordinarily used.

[270] St. Jerome rendered *debir* by *oraculum*, but some derive it from the Arabic root *dabar*, "to be behind," not from רָבַד, "to speak" (Munk, p. 290).

[271] In Zerubbabel's and Herod's Temples there was a curtain (*Parocheth*) before the Holiest; but we read of no such curtain in Solomon's, except in 2 Chron. iii. 14. The fact that the staves of the Ark were *visible* seems to show that there was not one. The chronicler speaks of "*the* vail" (2 Chron. iii. 14), showing, apparently, that there was only one; and does not mention the *Māsak*, which hung between the Porch and the Holy Place. Except in 2 Chron. iii. 14, the only mention of either is in the "Priestly Code." Since the Oracle had a door, one hardly sees why there should also have been a curtain. But the whole subject is obscure, and perhaps the chronicler is sometimes thinking of the second Temple.

[272] We read nothing, however, of any observance of the Day of Atonement till centuries later.

[273] 2 Sam. xxiv. 25 (LXX.); 1 Chron. xxii. 1; 2 Chron. iii. 1; Josephus, *Antt.*, I. xiii. 1, VII. xiii. 4; Targum of Onkelos on Gen. xii.

[274] "The Ark of the Lord," or "of the Testimony," or "of the Covenant," was an oblong chest of acacia wood, overlaid with gold, surmounted by a border of gold, and resting on four feet, to which (A.V. corners) were attached golden rings.

[275] 1 Kings viii. 9. The pot of manna and the budded rod of Aaron were placed before it (Exod. xvi. 34; Numb. xvii. 10), and the Book of the Law beside it (Deut. xxxi. 26). The Mercy-seat above was more sacred than the Ark itself (Lev. xvi. 2). It was the cover (*Kapporeth*. ἐπίθεμα) of the Ark, and was partly formed of two winged cherubim which gazed down upon it and faced each other.

[276] Stanley, ii. 203.

[277] The Tyrian adornments; the steps to the altar; the ten candlesticks, and tables; the lions and oxen.

[278] The Temple was finished in the eighth month of Solomon's eleventh year, and dedicated in the seventh month *Ethanim*, or Tisri) of the twelfth year. The first eight days (8th to 15th) were devoted to the Feast of Dedication, and then from the 15th to the 22nd they kept the Feast of Tabernacles. On the 23rd (the eighth day from the beginning of the Feast of Tabernacles, called *'atsereth*, 2 Chron. 10) Solomon dismissed the people. The עֲצֶרֶת, "solemn assembly," is not mentioned in Exodus or Deuteronomy, but in Lev. xxiii. 36.

[279] It was perhaps stored away in one of the Temple chambers (2 Macc. ii. 4). The Gibeonites (*Nethinim*) were at the same time transferred to Jerusalem. The chronicler (2 Chron. v. 6) says that *the Levites* took the Ark, according to the Levitic rule; but 1 Kings viii. 3 says that *the priests* bore it, as in Deut. xxxi. 9, and in all the præ-exilic histories (Josh. iii. 3, vi. 6; 2 Sam. xv. 24-29, etc.). W. Robertson Smith, p. 144.

[280] The sheykhs are heads of clans; the emîrs of tribes (Reuss, i. 444).

[281] The Greek Ἐπιφάνεια. Solomon seems to have had some jurisdiction there (2 Chron. viii. 6).

[282] The torrent (*nachal*) of Egypt.

[283] The Holiest, being an unlighted cube, must always have been dim; but, as we have seen, we have no proof that in Solomon's Temple the entrance to it was shrouded by a curtain. In 1 Kings viii. 12, for "The Lord said that He would dwell *in the thick darkness*," the Targum had "*In Jerusalem*."

[284] In 1 Kings viii. 4 we read that "the priests and the Levites" brought up to Jerusalem "the Tabernacle of the congregation." But the LXX. only has οἱ ἱερεῖς. In 2 Chron. v. 5 the Hebrew text has "the Levites" in some MSS., or "the priests, the Levites"—*i.e.*, the Levitic priests. For "the priests took up the ark" (1 Kings viii. 3) the chronicler has "the Levites" (comp. Numb. iii. 31, iv. 15). It is at least doubtful whether the distinction between priests

and Levites is older than the Priestly Code and the days of Ezekiel. Also, the LXX. in 1 Kings viii. 4 puts "witness" for "congregation," and some critics maintain that "congregation" (*'edah*) is post-exilic. (See Robertson Smith, Enc. Brit., s.v. Kings). See *infra*, pp. 189 , 190 .

[285] Some psalm, like Psalm cxxxvi., was probably sung by alternate choirs, but hardly in the attitude of prostration which followed the sudden blaze of glory (2 Chron. vii. 3).

[286] "The prayer" is of extreme beauty, but it belongs by its ideas to the seventh and not to the eleventh or tenth centuries b.c. (Ewald). It is probably added by a later editor who took the Deuteronomic standpoint. It is found, sometimes almost word for word, in Lev. xxvi. and Deut. xxviii.; but there are many variations between the Hebrew and the LXX., and Kings and Chronicles. Looking only at actual facts, not at *a priori* theories, we see that, as Professor Driver says (*Contemporary Review*, Feb. 1890), "the Hebrew historians used some freedom in attributing speeches to historical characters." Thus, both the syntax and vocabulary, to say nothing of the thoughts of various speeches attributed to David by the chronicler, are sometimes such as mark the latest period in the history of the language, and are often quite without precedent in præ-exilic literature. Some feelings which gathered round the Temple find expression in Psalms xxiv., xxvii., xlii., lxxii., lxxxiv., cxxii., and in more extravagant and less spiritual forms throughout the Talmud. *Soteh*, f. 48; *Berachoth*, f. 591; *Moed Qaton*, f. 261; etc.

[287] The Khalif Moktader sacrificed at Mecca 40,000 camels and 50,000 sheep (Burton's *Pilgrimage*, i. 318). Solomon offered burnt offerings (*oloth*) and thank offerings (*shellamim*). No mention is made of sin offerings; and it may be doubted whether they had any separate existence till the days of the Exile.

[288] 1 Kings viii. 66, "went unto their *tents*," is a reminiscence of earlier days. The chronicler (1) extends the feast to fourteen days, according to which there is an interpolation, "and seven days, even fourteen days," in verse 65; (2) he says that the sacrifices were consumed by fire from heaven.

[289] 1 Kings ix. 25. The Hebrew text seems to have been tampered with, and the allusions significantly disappear from 2 Chron. viii. 12, 13. The commentators assiduously try to clear away the difficulty.

[290] The scepticism of modern critics, who doubt whether there ever was a Tabernacle in the wilderness at all, seems to be insufficiently grounded.

[291] *Vit. Mos.*, iii.; *Antt.*, III. vi. 4, vii. 7; *B. J.*, VII. v. 5.

[292] *E.g.*, Origen (*Hom.*, ix.), Clement of Alexandria (*Strom.*, v.), Theodoret (*Qu.*, xl. *in Exod.*), Jerome (*Ep.*, lxiv.), and others. See Kalisch, *Exodus*, p. 495.

[293] Wisdom ix. 8: "A copy of the holy tabernacle which Thou didst prepare from the beginning."

[294] Exod. xxv. 40, xxvi. 30; Acts vii. 44; Heb. viii. 5.

[295] *More Nebochim*, iii, 45-49; Kalisch, *Exodus*, p. 497.

[296] The three names given to the Tabernacle are *Ohel* ("tent"), *Mishkan* ("tabernacle," "habitation," or "dwelling-place"), and *Baith* ("house"). It is undoubted that the Tabernacle followed the ordinary construction of the Oriental tent, with its two divisions, of which the interior could not be entered by strangers.

[297] Numb. xvii. 7, xviii. 2; 2 Chron. xxiv. 6; Acts vii. 44; Exod. xxix. 10, etc.; 1 Kings viii. 4; 2 Chron. viii. 13. The phrase "Tent of Meeting" in the R.V. removes the complete obscuring of the meaning involved by the A.V. rendering of "Tabernacle of the Congregation."

[298] Exod. xxv. 22.

[299] Exod. xxix. 42, 43.

[300] Kuenen's notion that the cherubim had come to the Jews through the Phœnicians from the Assyrians is quite improbable. The symbol was common throughout the East, whatever be the derivation of the word.

[301] Compare Ezek. i. 10 with x. 14, where "the face of an ox" is identical with "the face of a cherub." Perhaps this gave rise to the pagan calumnies that the Jews worshipped an ass. Josephus says (insincerely) that no man could tell or even conjecture the shape of the cherubim.

[302] Bähr, whose profound studies on symbolism command respect, says that "as standing on the highest step of created life, and uniting in themselves the most perfect created life, they are the most perfect revelation of God and the Divine" (*Symbolik*, i. 340).

[303] Compare the Homeric epithet νέποδες, and Milton's "smooth-gliding, without step."

[304] One of the Scriptural functions of the cherubim was *to guard treasure* (Ezek. xxviii. 13-15). This conception, too, was widely diffused throughout the East: —

"As when a Gryphon through the wilderness
Pursues the Arimaspian, who, by stealth,
Has from his watchful custody purloined
The guarded gold."
Milton.

[305] I follow the Rabbis in saying that the first broken slabs were in the Ark.

[306] Like the Greek images of the gods, they were made of olive, the least corruptible kind of wood, and overlaid with the purest gold.

[307] See, especially, Deut. xii. 5-19. In the later Priestly Code the centralisation of worship is not inculcated, but supposed to be already established. In the original Book of the Covenant it is not required at all.

[308] Judg. ii. 5, vi. 24, viii. 27, xx. 1, xxi. 2, 4; 1 Sam. vii. 9, x. 8, xi. 15, xiii. 9, xvi. 5, etc.

[309] ἡ νηστεία (Acts xxvii. 9); Philo, *Lib. de Septenariis*.

[310] Neh. viii. 17.

[311] Canon Cook in the *Speaker's Commentary* (Leviticus, p. 496) admits: "It is by no means unlikely there are insertions of a later date, which were written and sanctioned by the prophets and holy men who *after the captivity* arranged and edited the Scriptures of the Old Testament."

[312] *Book by Book*, p. 7.

[313] See Professor Robertson, *Book by Book*, p. 56. I quote Professor Robertson as one of the ablest and most competent opponents of extreme conclusions; but it does not seem to me that he touches on some of the arguments which constitute the main strength of the case against him.

[314] See 2 Kings xxii. 11; Ezra ix. 1, 7; Neh. ix. 3.

[315] "Sacrificia symbolicæ preces" (Outram, *De Sacrif.*, p. 108).

[316] *Yoma*, f. 21, *a*.

[317] On vast ancient holocausts, see Athen., *Deipnos.*, i. 5; Diod. Sic., xi. 72; Porph., *De abstin.*, ii. 60; Suet., *Calig.*, 14; Sen., *De Benef.*, iii. 27; Ammian. Marcel., xxii. 4, xxv. 4; and other passages collected by the diligence of commentators. See, too, Josephus (*B. J.*, VI. ix. 3) who reckons that at a passover in Nero's time 256,000 sacrifices were offered.

[318] Amos vi. 5; 1 Chron. xxiii. 5.

[319] Edersheim, *The Temple and its Services*, p. 54.

[320] The chronicler says that there were 38,000 Levites, of which 24,000 were "to oversee the work of the house of the Lord; and 6000 were officers and judges, and 4000 door-keepers; and 4000 praised the Lord with the instruments which I made," *said David*, "to praise therewith."

[321] Some of these titles of the Psalms are, however, very uncertain. Gesenius thinks that this last title (Psalm ix.) means that the Psalm "was to be sung by boys with virgins' voices." It is, to say the least, a very curious coincidence, that in 1 Chron. xxv. 4 the names of the sons of Heman, Giddalti and Romamti-ezer, Joshbekashah, Mallcthi, Hothir, Mahazioth, mean (omitting the strange Joshbekashah, for which the LXX. Cod. Alex. reads Σεβακαιτάν), consecutively, "I have given | great and high help: | I have spoken | visions | in abundance." Had the names any reference to tunes?

[322] Ezra ii. 65; Neh. vii. 67; Psalm lxxxvii. 7.

[323] Of these, perhaps, were "the children" who shouted their hosannas to Jesus in the Temple (Matt. xxi. 15).

[324] *The Temple and its Services*, p. 67.

[325] Exod. xix. 5, 6.

[326] Rev. xv. 6.

[327] Comp. Rev. i. 13, xv. 6.

[328] On this sagan, the later title for the "second priest," see 2 Kings xxv. 18; Jer. lii. 24.

[329] He refers to Wünsche, *Die Leiden des Messias.*

[330] Mark ix. 49.

[331] Lev. vi. 17, vii. 1, xiv. 13. On this whole subject see Edersheim, pp. 79-111.

[332] See Judg. vi. 19-21; 1 Sam. ii. 13, xiv. 35; 1 Kings xix. 21; 2 Kings v. 17.

[333] LXX., ὁλοκαύτωμα.

[334] LXX., περὶ ἁμαρτίας. *Chattath* and *Ashâm* both imply guilt, debt, sin. "The trespass offering affected rights of prcperty, but no precise definition of the two kinds of expiatory offerings can be based upon the statements made in the Pentateuch in respect to them. Perhaps they cannot all be referred to the same time and to one author; for they prescribe both sin and trespass offerings in cases of Levitical impurity, and also for moral offences. All Levites attempting to establish palpable distinctions between them must inevitably fail." (Kalisch, *Leviticus*, part ii., p. 272). The general scheme of sacrifices, as they now stand in the Pentateuch, is as follows:—

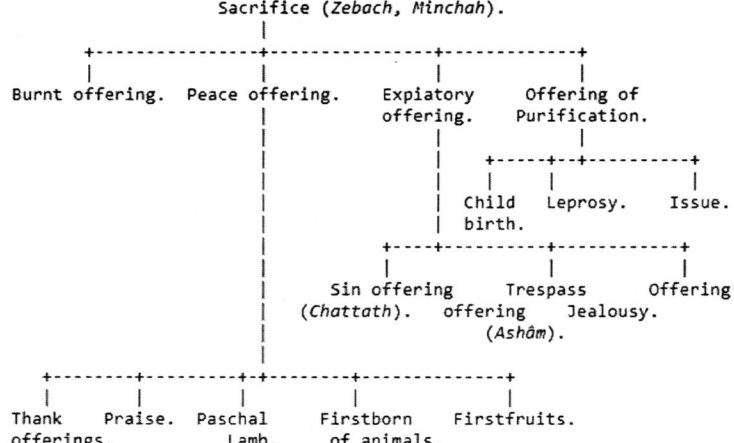

```
                            Sacrifice (Zebach, Minchah).
                                       |
        +---------------------+--------------------+------------+
        |                     |                    |            |
   Burnt offering.     Peace offering.        Expiatory    Offering of
                             |                offering.    Purification.
                             |                    |            |
                             |                    |       +-----+--+----------+
                             |                    |       |     |  |          |
                             |                    |       |   Child  Leprosy.  Issue.
                             |                    |       |   birth.
                             |                    |   +----+---------+----------+
                             |                    |   |              |          |
                             |              Sin offering       Trespass      Offering
                             |             (Chattath).         offering      Jealousy.
                             |                                  (Ashâm).
                             |
        +--------+---------+-+--------+---------------+
        |        |         |          |              |
      Thank    Praise.  Paschal    Firstborn     Firstfruits.
    offerings.          Lamb.      of animals.
```

[335] LXX., πλημμελεία.

[336] LXX., θυσία σωτηρίον.

[337] The phrase "wave offering" indicates the ceremony used by the priests in presenting peace offerings to God.

[338] For the full development of these views, see Wellhausen's *Prolegomena*.

[339] See Bishop Barry's article on Sacrifice in Smith's *Dictionary of the Bible*, to which, in this paragraph, I am much indebted.

[340] Lev. v. 11-13.

[341] See Kuenen, *Rel. of Israel*, ii. pp. 259-76.

[342] *Speaker's Commentary*, Leviticus, p. 508. In Lev. xvii. 11—"For the soul of the flesh is in the blood, and *I have ordained it for you upon the altar* to make atonement for your souls; for the blood it is which makes atonement by means of the soul"—Kurtz points out that the blood is simply *chosen as a symbol*, and the superstition that there is any atoning virtue in the blood itself is excluded.

[343] *Pæd.*, ii. 2, § 19.

[344] The Priestly Code is that part of the Pentateuch which is occupied with public worship and the function of priests—viz., most of Leviticus; Exod. xxv.-xl.; Numb. i.-x., xv.-xx., xxv.-xxxvi. (with inconsiderable exceptions)

[345] In Psalm xl. 6, "Sin offering hast Thou not required." The Psalm is perhaps of the age of Jeremiah.

[346] He argues that even in Chronicles it is not mentioned; and that there was no curtain (*Parocheth*) before the Holiest in Solomon's Temple (1 Kings vi. 31, 32. Comp. Ezek. xli. 23, 24; 1 Kings viii. 8). He considers that 2 Chron. iii. 14 (the only place in the Old Testament where *Parocheth* occurs except in the P.C.) cannot overthrow 1 Kings vi. 21, which speaks only of chains of gold between the Holy and the Holiest. (There was a curtain in Herod's Temple, Matt. xxvii. 51; Heb. ix. 3). But if there was no *Parocheth* in Solomon's Temple, the rule of Lev. xvi. 2, 12, 15 could not have been observed.

[347] This caused immense perplexity to the Rabbis. *Shabbath*, xiii. 2; *Chagigah*, xiii. 1; *Menachoth*, xlv. 1.

[348] 1 Sam. xv. 22.

[349] Amos v. 21-23.

[350] Micah vi. 6-8. Some suppose that the words are attributed to Balaam (see verse 5).

[351] Hosea vi. 6.

[352] Isa. i. 11-16.

[353] Jer. vii. 22, xi. 15.

[354] Jer. xxxiii. 14-26 seems to speak in a different tone, but is probably an interpolation. It is not found in the LXX.

[355] Psalm l. 8-14.

[356] Psalm li. 16, 17. It is difficult to believe that the two last verses of the Psalm are not a later addition.

[357] Psalm xl. 6.

[358] Prov. xxi. 3.

[359] Psalm lxix. 30, 31.

[360] Mark xii. 32, 33. So in the Talmud: "Acts of justice are more meritorious than all sacrifices" (*Succoth.*, lxix. 2).

[361] Matt. ix. 13.

[362] Matt. xii. 7.

[363] Rom. xii. 1; 1 Peter ii. 5.

[364] Heb. x. 4, 11.

[365] Heb. xiii. 16.

[366] Ecclus. xxxv. 1-15.

[367] Comp. Ov., *Trist.*, ii. 1, 75; Ep. xx. 81; Persius, ii. 45; Varro, *ap.* Arnob., *c. Natt.*, vii. 1. "Dii veri neque desiderant ea, neque deposcunt."

[368] Philo, *De Victimis*, 5.

[369] A. Geiger, *Judenthum und seine Geschichte*, Sect. 5.

[370] Vajikra R., 22 and 34 *b*. They got over Jer. xxxiii. 18 (in Yalkuth, on the passage) by saying, "He that doeth repentance it is counted to him as if he offered all the sacrifices of the land." They held that the place of sacrifices was taken by prayer, penitence, and good works. See Edersheim, *Jesus the Messiah*, i. 275.

[371] See Spencer, *De Legg. Ritual.*, iii.; *Dissert.*, ii., chap. 1.

[372] Evang. Ebion, *ap.* Epiph., *Hær.*, xxx. 16.

[373] Mark vii. 19.

[374] It was twice repaired—about b.c. 856 in the reign of Joash, and about two centuries later under Josiah.

[375] See Isa. xxix. 13, 14; Ezek. xxxiii. 31; Matt. xv. 7-9; Col. i. 20-22, etc. Comp. Wellhausen, pp. 77-79.

[376] Rev. xxi. 22.

[377] 1 Kings ix. 6-9. The phrase "at this house which is high" is uncertain. The Vulgate has "domus hæc erit in exemplum"; the Peshito and Arabic have "and this house shall be destroyed."

[378] To form some notion of these buildings, see the excellent illustrations in Stade, i. 318-25.

[379] The hill of Zion, the city of David, had become overcrowded, and the hill which lay to the north, which was called Millo, or "the border," had to be included in it. A narrow valley lay between them. "Mount Moriah, and its offshoot Ophel, remained outside the city, and the latter was inhabited by the remnant of the Jebusites" (Grätz, *Hist. of the Jews*, E. T., i. 121); Millo, LXX., ἡ ἄκρα. See 1 Macc. iv. 41, xiii. 49-52; Josephus, *Antt.*, XIII. vi. 7.

[380] 1 Kings ix. 19.

[381] The "linen yarn" of 1 Kings x. 28 seems to be an error. The Hebrew is מִקְוֵה; LXX., ἐκ Θεκουέ; Vulg., *de Coâ*; R.V., "in droves."

[382] 2 Chron. ix. 21.

[383] See Max Müller, *Lectures on Language*, i. 191. The names *Shen Habbim*, "ivory" (Sanskr. *ibhas*, "elephant"), *Kophim*, "apes" (Sanskr. *kapi*), *Tukkyim*, "peacocks" (Tamil, *togei*), "algum trees" (Sanskr. *Valgaka*, LXX.

πελεκητά, Alex. ἀπελέκητα, Vulg. *thyina*), all point to India. Aloes (*ahalim*, Psalm xlv. 8) are a fragrant tree of Malacca; cassia (Ind. *koost*), cinnamon (*cacyn-nama*) come from Ceylon. See Stanley, ii. 185. European history here first comes into contact with Sanskrit.

[384] See Eccles. ii. 4-6. See on the extensive water-works, Ewald, iii. 252-57.

[385] 2 Chron. ix. 21.

[386] שׁף; LXX., στακτή, "oil of myrrh."

[387] 1 Kings x. 25.

[388] See Cant. i. 9, iii. 6-11, iv. 8; 2 Chron. xi. 6; Josephus, *Antt.*, VIII. vii. 3; Psalm xlv.

[389] The great statue of Athene by Phidias was of this "Chryselephantine" work. Comp. "ivory palaces" (Psalm xlv. 8; 1 Kings xxii. 39; Amos iii. 15) and "ivory couches" (Amos vi. 4).

[390] Josephus, *Antt.*, VIII. v. 2; Hosea iv. 16; Jer. xxxi. 18, etc.

[391] Ezek. xxvii., xxviii.; Zech. ix. 3.

[392] The Abyssinian, confusing Sheba (Arabia Felix) with Seba (as do Origen and Augustine), call her Makeda, Queen of Abyssinia, and say that she had a son by Solomon named Melinek (Ludolphus, *Æthiop.*, ii. 3), from whom all their emperors down to Theodore were descended. The legend of the Queen of Sheba is related in the Qur'an, *Sura* xxvii. 20-40 (chapter of the Ant). The Arabs call her Balkis, whose legends are narrated by D'Herbelot (*Bibl. Or.*, s.v. Balki). Josephus identifies her with Nicaule (the Nitocris of Herod., ii. 100), Josephus, *Antt.*, VIII. vi. 2. In the New Testament she is called "the Queen of the South" (Matt. xii. 42).

[393] He had made two hundred large shields (*tzinnîm*, θυρεοί, *scuta*) and three hundred targets (*maginnîm*, ἀσπίδες, *clypei*) of gold at fabulous cost (1 Kings x. 16). They were all plundered by Shishak.

[394] 1 Kings x. 5, but "ascent" should perhaps be "burnt offering," as in margin of R.V. and in all the versions. Comp. 2 Chron. ix. 4 (LXX.). A special seat or platform of brass seems to have been assigned to Solomon in the Temple court (2 Kings xi. 14, xvi. 18, xxiii. 3; 2 Chron. vi. 13).

[395] Josephus says that she introduced the balsam plant into Palestine, which, in later years at Jericho, became a great source of revenue. Jer. viii. 22, xlvi. 11; Ezek. xxvii. 17; Josephus, *Antt.*, VIII. vi. 6, XIV. iv. 1, XV. iv. 2; Pliny, *H. N.*, xii. 54, xiii. 9 (but see Gen. xliii. 11).

[396] Psalm lxxii. 15. Spices, Herod., iii. 107-113. For one hundred and twenty talents we should probably read twenty (comp. Josephus, *Antt.*, VIII. vi. 6), *i.e.*, twelve thousand pounds. Into the riddles of Balkis (1 Kings x. 1, "hard questions"; LXX., αἰνίγματα), and all the strange Talmudic and Arabian legends which have gathered round her visit, we need not enter. I may perhaps refer to my little monograph on Solomon (pp. 134-37), in the Men of the Bible series.

[397] The 666 gold talents of his revenue are estimated at £3,613,500, and this is described as *his own* revenue, exclusive of tolls, tributes, etc. (1 Kings x. 15). Presents reached him from "kings of the mingled people" (Jer. xxv. 24), Pachas of the country (הַפֶּחָ Ezra v. 6; Neh. v. 14).

[398] See Weil, *Biblische Legenden*; D'Herbelot, *Bibl. Oriental*, s.v. Soliman ben-Daoud; Qur'an, *Suras* xxii., xxvii., xxviii., xxxiv. "Suleyman" means "Little Solomon," a term of affection.

[399] Stanley, *Lectures*, ii. 166, 167.

[400] See Euseb., *Præp. Evang.*, x. 11.

[401] Lev. xxv. 23, 24. See Judg. i. 31, 32.

[402] Hence, perhaps, the name "Galilee of the nations" (Isa. ix. 1). Comp. "Harosheth of the nations" (Judg. iv. 2, 13). Hazor was in this district.

[403] Milman, *Hist. of the Jews*, i. 321.

[404] 1 Kings ix. 10-13. There was a place called Cabul in Asher (Josh. xix. 27). Ewald thinks that Cabul was a sort of witticism meaning "as nothing." Josephus (*Antt.*, VIII. v. 3) says that in Phœnician χαβαλὼν means "not pleasing," and that Hiram would not take the cities. Nothing can be made of the allusion to this transaction in 2 Chron. viii. 1, 2. Why did Solomon re-occupy these cities? and why did Hiram give him one hundred and twenty talents of gold? The gloss put on the matter by late tradition cannot conceal the fact that Solomon tried to diminish his embarrassments by alienating some of the sacred territory.

[405] The later Jews chose the name "Alexander" as the Western equivalent for Solomon: hence the names "*Alexander* Jannæus," etc.

[406] 1 Kings iii. 15. See Ecclus. xlvii. 12-21.

[407] "L'amour du luxe et de la nouveauté le conduira peu à peu à défaire l'œuvre de son père, à ruiner le peuple dont il pouvait faire le bonheur, à detruire les institutions, et à dédaigner le culte national, auquel il avait d'abord cherché à donner le plus grand éclat." —Munk, *Palestine*, p. 285.

[408] 1 Kings ix. 25.

[409] Modern criticism generally regards the Book of Deuteronomy, or some elements of it, as "the Book of the Law" which was found in the Temple by the high priest Hilkiah in the reign of Josiah. We shall speak of this in the following volume (in 2 Kings). See Deut. xvii. 18.

[410] LXX., ἥν φιλογύνῃς. Vulg., *adamavit mulieres alienigenus.*

[411] Some suppose that this clause about Milcom is an interpolation from 2 Kings xxiii. 13.

[412] See Exod. xxxiv. 11-17; Deut. vii 1-4. The Talmud makes one of its dishonest attempts to get rid of the fact; Shabbath, p. 56, *b.* Sanhedrin, *ff.* 55, 56. Justin Martyr preserves a tradition (*Dial. c. Tryph.*, 34) that Solomon in taking a Sidonian wife worshipped idols at Sidon. Muslim tradition attributes Solomon's idolatry to the tricks of demons who assumed his form (Qur'an, *Sura* ii. 99; but see *Sura* xxxviii. 30).

[413] Prov. xxxi. 3.

[414] The Song of Solomon (vi. 8) gives him, besides the 'alamoth ("damsels") "without number," the sixty wives (*saroth*), and the eighty concubines, who were partly perhaps their slaves.

[415] Parmen. *ap.* Athen., *Deipnos.*, iii. 3. Comp. Quint. Curt., *Vit. Alex.*, iii. 3. Amehhate of Egypt had more than three hundred and seventeen wives (Brugsch, *Egypt*, iii. 607, E.T.). Rehoboam, who had eighteen wives and sixty concubines, left twenty-eight sons and sixty daughters. Solomon, so far as we know, had only one son and two daughters.

[416] Cant. vi. 8.

[417] The Vatican MS. of the LXX. adds Syrian and Amorite princesses to the number. Marriages with Sidonians and Hittites are expressly forbidden in Exod. xxxiv. 12-16, and with Canaanites in Deut. vii. 3 (comp. Ezra ix. 2 and Neh. xiii. 23).

[418] Numb. xxv. 3.

[419] See Prov. ii. 10-22, v. 1-14, vi. 24-35, etc. (contrast Psalm cxliv. 12-15).

[420] In 1 Kings xi. 9-25 the mischief inflicted by Rezon and Hadad is represented as a punishment for Solomon's apostasy. It has been said that here "the pragmatism belongs to the redactor," because these enemies sprang into existence when he came to the throne. But, as I have here represented it, nothing seems more probable than that Rezon and Hadad were practically

impotent to inflict much damage before the period of Solomon's decline. (Verse 23 is omitted in some MSS. of the LXX.)

[421] An isolated anecdote of the exterminating war is preserved in 1 Chron. xi. 22, 23, from which it would seem that Egypt had interfered in favour of Edom.

[422] Renan conjectures that the real Egyptian name is Ahotepnes. The LXX. wrongly calls this Pharaoh Sheshonk (Σουσακείμ), who came later, and whose queen's name was Karaäma (not Thekemina, as the LXX. says).

[423] Canon Rawlinson (*Speaker's Commentary, ad loc.*) points out that fugitives once received at Eastern courts found it very difficult to get away, *e.g.*, Democedes, Herod., iii. 132-37. Histiæus, in leaving the court of Persia, has expressly to say that he had lacked nothing—τεῦ δὲ ἐνδεὴς ὤν; Herod., v. 106; comp. 1 Kings xi. 22.

[424] 1 Kings xi. 14: "The Lord stirred up an adversary" (וַיָּקֶם).

[425] Stade, i. 302. In 1 Kings xi. 22, 25 the text is corrupt. Verse 25 should partly be transferred to the end of verse 22, and should run, "And Hadad returned to his own land," *i.e.*, to *Edom*. (Edom has been confused with "Aram.")

[426] The additions to the LXX. call her Sarira. But the names "Sarira," "Enlamite," "Ano" are all suspicious; and possibly the LXX. additions may be only part of some Alexandrian Haggadah.

[427] In 2 Chron. ix. 29 the LXX. reads "Joel." He wrote "visions" against Jeroboam, a life of Ahijah, and a book "on (or after the manner of) genealogies" (2 Chron. ix. 29, xii. 15, xiii. 22). Jerome (on 2 Chron. xv. 1) identifies him with Oded.

[428] 2 Chron. ix. 29. Perhaps 1 Kings xi. may be borrowed from the historic records of Ahijah.

[429] For in the LXX. 1 Kings xi. 29-39 is absent in some MSS., as well as 1 Kings xiv. (Ahijah and Abijah), which has been added from the Greek version of Aquila. In verse 29, for "Ahijah the Shilonite" we have in some MSS. of the LXX. "Shemaiah the Elamite" or "Eulamite."

[430] 1 Kings xi. 29, addition of LXX.

[431] The square cloth worn over the other dress, and now called *abba*, seems to represent the *salemâh* (הַשַּׂלְמָה) here mentioned.

[432] The story is usually made to apply to *Jeroboam's* new robe; but in the addition to the LXX., where the action is ascribed to Shemaiah, the word of the Lord says to him, λάβε σεαυτῷ ἱμάτιον καινὸν τὸ οὐκ εἰσεληλυθὸς

εἰς ὕδωρ κ. τ. λ. The method of "acted parables" was common among the Hebrew prophets (See Jer. xiii., xix., xxvii.; Ezek. iii., iv., v., etc.); but this is the earliest recorded instance of the kind.

[433] Not "two tribes," as the LXX. says. But neither the number 1 nor the number 2 are literally exact, for certainly Jeroboam did not command the territory of Simeon, south of Judah. The adherence of Benjamin, or part of Benjamin, to Judah was mainly a geographical accident, due to the fact that Jerusalem lay in both tribes (Josh. xv. 8, xviii. 16; Jer. xx. 2). Late in David's reign a Benjamite (Sheba, son of Bichri) had headed a revolt against David (2 Sam. xx. 1).

[434] 1 Kings xi. 34-39.

[435] The story occurs in the additions to the LXX., and is highly improbable. Shishak came to the throne, according to R. S. Poole, about b.c. 972; others date his accession in 975 or 988. No such name as Tahpanes or Thekemina is found in the Egyptian records, and the wife of Shishak was Karaämat.

[436] Compare the names Eshbaal, Meribaal, Jerubbaal, Baaljada, with Ishjo (LXX. 1 Sam. xiv. 49, Heb.), Mephibosheth Eliada. In later days Baal was changed into the nickname *Bosheth*, "shame": hence Ishbosheth, Jerubesheth, Mephibosheth. See Kittel, ii. 87.

[437] See Kittel, *Gesch. der Hebr.*, ii. 169-76.

[438] See Buddæus, *Hist. Eccl.*, ii. 237.

[439]

> "The fifth light shining with a beauty pure
> Breathes from such love that all the world below
> Craves to have tidings of him true and sure.
> Within it is the lofty mind, where so
> Deep knowledge dwelt, that, if the truth be true,
> Such insight ne'er a second rose to know."
> *Parad.*, x. 109-114, and Dean Plumtre's notes.

[440] Qur'an, xxxiv. 10; Chapter of Sebâ (Palmer's translation, p. 151).

[441] Sale's Koran, ii. 287; Palmer's Qur'an, ii. 152.

[442] The Earl of Lytton.

[443] "Rehoboam" means "enlarger of the people" (comp. Eurudemos); Jeroboam, "whose people is many" (Poludemos; comp. Thiodric, Thierry). But Cheyne makes it mean "the kingdom contendeth" (Kleinert, *Volkstreiter*).

[444] So we read in the LXX. Cod. Vat., and (partly) in the Vulgate (see Robertson Smith, *The Old Testament*, p. 117). Unless Jeroboam had spontaneously returned from Egypt on hearing of the death of Solomon, there would hardly have been time to summon him thence. 2 Chron. x. 2 represents the matter thus. Possibly his name has crept by error into 1 Kings xii. 3. See Wellhausen-Bleek's *Einleitung*, p. 243.

[445] In the LXX. the Ephraimites complain of the expensive provision for Solomon's table. "Thy father made his yoke grievous upon us, and made grievous to us the meats of his table." LXX. (Cod. Vat.), καὶ ἐβάρυνε τὰ βρώματα τῆς τραπέζης αὐτοῦ.

[446] Dante, *Inferno*, Cant. xxvii.

[447] They are called *yeladim*, which surely cannot apply to men of forty, so that Rehoboam was probably little more than a youth, *na'ar* (2 Chron. xiii. 7; comp. Gen. xxxiii. 13).

[448] Herod., ii. 124-28.

[449] "My little finger." Heb., "my littleness"; LXX., ἡ μικρότης μου. But the paraphrase is perfectly correct (Vulg., Pesh., Josephus, and the Rabbis).

[450] "Virga si est nodosa et aculeata scorpios vocatur, quia arcuato vulnere in corpus infigitur" (Isodore., *Orig.*, i. 175).

[451] 2 Sam. xx. 1.

[452] Or, "Now feed thine own house" (LXX., βόσκε, reading העָר for האר); and the LXX. adds, "For this man is not (fit) to be a ruler, nor to be a prince." Evidently the revolt was the culmination of those jealousies which the haughty tribe of Ephraim had already manifested in the lives of Gideon, Abimelech, and David.

[453] Heb., "strengthened himself."

[454] In fact, the δωδεκάφυλον became more of a reminiscence than anything else. Simeon, for instance, practically disappeared (1 Chron. iv. 24-43).

[455] 1 Kings xii. 17.

[456] In 1 Kings xix. 3 it is reckoned as belonging to Judah (comp. Josh. xv. 28), being really a town of Simeon (Josh. xix. 2); but from Amos v. 5, viii. 14, we should infer that it was at any rate largely frequented by Israelites.

[457] 1 Kings xvi. 34; 2 Kings ii. 4.

[458] See Stanley, *Lectures on the Jewish Church*, ii. 269-71.

[459] Amos v. 11, vi. 4-6.

[460] 2 Kings iv. 18, 22, viii. 1-6; Stanley, ii. 271.

[461] See Ewald, iv. 9 (E. T.).

[462] 2 Chron. xx. 37.

[463] Zech. xi. 4-17, xiii. 7-9.

[464] If we may regard Kobolam as a real person (2 Kings xv. 10, LXX.). Thus, in the Northern Kingdom twenty kings belong to *nine* different dynasties in two hundred and forty-five years; and in the Southern only nineteen kings of *one* dynasty rule for three hundred and forty-five years.

[465] Jeroboam lived for a time at Penuel, on the east of the Jordan, perhaps to escape all danger from Shishak's invasion. For Penuel, on the eastern side of the Jabbok, see Gen. xxxii. 22, 30; Judg. viii. 8, 17. It was important as commanding the caravan route from Damascus to Shechem.

[466] Zech. x. 4 (R.V., "exactors").

[467] *Hist. of Isr.*, iv. 12.

[468] It recurs twenty-three times: 1 Kings xiv. 16, xv. 26, 30, 34, xvi. 2, 19, 26, 31, xxi. 22, xxii. 52; 2 Kings iii. 3, x. 29, 31, xiii. 2, 6, xiv. 24, xv. 9, 18, 24, 28, xvii. 21, 22, xxiii, 15.

[469] Literally, *"he filled the hand,"* because the priests were consecrated by putting into their hands the parts of the sacrifice which were to be presented to God on the altar (Exod. xxviii. 41, xxix. 9-35; Lev. viii. 27).

[470] Such is the true reading. The "Manasseh" of our existing text is a Jewish falsification of the text timidly and tentatively introduced to protect the memory of Moses (see Judg. xviii. 26 ff.).

[471] For the sanctity of Bethel, "House of God," where God had twice appeared to Jacob, see Gen. xxviii. 11-19, xxxv. 9-15. The Ark had once rested there under Phinehas (Judg. xx. 26-28), and it had been the home of Samuel (1 Sam. vii. 16). Dan, too, was "a holy city" (Judg. xviii. 30, 31; Tobit i. 5, 6). In 1 Kings xii. 30 ("the people went to worship before the one, even unto Dan") some words may have dropped out. Klostermann adds, "and neglected Bethel"; but is that the fact? The LXX. adds, καὶ εἴασαν τὸν ἄκον Κυρίου. On the other hand, the clause has been taken to imply the opposite—*i.e.*, that even as far as Dan some were found who went in preference to Bethel, "the king's chapel" (Amos vii. 13). In 1 Kings xii. 28 the fairer rendering would be, "These are thy God," not "gods."

[472] Lev. xxiii. 39. There is no hint about the other two annual feasts of Passover and Pentecost. Josephus implies that Jeroboam's feast was in the *seventh* month, as in Judah (*Antt.*, VIII. viii. 5).

[473] 2 Sam. iv. 7.

[474] Conceivably there may have been a reference to the heraldic sign of Ephraim (Deut. xxxiii. 17), as Klostermann supposes.

[475] Exod. xx. 23, xxxii. 4, 8. See Professor Paul Cassel, *König Jeroboam*, p. 6. The identity of Jeroboam's words with Exod. xxxii. 4 may be due to the narrator.

[476] It has been considered probable that he found an additional sanction for these material symbols in an ancient existing image at Gilgal, to which there may be obscure allusion in the Prophet Hosea (iv. 15, ix. 15).

[477] See 2 Chron. xi. 15, where the chronicler in his flaming hatred calls them devils (*i.e.*, "satyrs," *Feldtäufel*, Isa. xiii. 21; comp. Hosea viii. 5, xiii. 2). They were probably two young bulls of brass overlaid with gold (see Psalm cvi. 19; Isa. xl. 19).

[478] Tobit i. 5.

[479] Ἡ δάμαλις Βάαλ. If this be the right reading, not δύναμις, the feminine implies special scorn, either implying ἡ αἰσχύνη (*Bosheth*), or pointing, as Baudissin thinks, to an androgynous deity. Grätz thinks that "Bethel" may be the true reading.

[480] Josh. xxiv. 1; 1 Sam. x. 19; 2 Sam. v. 1-3; 1 Kings viii. 1-5, 62.

[481] Vilmar.

[482] Now Talura, six miles north of Nablus.

[483] So, too, Jarchi. No doubt they were guided by the remark in 2 Chron. ix. 29, "the visions of Iddo the seer against Jeroboam." But it is not possible, for Iddo lived to a later date (2 Chron. xiii. 22). Ephrem Syrus and Tertullian suppose him to have been Shemaiah (comp. 2 Chron. xii. 5). These are untenable guesses. Epiphanius calls him Joas; Clement, Abdadonai; Tertullian, Sameas.

[484] Not *"by* the altar," as in A.V. LXX., ἐπὶ τὸ θυσιαστήριον; Vulg., *super altare.*

[485] The ashes of the animal offerings (דֶּשֶׁן) used to be carried away to a clean place (Lev. vi. 11).

[486] Amos ix. 1. The Vatican LXX. distinctly makes the sign a *future* one (1 Kings xiii. 3), καὶ δώσει ἐν τῇ ἡμέρᾳ ἐκείνῃ τέρας. The narrative

seems to *suppose*, but it does not assert that the altar was rent *then and there.* Had these miracles immediately followed, it is difficult to imagine that no deeper impression should have been made. As it was the new cult does not seem to have been interrupted for a single day.

[487] The mention by name of a king three centuries before he was even born is wholly alien from every characteristic of Jewish prophecy, and, as in the case of Cyrus (Isa. xliv. 28), it would be false to say that we have even a particle of evidence to show that the name was not added from a marginal gloss or by the latest redactor. He also makes the mistake of putting into the old prophet's mouth the phrase "all the cities of Samaria" at least fifty years before Samaria existed (1 Kings xvi. 24). Keil's remark that *"Josiah"* is only used appellatively for one whom Jehovah will support (!) is one of the miserable expedients of reckless harmonists. Even Bähr, *ad loc.*, admits that the narrative is of later date, and has received a traditional colouring. In 2 Kings xxiii. 15-18 there is no hint that Josiah had been prophesied of by name.

[488] 1 Kings xiii. 6, "Intreat now" (*lit.*, "make soft") "the face of the Lord." Klostermann, "Besänftige noch das Angesicht Jahve's."

[489] Gal. i. 8.

[490] Klostermann, in his *Kurzgefasster Kommentar,* gets rid of the lion altogether by one of his sweeping emendations of the text, p. 352. He considers that the whole story comes from a book of edifying anecdotes for the use of young prophets in the schools; and that it may have some connexion with the threat of another Jewish prophet against the altar at Bethel in the days of another Jeroboam (Amos iii. 14, vii. 9).

[491] Comp. Jer. xxii. 18.

[492] The older expositors at any rate see in the prophet's rest under the terebinth, so near Bethel, "peccati initium; moras utique nectere non debuit." It was like Eve's lingering near the place where temptation lay.

[493] "'Whom the gods love die young' was said of yore" (Byron). It was said by Menander: "Ὃν γὰρ θεοὶ φιλοῦσιν ἀποθνῄσκει νέος"; and by Plautus: "Quem dii diligunt, adolescens moritur" (*Bacch.*, iv. 7, 18). A similar thought is found in Plutarch, in St. Chrysostom, and many others.

[494] Ahijah had not followed the example of the Levites and pious persons who, the chronicler says, went in numbers to the Southern Kingdom.

[495] Nikuddim (only elsewhere in Josh. ix. 5-12); LXX., κολλυρίδες; Vulg., *crustula*; A.V., "cracknels." They were some sort of cakes. Presents

to prophets were customary (see 1 Sam. ix. 7, 8; 1 Kings xiii. 7; 2 Kings v. 5, viii. 8, 9).

[496] Heb., "His eyes stood" (comp. 1 Sam. iv. 15). It seems to imply *amaurosis.*

[497] This tremendous expression only occurs elsewhere in Ezek. xxiii. 35; but comp. Psalm l. 17; Neh. ix. 26.

[498] The coarse expression of 1 Kings xiv. 10 (1 Sam. xxv. 22; 2 Kings ix. 8) means "every male." The phrase "him that is shut up and him that is left in Israel" (Deut. xxxii. 36) is obscure and alliterative. It has been variously explained to mean, (1) "bond and free," (2) "imprisoned or released," (3) "kept in by legal impurity or at large" (Jer. xxxvi. 5), (4) "under or over age," (5) "married or unmarried." (Reuss renders the paronomasia, "qu'il soit caché ou lâché en Israel.") LXX. ἐχόμενον καὶ ἐγκαταλελειμμένον; Vulg. *clausum et novissimum.*

[499] In ancient days this was regarded as the most terrible of calamities.

> "Ἀλλ᾽ ἄρα τόνγε κύνες τε καὶ οἰωνοὶ κατέδαψαν
> Κείμενον ἐν πεδίῳ ἑκὰς ἄστεος, οὐδέ κέ τίς μιν
> Κλαῦσεν Ἀχαιϊάδων· μάλα γὰρ μέγα μήσατο ἔργον."
> Hom., *Od.,* iii. 258.

Comp. Deut. xxviii. 26; 1 Sam. xvii. 44, 45. And after in Jeremiah (vii. 33, viii. 2, ix. 22, etc.) and Ezekiel (xxix. 5, xxxix. 17, etc.).

[500] 1 Kings xiv. 14: "That day: but what? even now."

[501] It is almost identical with the message of doom pronounced on other kings, like Baasha (1 Kings xvi. 3-5) and Ahab (1 Kings xxi. 19-23).

[502] Ewald pronounces them to be clearly an addition of the Deuteronomist.

[503] LXX., εἰς γῆν Σαριρά. The additions to the LXX. have the touching incident, "Καὶ ἐγένετο ὡς εἰσῆλθεν εἰς τὴν Σαριρὰ καὶ τὸ παιδάειον ἀπέθανεν, καὶ ἐξῆλθεν ἡ κραυγὴ εἰς ἀπαντήν."

[504] Verg., *Æn.,* vi. 870.

[505] See Job xii. 12; Psalm xxi. 4; Prov. iii. 2-16.

[506] Wisdom iv. 8-14.

[507] Josh. xix. 44, xxi. 23; 1 Kings xv. 27, xvi. 15.

[508] His father therefore could not have been Ahijah the prophet, who was an Ephraimite. He was the only ruler who came from slothful Issachar (Gen. xlix. 14, 15) except the unknown Tola (Judg. x. 1).

[509] For any other records of Nadab the writer refers to "the Chronicles of the Kings of Israel."

[510] 2 Chron. xvi. 7-10.

[511] 2 Chron. xx. 34.

[512] Comp. Hosea vii. 3-7.

[513] If Zimri was a descendant of the House of Saul, as is possible from the occurrence of the name in the number of Saul's descendants (1 Chron. viii. 36), we perhaps see an excuse for his ill-considered conspiracy. He acted, says Grotius, upon the principle, "Νήπιος ὃς πατέρα κτείνας υιοὺς καταλείπει."

[514] Comp. 2 Kings ix. 7 with Hosea i. 4. Thus Babylon is at once commissioned to punish, and condemned for ruthlessness: Isa. xlvii. 6.

[515] According to the LXX. she was a daughter of Hanun, son of Naash, King of Ammon (2 Sam. x. 1).

[516] Canon Rawlinson, *Kings of Israel and Judah.*

[517] 1 Kings xiv. 21. "A boy and faint-hearted" (2 Chron. xiii. 7). The additions to the LXX. say that he was sixteen, and reigned twelve years.

[518] In the LXX. additions it was a little before this occasion (after the revolt) that "Shemaiah the Enlamite" tore his new cloak and gave ten parts to Jeroboam.

[519] The *Chammanim* were, according to some, pillars to Baal-Hammon. For the *Asherim*, see Deut. xvi. 21; 2 Kings xxi. 3. They were wooden pillars to Asherah, and were called *Asherim* just as statues of the Virgin are called "Virgins." *Asheroth* seem to be various forms of the Nature-goddess herself (2 Chron. xxxiii. 3). Asherah = Ὀρθία. Like the other kings of Judah, Rehoboam had an exaggerated harem and provided for the young princes by settling them in separate cities as governors.

[520] Jerome compares them to the horrible *Galli* of the Syrian goddess. LXX., τετελεσμένοι ("initiated"); Aquila, ἐνηλλαγμένοι ("changed"); Theodotion, κεχωρισμένοι ("set apart"); Symmachus, ἑταιρίδες. They were also called "dogs" (comp. Deut. xxiii. 18).

[521] According to the chronicler Rehoboam's defection only began in the fourth year of his reign.

[522] He was the first king of the twenty-second dynasty of Bubastis or Pibeseth, and succeeded about b.c. 988 in the fourteenth year of Solomon. The Egyptians (Manetho) called him Shesonk (Sesonsochosis) Sasychis, Herod., ii. 136; LXX., Σουσακίμ; Vulg., *Sesac.*

[523] He was of alien, perhaps of Assyrian, race. His family had settled at Bubastis, and his grandfather had married the daughter of the Pharaoh. His son Osorkhon also married the Princess Keramat, a daughter of the last Tanite king. Imitating the example of Hir-hor, he combined many offices, and then quietly seized the crown.

[524] Brugsch, *Geogr. Inschriften altägyptischer Denkmäler*, ii. 58; Lepsius, *Denkmäler*, iii. 252; *Story of the Nations: Egypt*, pp. 228-307; Stade, i. 354 (who reproduces the sculptures). They are carved on the wall of a Temple of Amon on the southern side of a smaller temple (built by Rameses III.). Shishak is smiting with his club a number of captive Jews, whom he grasps by the hair. The names of the towns and districts are paraded in two long rows, each name being enclosed in a shield. Amon is delivering them all to his beloved son "Shashonq." These smitten people are described as "the *Am* of a distant land, and the Fenekh" (Phœnicians).

[525] *Lit.*, "Judah-king." Brugsch thinks it is the name of a town. It cannot mean, as Champollion thought, "King of Judah."

[526] See Shishak in *Bibl. Dict.* It is extremely difficult to believe that these cities were taken by the Egyptian army in order to help Jeroboam.

[527] Josephus says that Shishak did all this ἀμαχητὶ (*Antt.*, VIII. x. 2, 3), but he confuses Shishak with Sesostris (Herod., ii. 102, 106).

[528] 1 Kings x. 17.

[529] LXX., 2 Sam. viii. 7; 1 Kings x. 17. A timely humiliation saved Rehoboam from extinction, but he practically became a vassal of Egypt (2 Chron. xii. 5).

[530] אֵת (Ezek. xl. 7).

[531] Ratzim; comp. "*Celeres*," Liv., i. 14. We hear no more of Cherethites and Pelethites. The later kings could not afford to keep up these mercenaries.

[532] *Jewish Church*, ii. 385.

[533] Renan.

[534] 2 Chron. xii. 16; comp. Abiel (1 Sam. ix. 1).

[535] Abijam seems to mean "father of the sea"; *vir maritimus*, Gesenius.

[536] So perhaps, for the same reason, Jehoahaz was shortened into Ahaz. See Canon Rawlinson on 2 Kings xv. 38 (*Speaker's Commentary*). But Simonis, *Onomasticon*, regards the final *m* as intensive.

[537] 2 Chron. xi. 18-23. Rehoboam had eighteen wives, sixty concubines, twenty-eight sons, and sixty daughters. A fragment of the *Stemma Davidis* may make things clearer to the reader:—

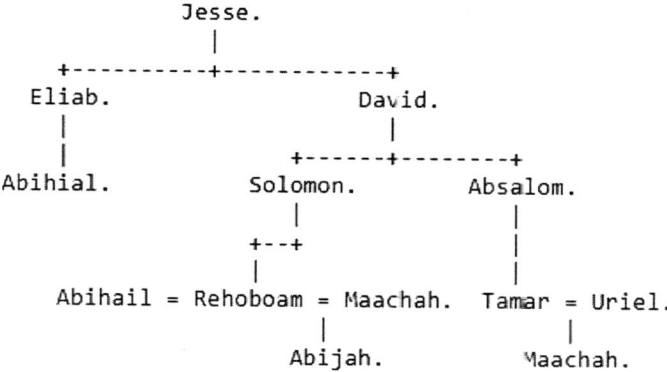

```
                        Jesse.
                          |
      +----------+-----------+
   Eliab.                  David.
      |                      |
      |              +-----+--------+
  Abihial.       Solomon.        Absalom.
                    |                |
                  +--+               |
                    |                |
  Abihail = Rehoboam = Maachah.  Tamar = Uriel.
                    |                |
                 Abijah.          Maachah.
```

Thus on both sides, as a great-grandson and great-great-grandson, Abijah was descended from David.

[538] The lamp (LXX., κατάλειμμα; in xi. 36, θέσις) is the sign of home (1 Kings xi. 36; 2 Kings viii. 19. Comp. Psalm xviii. 28, cxxxii. 17). There was, as the chronicler boldly expressed it, "a covenant of salt" between God and the House of David (2 Chron. xiii. 5; comp. Numb. xviii. 19).

[539] Chron. xiii. 22.

[540] Zemaraim was in Benjamin near Bethel (Josh. xviii. 22), apparently Kirbet *el-Szomer* in the Jordan valley, four miles north of Jericho.

[541] 2 Chron. xiii. 3-19. So that the golden calf and its chapel and its priests must, if the account be true, have fallen into his power. But it does not seem to have made the least difference. It is certain that "the calf" remained undisturbed till the days of the Assyrian invasion.

[542] How atrocious these "abominations were" may be seen from the Pentateuch (Lev. xviii. 3-25, xx. 1-23; Deut. xviii. 6-12).

[543] 1 Kings xv. 15.

[544] Ewald, iv. 49.

[545] Comp. the *Madame Mère* in the French court.

[546] The LXX. (Vat.) calls her Ana.

[547] That it was not perfectly successful we see from 1 Kings xxii. 46.

[548] The word is an ἅπαξ λεγόμενον. It is only applied to this grotesque and obscene figure (1 Kings xv. 13; 2 Chron. xv. 16).

[549] 2 Kings xi. 16, xxiii. 4, 6, 12; 2 Chron. xxix. 16, xxx. 14. Vulg., *in Sacris Priapi*. Jerome (*ad Hos.*, i. 4) calls Maachah's "horror" a *Simulacrum Priapi* (see Selden, *De Dis Syris Syntagma*, ii. 5).

[550] 2 Chron. xvi. 8. Zarkh, perhaps Osorkhon I. (O-*serek*-on, "Ammon's darling"), was the feebler successor of Shesonk, Maspero, p. 362; Ewald, iii. 470. Shishak's army also consisted of Sushim and Lubim (2 Chron. xii. 3).

[551] The defeat had important consequences. Egypt did not again attack Palestine till three centuries later, under Pharaoh Nechoh (b.c. 609). The defeat weakened the Bubastite dynasty (Rawlinson, p. 36), though it continued to reign for two centuries. The "invasion" may have been a mere raid. The Pharaohs always seem to have degenerated from the founders of their dynasty, both in personal beauty and intellectual force.

[552] Josh. xviii. 25, now Er-Ram. No great importance can be attached to the dates, which are often self-contradictory.

[553] Ben-Hadad, "son of Hadad," the Sun-god (Macrob., *Saturn*, i. 24). Tabrimmon, "Rimmon is good." According to Sayce (*Hibbert Lectures*, p. 42), Rimmon—an Accadian name, which became, in Semitic, Rammânu, "the exalted"—was identified by the Syrians with the Sun-god Hadad, whom Shahmanaser called *Dada*. In Assyrian *Dadu* ("dear child") is akin to David and to Dido.

[554] Ijon is probably Merj Ayion, "the meadow of the House of Maachah"; called also, Abel-maim, "the meadow of the waters"; "a city and a mother in Israel" (2 Sam. xx. 19); now Abil in the Ard-el-Huleh.

[555] See Numb. xxxiv. 11; Josh. xiii. 27.

[556] Josh. xxi. 17; 2 Kings xxiii. 8.

[557] LXX., ἡ σκοπία. Jer. xli. 5-9. Into this well Ishmael flung the corpses of the murdered adherents of Gedaliah.

[558] Renan, *Hist. du Peuple Israel,* ii. 248. Comp. Rephaiah.

[559] 2 Chron. xv. 1-15.

[560] 2 Chron. xvi. 9, 10.

[561] Following the precedent set by Rehoboam, he established his six younger sons in castles and fenced cities. Athaliah must have found it difficult to exterminate their families if she attempted this.

[562] The Nitzab or Præfect of Edom was allowed the barren title of king.

[563] 2 Chron. xx. 37. His name faintly recalls that of Eleazar, son of Dodo (2 Sam. xxiii. 9). Dodavahu means "friend of God."

[564] 2 Chron. xx. 36, 37. It would be monstrous to send ships to circumnavigate Africa in order to reach Tartessus. The last resource of the harmonists (*e.g.*, Keil) to save the accuracy of the chronicler is to suppose that Jehoshaphat meant to drag the whole fleet across the Isthmus of Suez, and so to sail from one of the havens of Palestine!

[565] "Cette version," says Munk (*Palestine*, p. 314), "a probablement pris naissance dans l'esprit de rigorisme qui animait plus tard les écrivans Juifs." "This," says Dr. Robertson Smith, "is a mere pragmatical inference from the story in Kings." See his further remarks in *The Old Testament in the Jewish Church*, chap. ii., p. 146. He regards parts of the Books of Chronicles as being, in fact, a Jewish *Midrash*. "It is not History, but *Haggada*, moralising romance. And the chronicler himself gives the name of *Midrash* (R.V., 'story') to two of the sources from which he drew (2 Chron. xiii. 22, xxiv. 27), so that there is really no mystery as to the nature of the work when it departs from the old canonical histories" (p. 148).

[566] We shall have further glimpses of Jehoshaphat in the reigns of Ahab and even of Jehoram.

[567] See 1 Chron. xvi. 34; 2 Chron. v. 13, vii. 3, xx. 21; Psalms cvi., cvii., cxviii., etc. The eighty-third Psalm may owe its origin to this deliverance, and Hengstenberg thinks Psalms xlvii. and xlviii. also.

[568] The title "valley of Jehoshaphat" is thought also to have derived its origin from these events. Comp. Joel iii. 2.

[569] 2 Chron. xxi. 2, 3.

[570] There is a little exaggeration here.

[571] 2 Kings ix. 31.

[572] R.V., "the *castle* of the king's house."

[573] Justin, *Hist.*, i. 3; cf. Herod., i. 176, vii. 107; Liv., xxi. 14. Ewald elaborates out of his own consciousness an extraordinary romance about Zimri and the queen-mother.

[574] Josephus (*Antt.*, VIII. xii. 5) says that Tibni was assassinated, as does the Rabbinic *Seder Olam Rabba*, chap. xvii. LXX., καὶ ἀπέθανε Θαβνὶ καὶ Ἰωρὰμ ὁ ἀδελφὸς αὐτοῦ.

[575] Athaliah is called "the daughter of Omri."

[576] The Aramæans have come to be incorrectly called Syrians because the Greeks confused them with the Assyrians.

[577] 1 Kings xx. 34.

[578] 2 Kings iii. 4.

[579] 1 Kings xvi. 25.

[580] Micah vi. 16.

[581] Isa. xxviii. 1-4.

[582] Stanley, *Lectures*, ii. 242.

[583] 1 Kings xx. 1; 2 Kings vi. 24.

[584] Josephus, *Antt.*, XV. vii. 7. One of the few instances in Palestine where the ancient name has been superseded by a more modern one. The early Assyrians call it Beth-Khumri, "House of Omri"; but the name Sammerin occurs in the monument of Tiglath-Pileser II.

[585] About £800 of our money.

[586] LXX., Σκοπία; רָמַשׁ, "to watch."

[587] Meyer, *Gesch. d. Alt.*, 331; Kittel, ii. 221; Schrader, *Keilinschr.*, i. 165.

[588] וּתְרוּבְנ (1 Kings xvi. 27).

[589] It is needless in each separate case to enter into the chronological minutiæ about which the historian is little solicitous. A table of the chronology so far as it can be ascertained is furnished, *infra*.

[590] 1 Kings xx. 5; 2 Kings x. 7.

[591] Hitzig thinks that Psalm xlv. was an epithalamium on this occasion, from the mention of "ivory palaces" and "the daughter of Tyre." Had it been composed for the marriage of Solomon, or Jehoram and Athaliah, or any king of Judah, there would surely have been an allusion to Jerusalem. Moreover, the queen is called לֵגֶשׁ, which is a Chaldee (Dan. v. 2), or perhaps a North Palestine word. The word in Judah was Gebira.

[592] Ἰθόβαλος, Josephus, *Antt.*, VIII. xiii. 1; *c. Ap.*, I. 18 (quoting the heathen historian Menander of Ephesus). It may, however, be "Man of Baal," like Saul's son Ishbaal (Ishbosheth). In Tyre the high priest was only second to the king in power (Justin, *Hist.*, xviii. 4), and Ethbaal united both dignities. He died aged sixty-eight. Another Ethbaal was on the throne during the siege of Tyre by Nebuchadnezzar (Josephus, *Antt.*, X. xi. I).

[593] Josephus, *c. Ap.*, I. 18. The genealogy is:—

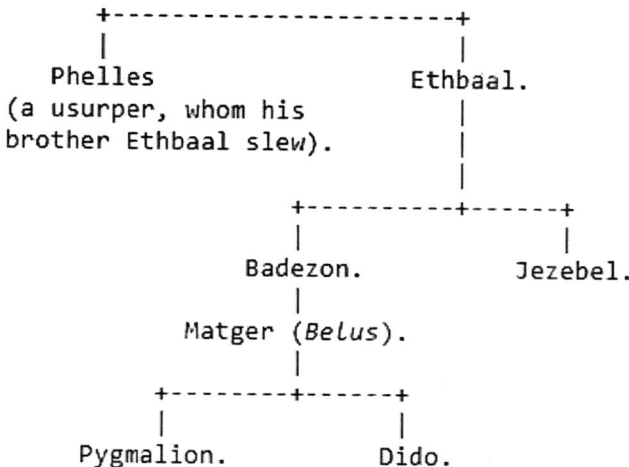

```
+------------------------+
|                        |
Phelles                Ethbaal.
(a usurper, whom his     |
brother Ethbaal slew).   |
                         |
                         |
            +-----------+------+
            |                  |
         Badezon.            Jezebel.
            |
       Matger (Belus).
            |
     +--------+------+
     |               |
  Pygmalion.        Dido.
```

See Canon Rawlinson, *Speaker's Commentary, ad loc.*

[594] Plaut., *Pænul.,* V. ii. 6, 7. Phœnician names abound in the element "Baal."

[595] Ahaziah ("Jehovah supports"), Jehoram ("Jehovah is exalted"), Athaliah (?). The word Baal merely meant "Lord"; and perhaps the fact that at one time it had been freely applied to Jehovah Himself may have helped to confuse the religious perceptions of the people. Saul, certainly no idolater, called his son Eshbaal ("the man of Baal"); and it was only the hatred of the name Baal in later times which led the Jews to alter Baal into Bosheth ("shame"), as in Ishbosheth, Mephibosheth. David himself had a son named Beeliada ("known to Baal"), which was altered into Eliada (1 Chron. xiv. 7, iii. 8; 2 Sam. v. 16; comp. 2 Chron. xvii. 17). We even find the name Bealiah ("Baal is Jah") as one of David's men (1 Chron. xii. 5). Hoshea too records that Baali ("my Lord") was used of Jehovah, but changed into Ishi ("my husband") (Hosea ii. 16, 17). It is used simply for owner ("the baal of an ox") in "the Book of the Covenant" (Exod. xxi. 28). See Robertson Smith, *Rel. of the Semites,* 92.

[596] Ethbaal is called King of Sidon (1 Kings xvi. 31), and was also King of Tyre (Menander *ap.* Josephus, *Antt.,* VIII. xiii. 1).

[597] 1 Kings xvi. 23; 2 Kings iii. 2, x. 27.

[598] *Asherim* seem to be upright wooden stocks of trees in honour of the Nature-goddess Asheroth. The Temple of Baal at Tyre had no image, only two *Matstseboth,* one of gold given by Hiram, one of "emerald" (Dius and Menander *ap.* Josephus, *Antt.,* VIII. v. 3; *c. Ap.,* I. 18; Herod., ii. 66).

[599] Döllinger, *Judenth. u. Heidenthum* (E. T.), i. 425-29.

[600] 2 Sam. x. 5; Judg. iii. 28.

[601] 2 Chron. xxviii. 15.

[602] Comp. Josh. vi. 26; 2 Sam. x. 5.

[603] Rev. ii. 20.

[604] 1 Kings xxi. 25, 26.

[605] Henry Smith, *The Trumpet of the Lord sounding to Judgment.*

[606] Tobit i. 2.

[607] Josephus, *Antt.*, VIII. xiii. 2; Vat. (LXX.), Θεσβίτης ὁ ἐκ Θεσβῶν. The Alex. LXX. omits Θεσβίτης. An immense amount has been written about Elijah. Among others, see Knobel, *Der Prophetismus*, ii. 73; Köster, *Der Thesbiter*; Stanley, ii., lect. xxx.; Maurice, *Prophets and Kings*, serm. viii.; F. W. Robertson, ii., serm. vi.; Milligan, *Elijah* (Men of the Bible).

[608] See 1 Chron. ii. 55.

[609] See Cheyne, *The Hallowing of Criticism*, p. 9.

[610] Zech. xiii. 4.

[611] The word also means "sea-mist" (Cheyne, p. 15).

[612] Lev. xxvi. 19; Psalm cxxxiv. 1; Heb. x. 11.

[613] So too Ecclus. xlviii. 2, "He *brought* a sore famine upon them, and by his zeal he diminished their number"; but the writer adds, "*By the word of the Lord he shut up the heavens.*" Deut. xxviii. 12; Amos iv. 7.

[614] 2 Sam. xxi. 1.

[615] 2 Sam. xxiv. 13. "Three," not "seven," is probably here the true reading.

[616] Not "by," as in the A.V. Cherith means "cut off" (1 Kings xvii. 3). "The Lord hid him" (Jer. xxxvi. 26). "In famine he shall redeem thee from death.... At famine and destruction thou shalt laugh" (Job v. 20-22).

[617] Robinson.

[618] Benjamin of Tudela.

[619] Marinus Sanutus (1321).

[620] The ravens were unclean birds (Deut. xiv. 14), and this naturally startled and offended the Rabbis.

[621] Prov. xxx. 17.

[622] Orbo was a small town near the Jordan and Bethshan.

[623] On the other side, Bunsen (*Bibelwerk*, v. 2, 540) speaks too strongly when he says that "nothing but boundless ignorance, or, where historical criticism has not died out, an hierarchical dilettanti reaction, foolhardy hypocrisy, and weak-hearted fanaticism would wish to demand the faith of a Christian community in the historic truths of these miracles as if they had actually taken place." He regards the whole narrative as a "popular epic— the fruit of an inspiration, which he, as it were some superhuman being, awakened in his disciples."

[624] I append the remarks of Professor Milligan, a theologian of unimpeachable orthodoxy. "The miracle," he says, "is so remarkable, so much out of keeping with most of the other miracles of Scripture, that even pious and devout minds may well be perplexed by it, and we can feel no surprise at the attempts made to explain it. Such attempts are not inconsistent with the most devout reverence for the word of God. They are rather, not unfrequently, the result of a just persuasion that the Eastern mind did not express itself in forms similar to those of the West" (*Elijah*, p. 22). He proceeds to protest against the harsh condemnation of those who thus only try to interpret the real ideas present in the mind of the writer. He regards it as perhaps a highly poetic and figurative representation of the truth that the God of Nature was with Elijah. "The value of the Prophet's experience is neither heightened by a literal, nor diminished by a figurative, interpretation of what passed" (p. 24).

[625] 1 Kings xvii. 7. Perhaps years (Lev. xxv. 29; 1 Sam. xxvii. 7).

[626] Job vi. 17.

[627] Menander, quoted by Josephus, *Antt.*, VIII. xiii. 2. He says it lasted for a year.

[628] LXX., "My sons"—perhaps with reference to "her house" in verse 15.

[629] Perhaps the language of the Hebrew is not actually decisive. Josephus says, τὴν ψυχὴν ἀφεῖναι καὶ δόξαι νεκρόν. In any case his recovery was due to Elijah's prayer.

[630] The phrase "man of God" is characteristic of the Book of Kings, in which it occurs fifty-three times. It became a normal description of Elijah and Elisha. "What have I to do with thee?" Comp. 2 Sam. xvi. 10; Luke v. 8. It was a common superstition that death always followed the appearance of superhuman beings.

[631] Compare the similar revivals of life wrought by Elisha (2 Kings iv. 34), and by St. Paul (Acts xx. 10).

[632] Amos ix. 3: "And though they hide themselves in the top of Carmel, I will search and take them out thence." The phrase shows the security and seclusion of these caves and thickets, the haunt once of lions and bears, and still of leopards and hyænas.

[633] The LXX. adds that he inflicted vengeance because Elijah was not found: "Καὶ ἐνέπρησε τὴν βασιλείαν καὶ τὰς χώρας αὐτῆς ὅτι οὐχ εὗρηκέ σε" (1 Kings xviii. 10).

[634] Obadiah seems to have believed in miraculous transference of the Prophet from place to place. Comp. Ezek. iii. 12-14 (where "the spirit" may be rendered "a spirit," or "a wind"), viii. 3; 2 Kings ii. 16; Acts viii. 39; and the Ebionite Gospel of St. Matthew. "My mother, the Holy Ghost, took me by a hair of the head, and carried me to Mount Tabor" (Orig. *in Joann.*, ii., § 6; and Jer. *in Mic.* vii. 6). So in Bel and the Dragon 33-36 (Abarbanel, *Comm. in Habakkuk*) the prophet Habakkuk is said to have been taken invisibly to supply food to Daniel in the den of lions. "Then the angel of the Lord took him by the crown and bare him by the hair of his head, and through the vehemency of his spirit" (*Midr. Robshik Rabba, "in the might of the Holy Ghost"*) "set him in Babylon."

[635] 1 Kings xviii. 15, LXX., "The Lord God of Israel" has now become to him more prominently "the Lord God of Hosts."

[636] The phrase had already been applied to Achan (Josh. vii. 25).

[637] *I.e.*, were maintained at Jezebel's expense. The subsequent narration is silent as to the presence of the prophets of the Asherah, and Wellhausen thinks that the words here are an interpolation.

[638] Isa. xxxiii. 9, xxxv. 2; Micah vii. 14. Its beauty and fruitfulness are alluded to in Jer. xlvi. 18, l. 19; Amos i. 2, ix. 3; Nahum i. 4; Cant. vii. 5.

[639] Sir George Grove, to whose excellent article in Smith's *Dict. of Bible* (i. 279) I am indebted, quotes Martineau (i. 317), Porter's *Handbook*, Van de Velde, etc. See, too, Stanley, *Sinai and Palestine*, pp. 353-56.

[640] On these *Lapides judaici*, see my *Life of Christ*, i. 129. Illustrations are given in the illustrated edition.

[641] Jambl., *Vit. Pythag.*, iii.; Suet., *Vesp.*, 5; Tac., *Hist.*, ii. 78; Reland, *Palest.*, pp. 327-30.

[642] Megiddo lies in the plain below, and this scene of conflict between good and the powers of evil was an anticipated Armageddon.

[643] Isa. xlix. 2; Cheyne, p. 16.

[644] LXX., 1 Kings xviii. 21, ἕως πότε ὑμεῖς χωλανεῖτε ἐπ' ἀμφοτέραις ταῖς ἰγνύαις. Vulg., *usquequo claudicatis in duas partes?* Cheyne renders it: "How long will ye go lame upon tottering knees?" In Psalm cxix. 113, סֵעֲפִים are "the double-minded." In Ezek. xxxi. 6, תוֹפֿעֹת, "diverging branches." In Isa. ii. 21, יַסְעֵף, "clefts of rocks" (Bähr).

[645] Herodian (*Hist.*, v. 3) describes the dance of Heliogabalus round the altar of the Emesene Sun-god, and Apuleius describes at length the fanatic leapings and gashings of the execrable *Galli*—the eunuch-mendicant priests of the Syrian goddess. From these sources and from allusions in Seneca, Lucian, Statius, Arnobius, etc., Movers (*Phöniz.*, i. 682) derives his description (quoted by Keil, *ad loc.*, E.T., p. 281): "A discordant howling opens the scene. Now they fly wildly through one another, with the head sunk down to the ground, but turning round in circles, so that the loose flowing hair drags through the mire. Thereupon they first bite themselves on the arm, and at last cut themselves with two-edged swords, which they are wont to carry. Then begins a new scene. One of them who surpasses all the rest in frenzy, begins to prophesy with sighs and groans, openly accuses himself of past sins, which he now wishes to punish by the mortifying of the flesh, takes the knotted whip which the Galli are wont to bear, lashes his back, cuts himself with swords, till the blood trickles down from his mangled body."

[646] Verse 27. Others render it "meditating" (De Wette Thenius) or "peevish" (Bähr). Comp. Hom., *Il.*, i. 423; *Od.*, i. 22, etc.

[647] This instance of "grim sarcastic humour" is almost unique in Scripture. It was made more mordant by the paronomasia (2 Sam. i. 22) וּל גִּישׁ־יָכִן חִישׁ־יִכ.

[648] Plutarch (*De Superstit.*, p. 170) says: "The priests of Bellona offered their own blood, which was deemed powerful to move their gods." Comp. Herod., ii. 61; Lucian, *De Dea Syra*, 50; Apul., *Metam.*, viii. 28.

[649] הַחֶנְמַה תוֹלֲעַל דַע, "till towards (Numb. xxviii 4) the offering of the Minchah." LXX., θυσία; Vulg., *sacrificium* and *holocaustum*. In verse 39 it is omitted in the LXX. "There is a great concurrence of evidence that the evening sacrifice of the first Temple was not a holocaust, but a cereal oblation" (Robertson Smith, p. 143, quoting 1 Kings xviii. 34; 2 Kings xvi. 15; Ezek. ix. 4, Heb).

[650] Heb., וַיִּתְנַבְּאוּ; LXX., διέτρεχον; Vulg., *transiliebant*. Literally, they acted like frantic prophets (1 Sam. xviii. 10; Jer. xxix. 26).

[651] LXX., θαλάσσαν, or "sea"—the name given to Solomon's molten laver; but the description, "as great as would contain two *seahs* of seed," is curious, for a seah was only the third of an ephah.

[652] Blunt (*Undesigned Coincidences*, II. xxxii.) thinks that as the drought had been so intense the water must have been sea-water. But Josephus says it was drawn ἀπὸ τῆς κρήνης (*Antt.*, VIII. xiii. 5); and the well still exists.

[653] Priests, both pagan and mediæval, have been adepts at deception. At the Reformation the mechanism of winking Madonnas, etc., was exposed to the people. At Pompeii may still be seen the secret staircase behind the altar, and the pipes let into the head of Isis from behind, through which the priests spoke her pretended oracles. St. Chrysostom (*Orat. in. Petr. et Eliam*, which is of uncertain genuineness) tells us that he had himself seen (θεάτης αὐτὸς γενομένος) altars with concealed hollows in the middle, into which the unsuspected operator crept, and blew up a fire which the people were assured was self-kindled (see Keil, p. 282). One legend says that on this occasion a man was suffocated, who had been concealed by the Baal priests inside their altar.

[654] 1 Kings xviii. 36.

[655] Comp. Lev. ix. 24. Analogous stories existed among pagans (Hom., *Il.*, ii. 305; *Od.*, ii. 143; Verg., *Ecl.*, viii. 105). Pliny says that annals recorded the eliciting of lightning by prayers and incantations (*H. N.*, ii. 54; Winer, *Realwörterb.* 371).

[656] It is after Elijah's time, and probably from his influence, that from this time proper names compounded with Jehovah become almost the rule—as in Ahaziah, Jehoram, Jehu, Jehoahaz, Joash, Pekahiah, etc.

[657] 1 Kings xix. 1, בְּרָחַב; LXX., ἐν ῥομφαίᾳ.

[658] Renan, *Vie de Jésus*, 100.

[659] Matt. xii. 19, 20; Isa. xlii. 2, 3; Ezek. xxxiv. 16.

[660] LXX., ὅτι φωνὴ τῶν ποδῶν τοῦ ὑετοῦ. Perhaps, with reference to this reading, Josephus afterwards describes "the little cloud" as "no bigger than a human footstep" (οὐ πλέον ἴχνους ἀνθρωπίνου).

[661] LXX., τῷ παιδαρίῳ αὐτοῦ.

[662] LXX., 1 Kings xviii. 45, Καὶ ἔκλαιε καὶ ἐπορεύετο Ἀχαὰβ ἕως Ιεζράελ.

[663] Menander of Ephesus (Josephus, *Antt.*, VIII. xiii. 2).

[664] Eisenlohr, *Das Volk Israel,* p. 162.

[665] He refers to Gibbon, iv. 232.

[666] See Mrs. Gaskell's *Life of Charlotte Brönte.*

[667] LXX., 1 Kings xix. 2.

[668] The touch "which belongeth to Judah" shows that the Elijah-narrative emanated from some prophet in the northern schools. In later days it was much visited by pilgrims from the Northern Kingdom (Amos v. 5, viii. 14).

[669] Matt. xxvi. 36.

[670] 1 Kings xix. 4, 5, תַּחַת אַ רֹתֶם; Vulg., *subter unam juniperum.* The plant is the *Genista monosperma,* with papilionaceous flowers. Not "juniper," as in Luther (*Wachholder*) and the A.V. LXX., ῥαθμὲν φύτον. See Robinson, *Researches,* i. 203, 205. It gave its name to the station Rithmah (Numb. xxxiii. 18) and the Wadies Retemît and Retâmah.

[671] Comp. Moses (Numb. xi. 15), Jonah (Jonah iv. 3).

[672] Pope's epitaph on Mrs. Elizabeth Corbet, in St. Margaret's Westminster.

[673] Jer. xx. 1-18.

[674] Psalm cii. 6, 8.

[675] Psalm xxxviii. 11, 12.

[676] Jer. v. 31, xxix. 9.

[677] John xvi. 32.

[678] Krummacher.

[679] The *coals* (*reshaphim*) for the cake (LXX., ἐγκρυφίας ὀλυρίτης; Vulg., *subcinericius panis*) were the dry twigs of the broom plant, still sold for that purpose in the markets of Cairo. Comp. Psalm cxx. 4; "*coals of juniper.*"

[680] 1 Kings xix. 5. מַלְאָךְ means "a messenger," and in verse 2 is used of the messenger of Jezebel.

[681] Exod. xxxiii. 22.

[682] *Bible Educator,* iii. 135.

[683] The use of the plural, and the absence of any objections to an uncentralised worship, are proofs of the northern origin of the Elijah-episode.

[684] LXX., αὔριον; Josephus, *Antt.*, VIII. xiii. 7; Comp. Exod. xxxiv. 2. It is hardly likely that the stupendous vision would follow instantly and without a moment's preparation.

[685] Deut. iv. 12, 15, (comp. v. 4, 22, 23). Of Moses, on the other hand, it is said, "the similitude of the Lord shall he behold" (Numb. xii. 8; Exod. xxxiii. 11; Deut. xxxiv. 10).

[686] מקום, τόπος, "place," was a sort of recognised euphemism for God in Rabbinic and Alexandrian exegesis. Thus, in Exod. xxiv. 10, for "they saw *the God of Israel*," the LXX. have εἶδον τὸν τόπον οὗ εἱστήκει ὁ Θεός. Philo says, "God Himself is called Place" (*De Somn.*, i. 525). Rabbi Isaac says, "God is not in Makom, but Makom is in God." See my Bampton Lectures on *Hist. of Interpretation*, p. 120; *Early Days of Christianity*, i. 261.

[687] Psalm civ. 4; Heb. i. 7. This intermediacy of angels is prominently alluded to in Acts vii. 53; Gal. iii. 19; Heb. ii. 2, 3; Deut. xxxiii. 2; Psalm lxviii. 17.

[688] The anthropomorphism which the Targumists disliked vanishes in the Chaldee: "And before Him was a host of angels of the wind rending the mountains, and breaking the rocks, before the Lord but the Shechinah was not in the hosts of the angels of the wind, and after the hosts of the angels of the wind was the host of the angel of the earthquake, etc."

[689] Job xxxviii. 1, xl. 6.

[690] Ezek. i. 4.

[691] Jer. xxiii. 19, 20, xxv. 32, xxx. 23.

[692] Psalms xviii. 10, civ. 3, 5.

[693] Nahum i. 3, 5.

[694] Psalm xviii. 7, lxxvii. 18, xcvii. 4; Judg. v. 4; 2 Sam. xxii. 8.

[695] Hab. iii. 3-16.

[696] 1 Kings xix. 12; LXX., φωνὴ αὔρας λεπτῆς; Vulg., *Sibilus auræ tenuis*; Chaldee, "a voice of angels singing in silence."

[697] Jehu was the grandson of Nimshi, and was the son of Jehoshaphat (2 Kings ix. 2).

[698] Isa. xi. 4, xlix. 2; comp. Jer. i. 10, xviii. 7.

[699] Comp. Rom. xii. 5. Kissing images was a sign of idolatry then as it is now. The foot of the statue of St. Peter in Rome is worn away with kisses. Hosea xiii. 2 tells us of the custom of kissing the calves. Comp. Psalm ii. 12. Cicero tells us that the lovely brazen statue of Hercules at Agrigentum had

the mouth and chin partly worn away by the kisses of the devout (in *Verr.*, iv. 43).

[700] Herder, who was a devout poet, and therefore a true imaginative interpreter of devout poetry, says: "The vision was to show the fiery zeal of the Prophet that would amend everything by the storm, the mild process of God, and proclaim His longsuffering tender nature as previously the voice did to Moses: hence the scene was so beautifully changed." Long before him the wise Theodoret had said: Διὰ δὲ τούτων ἔδειξεν ὅτι μακροθυμία καὶ φιλανθρωπία μόνη φίλη Θεῷ. Irenæus, still earlier (c. *Hær.*, iv. 27), saw in the vision an emblem of the difference between the law and the gospel; and Grotius, following him, says, "Evangelii figuratio, quod non venit cum vento, terræ motu, et fulminibus ut lex," Exod. xix. 16 (see Keil, *ad loc.*, whose illustrations are often valuable when his exegesis is false and obsolete).

[701] Psalm xviii. 7-9; comp. 2 Sam. xxii. 8-11.

[702] Isa. xiii. 13.

[703] Isa. xxix. 6; comp. Ecclus. xxxix. 28.

[704] W. S. Landor.

[705] 1 Kings iv. 12. It was in the north part of the Jordan valley.

[706] 1 Kings xix. 19.

[707] The Hebrew can hardly bear the meaning that he was finishing the twelfth furrow in his field, ploughed by his single yoke of oxen.

[708] For these particulars, and the following translations, see Dr. Ginsburg in *Records of the Past*, xi. 163; and Dr. Neubauer, *id.*, New Series, ii. 194; *The Moabite Stone*, Second Edition (Reeves & Turner), 1871; Dr. Schlottmann, *Die Sieggessaüle Mesas*, 1870; Nöldeke, *Die Inschrift der König Mesa,* 1870; Stade, i. 534; Kittel, ii. 193, etc.

[709] Chemosh-Gad perhaps came to the throne in the fourth year of Omri, about b.c. 926, and reigned till the close of Ahaziah's reign (b.c. 896).

[710] Comp. 1 Sam. vii. 12.

[711] For it is indirectly mentioned that "*his father*" had taken cities from Omri.

[712] LXX., Exod. iii. 16.

[713] Comp. Josh. ix. 18; Judg. xi. 11.

[714] 1 Kings xx. 10. Elohim here, doubtless, means the false gods of Benhadad. Vat. LXX., ὁ θεός; but Chaldee, "the terrors."

[715] "Fanfaronnade, qui veut dire; je réduirai cette bicoque en poussière; j'ai avee moi plus de monde qu'il ne faudra pour l'emporter tout entière" (Reuss). Comp. Herod., viii. 226, where Dieneces answers the braggart vaunt of the Medes.

[716] Reuss renders it, "Ceignant n'est pas encore gaignant." The proverb resembles in different aspects the precept of Solon, τέρμα ὁρᾶν βιότοιο, and "Praise a fair day at night"; and the Italian, "Capo ha cosa fatta"; and the Latin, "Ne triumphum canas ante victoriam"; and the French, "Il ne faut pas vendre le peau de l'ours avant de l'avoir tué."

[717] A.V., "pavilions"; but the word (sukkoth) implies that they were temporary booths rather than tents. They resembled the birchwood pavilions made for the Turkish pachas in campaigns (Keil).

[718] A.V., "Set yourselves in array." LXX., οἰκοδομήσατε χάρακα; Vulg., circumdate civitatem.

[719] Now in the British Museum.

[720] 1 Kings xx. 14 (מְיַרְעֵן).

[721] Jarchi—more Rabbinico—says that these were the seven thousand who had not bowed the knee to Baal.

[722] 1 Kings xx. 20, LXX., καὶ ἐδευτέρωσεν ἕκαστος τὸν παρ᾽ αὐτοῦ.

[723] Or, "pell-mell." The Hebrew in 1 Kings xx. 20 is, מְיֹשָׁרְפוּ סוּס־לֹע, "on a horse with (some) horsemen." Klostermann would supply אוּה. Jonathan takes מְיֹשָׁרְפוּ as a dual—"and two riders with him"; LXX., ἐφ᾽ ἵππων ἱππέων; Vulg., in equo cum equitibus suis; Luther, "sammt Rossen und Reitern."

[724] See 2 Sam. xi. 1. The custom of all countries in the ancient world was to devote the summer months only to campaigns. There were few or no standing armies, and the citizen-conscripts had to look after their farms, or the nation would have starved. The Assyrians, Babylonians, and Persians introduced a gradual revolution in these respects.

[725] 1 Kings xx. 24. LXX., σατράπας.

[726] R.V., "and were victualled," not, as in A.V., "and were all present." Alex. LXX., διοικήθησαν; Vulg., acceptis cibariis.

[727] Why two? No explanation is given. It has been conjectured that Judah had sent a separate contingent to help them in their distress.

[728] Some have supposed that an earthquake occurred, and Canon Rawlinson mentions (Speaker's Commentary) that the earthquake of Lisbon is said to have destroyed sixty thousand persons in five minutes.

[729] רְחֶבׁ רְחֶב. Comp. for similar phrases, (Heb.) Lev. xxv. 53; Deut. xv. 20; 1 Kings xxii. 25; 2 Chron. xxviii. 26. Klostermann, with one of his amazing conjectures, reads "by the spring Harod in Harod"! LXX., εἰς τὸν οἶκον τοῦ κοιτῶνος, εἰς τὸ ταμεῖον; Vulg., *in cubiculum quod erat intra cubiculum.* Josephus makes it a cellar (εἰς ὑπόγαιον οἶκον ἐκρύβη), "like the modern *serdaubs* in which the inhabitants of many Eastern cities live in the summer" (Rawlinson).

[730] The accidental sigh of the engineer was sufficient to prevent the colossal Egyptian statue of a Pharaoh from being moved to its destination. Even Rome shared the immemorial superstition.

[731] Suet., *Claud.*

[732] xx. 33, וִשְׁחֲנִי, from שָׁחַנ, "an augury"; LXX., ἀνελέξαντο τὸν λόγον (οἰωνίσαντο); Vulg., *quod acceperunt viri pro omine.*

[733] Layard, *Nineveh*, 317-19.

[734] The compact is vainly dignified with the name of a תִּירְב, or "covenant."

[735] תוֹצָח. Compare the *Lombard* Streets, and the *Jewries* in London and Paris.

[736] Clericus says, rightly: "Factum Ahabi, quamvis clementiæ speciem præ se ferret, non erat veræ clementiæ, quæ non est erga latrones exercenda; qui si dimittantur multo magis nocebunt."

[737] The object and necessity of this for his purpose is by no means apparent. Perhaps it was to figure the wound which Ahab had by his conduct wilfully inflicted on himself or on Israel.

[738] Verse 38. This, and not "with ashes upon his face," is the meaning of the Hebrew רֵפֶא. LXX., τελαμών, "a headband"; Vulg., *aspersione pulveris*; and so, too, Peshito, Aquila, and Symmachus.

[739] 1 Kings xx. 39. רש in the sense of רַס, according to Ewald's reading.

[740] About £350. Evidently, therefore, the captive is supposed to be a very important person.

[741] יִמְרֵח שִׂיא.

[742] וְּתֵעֶזֵו רַס; Vulg., *indignans, et frendens*, a phrase only used of Ahab (xxi. 4-5). Josephus (*Antt.*, XIII. xv. 5) says that Ahab imprisoned and punished the prophet, whom, with the Rabbis, he identifies with Micaiah.

[743] Zech. xiii. 4.

[744] On this defection and imposture of prophets, see Jer. xxiii. 21-40. Isa. xxx. 9, 10; Ezek. xiii. 7-9; Micah ii. 11; Deut. xviii. 20.

[745] Jer. xxii. 17.

[746] *De Gubernat. Dei.*, viii.; Ambrose, *Ep.*, xli.; Cassian, *De Instit. Monastic. passim.* See chap. xvi. of my *Lives of the Fathers* (St. Jerome), and Zöckler, *Gesch. der Askese*, for many authorities.

[747] See my *Lives of the Fathers*, vol. i. (St. Martin of Tours).

[748] See Jer. xxiii. 20-40.

[749] The Alex. LXX. throughout calls Naboth "an Israelite," not "a Jezreelite."

[750] Both the Hebrew text of 1 Kings xxi. 1 and Josephus (*Antt.*, XIII. xv. 6) locate the vineyard of Naboth at Jezreel. The LXX., however, place it apparently near the threshing-floor of Ahab in Samaria (παρὰ τῇ ἅλῳ Ἀχαὰβ βασίλεως Σαμαρείας), which is the same as the "void place" of 1 Kings xxii. 10. At both cities Ahab's palace was on the city wall, and on either supposition Naboth's vineyard was close by the palace.

[751] Lev. xxv. 23, "The land shall not be sold for ever, for the land is Mine." Numb. xxxvi. 7; Ezek. xlvi. 18.

[752] 2 Sam. xxiv. 24; 1 Kings xvi. 24.

[753] The word rendered "sad" is rendered "mutinous" by Thenius.

[754] LXX., 1 Kings xxi. 7, Σὺ νῦν οὕτως ποιεῖς βασιλέα ἐπὶ Ἰσραήλ·

[755] The signet was carved with the king's name. Rawlinson aptly compares Lady Macbeth's "Infirm of purpose give me the daggers!"

[756] Josephus calls it an ἐκκλησία. "Set Naboth on high" (Heb.) "at the head of the people"; LXX., ἐν ἀρχῇ τοῦ λαοῦ; Vulg., *inter primos populi.*

[757] The charge was that "he cursed God and the king." LXX. (by euphemism), εὐλόγησε; Vulg., *Benedixit.* The Hebrew word has both meanings (comp. Exod. xxii. 28, where some would render *Elohim* not "God," but "the judges." See marg. of R.V.). Stoning was the punishment of blasphemy (Lev. xxiv. 16), and took place outside the city (Acts vii. 58).

[758] 2 Kings ix. 26.

[759] 2 Sam. xvi. 4.

[760] In 1 Kings xxi. 16 the LXX. curiously says, that "when Ahab heard that Naboth was dead he rent his garments, and clothed himself in sackcloth; and after this he also arose," etc. This mourning for the *means*

but acceptance of the *fact* would not be in disaccord with Ahab's moral weakness.

[761] 2 Kings ix. 25, 36.

[762] LXX.

[763] 2 Kings ix. 36. LXX., ἐν τῷ προτειχίσματι. The לֵח of an Eastern city is the desert space outside the walls where the "pariah dogs prowl on the mounds."

[764] שׁוּ, LXX., κλαίων; Josephus, Chaldee, and Peshito, "shoeless."

[765] 1 Kings xxi. 27. καὶ περιεβάλετο σάκκον ἐν τῇ ἡμέρᾳ ᾗ ἐπάταξε Ναβουθαί.

[766] Psalm cix. 17, 18.

[767] 2 Chron. xviii. 2.

[768] 2 Kings iii. 7.

[769] 1 Kings xxii. 10 (Peshito).

[770] The LXX. has, "The Lord shall deliver into thy hands *even the king of Syria.*" At first they all said, "*Adonai* shall deliver it"; but afterwards, perhaps stung by the doubts of Jehoshaphat, or encouraged by the audacity of Zedekiah, they said, "*Jehovah* shall deliver it."

[771] Deut. xxxiii. 17. "His glory is like the firstling of his bullock, and his horns are like the horns of unicorns: with them he shall push the people altogether to the ends of the earth."

[772] The LXX., omitting "besides," implies Jehoshaphat's opinion that these were not true prophets of Jehovah. So, too, the Vulg., "Non est hic *propheta Domini quispiam?*"

— [773] Compare Agamemnon's bitter complaint of Calchas.

[774] 1 Kings xxii. 9. LXX., εὐνοῦχον ἕνα. And this is probably the meaning of סָרִים, not "officer," as in A.V.

[775] For he had seventy sons, besides daughters (2 Kings x. 7)

[776] The words implied that the king would fall, though the army would escape (1 Kings xxii. 17, מוֹשֵׁב). Comp. Numb. xxvii. 16, 17 "Let the Lord ... set a man over the congregation, ... who may lead them out and in; that the *congregation of the Lord be not as sheep which have no shepherd.*"

[777] Theodoret explains it as anthropomorphism, and condescension to human modes of speech (προσωποποιΐα τίς ἐστι διδάσκουσα τὴν θείαν συγχώρησιν).

[778] 1 Kings xxii. 21. It is "the," not "a" spirit, *i.e.*, the unclean spirit of deception (τὸ πνεῦμα τῆς πλάνης, 1 John iv. 6). Comp. Zech. xiii. 2, "Also I will cause *the prophets and the unclean spirit* to pass out of the land." St. Paul says in 2 Thess. ii. 11: "God shall send them strong delusion that they should believe the lie."

[779] The worst of insults (Job xvi. 10; Lam. iii. 30).

[780] The words (verse 28) "And he said, Hearken, O people, every one of you," are believed by Nöldeke, Klostermann, and others to be an interpolation from Micah i. 2, by some one who confused Micaiah with Micah. They are omitted in the LXX.

[781] We have no reason to accuse Ahab of any bad or selfish motives here. No doubt Micaiah's prophecy of his approaching death had made him anxious. If the LXX. reading, "but put thou on *my* robes," were right, the case would be different.

[782] We see in this order a trace of the single combats which mark the Homeric battles.

[783] 2 Chron. xviii. 31: "And the Lord helped him, and God moved them from him."

[784] So Jarchi. Josephus calls him Aman.

[785] 1 Kings xxii. 34. "At a venture"; marg., "in his simplicity"; comp. 2 Sam. xv. 11.

[786] What the French call *le défaut de la cuirasse* (Keil). Luther has, *zwischen den Panzer und Hengel.*

[787] Josephus, *Antt.*, VIII. xv. 6.

[788] Köster thinks that there may be reference to the fact that the name "dog" was given to the unchaste.

[789] Amos iii. 15; Psalm xlv. 8; Hom., *Od.*, iv. 72.

[790] It is supposed that Mohammed alludes to Elijah in the Qur'an, *Sura* xxi. 85: "And Ishmael, and Idris, and *Dhu'l Kifl* ("he of the portion") — all these were of the patient; and we made them enter into our mercy; verily they were among the righteous" (Palmer's Qur'an, ii. 53).

[791] See W. Robertson Smith, *Journ. of Philology*, x. 20.

[792] See Reuss, *Hist. d'Israel*, i. 101-103.